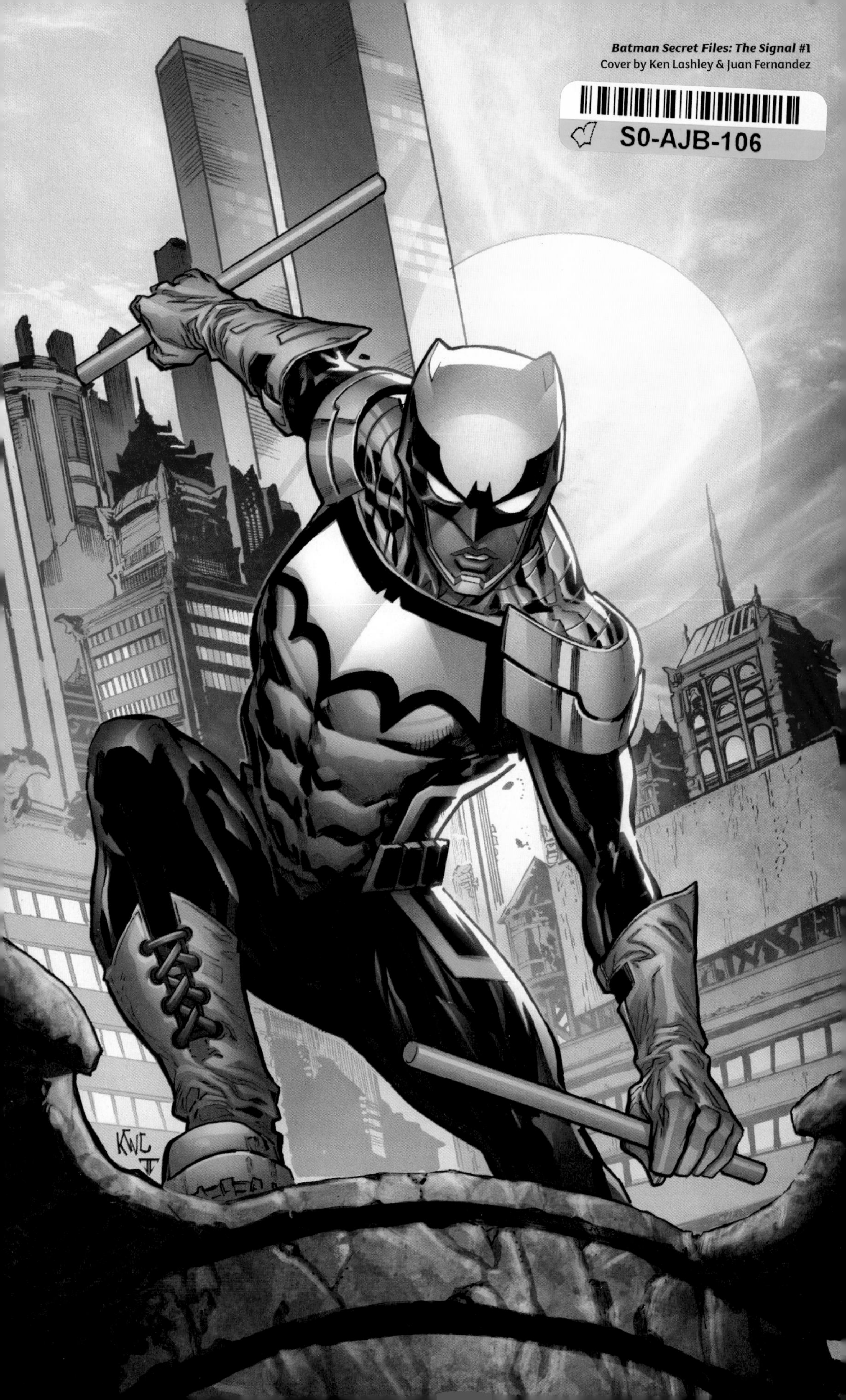

Batman Secret Files: The Signal #1
Cover by Ken Lashley & Juan Fernandez

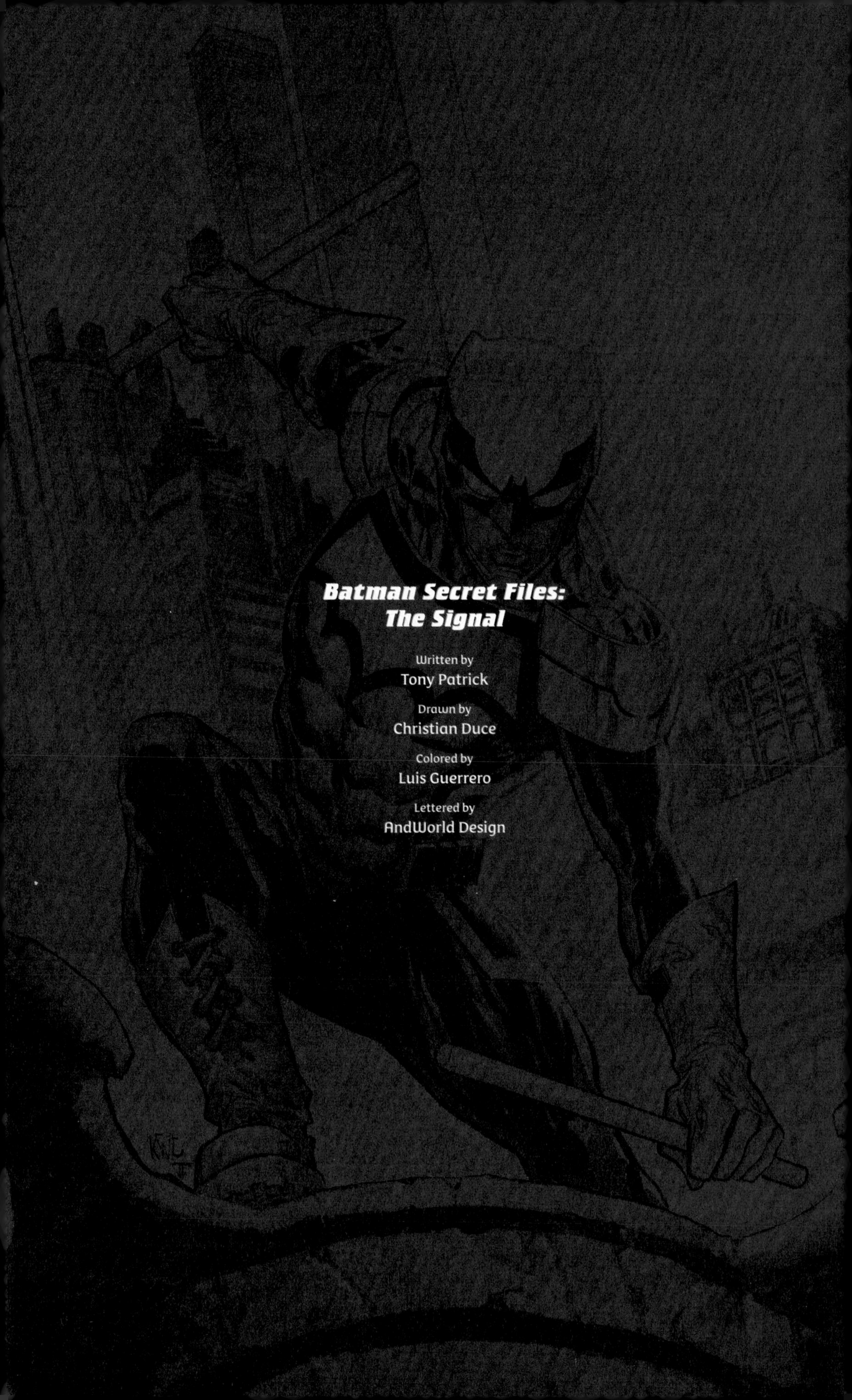

Batman Secret Files: The Signal

Written by
Tony Patrick

Drawn by
Christian Duce

Colored by
Luis Guerrero

Lettered by
AndWorld Design

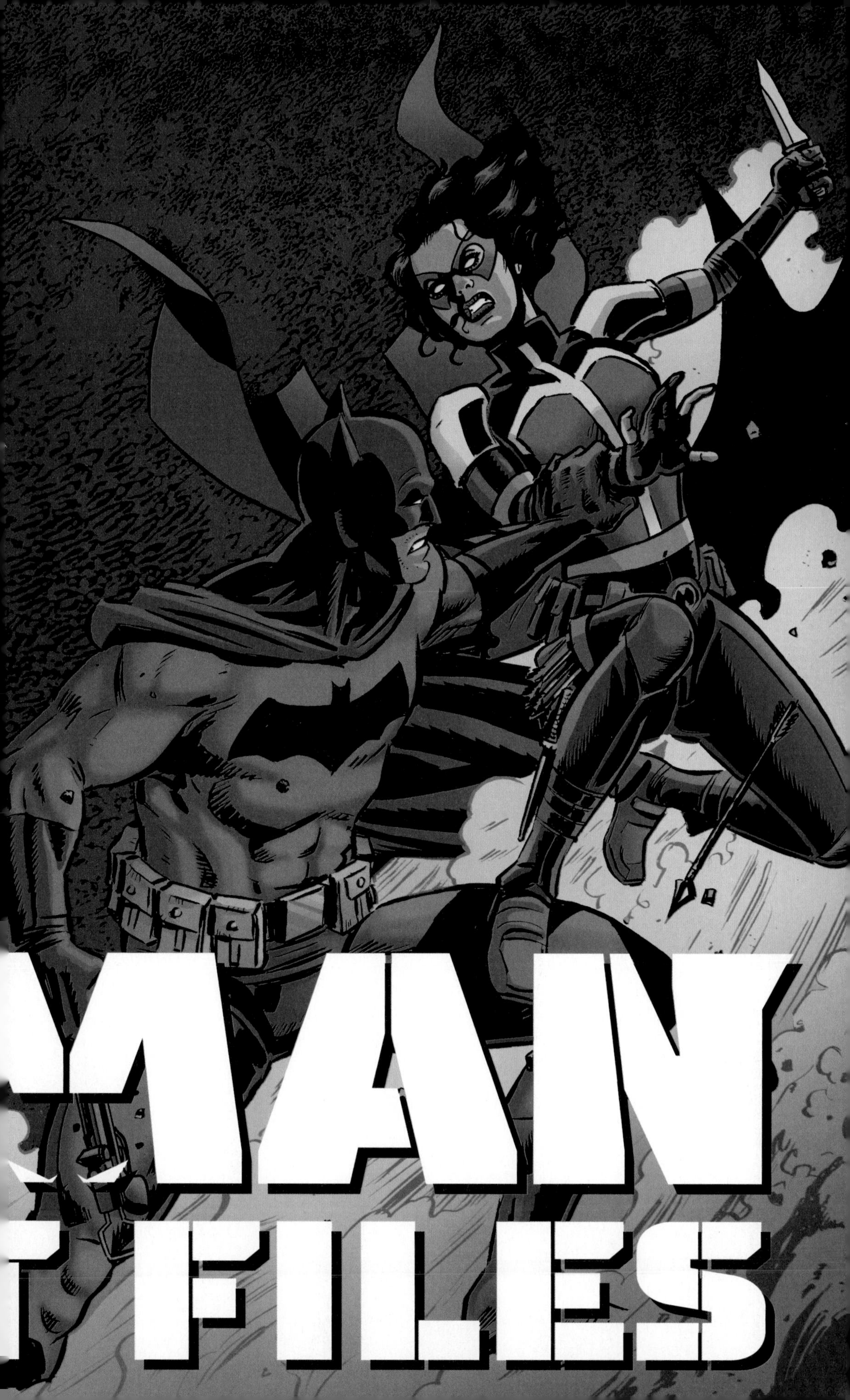
MAN
FILES

Ben Abernathy, Paul Kaminski, Dave Wielgosz
Editors – Original Series
Ben Meares
Associate Editor – Original Series
Amedeo Turturro
Editor – Original Series & Collected Edition
Steve Cook
Design Director – Books
Megen Bellersen
Publication Design
Erin Vanover
Publication Production

Marie Javins
Editor-in-Chief, DC Comics

Anne DePies
Senior VP – General Manager
Jim Lee
Publisher & Chief Creative Officer
Don Falletti
VP – Manufacturing Operations & Workflow Management
Lawrence Ganem
VP – Talent Services
Alison Gill
Senior VP – Manufacturing & Operations
Jeffrey Kaufman
VP – Editorial Strategy & Programming
Nick J. Napolitano
VP – Manufacturing Administration & Design
Nancy Spears
VP – Revenue

BATMAN: SECRET FILES

DC Comics, 2900 West Alameda Ave., Burbank, CA 91505
Printed by Solisco Printers, Scott, QC, Canada. 6/10/22. First Printing.
ISBN: 978-1-77951-711-1

Library of Congress Cataloging-in-Publication Data is available.

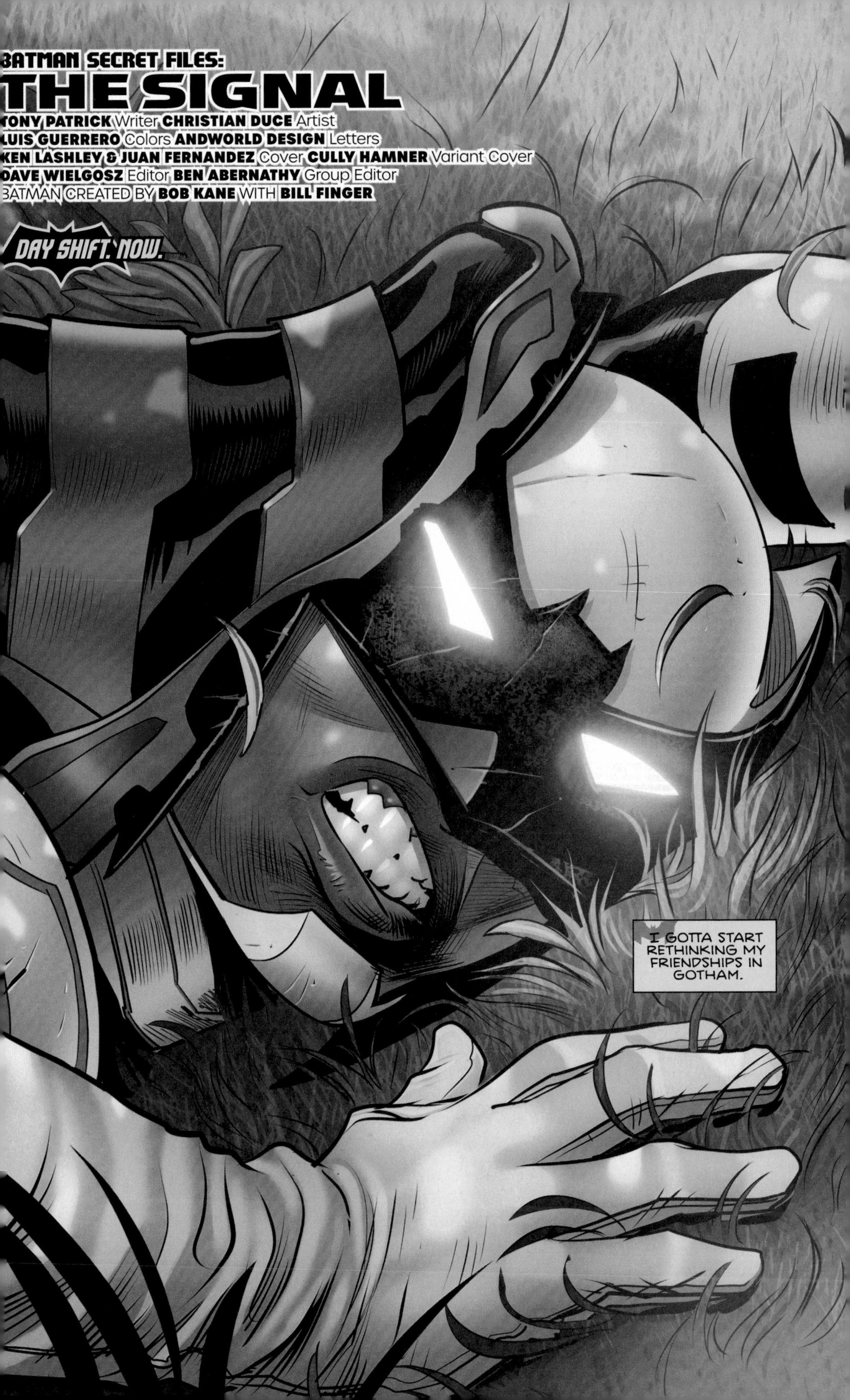
BATMAN SECRET FILES:
THE SIGNAL
TONY PATRICK Writer CHRISTIAN DUCE Artist
LUIS GUERRERO Colors ANDWORLD DESIGN Letters
KEN LASHLEY & JUAN FERNANDEZ Cover CULLY HAMNER Variant Cover
DAVE WIELGOSZ Editor BEN ABERNATHY Group Editor
BATMAN CREATED BY BOB KANE WITH BILL FINGER
DAY SHIFT. NOW.
I GOTTA START RETHINKING MY FRIENDSHIPS IN GOTHAM.

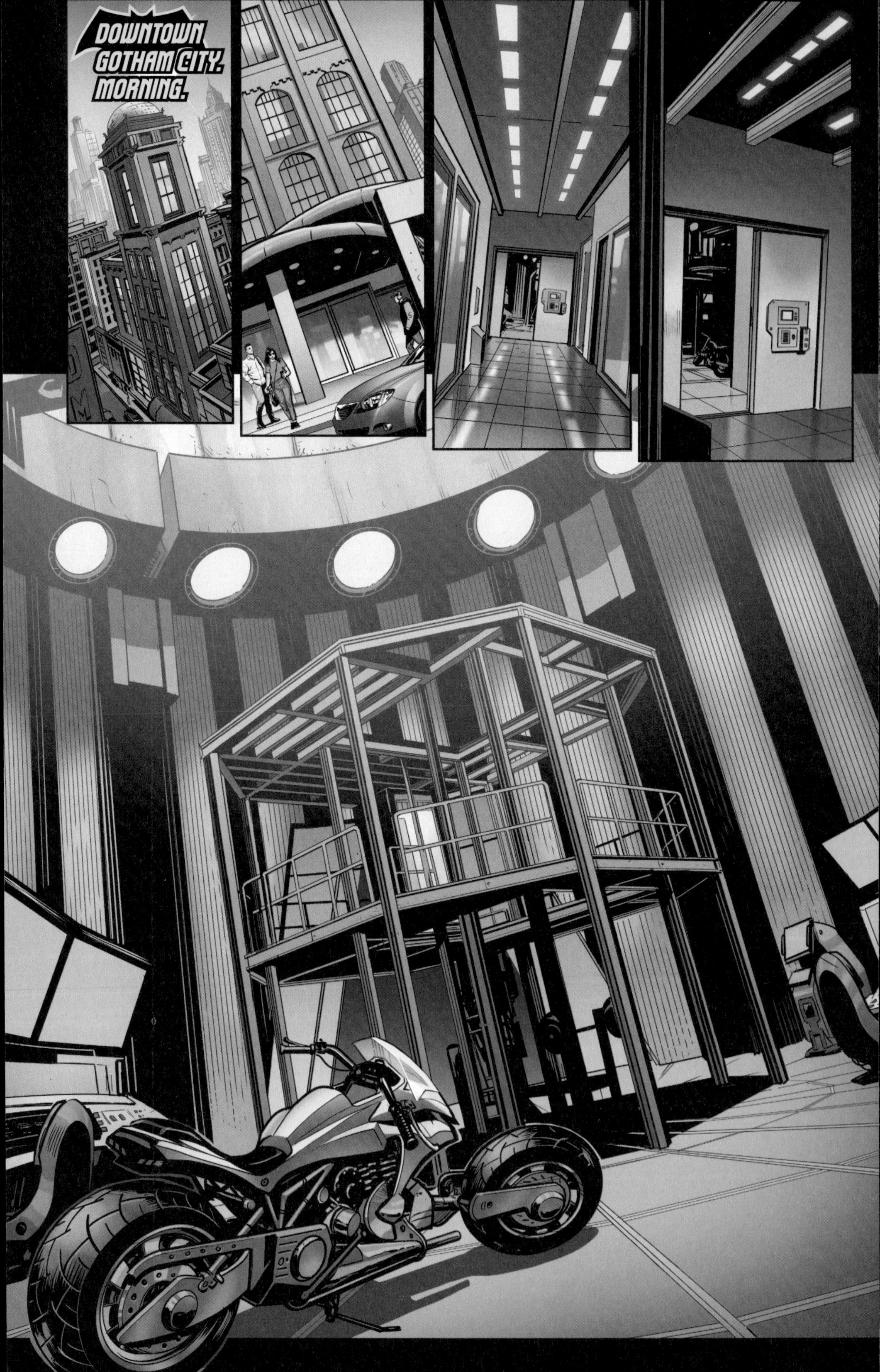
DOWNTOWN GOTHAM CITY. MORNING.

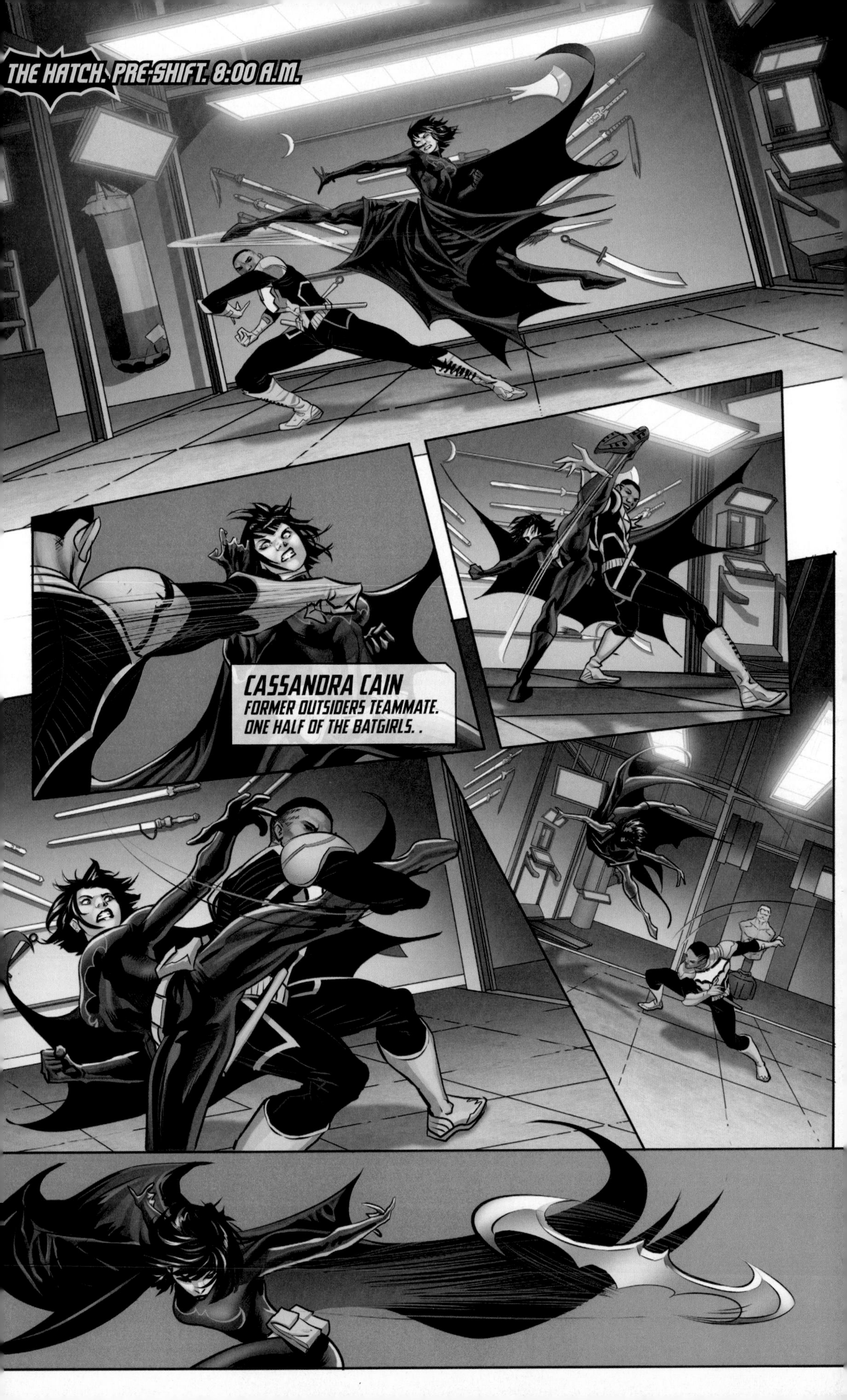
THE HATCH. PRE-SHIFT. 8:00 A.M.
CASSANDRA CAIN
FORMER OUTSIDERS TEAMMATE.
ONE HALF OF THE BATGIRLS. .

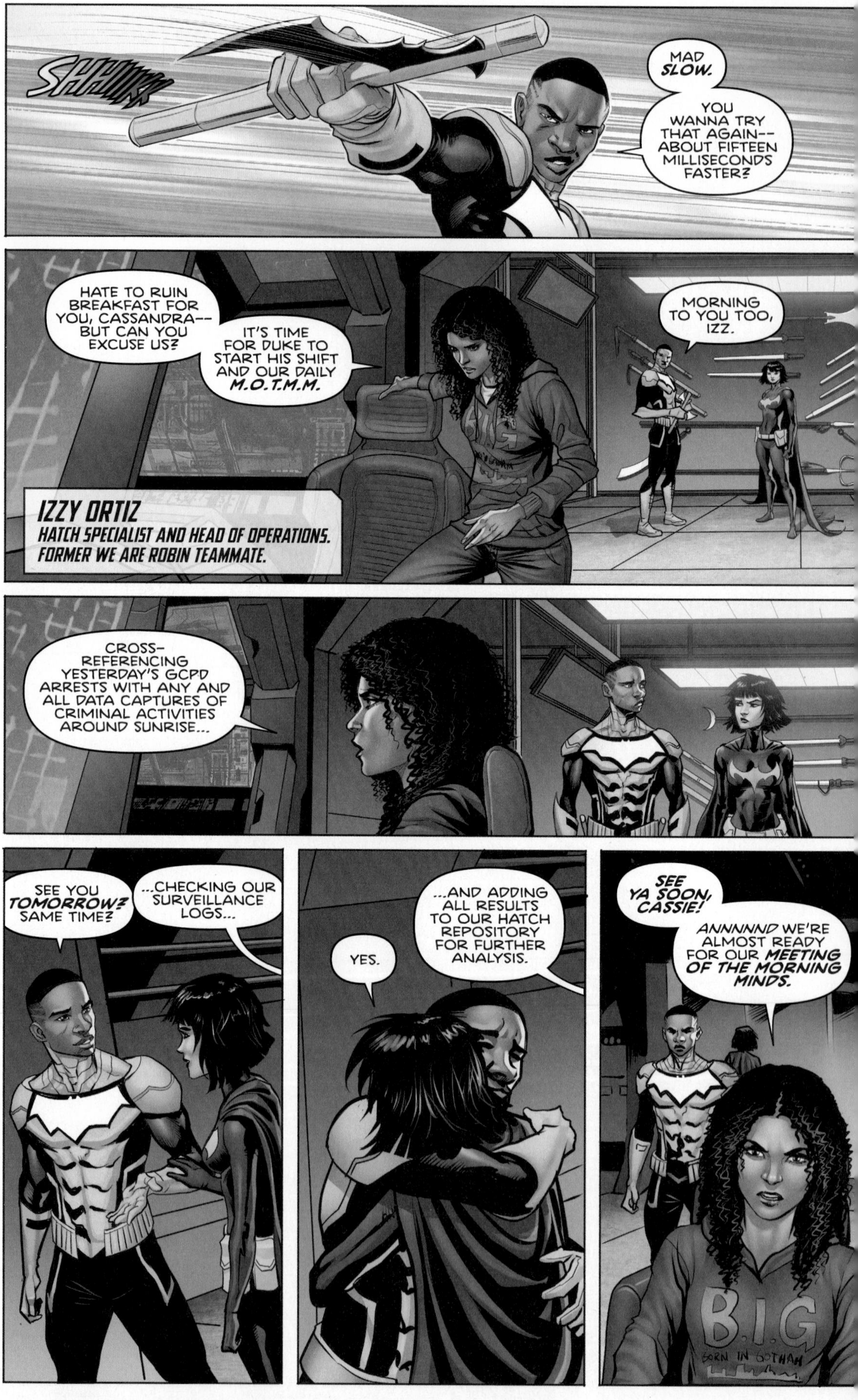
SHHHKK
MAD SLOW.
YOU WANNA TRY THAT AGAIN-- ABOUT FIFTEEN MILLISECONDS FASTER?
HATE TO RUIN BREAKFAST FOR YOU, CASSANDRA-- BUT CAN YOU EXCUSE US?
IT'S TIME FOR DUKE TO START HIS SHIFT AND OUR DAILY M.O.T.M.M.
MORNING TO YOU TOO, IZZ.
IZZY ORTIZ
HATCH SPECIALIST AND HEAD OF OPERATIONS. FORMER WE ARE ROBIN TEAMMATE.
CROSS-REFERENCING YESTERDAY'S GCPD ARRESTS WITH ANY AND ALL DATA CAPTURES OF CRIMINAL ACTIVITIES AROUND SUNRISE...
SEE YOU TOMORROW? SAME TIME?
...CHECKING OUR SURVEILLANCE LOGS...
...AND ADDING ALL RESULTS TO OUR HATCH REPOSITORY FOR FURTHER ANALYSIS.
YES.
SEE YA SOON, CASSIE!
ANNNNND WE'RE ALMOST READY FOR OUR MEETING OF THE MORNING MINDS.
B.I.G
BORN IN GOTHAM

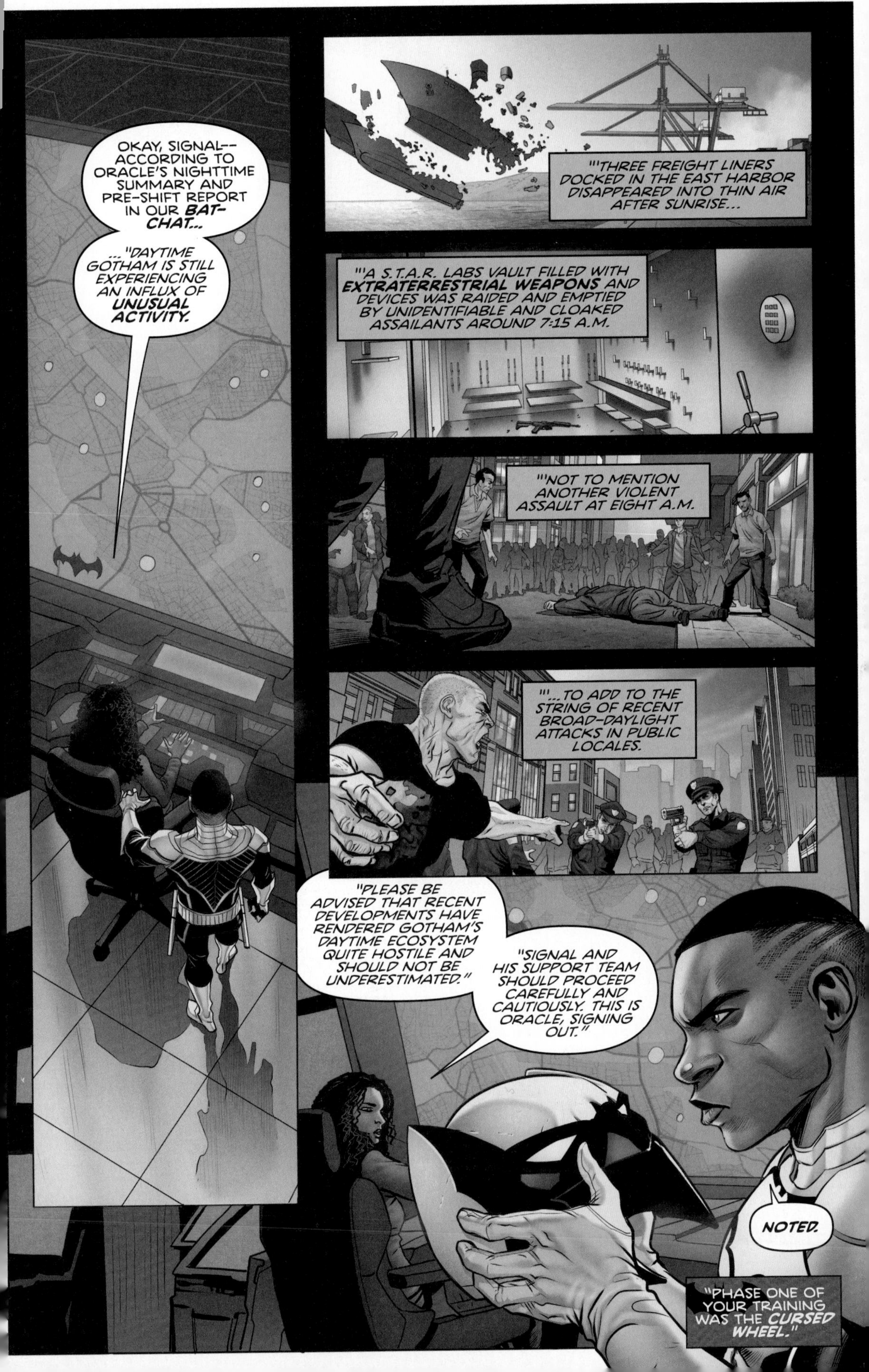
OKAY, SIGNAL-- ACCORDING TO ORACLE'S NIGHTTIME SUMMARY AND PRE-SHIFT REPORT IN OUR BAT-CHAT...
..."DAYTIME GOTHAM IS STILL EXPERIENCING AN INFLUX OF UNUSUAL ACTIVITY.
"THREE FREIGHT LINERS DOCKED IN THE EAST HARBOR DISAPPEARED INTO THIN AIR AFTER SUNRISE...
"A S.T.A.R. LABS VAULT FILLED WITH EXTRATERRESTRIAL WEAPONS AND DEVICES WAS RAIDED AND EMPTIED BY UNIDENTIFIABLE AND CLOAKED ASSAILANTS AROUND 7:15 A.M.
"NOT TO MENTION ANOTHER VIOLENT ASSAULT AT EIGHT A.M.
"...TO ADD TO THE STRING OF RECENT BROAD-DAYLIGHT ATTACKS IN PUBLIC LOCALES.
"PLEASE BE ADVISED THAT RECENT DEVELOPMENTS HAVE RENDERED GOTHAM'S DAYTIME ECOSYSTEM QUITE HOSTILE AND SHOULD NOT BE UNDERESTIMATED."
"SIGNAL AND HIS SUPPORT TEAM SHOULD PROCEED CAREFULLY AND CAUTIOUSLY. THIS IS ORACLE, SIGNING OUT."
NOTED.
"PHASE ONE OF YOUR TRAINING WAS THE CURSED WHEEL."

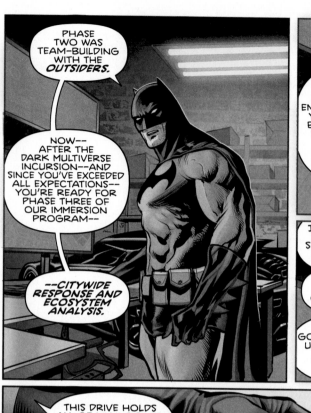

PHASE TWO WAS TEAM-BUILDING WITH THE *OUTSIDERS.*

NOW-- AFTER THE *DARK MULTIVERSE* INCURSION--AND SINCE YOU'VE EXCEEDED ALL EXPECTATIONS-- YOU'RE READY FOR PHASE THREE OF OUR IMMERSION PROGRAM--

--CITYWIDE RESPONSE AND ECOSYSTEM ANALYSIS.

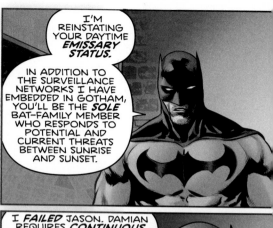

I'M REINSTATING YOUR DAYTIME *EMISSARY STATUS.*

IN ADDITION TO THE SURVEILLANCE NETWORKS I HAVE EMBEDDED IN GOTHAM, YOU'LL BE THE *SOLE* BAT-FAMILY MEMBER WHO RESPONDS TO POTENTIAL AND CURRENT THREATS BETWEEN SUNRISE AND SUNSET.

I *FAILED* JASON. DAMIAN REQUIRES *CONTINUOUS* SUPERVISION. DICK HAD TO *LEAVE* TO FIND HIS OWN IDENTITY AND CITY.

BUT YOU? YOU REPRESENT GOTHAM'S *BEST.*

A BORN-AND-BRED GOTHAM METAHUMAN WITH UNPARALLELED DETECTIVE SKILLS WHO WILL BE TRAINED FOR LEAGUE-LEVEL LEADERSHIP?

THAT'S A LEGACY WORTH FIGHTING FOR.

THIS DRIVE HOLDS ALL OF MY INSIGHTS, CONTINGENCY PLANS, AND JOURNALS FROM THE PAST FEW YEARS.

STUDY IT, ABSORB IT, USE IT TO YOUR ADVANTAGE--TO BECOME YOUR OWN HERO.

YOU'LL NEED TO BRING THE HATCH BACK ONLINE AND RE-UP YOUR OPS SUPPORT.

IZZY ORTIZ AND RIKO SHERIDAN ALREADY HAVE CLEARANCE--SO I WOULD ASK THEM FOR THEIR SUPPORT AGAIN IF I WERE YOU.

AND I'LL EXPECT A DAILY DEBRIEF IN THE CAVE AT NINETEEN HUNDRED WHICH WILL SIGNAL THE END OF YOUR SHIFT. UNDERSTOOD?

YEAH...UH... *UNDERSTOOD.* AND...THANK YOU?

NO NEED FOR THANKS--JUST PROVE THE NAYSAYERS WRONG AND PROVE MY INVESTMENT IN YOU... CORRECT.

"YOU ZONED OUT THERE FOR A MINUTE."

BUT I'LL SAY IT AGAIN--HAVE A GREAT SHIFT.

MAYBE WE CAN WATCH A MOVIE LATER IF YOUR COUSIN JAY DOESN'T FALL ASLEEP ON THE COUCH AGAIN? BUT FOR NOW--

--YOU NEED TO RESPOND TO A DISTURBANCE IN *ROBINSON PARK* AND THEN CONDUCT YOUR MORNING PATROL.

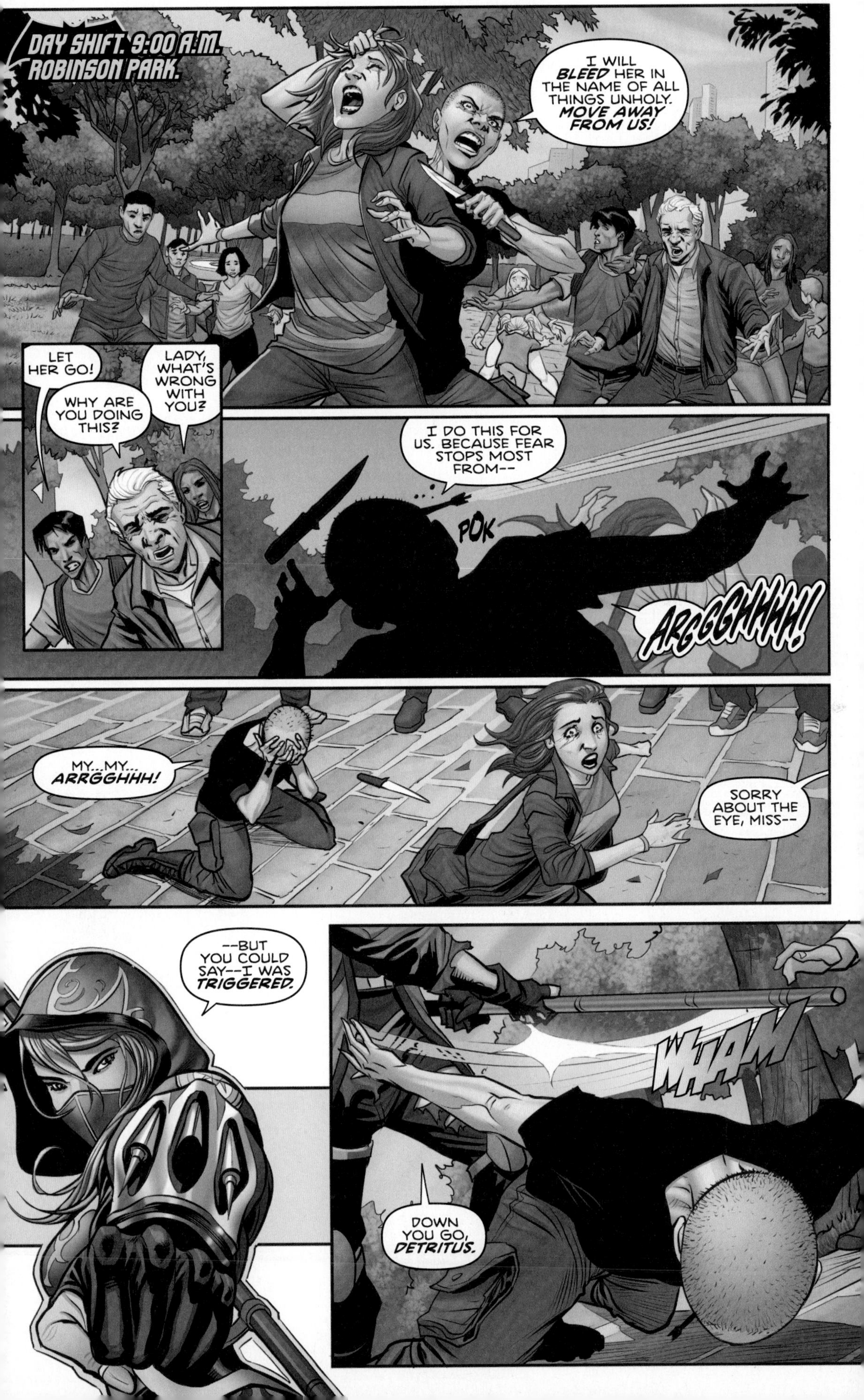
DAY SHIFT. 9:00 A.M. ROBINSON PARK.
I WILL BLEED HER IN THE NAME OF ALL THINGS UNHOLY. MOVE AWAY FROM US!
LET HER GO!
WHY ARE YOU DOING THIS?
LADY, WHAT'S WRONG WITH YOU?
I DO THIS FOR US. BECAUSE FEAR STOPS MOST FROM--
POK
ARGGGHHHH!
MY...MY... ARRGGHHH!
SORRY ABOUT THE EYE, MISS--
--BUT YOU COULD SAY--I WAS TRIGGERED.
WHAM
DOWN YOU GO, DETRITUS.

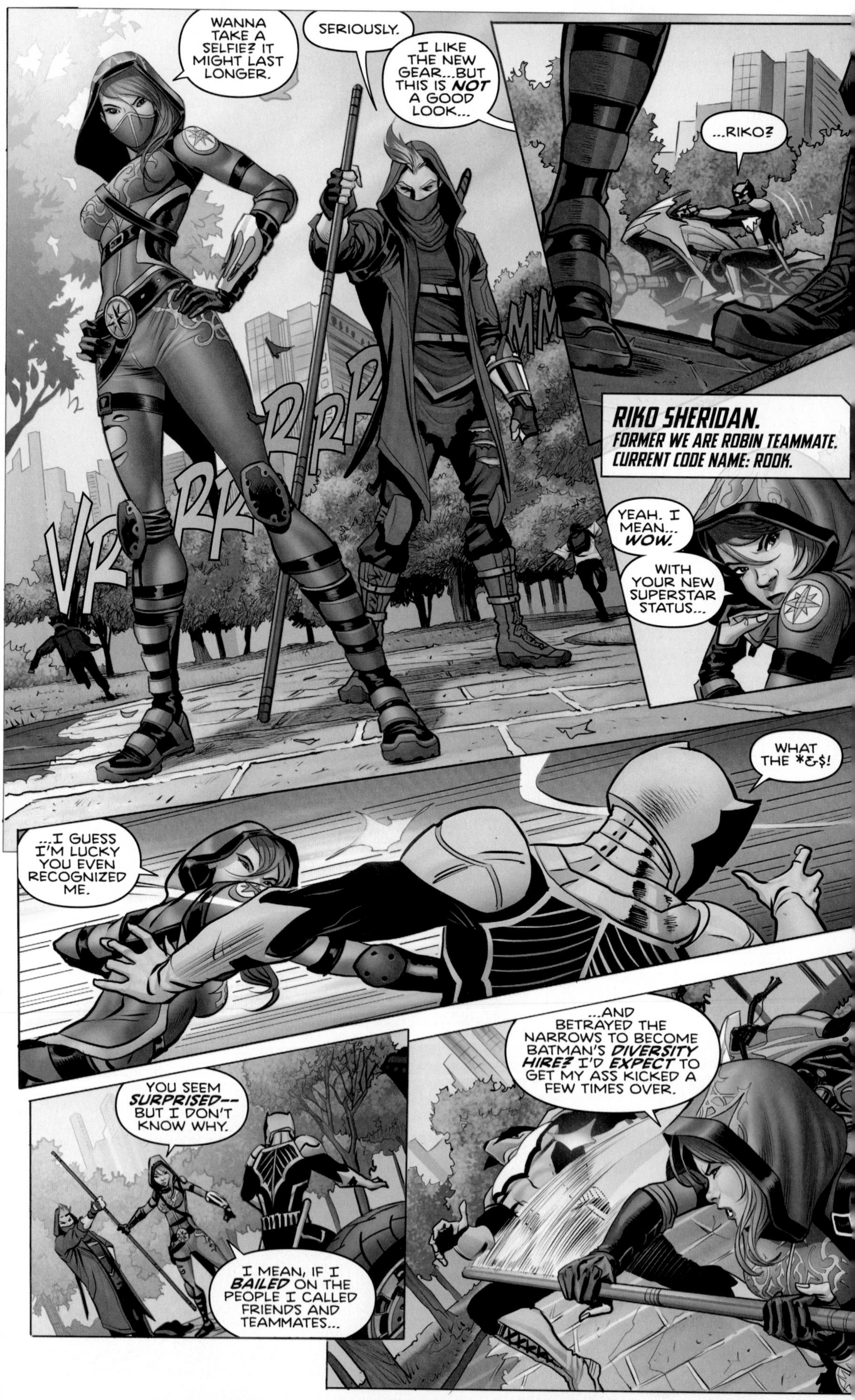
WANNA TAKE A SELFIE? IT MIGHT LAST LONGER.
SERIOUSLY.
I LIKE THE NEW GEAR...BUT THIS IS NOT A GOOD LOOK...
VRRRRRMMM
...RIKO?
RIKO SHERIDAN.
FORMER WE ARE ROBIN TEAMMATE.
CURRENT CODE NAME: ROOK.
YEAH. I MEAN... WOW.
WITH YOUR NEW SUPERSTAR STATUS...
WHAT THE *&$!
...I GUESS I'M LUCKY YOU EVEN RECOGNIZED ME.
YOU SEEM SURPRISED-- BUT I DON'T KNOW WHY.
I MEAN, IF I BAILED ON THE PEOPLE I CALLED FRIENDS AND TEAMMATES...
...AND BETRAYED THE NARROWS TO BECOME BATMAN'S DIVERSITY HIRE? I'D EXPECT TO GET MY ASS KICKED A FEW TIMES OVER.

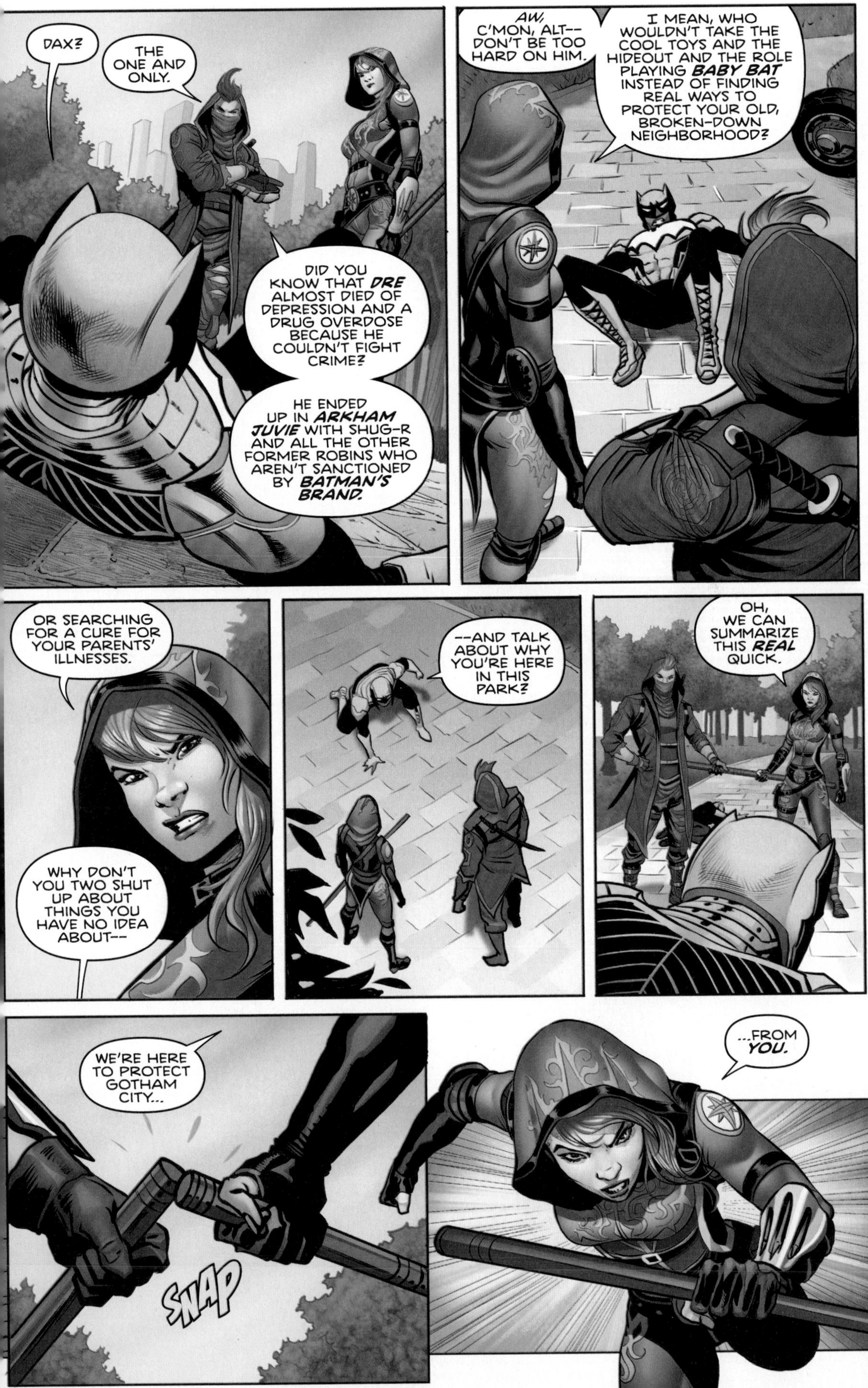
DAX?
THE ONE AND ONLY.
DID YOU KNOW THAT DRE ALMOST DIED OF DEPRESSION AND A DRUG OVERDOSE BECAUSE HE COULDN'T FIGHT CRIME?
HE ENDED UP IN ARKHAM JUVIE WITH SHUG-R AND ALL THE OTHER FORMER ROBINS WHO AREN'T SANCTIONED BY BATMAN'S BRAND.
AW, C'MON, ALT-- DON'T BE TOO HARD ON HIM.
I MEAN, WHO WOULDN'T TAKE THE COOL TOYS AND THE HIDEOUT AND THE ROLE PLAYING BABY BAT INSTEAD OF FINDING REAL WAYS TO PROTECT YOUR OLD, BROKEN-DOWN NEIGHBORHOOD?
OR SEARCHING FOR A CURE FOR YOUR PARENTS' ILLNESSES.
WHY DON'T YOU TWO SHUT UP ABOUT THINGS YOU HAVE NO IDEA ABOUT--
--AND TALK ABOUT WHY YOU'RE HERE IN THIS PARK?
OH, WE CAN SUMMARIZE THIS REAL QUICK.
WE'RE HERE TO PROTECT GOTHAM CITY...
SNAP
...FROM YOU.

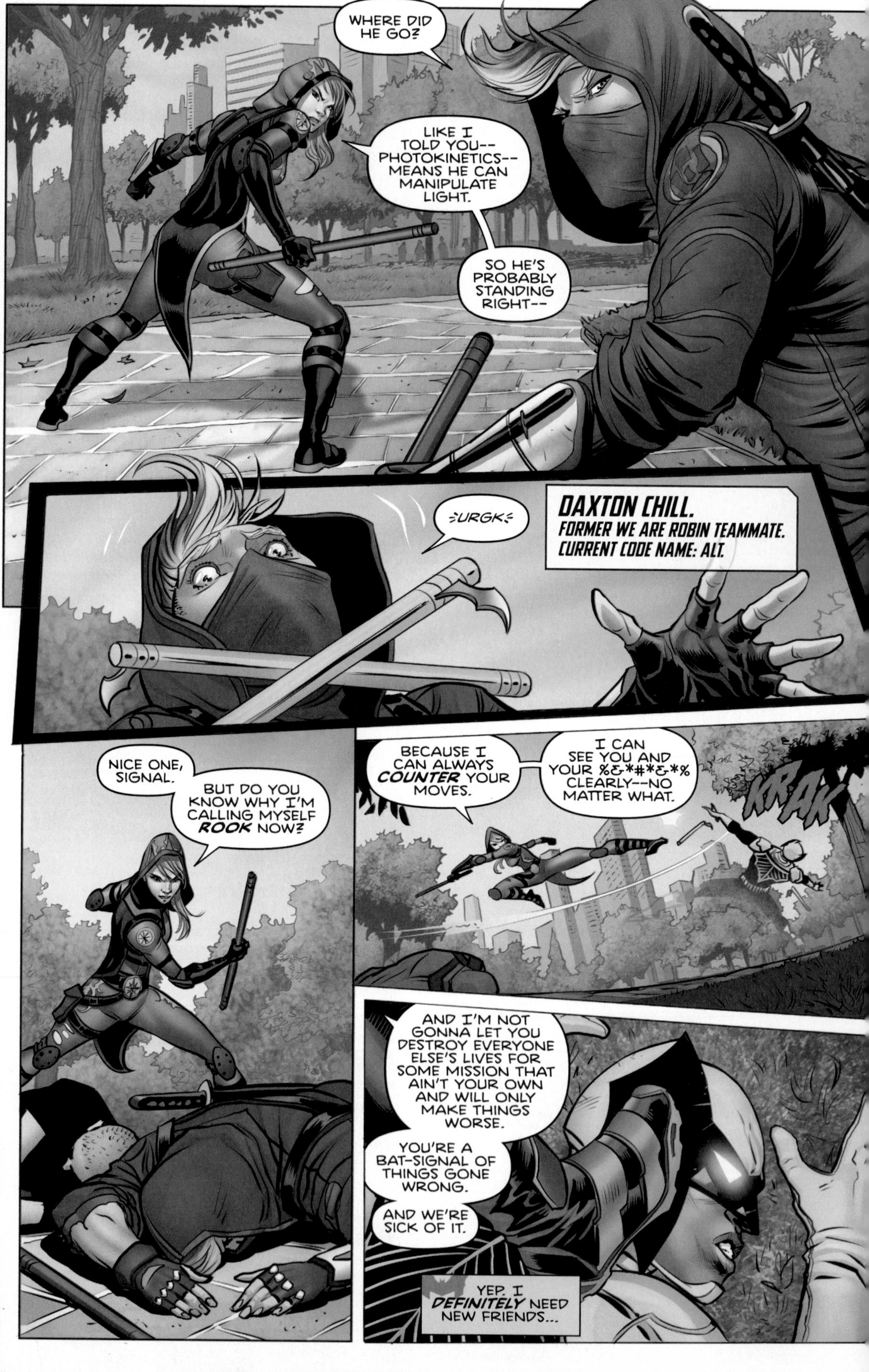
WHERE DID HE GO?
LIKE I TOLD YOU-- PHOTOKINETICS-- MEANS HE CAN MANIPULATE LIGHT.
SO HE'S PROBABLY STANDING RIGHT--
URGK
DAXTON CHILL. FORMER WE ARE ROBIN TEAMMATE. CURRENT CODE NAME: ALT.
NICE ONE, SIGNAL.
BUT DO YOU KNOW WHY I'M CALLING MYSELF ROOK NOW?
BECAUSE I CAN ALWAYS COUNTER YOUR MOVES.
I CAN SEE YOU AND YOUR %&*#*&*% CLEARLY--NO MATTER WHAT.
KRAK
AND I'M NOT GONNA LET YOU DESTROY EVERYONE ELSE'S LIVES FOR SOME MISSION THAT AIN'T YOUR OWN AND WILL ONLY MAKE THINGS WORSE.
YOU'RE A BAT-SIGNAL OF THINGS GONE WRONG.
AND WE'RE SICK OF IT.
YEP. I DEFINITELY NEED NEW FRIENDS...

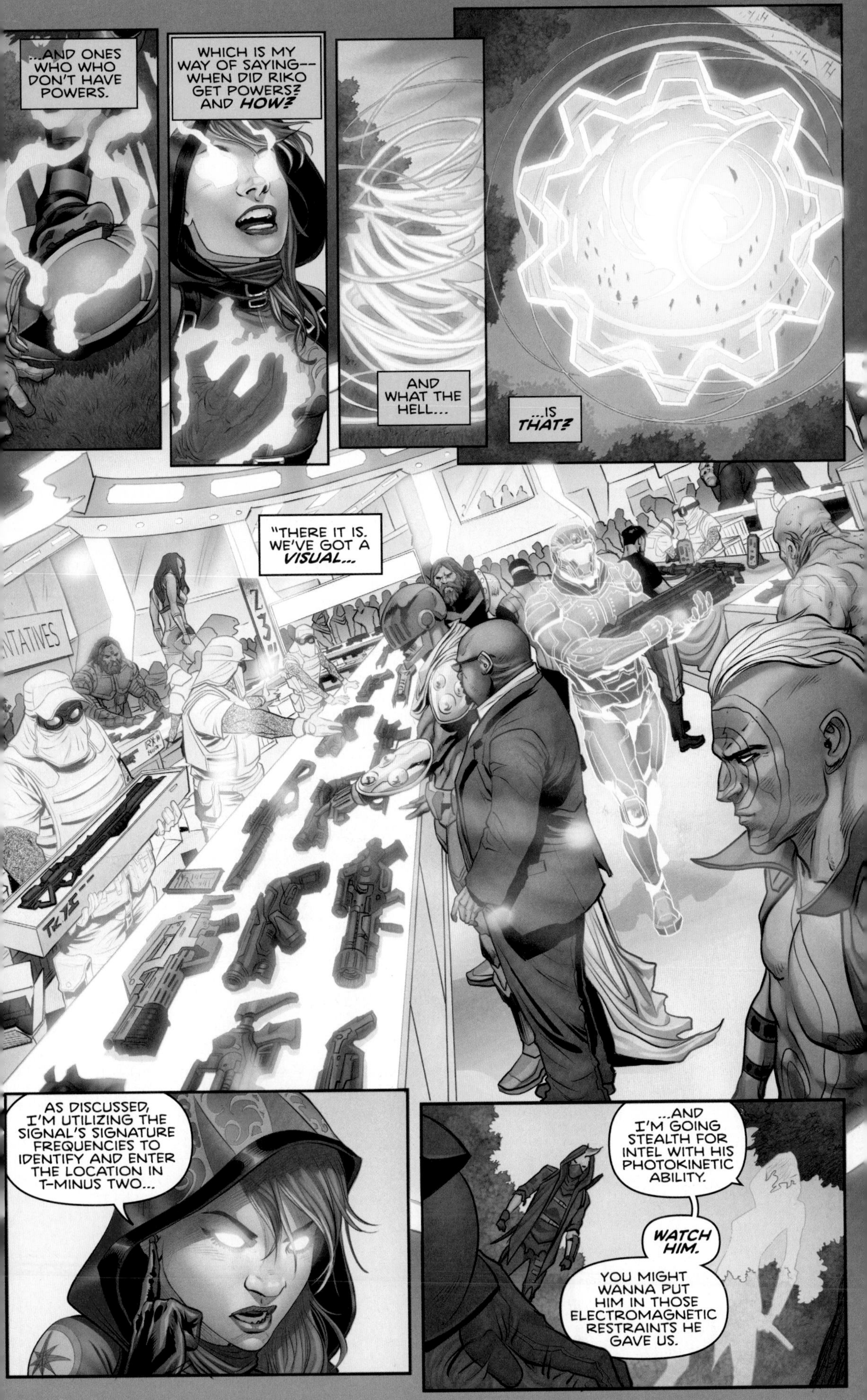
...AND ONES WHO WHO DON'T HAVE POWERS.
WHICH IS MY WAY OF SAYING-- WHEN DID RIKO GET POWERS? AND *HOW?*
AND WHAT THE HELL...
...IS *THAT?*
"THERE IT IS. WE'VE GOT A *VISUAL*...
AS DISCUSSED, I'M UTILIZING THE SIGNAL'S SIGNATURE FREQUENCIES TO IDENTIFY AND ENTER THE LOCATION IN T-MINUS TWO...
...AND I'M GOING STEALTH FOR INTEL WITH HIS PHOTOKINETIC ABILITY.
WATCH HIM.
YOU MIGHT WANNA PUT HIM IN THOSE ELECTROMAGNETIC RESTRAINTS HE GAVE US.

WERD?

WOWWWW-- ROOK--YOU TWO KEEP IT **ONE HUNDRED,** HUH?

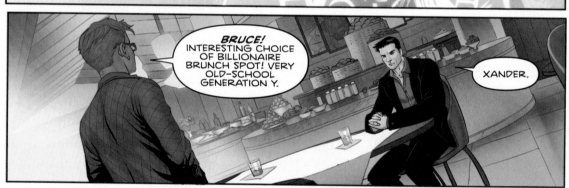

I NEED A **FULL CAPTURE** OF EVERYTHING. MOST PEOPLE IN THE OTHER MARKETS DON'T EVEN BELIEVE THAT THE **WHITE MARKET** EXISTS.

GOT IT. ROOK OUT.

BRUCE! INTERESTING CHOICE OF BILLIONAIRE BRUNCH SPOT! VERY OLD-SCHOOL GENERATION Y.

XANDER.

VERY COOL TO INVITE ME HERE TO NOGO HOUSE FOR A FACE-TO-FACE...BUT I MEAN, THE ONLINE MENU SAYS THE PRICES HERE...ARE, UM... VERY **PRICEY.**

AND I MEAN, WITH YOU **LOSING** YOUR COMPANY AND ALMOST **ALL** OF YOUR FORTUNE...

...ARE YOU SURE YOU CAN AFFORD THE **MAINE LOBSTER** HERE?

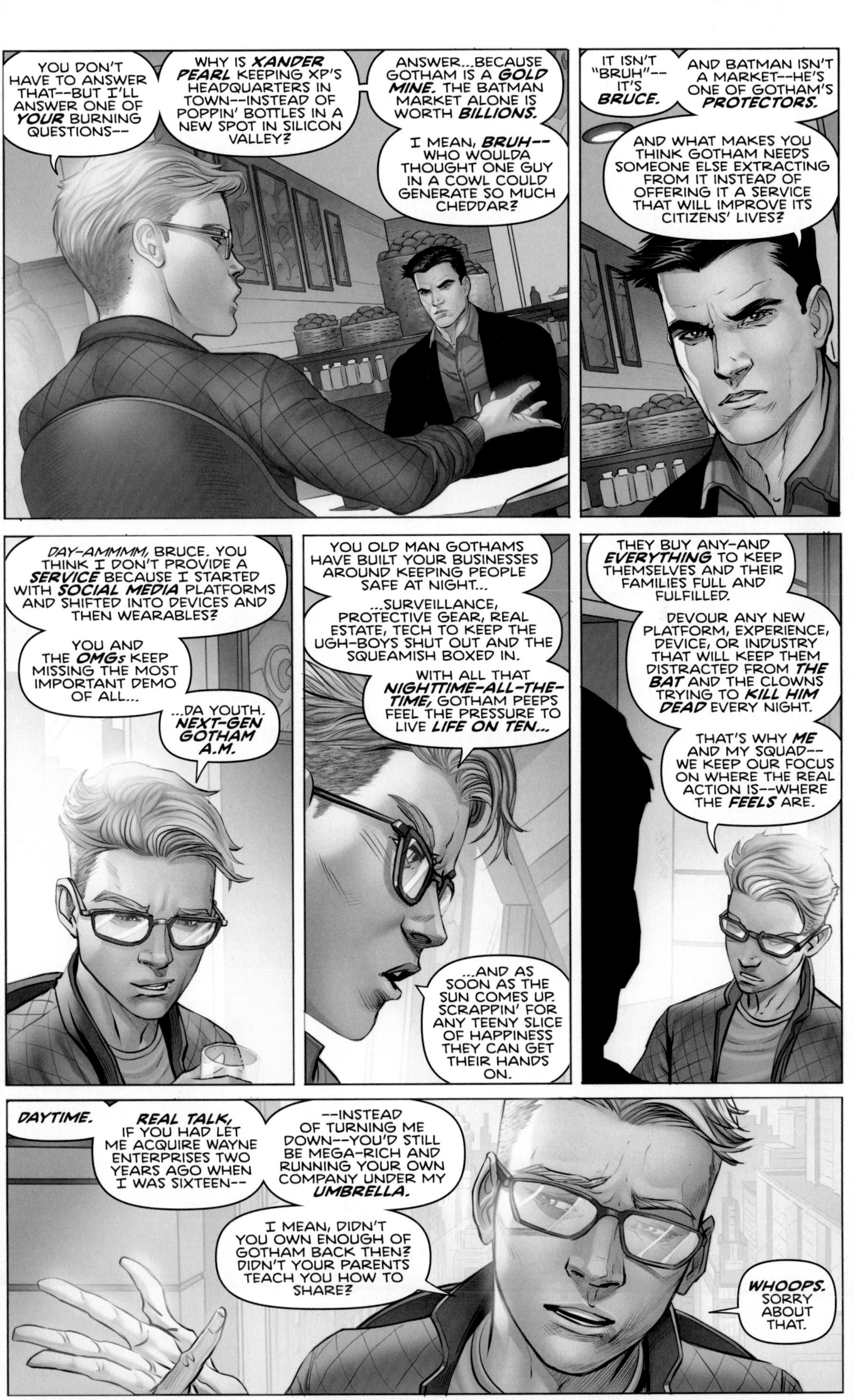
YOU DON'T HAVE TO ANSWER THAT--BUT I'LL ANSWER ONE OF YOUR BURNING QUESTIONS--
WHY IS XANDER PEARL KEEPING XP'S HEADQUARTERS IN TOWN--INSTEAD OF POPPIN' BOTTLES IN A NEW SPOT IN SILICON VALLEY?
ANSWER...BECAUSE GOTHAM IS A GOLD MINE. THE BATMAN MARKET ALONE IS WORTH BILLIONS.
I MEAN, BRUH--WHO WOULDA THOUGHT ONE GUY IN A COWL COULD GENERATE SO MUCH CHEDDAR?
IT ISN'T "BRUH"--IT'S BRUCE.
AND BATMAN ISN'T A MARKET--HE'S ONE OF GOTHAM'S PROTECTORS.
AND WHAT MAKES YOU THINK GOTHAM NEEDS SOMEONE ELSE EXTRACTING FROM IT INSTEAD OF OFFERING IT A SERVICE THAT WILL IMPROVE ITS CITIZENS' LIVES?
DAY-AMMMM, BRUCE. YOU THINK I DON'T PROVIDE A SERVICE BECAUSE I STARTED WITH SOCIAL MEDIA PLATFORMS AND SHIFTED INTO DEVICES AND THEN WEARABLES?
YOU AND THE OMGs KEEP MISSING THE MOST IMPORTANT DEMO OF ALL...
...DA YOUTH. NEXT-GEN GOTHAM A.M.
YOU OLD MAN GOTHAMS HAVE BUILT YOUR BUSINESSES AROUND KEEPING PEOPLE SAFE AT NIGHT...
...SURVEILLANCE, PROTECTIVE GEAR, REAL ESTATE, TECH TO KEEP THE UGH-BOYS SHUT OUT AND THE SQUEAMISH BOXED IN.
WITH ALL THAT NIGHTTIME-ALL-THE-TIME, GOTHAM PEEPS FEEL THE PRESSURE TO LIVE LIFE ON TEN...
...AND AS SOON AS THE SUN COMES UP. SCRAPPIN' FOR ANY TEENY SLICE OF HAPPINESS THEY CAN GET THEIR HANDS ON.
THEY BUY ANY-AND EVERYTHING TO KEEP THEMSELVES AND THEIR FAMILIES FULL AND FULFILLED.
DEVOUR ANY NEW PLATFORM, EXPERIENCE, DEVICE, OR INDUSTRY THAT WILL KEEP THEM DISTRACTED FROM THE BAT AND THE CLOWNS TRYING TO KILL HIM DEAD EVERY NIGHT.
THAT'S WHY ME AND MY SQUAD--WE KEEP OUR FOCUS ON WHERE THE REAL ACTION IS--WHERE THE FEELS ARE.
DAYTIME.
REAL TALK, IF YOU HAD LET ME ACQUIRE WAYNE ENTERPRISES TWO YEARS AGO WHEN I WAS SIXTEEN--
--INSTEAD OF TURNING ME DOWN--YOU'D STILL BE MEGA-RICH AND RUNNING YOUR OWN COMPANY UNDER MY UMBRELLA.
I MEAN, DIDN'T YOU OWN ENOUGH OF GOTHAM BACK THEN? DIDN'T YOUR PARENTS TEACH YOU HOW TO SHARE?
WHOOPS. SORRY ABOUT THAT.

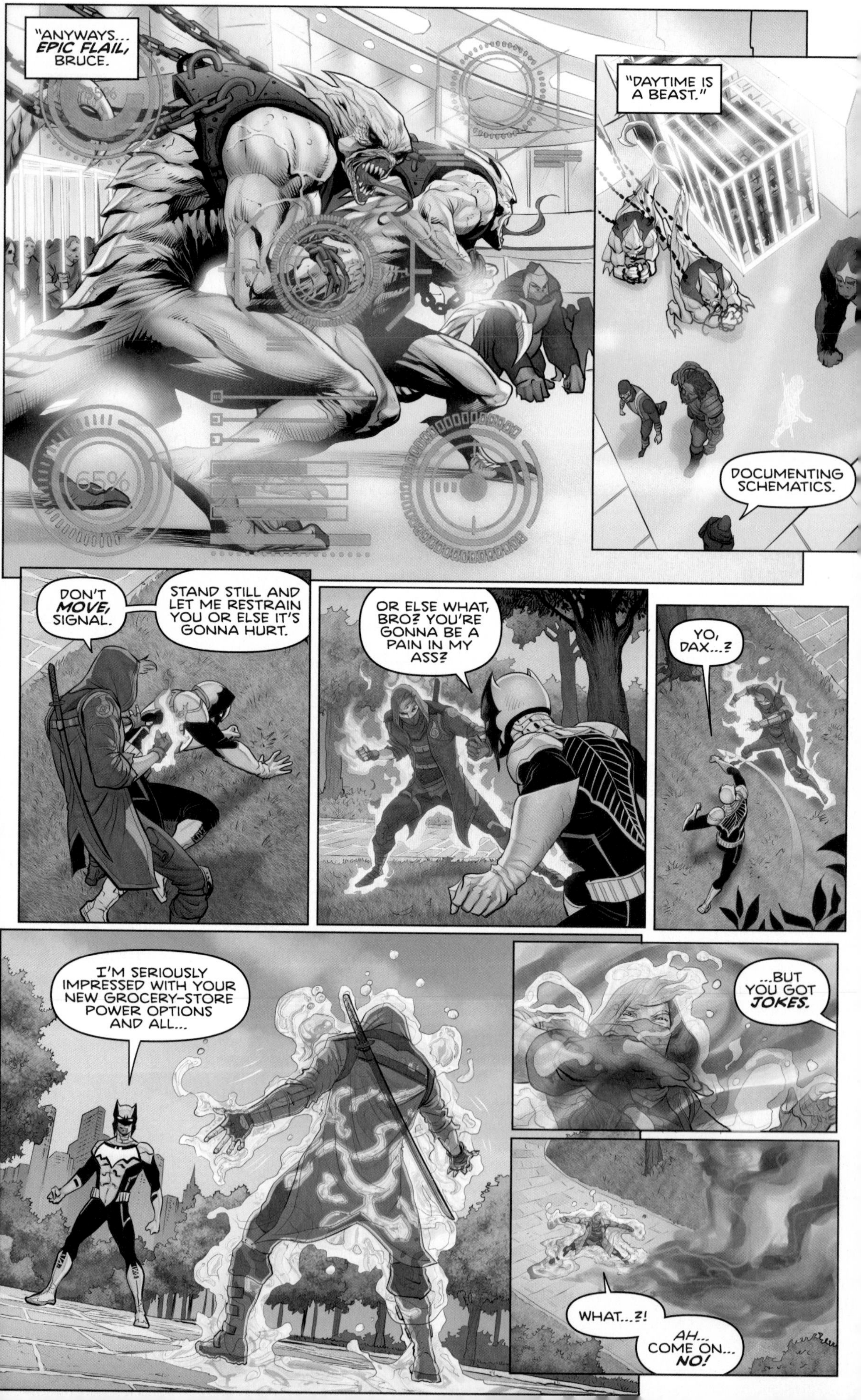
"ANYWAYS... EPIC FLAIL, BRUCE.
65%
"DAYTIME IS A BEAST."
DOCUMENTING SCHEMATICS.
DON'T MOVE, SIGNAL.
STAND STILL AND LET ME RESTRAIN YOU OR ELSE IT'S GONNA HURT.
OR ELSE WHAT, BRO? YOU'RE GONNA BE A PAIN IN MY ASS?
YO, DAX...?
I'M SERIOUSLY IMPRESSED WITH YOUR NEW GROCERY-STORE POWER OPTIONS AND ALL...
...BUT YOU GOT JOKES.
WHAT...?!
AH... COME ON... NO!

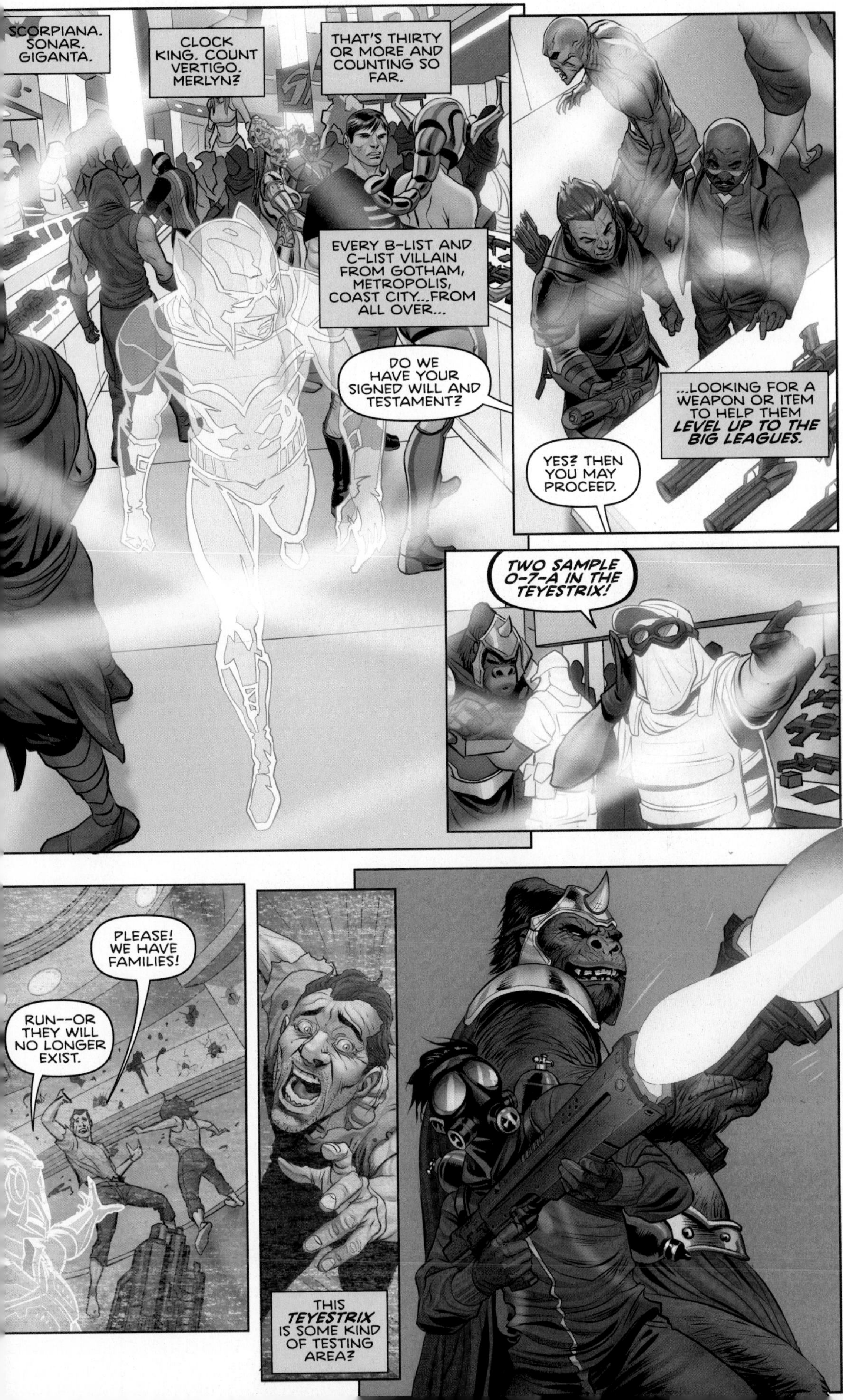
SCORPIANA. SONAR. GIGANTA.
CLOCK KING. COUNT VERTIGO. MERLYN?
THAT'S THIRTY OR MORE AND COUNTING SO FAR.
EVERY B-LIST AND C-LIST VILLAIN FROM GOTHAM, METROPOLIS, COAST CITY...FROM ALL OVER...
DO WE HAVE YOUR SIGNED WILL AND TESTAMENT?
...LOOKING FOR A WEAPON OR ITEM TO HELP THEM *LEVEL UP TO THE BIG LEAGUES.*
YES? THEN YOU MAY PROCEED.
TWO SAMPLE O-7-A IN THE TEYESTRIX!
PLEASE! WE HAVE FAMILIES!
RUN--OR THEY WILL NO LONGER EXIST.
THIS *TEYESTRIX* IS SOME KIND OF TESTING AREA?

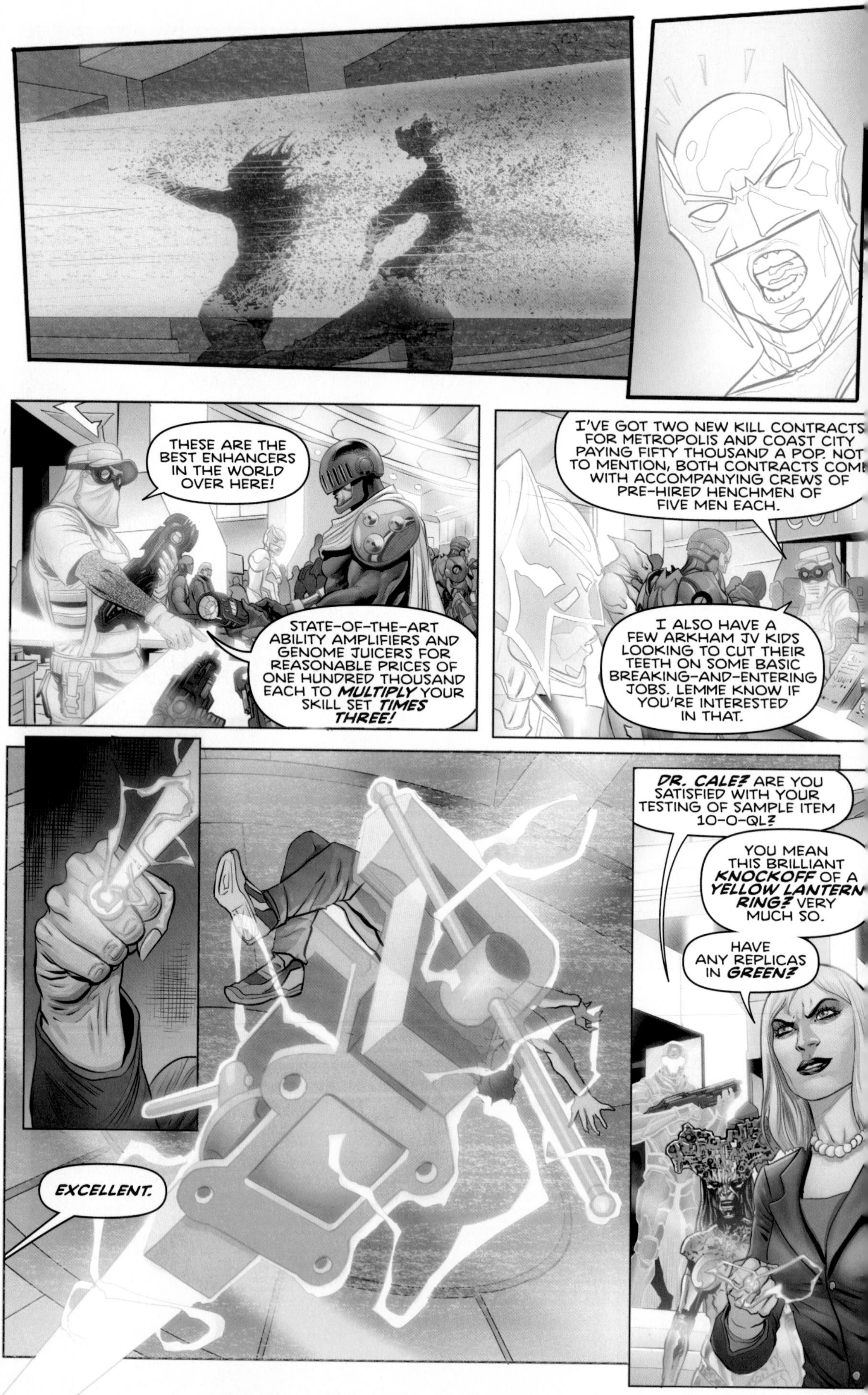

THESE ARE THE BEST ENHANCERS IN THE WORLD OVER HERE!
STATE-OF-THE-ART ABILITY AMPLIFIERS AND GENOME JUICERS FOR REASONABLE PRICES OF ONE HUNDRED THOUSAND EACH TO *MULTIPLY* YOUR SKILL SET *TIMES THREE!*
I'VE GOT TWO NEW KILL CONTRACTS FOR METROPOLIS AND COAST CITY PAYING FIFTY THOUSAND A POP. NOT TO MENTION, BOTH CONTRACTS COME WITH ACCOMPANYING CREWS OF PRE-HIRED HENCHMEN OF FIVE MEN EACH.
I ALSO HAVE A FEW ARKHAM JV KIDS LOOKING TO CUT THEIR TEETH ON SOME BASIC BREAKING-AND-ENTERING JOBS. LEMME KNOW IF YOU'RE INTERESTED IN THAT.
DR. CALE? ARE YOU SATISFIED WITH YOUR TESTING OF SAMPLE ITEM 10-O-QL?
YOU MEAN THIS BRILLIANT *KNOCKOFF* OF A *YELLOW LANTERN RING?* VERY MUCH SO.
HAVE ANY REPLICAS IN *GREEN?*
EXCELLENT.

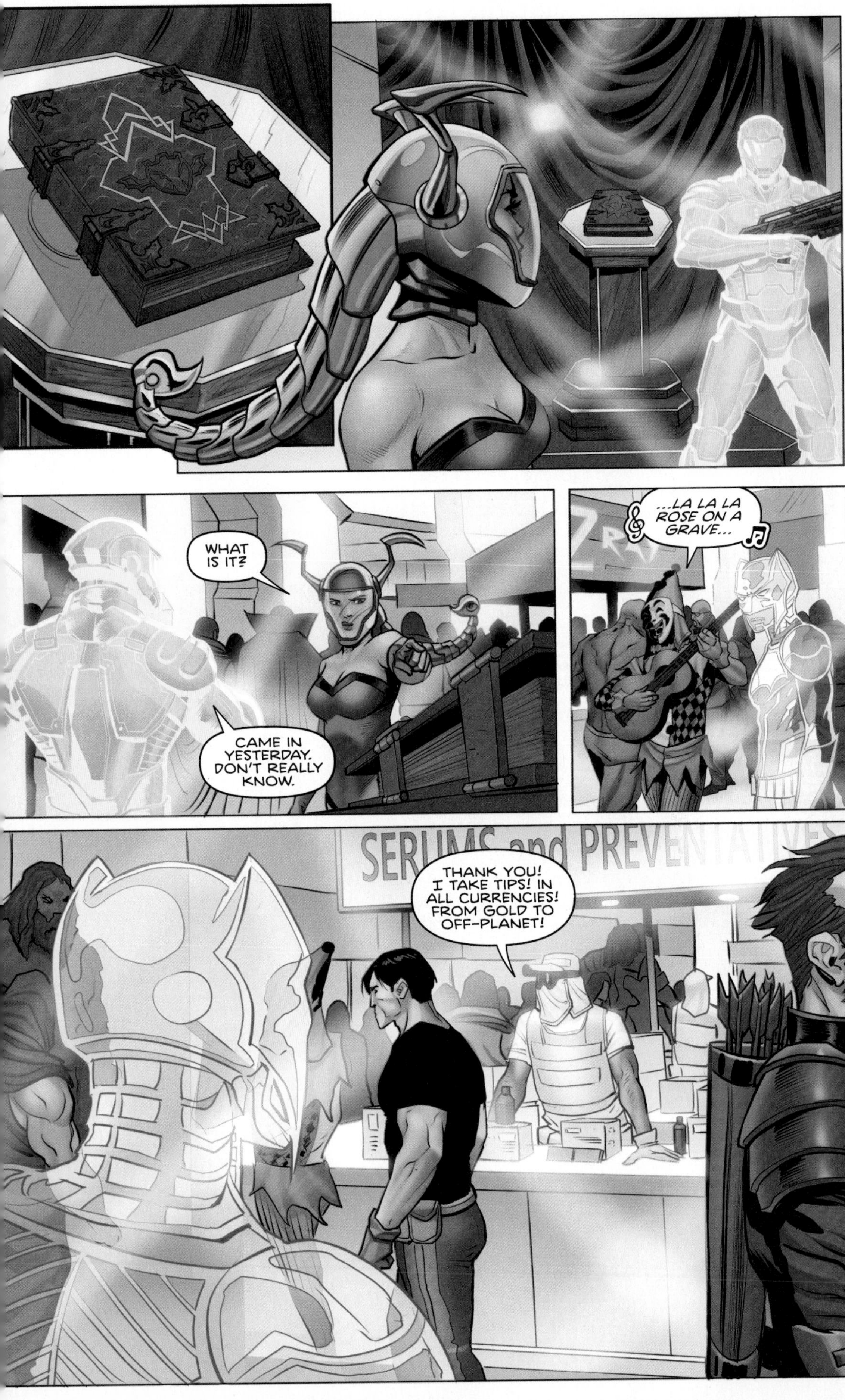
WHAT IS IT?
CAME IN YESTERDAY. DON'T REALLY KNOW.
...LA LA LA ROSE ON A GRAVE...
SERUMS and PREVENTATIVES
THANK YOU! I TAKE TIPS! IN ALL CURRENCIES! FROM GOLD TO OFF-PLANET!

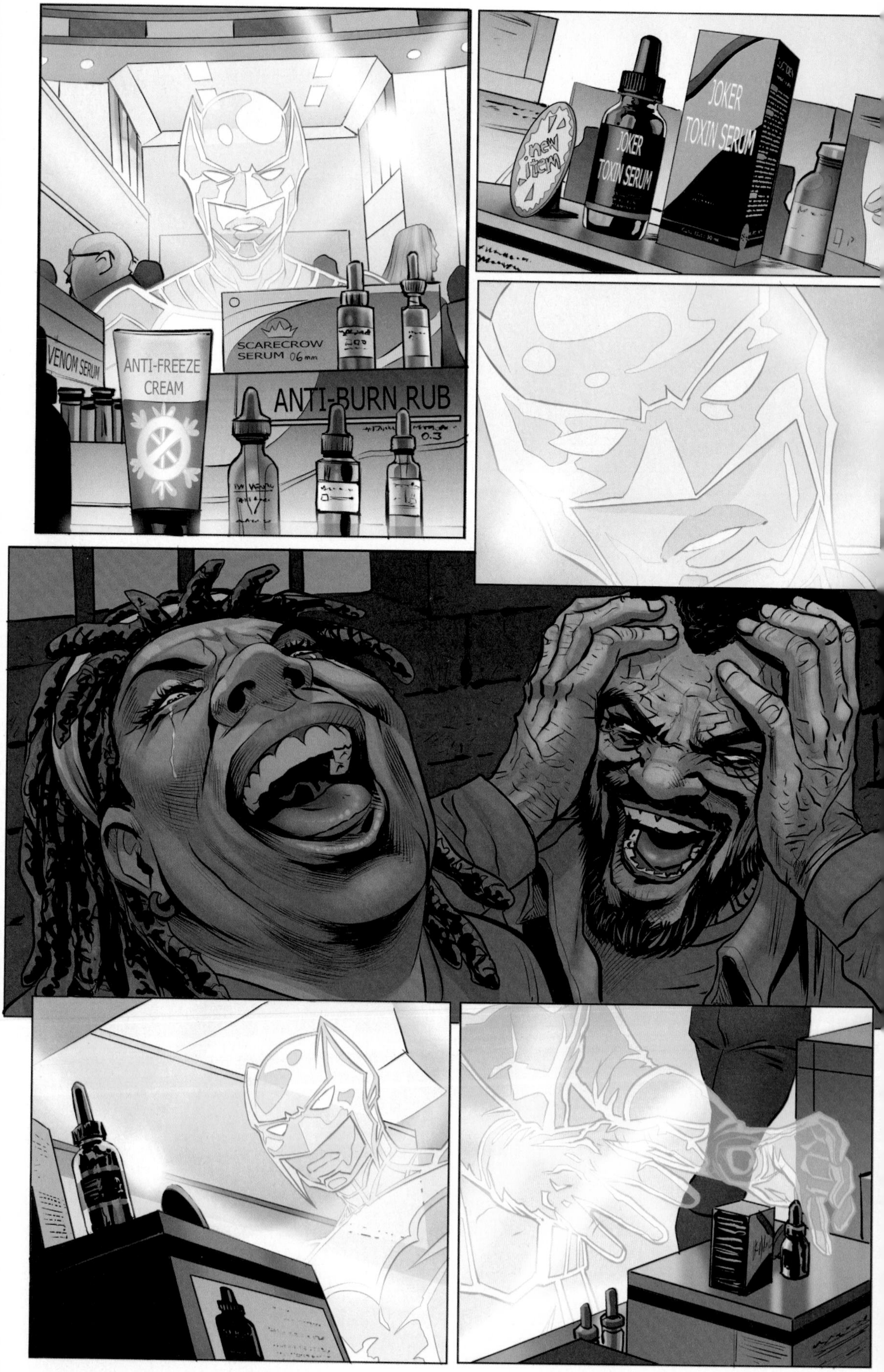
SCARECROW
SERUM 06mm
VENOM SERUM
ANTI-FREEZE
CREAM
ANTI-BURN RUB
0.3
new
item
JOKER
TOXIN SERUM
JOKER
TOXIN SERUM

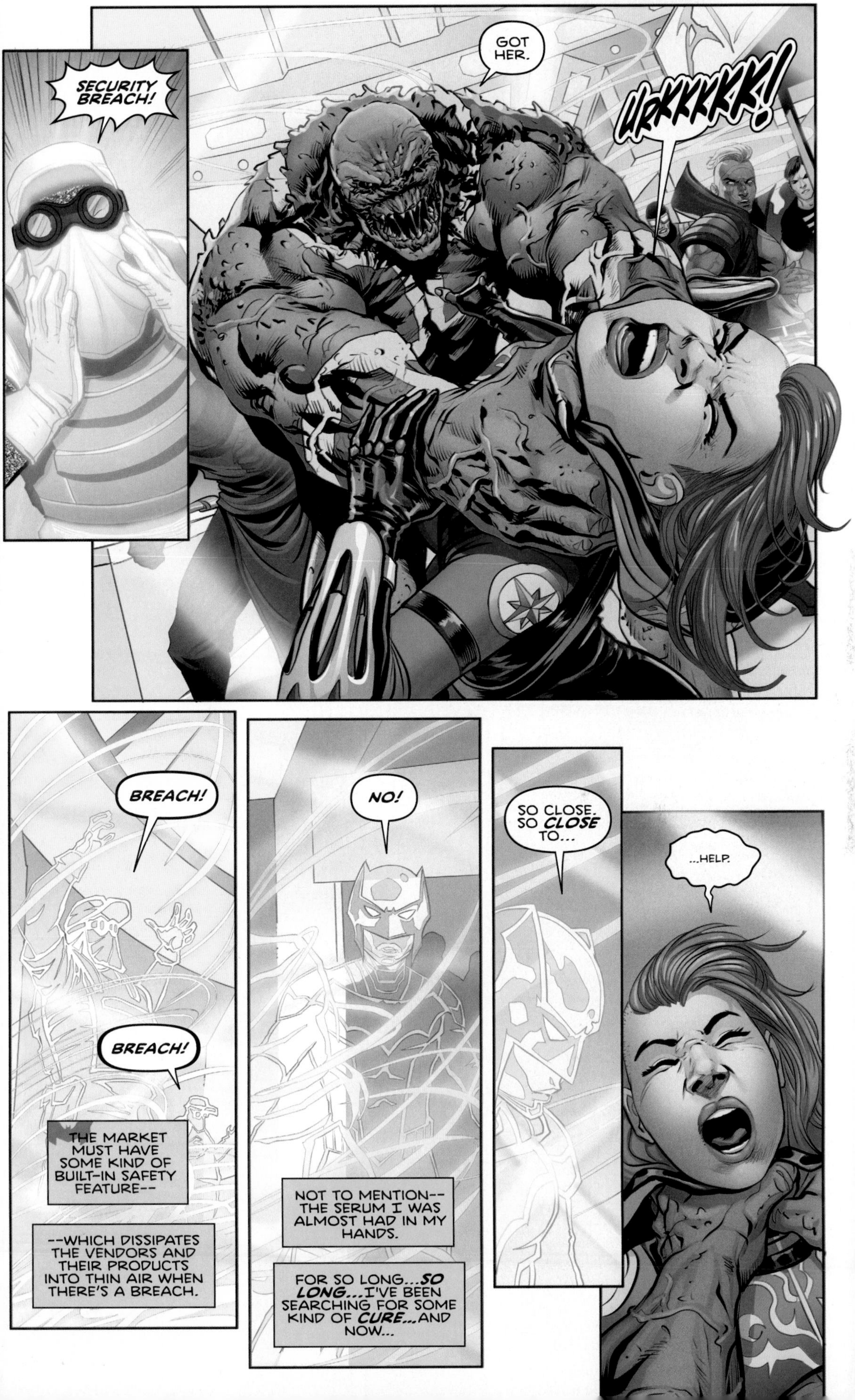
SECURITY BREACH!
GOT HER.
URKKKKKK!
BREACH!
BREACH!
THE MARKET MUST HAVE SOME KIND OF BUILT-IN SAFETY FEATURE--
--WHICH DISSIPATES THE VENDORS AND THEIR PRODUCTS INTO THIN AIR WHEN THERE'S A BREACH.
NO!
NOT TO MENTION-- THE SERUM I WAS ALMOST HAD IN MY HANDS.
FOR SO LONG...SO LONG...I'VE BEEN SEARCHING FOR SOME KIND OF CURE...AND NOW...
SO CLOSE. SO CLOSE TO...
...HELP.

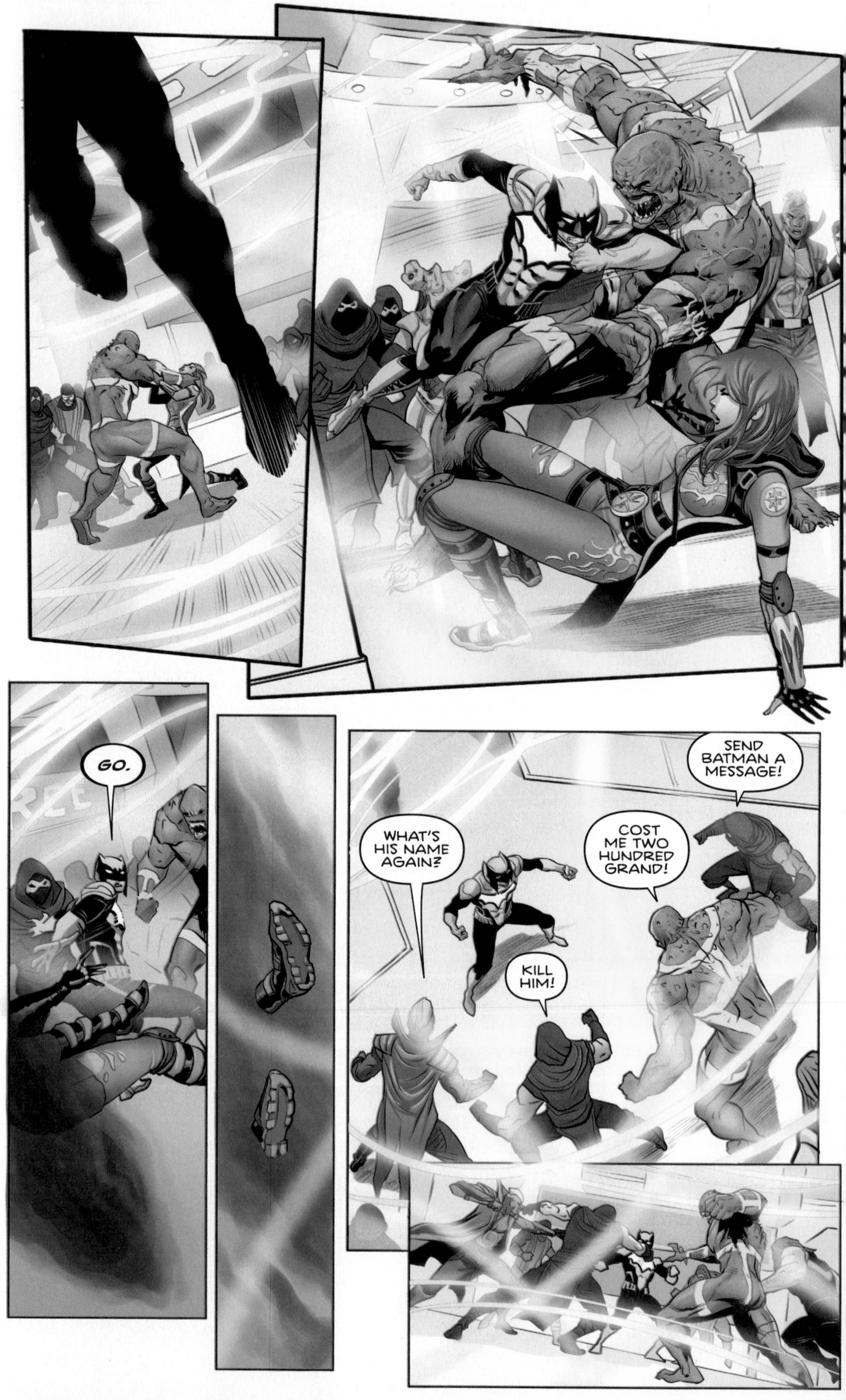
GO.
SEND BATMAN A MESSAGE!
WHAT'S HIS NAME AGAIN?
COST ME TWO HUNDRED GRAND!
KILL HIM!

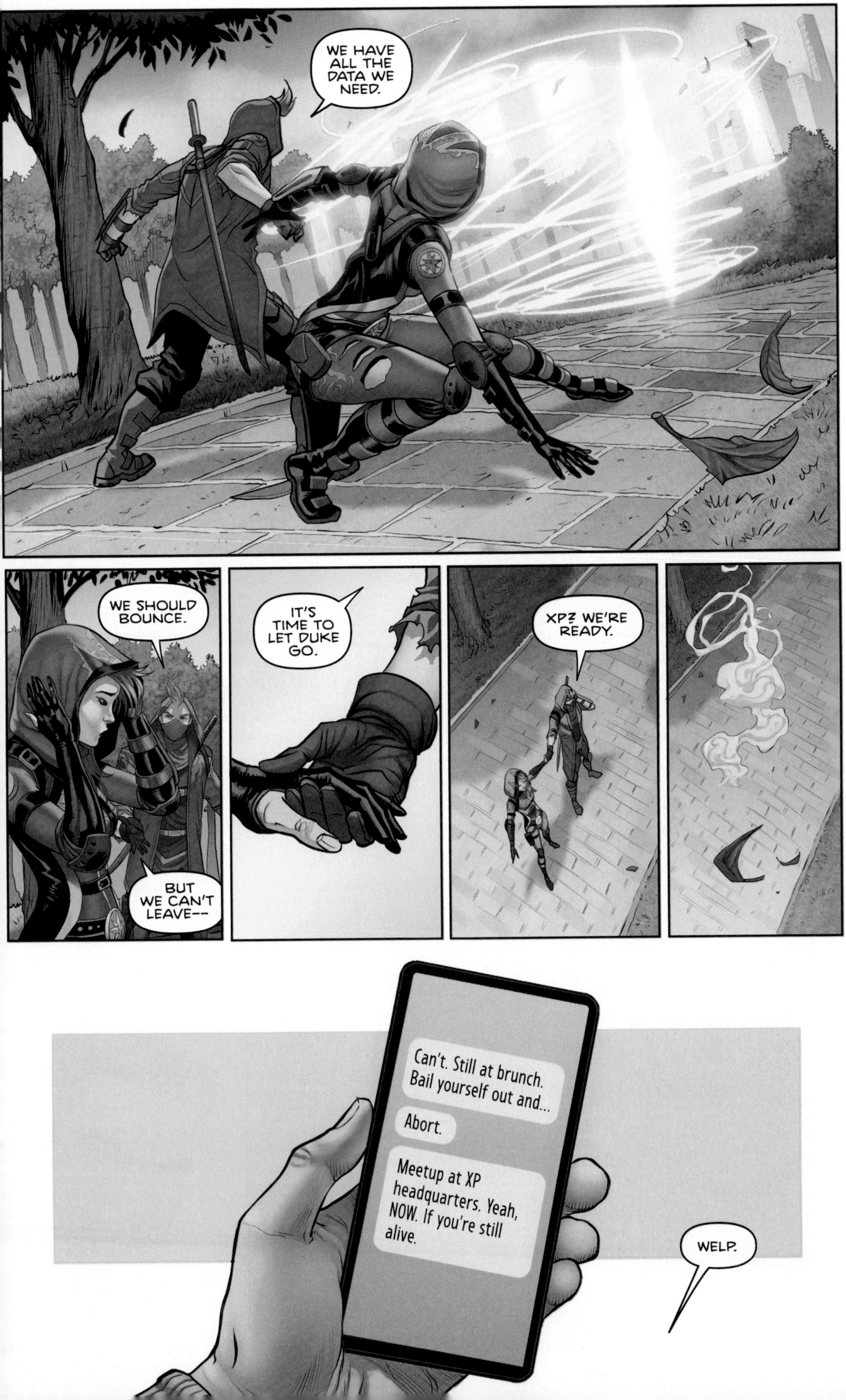
WE HAVE ALL THE DATA WE NEED.
WE SHOULD BOUNCE.
BUT WE CAN'T LEAVE--
IT'S TIME TO LET DUKE GO.
XP? WE'RE READY.
Can't. Still at brunch. Bail yourself out and...
Abort.
Meetup at XP headquarters. Yeah, NOW. If you're still alive.
WELP.

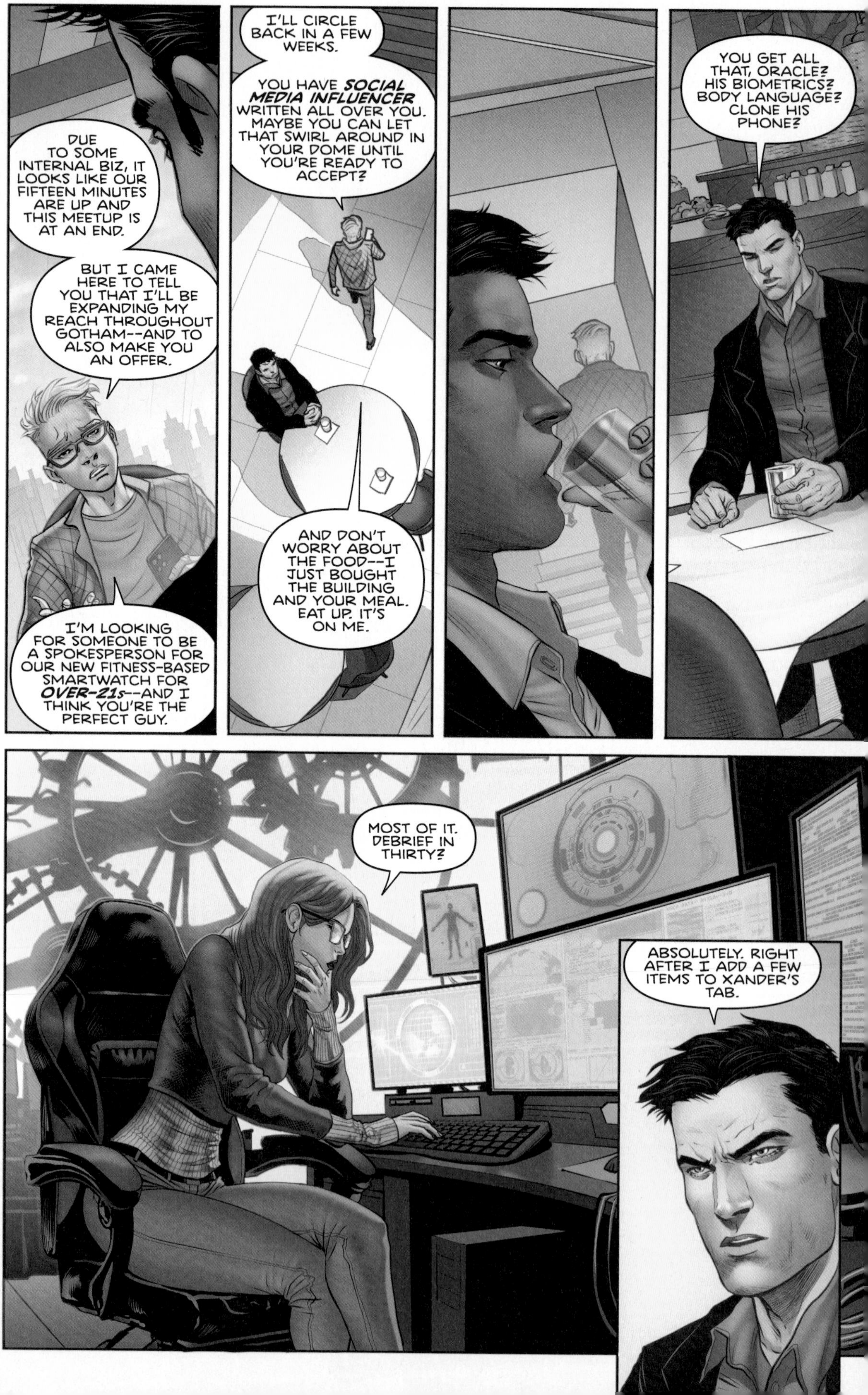
DUE TO SOME INTERNAL BIZ, IT LOOKS LIKE OUR FIFTEEN MINUTES ARE UP AND THIS MEETUP IS AT AN END.
BUT I CAME HERE TO TELL YOU THAT I'LL BE EXPANDING MY REACH THROUGHOUT GOTHAM--AND TO ALSO MAKE YOU AN OFFER.
I'M LOOKING FOR SOMEONE TO BE A SPOKESPERSON FOR OUR NEW FITNESS-BASED SMARTWATCH FOR *OVER-21s*--AND I THINK YOU'RE THE PERFECT GUY.
I'LL CIRCLE BACK IN A FEW WEEKS.
YOU HAVE ***SOCIAL MEDIA INFLUENCER*** WRITTEN ALL OVER YOU. MAYBE YOU CAN LET THAT SWIRL AROUND IN YOUR DOME UNTIL YOU'RE READY TO ACCEPT?
AND DON'T WORRY ABOUT THE FOOD--I JUST BOUGHT THE BUILDING AND YOUR MEAL. EAT UP. IT'S ON ME.
YOU GET ALL THAT, ORACLE? HIS BIOMETRICS? BODY LANGUAGE? CLONE HIS PHONE?
MOST OF IT. DEBRIEF IN THIRTY?
ABSOLUTELY. RIGHT AFTER I ADD A FEW ITEMS TO XANDER'S TAB.

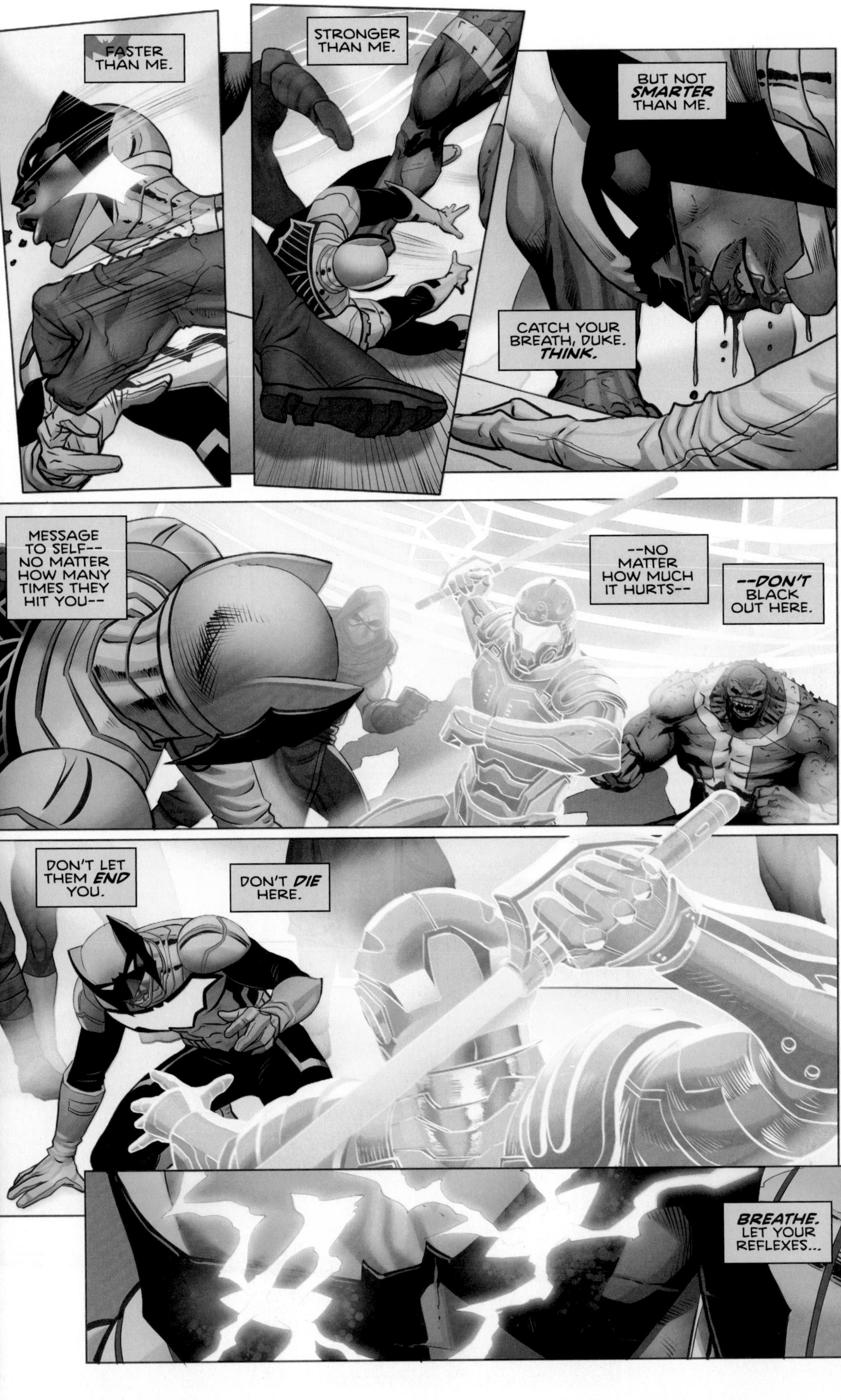

FASTER THAN ME.
STRONGER THAN ME.
BUT NOT SMARTER THAN ME.
CATCH YOUR BREATH, DUKE. THINK.
MESSAGE TO SELF-- NO MATTER HOW MANY TIMES THEY HIT YOU--
--NO MATTER HOW MUCH IT HURTS--
--DON'T BLACK OUT HERE.
DON'T LET THEM END YOU.
DON'T DIE HERE.
BREATHE. LET YOUR REFLEXES...

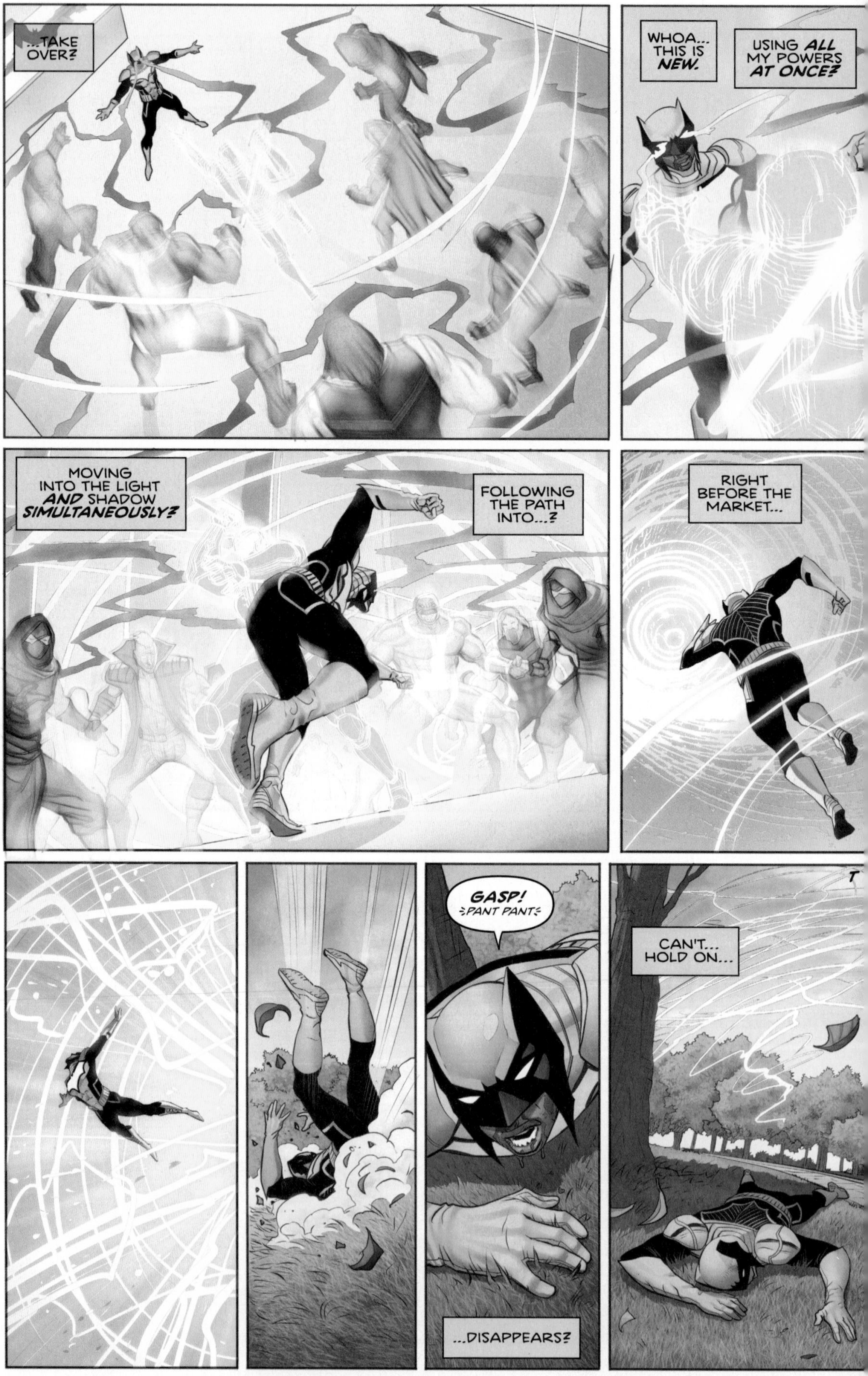
...TAKE OVER?
WHOA... THIS IS NEW.
USING ALL MY POWERS AT ONCE?
MOVING INTO THE LIGHT AND SHADOW SIMULTANEOUSLY?
FOLLOWING THE PATH INTO...?
RIGHT BEFORE THE MARKET...
GASP! PANT PANT
...DISAPPEARS?
CAN'T... HOLD ON...

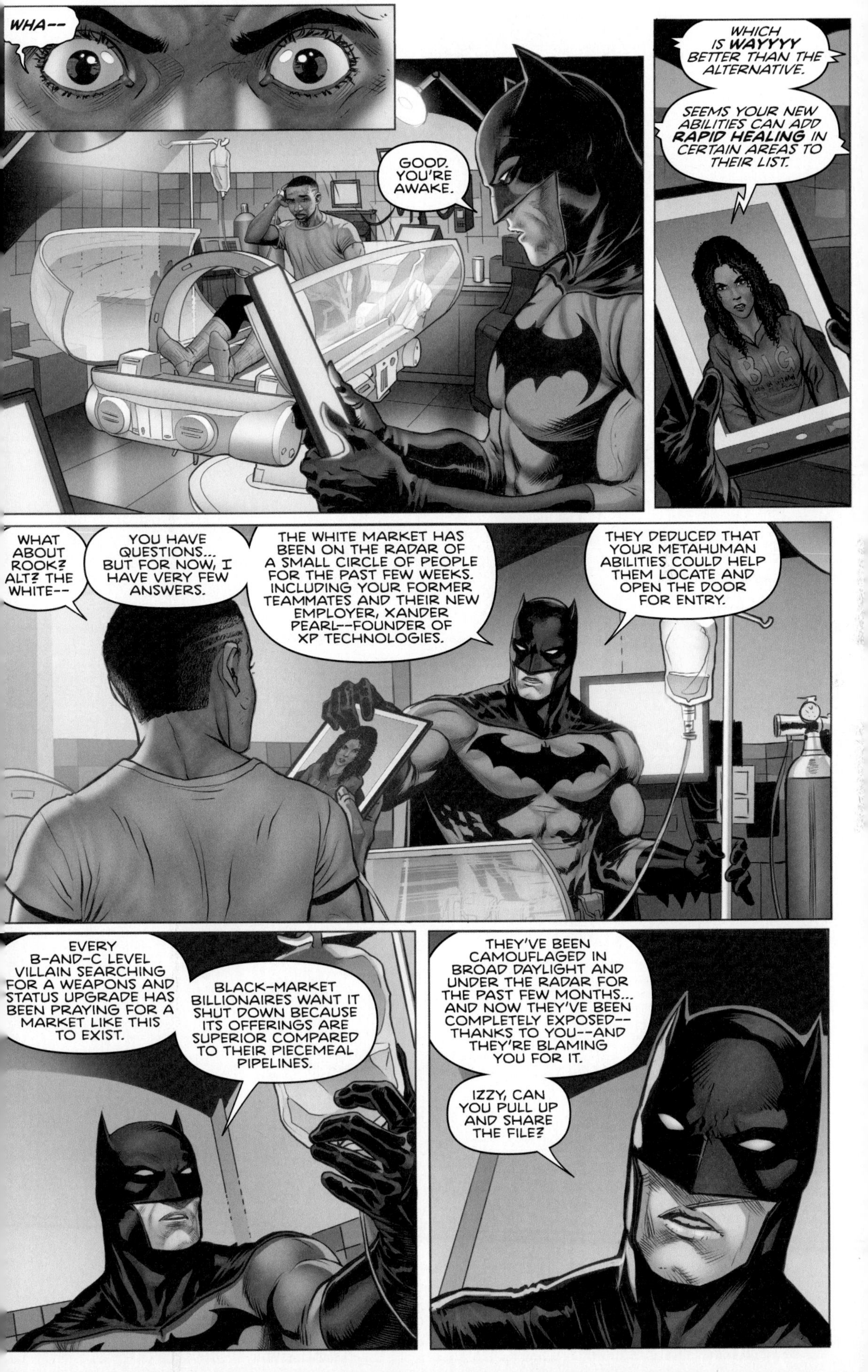
WHA--
GOOD. YOU'RE AWAKE.
WHICH IS WAYYYY BETTER THAN THE ALTERNATIVE.
SEEMS YOUR NEW ABILITIES CAN ADD RAPID HEALING IN CERTAIN AREAS TO THEIR LIST.
WHAT ABOUT ROOK? ALT? THE WHITE--
YOU HAVE QUESTIONS... BUT FOR NOW, I HAVE VERY FEW ANSWERS.
THE WHITE MARKET HAS BEEN ON THE RADAR OF A SMALL CIRCLE OF PEOPLE FOR THE PAST FEW WEEKS. INCLUDING YOUR FORMER TEAMMATES AND THEIR NEW EMPLOYER, XANDER PEARL--FOUNDER OF XP TECHNOLOGIES.
THEY DEDUCED THAT YOUR METAHUMAN ABILITIES COULD HELP THEM LOCATE AND OPEN THE DOOR FOR ENTRY.
EVERY B-AND-C LEVEL VILLAIN SEARCHING FOR A WEAPONS AND STATUS UPGRADE HAS BEEN PRAYING FOR A MARKET LIKE THIS TO EXIST.
BLACK-MARKET BILLIONAIRES WANT IT SHUT DOWN BECAUSE ITS OFFERINGS ARE SUPERIOR COMPARED TO THEIR PIECEMEAL PIPELINES.
THEY'VE BEEN CAMOUFLAGED IN BROAD DAYLIGHT AND UNDER THE RADAR FOR THE PAST FEW MONTHS... AND NOW THEY'VE BEEN COMPLETELY EXPOSED-- THANKS TO YOU--AND THEY'RE BLAMING YOU FOR IT.
IZZY, CAN YOU PULL UP AND SHARE THE FILE?

IN THE DRIVE BATMAN SHARED--IT SEEMS THAT AT LEAST ONE POSSIBLE FUNDER OF THE MARKET...IS **THE ORDER OF THE STONE.**

A SECT OF THE RELIGION OF CRIME.

CENTERED AROUND A BOOK OF HISTORICAL DARK DEEDS CALLED THE CRIME BIBLE.

BASED ON THE DATA FROM RECENT DAYTIME ATTACKS, THEY'VE RETURNED TO GOTHAM.

WHICH PROMPTS ME TO ASK--ARE YOU UP FOR MORE FIELD RESEARCH IN THE NEXT FEW DAYS?

I CAN UNDERSTAND IF YOU SAY NO.

YOU CAN'T KEEP DOING THIS ALONE, DUKE.

IZZY, YOU SAID YOU'RE NOT READY TO GO BACK INTO THE FIELD. AND BESIDES, YOU HAVEN'T DECIDED ON A NEW IDENTITY AND CODE NAME...

SO FOR NOW--THE SIGNAL WILL RESUME HIS DAYTIME DUTIES... **SOLO.**

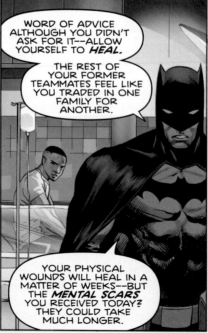

WORD OF ADVICE ALTHOUGH YOU DIDN'T ASK FOR IT--ALLOW YOURSELF TO *HEAL.*

THE REST OF YOUR FORMER TEAMMATES FEEL LIKE YOU TRADED IN ONE FAMILY FOR ANOTHER.

YOUR PHYSICAL WOUNDS WILL HEAL IN A MATTER OF WEEKS--BUT THE *MENTAL SCARS* YOU RECEIVED TODAY? THEY COULD TAKE MUCH LONGER.

I'M LOOKING FORWARD TO YOUR NEXT SHIFT.

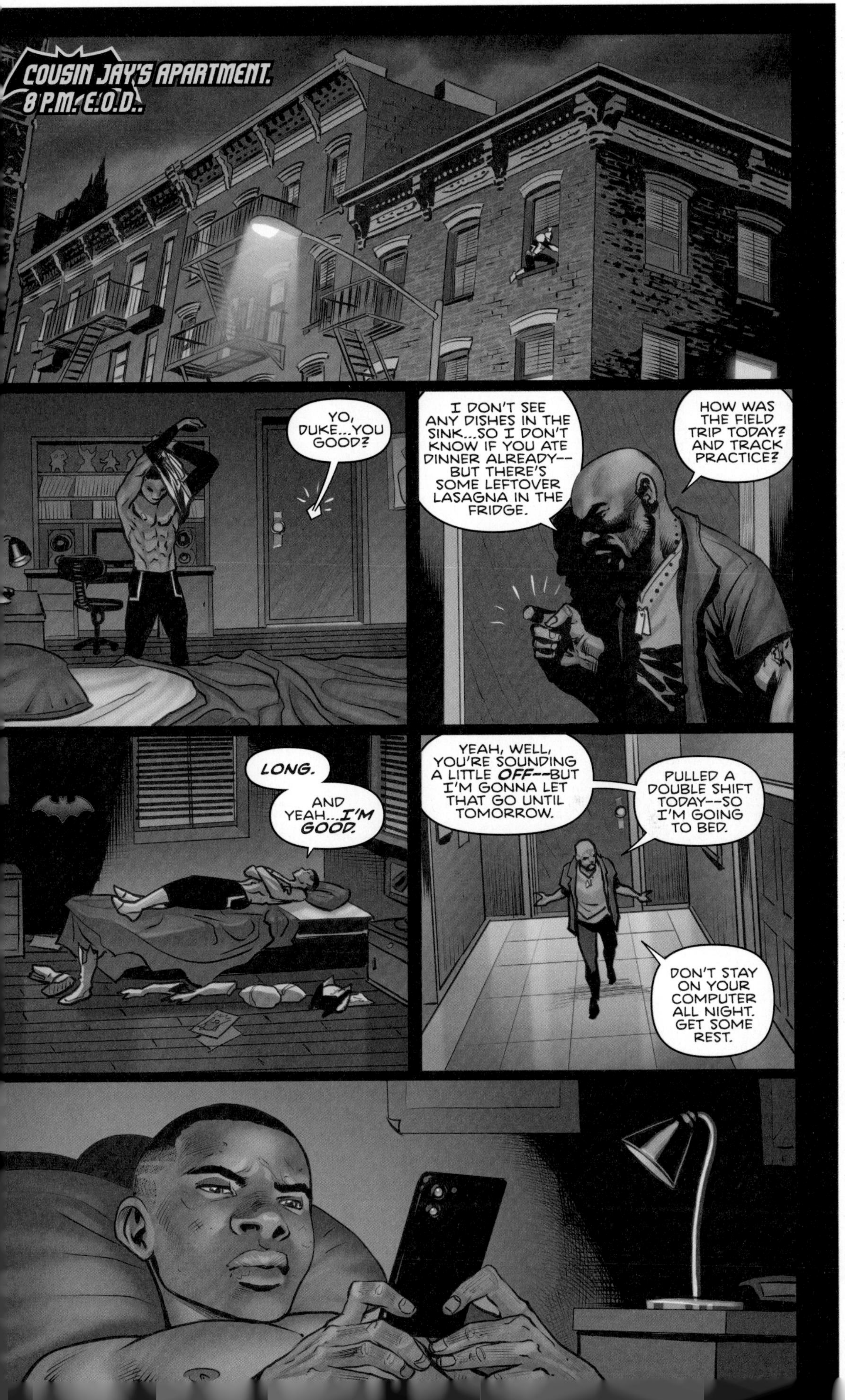
COUSIN JAY'S APARTMENT. 8 P.M. E.O.D..
YO, DUKE...YOU GOOD?
I DON'T SEE ANY DISHES IN THE SINK...SO I DON'T KNOW IF YOU ATE DINNER ALREADY--BUT THERE'S SOME LEFTOVER LASAGNA IN THE FRIDGE.
HOW WAS THE FIELD TRIP TODAY? AND TRACK PRACTICE?
LONG.
AND YEAH...I'M GOOD.
YEAH, WELL, YOU'RE SOUNDING A LITTLE OFF--BUT I'M GONNA LET THAT GO UNTIL TOMORROW.
PULLED A DOUBLE SHIFT TODAY--SO I'M GOING TO BED.
DON'T STAY ON YOUR COMPUTER ALL NIGHT. GET SOME REST.

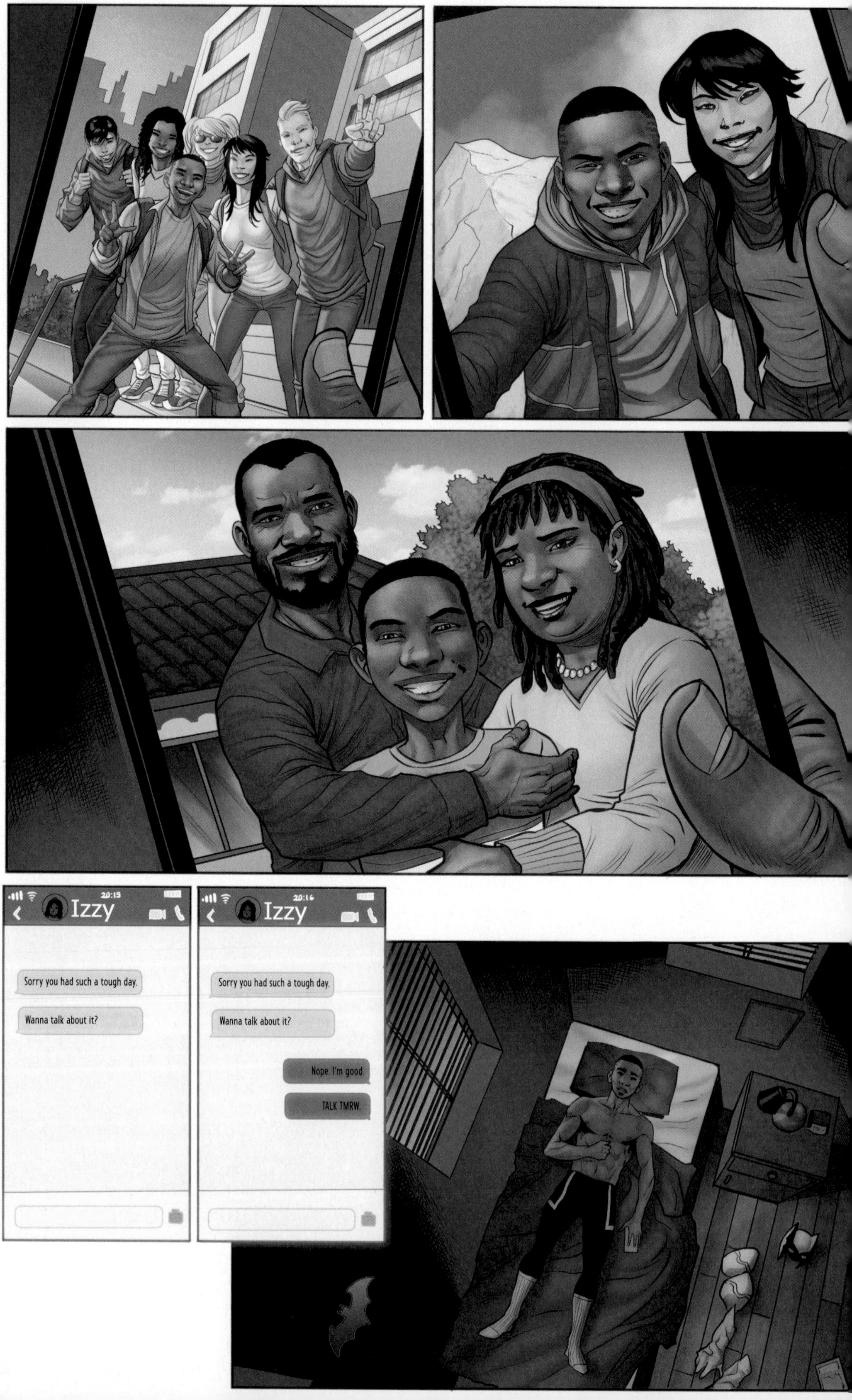
20:15
Izzy
Sorry you had such a tough day.
Wanna talk about it?
20:16
Izzy
Sorry you had such a tough day.
Wanna talk about it?
Nope. I'm good
TALK TMRW.

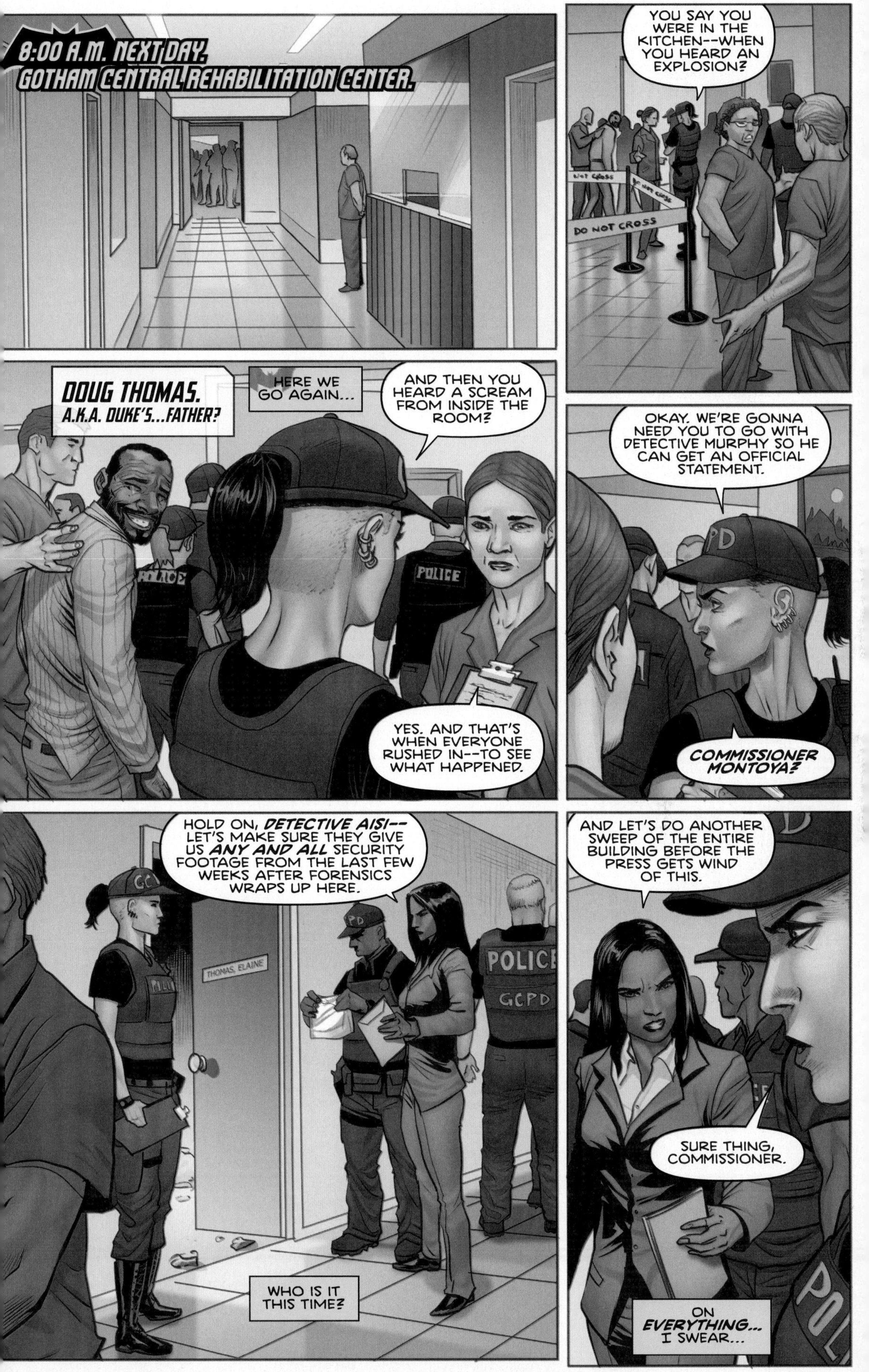
8:00 A.M. NEXT DAY.
GOTHAM CENTRAL REHABILITATION CENTER.
YOU SAY YOU WERE IN THE KITCHEN--WHEN YOU HEARD AN EXPLOSION?
DO NOT CROSS
DOUG THOMAS.
A.K.A. DUKE'S...FATHER?
HERE WE GO AGAIN...
AND THEN YOU HEARD A SCREAM FROM INSIDE THE ROOM?
POLICE
YES. AND THAT'S WHEN EVERYONE RUSHED IN--TO SEE WHAT HAPPENED.
OKAY. WE'RE GONNA NEED YOU TO GO WITH DETECTIVE MURPHY SO HE CAN GET AN OFFICIAL STATEMENT.
COMMISSIONER MONTOYA?
HOLD ON, DETECTIVE AISI-- LET'S MAKE SURE THEY GIVE US ANY AND ALL SECURITY FOOTAGE FROM THE LAST FEW WEEKS AFTER FORENSICS WRAPS UP HERE.
THOMAS, ELAINE
POLICE
GCPD
WHO IS IT THIS TIME?
AND LET'S DO ANOTHER SWEEP OF THE ENTIRE BUILDING BEFORE THE PRESS GETS WIND OF THIS.
SURE THING, COMMISSIONER.
ON EVERYTHING... I SWEAR...

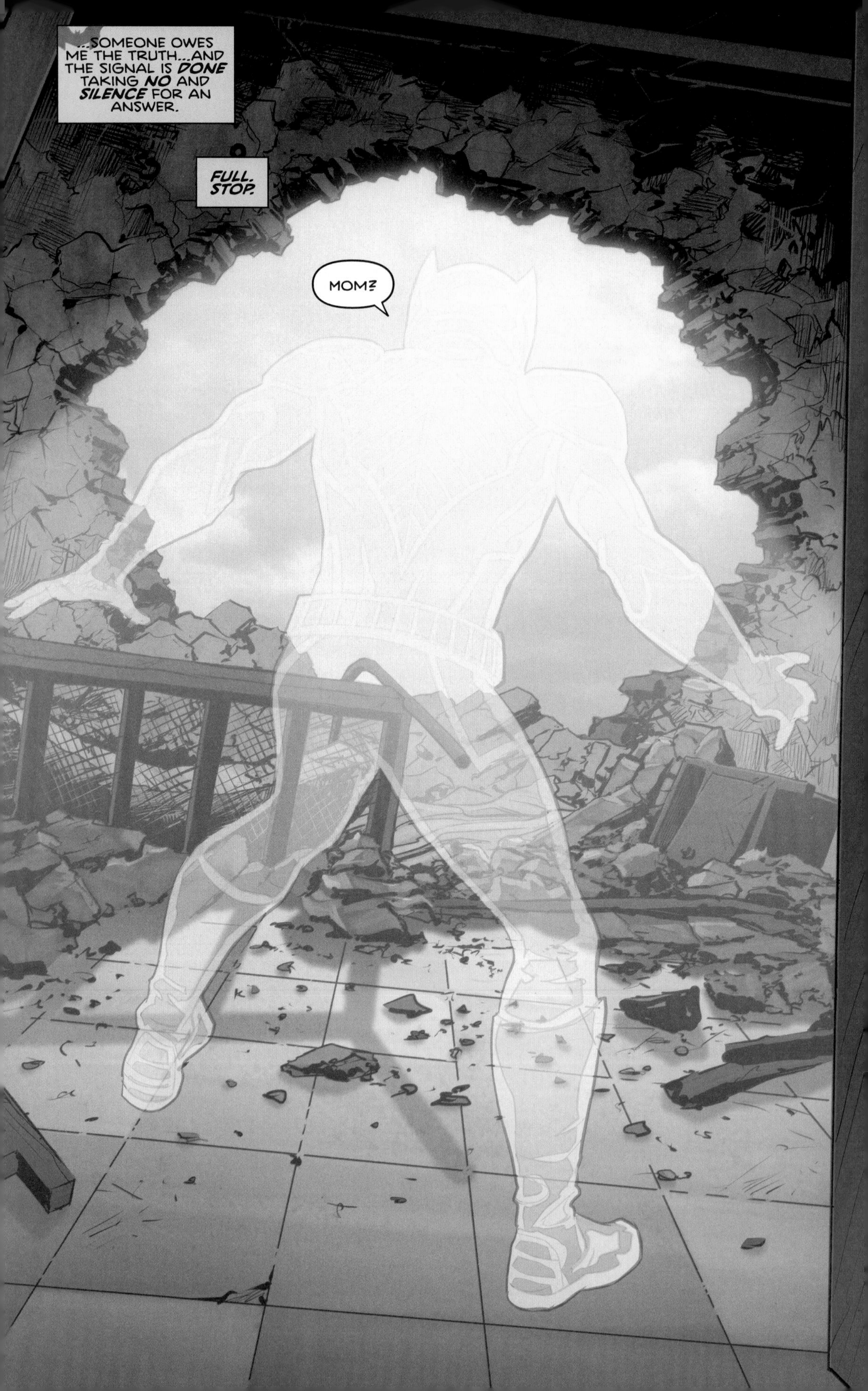
...SOMEONE OWES ME THE TRUTH...AND THE SIGNAL IS DONE TAKING NO AND SILENCE FOR AN ANSWER.
FULL. STOP.
MOM?

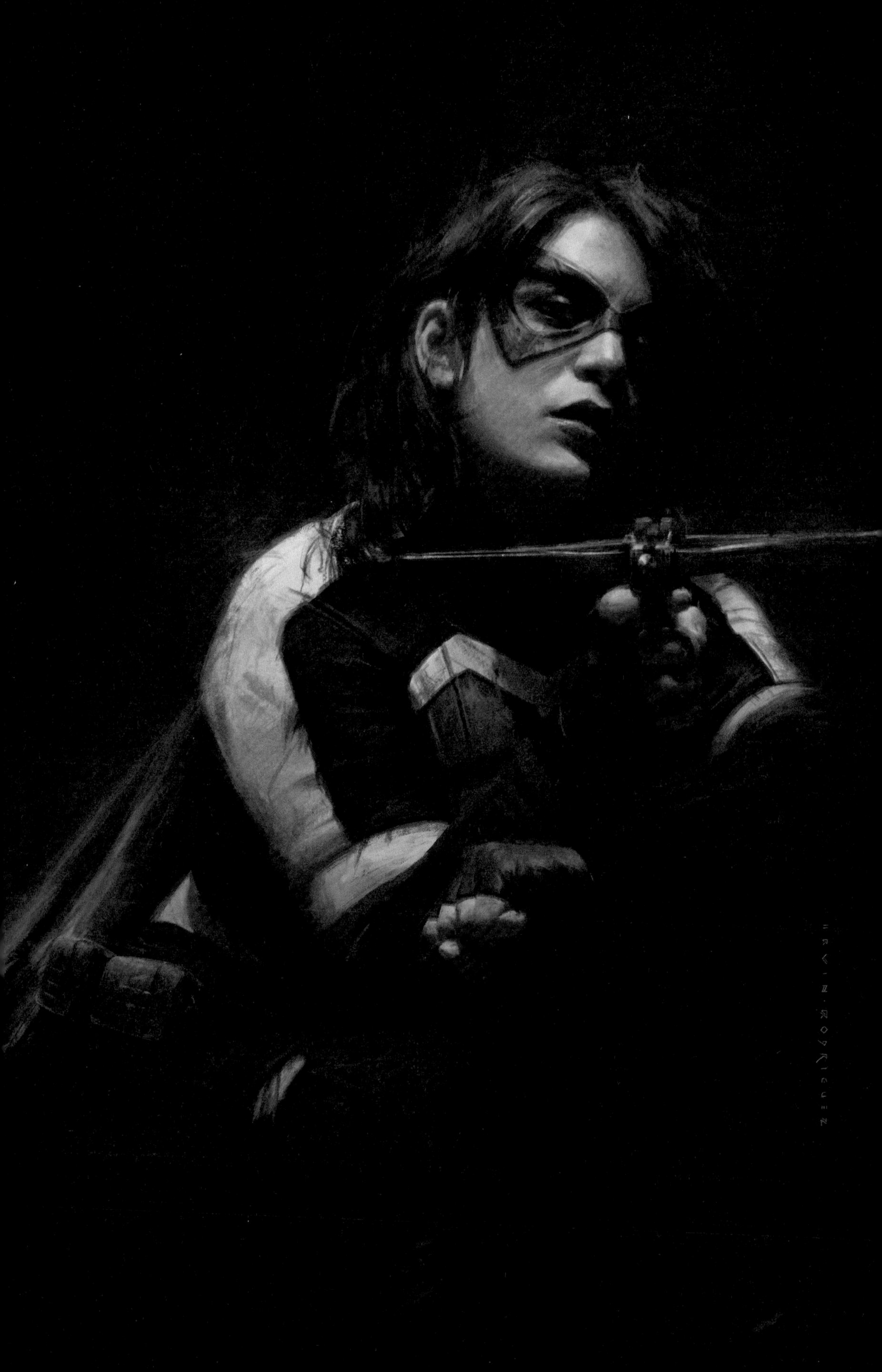

Batman Secret Files: Huntress #1
Cover by Irvin Rodriguez

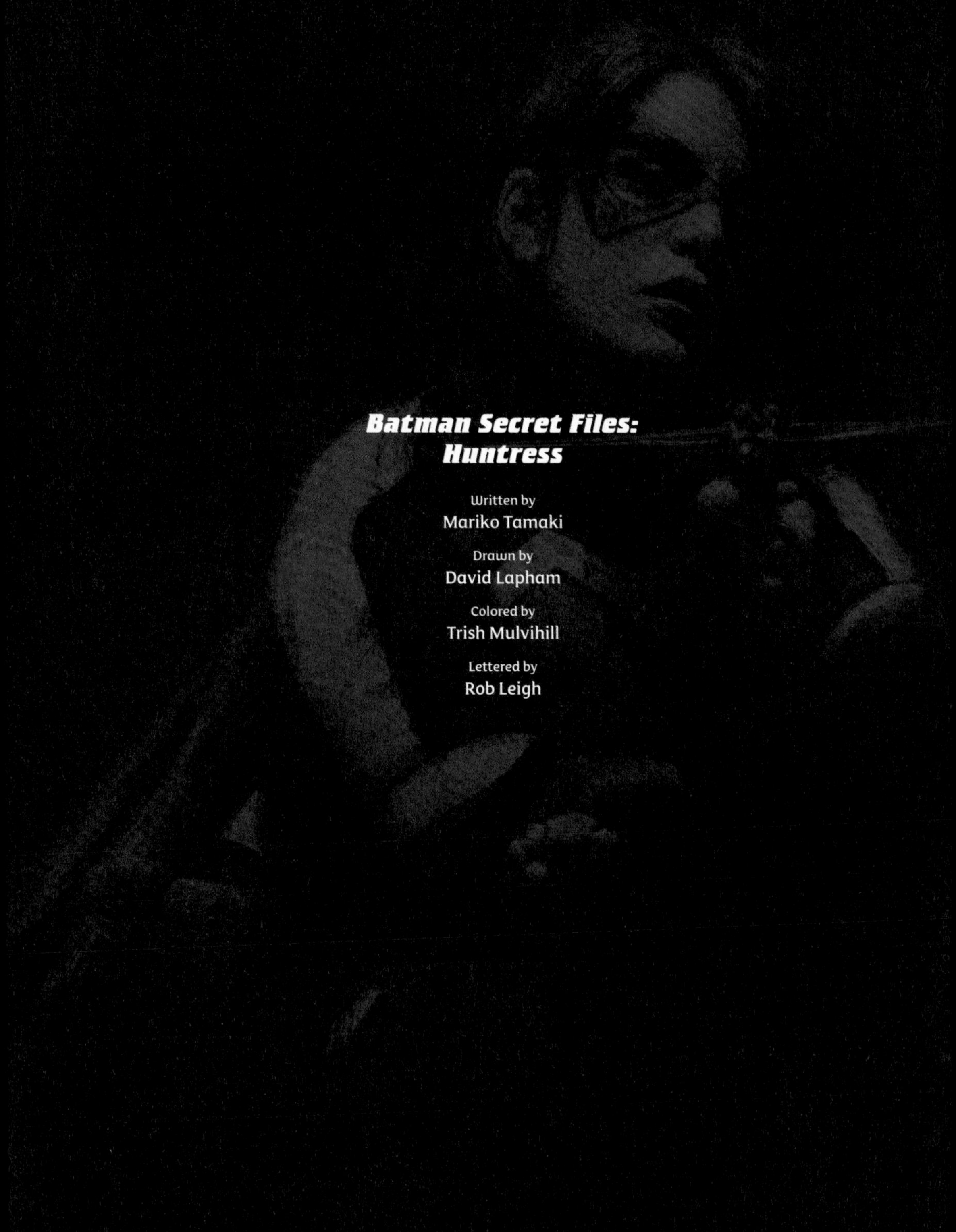

Batman Secret Files: Huntress

Written by
Mariko Tamaki

Drawn by
David Lapham

Colored by
Trish Mulvihill

Lettered by
Rob Leigh

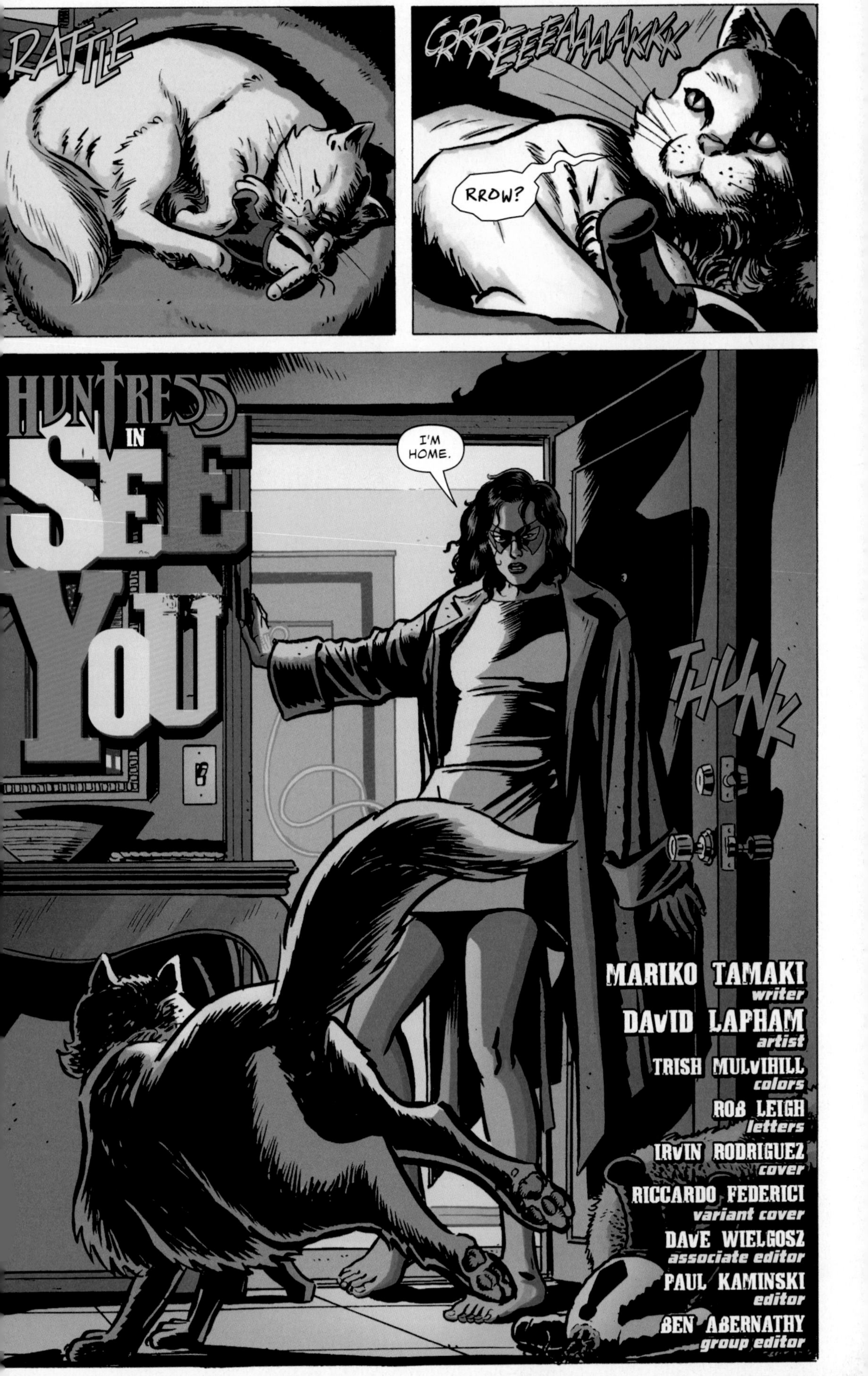
RATTLE
CRRREEEEAAAAKKK
RROW?
HUNTRESS IN
SEE YOU
I'M HOME.
THUNK
MARIKO TAMAKI
writer
DAVID LAPHAM
artist
TRISH MULVIHILL
colors
ROB LEIGH
letters
IRVIN RODRIGUEZ
cover
RICCARDO FEDERICI
variant cover
DAVE WIELGOSZ
associate editor
PAUL KAMINSKI
editor
BEN ABERNATHY
group editor

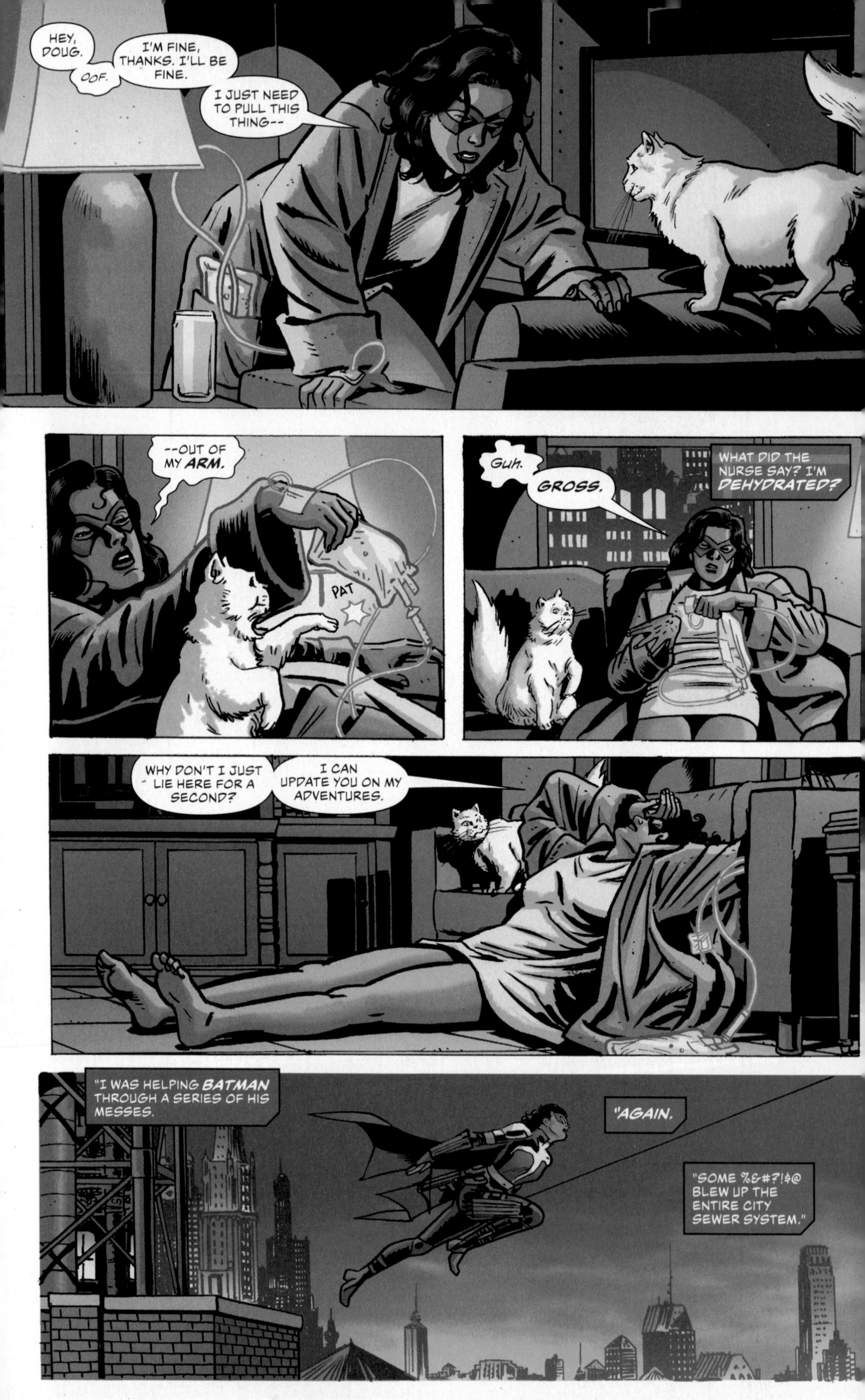
HEY, DOUG.
OOF.
I'M FINE, THANKS. I'LL BE FINE.
I JUST NEED TO PULL THIS THING--
--OUT OF MY ARM.
PAT
Guh.
GROSS.
WHAT DID THE NURSE SAY? I'M DEHYDRATED?
WHY DON'T I JUST LIE HERE FOR A SECOND?
I CAN UPDATE YOU ON MY ADVENTURES.
"I WAS HELPING BATMAN THROUGH A SERIES OF HIS MESSES.
"AGAIN.
"SOME %&#?!$@ BLEW UP THE ENTIRE CITY SEWER SYSTEM."

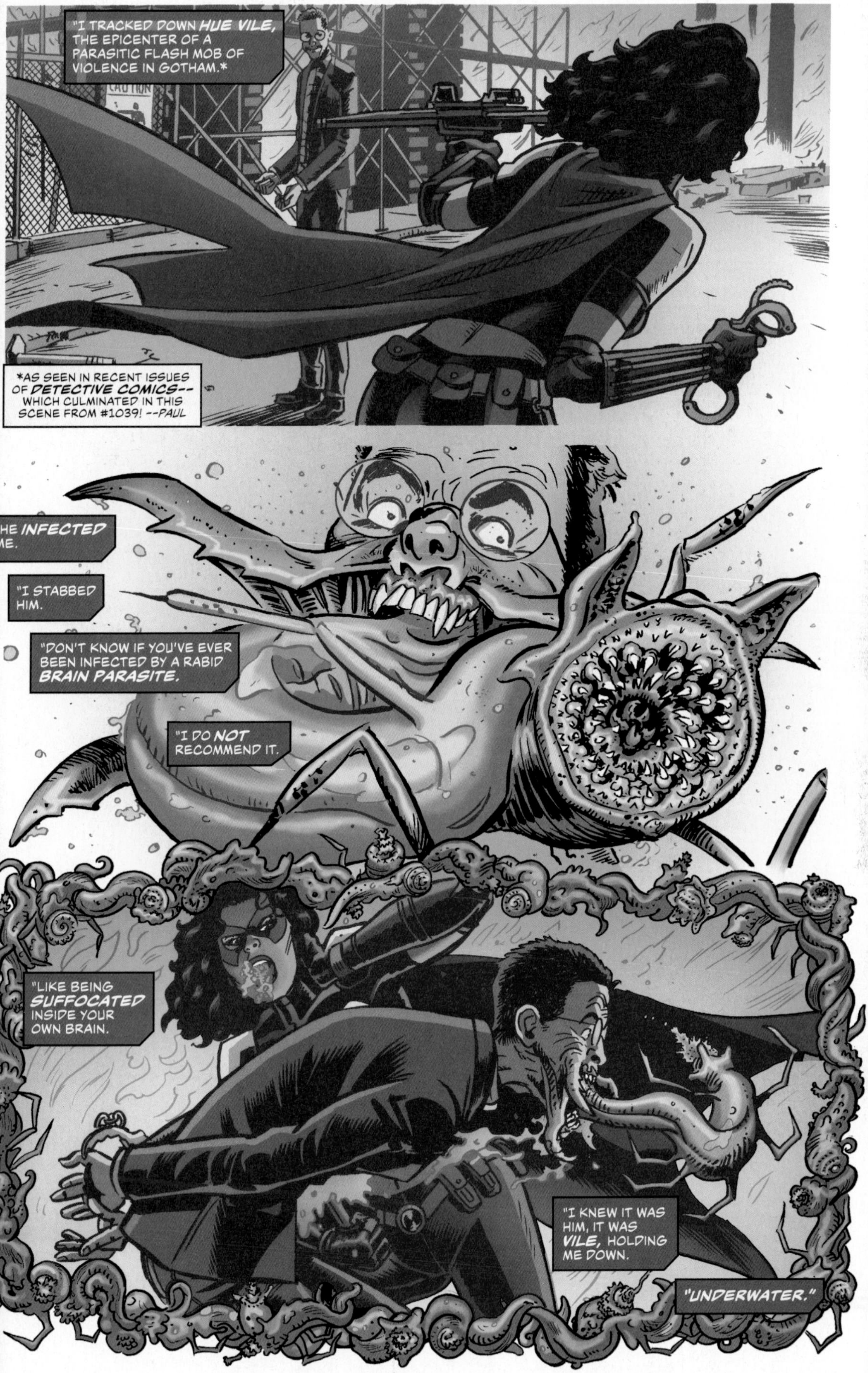
"I TRACKED DOWN HUE VILE, THE EPICENTER OF A PARASITIC FLASH MOB OF VIOLENCE IN GOTHAM.*
CAUTION
*AS SEEN IN RECENT ISSUES OF DETECTIVE COMICS-- WHICH CULMINATED IN THIS SCENE FROM #1039! --PAUL
HE INFECTED ME.
"I STABBED HIM.
"DON'T KNOW IF YOU'VE EVER BEEN INFECTED BY A RABID BRAIN PARASITE.
"I DO NOT RECOMMEND IT.
"LIKE BEING SUFFOCATED INSIDE YOUR OWN BRAIN.
"I KNEW IT WAS HIM, IT WAS VILE, HOLDING ME DOWN.
"UNDERWATER."

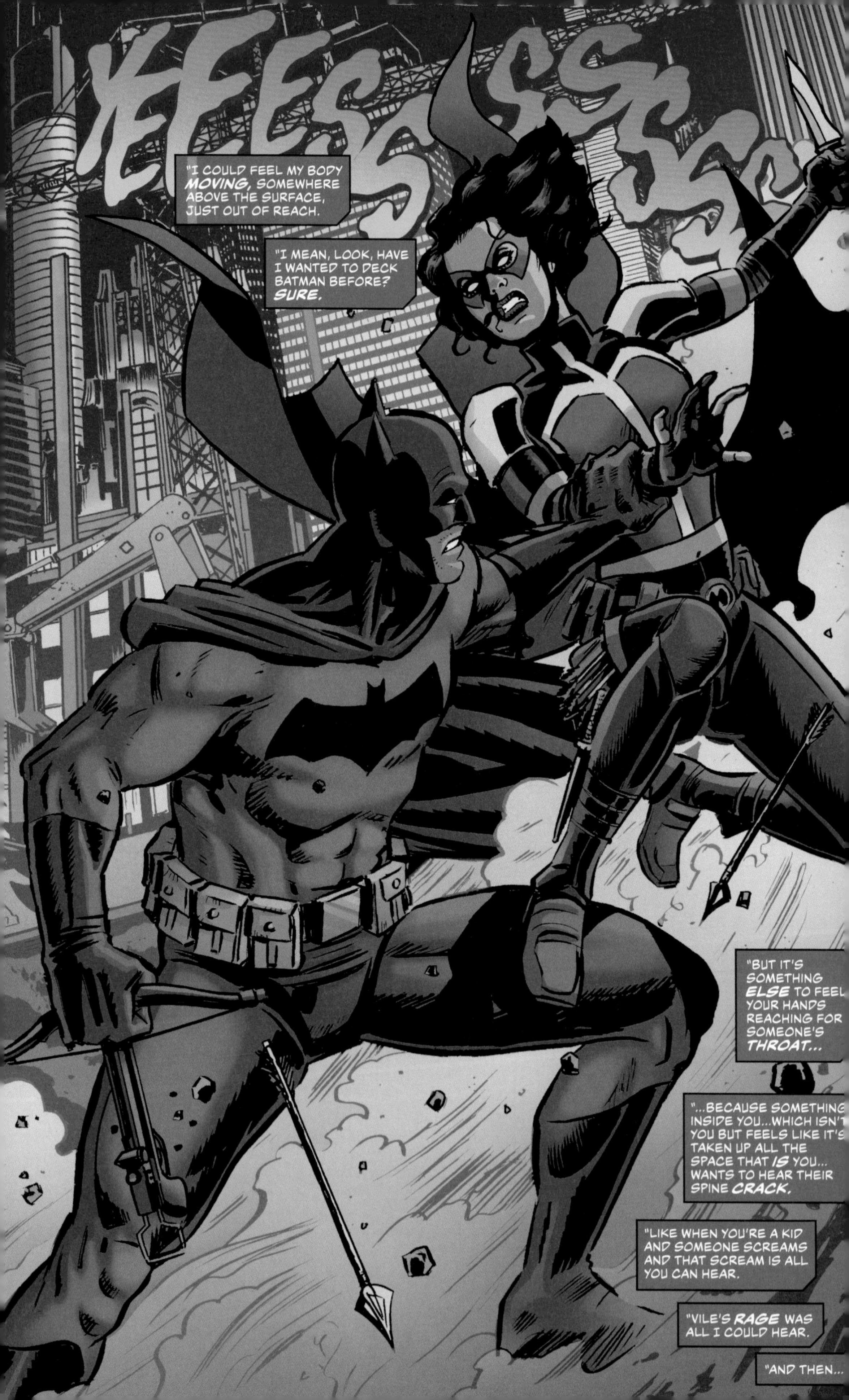
YEEESSSSSSSCC
"I COULD FEEL MY BODY MOVING, SOMEWHERE ABOVE THE SURFACE, JUST OUT OF REACH.
"I MEAN, LOOK, HAVE I WANTED TO DECK BATMAN BEFORE? SURE.
"BUT IT'S SOMETHING ELSE TO FEEL YOUR HANDS REACHING FOR SOMEONE'S THROAT...
"...BECAUSE SOMETHING INSIDE YOU...WHICH ISN'T YOU BUT FEELS LIKE IT'S TAKEN UP ALL THE SPACE THAT IS YOU... WANTS TO HEAR THEIR SPINE CRACK.
"LIKE WHEN YOU'RE A KID AND SOMEONE SCREAMS AND THAT SCREAM IS ALL YOU CAN HEAR.
"VILE'S RAGE WAS ALL I COULD HEAR.
"AND THEN...

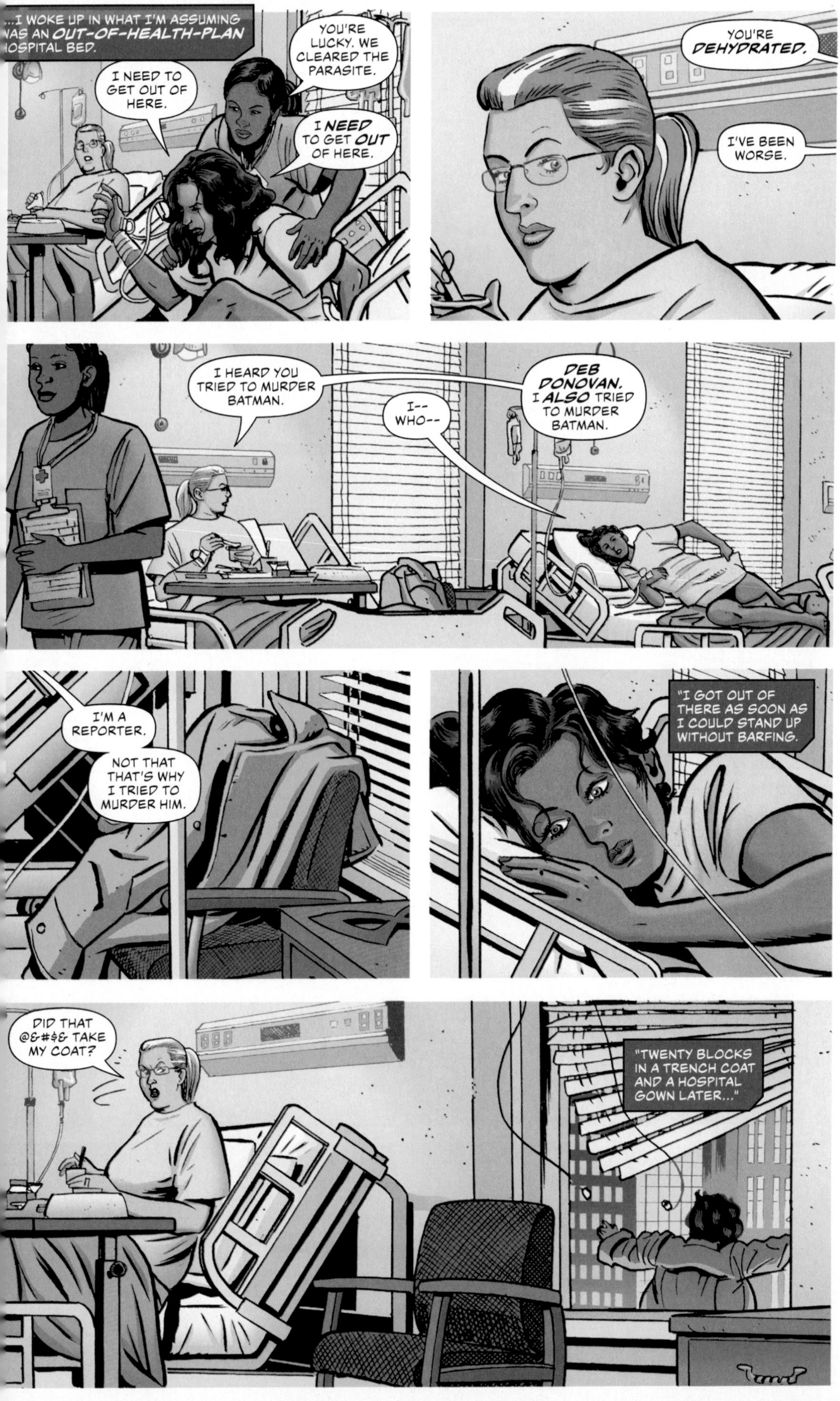
...I WOKE UP IN WHAT I'M ASSUMING WAS AN OUT-OF-HEALTH-PLAN HOSPITAL BED.
YOU'RE LUCKY. WE CLEARED THE PARASITE.
I NEED TO GET OUT OF HERE.
I NEED TO GET OUT OF HERE.
YOU'RE DEHYDRATED.
I'VE BEEN WORSE.
I HEARD YOU TRIED TO MURDER BATMAN.
I-- WHO--
DEB DONOVAN. I ALSO TRIED TO MURDER BATMAN.
I'M A REPORTER.
NOT THAT THAT'S WHY I TRIED TO MURDER HIM.
"I GOT OUT OF THERE AS SOON AS I COULD STAND UP WITHOUT BARFING.
DID THAT @&#$& TAKE MY COAT?
"TWENTY BLOCKS IN A TRENCH COAT AND A HOSPITAL GOWN LATER..."

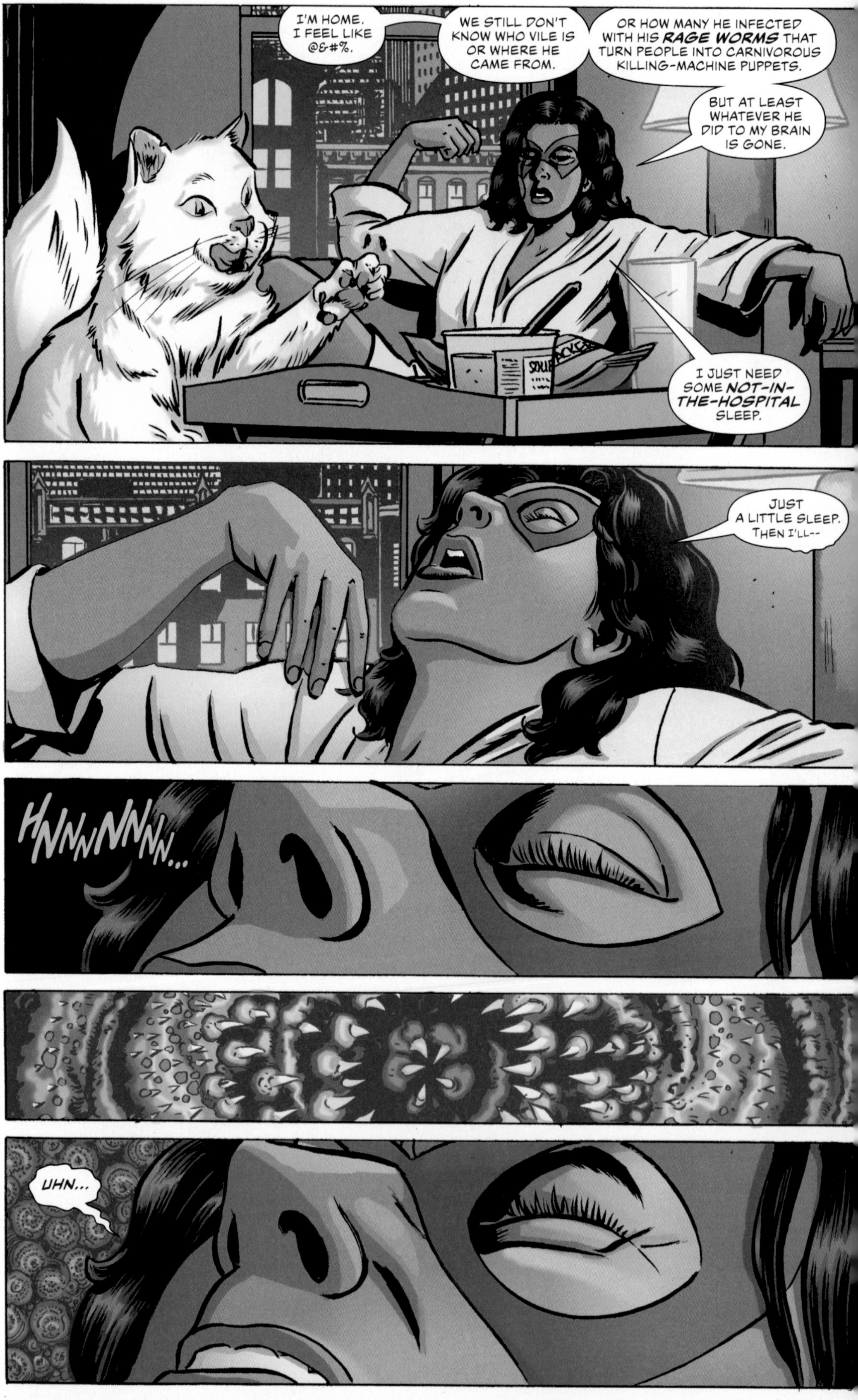
I'M HOME. I FEEL LIKE @&#%.
WE STILL DON'T KNOW WHO VILE IS OR WHERE HE CAME FROM.
OR HOW MANY HE INFECTED WITH HIS RAGE WORMS THAT TURN PEOPLE INTO CARNIVOROUS KILLING-MACHINE PUPPETS.
BUT AT LEAST WHATEVER HE DID TO MY BRAIN IS GONE.
I JUST NEED SOME NOT-IN-THE-HOSPITAL SLEEP.
JUST A LITTLE SLEEP. THEN I'LL--
HNNNNNNN...
UHN...

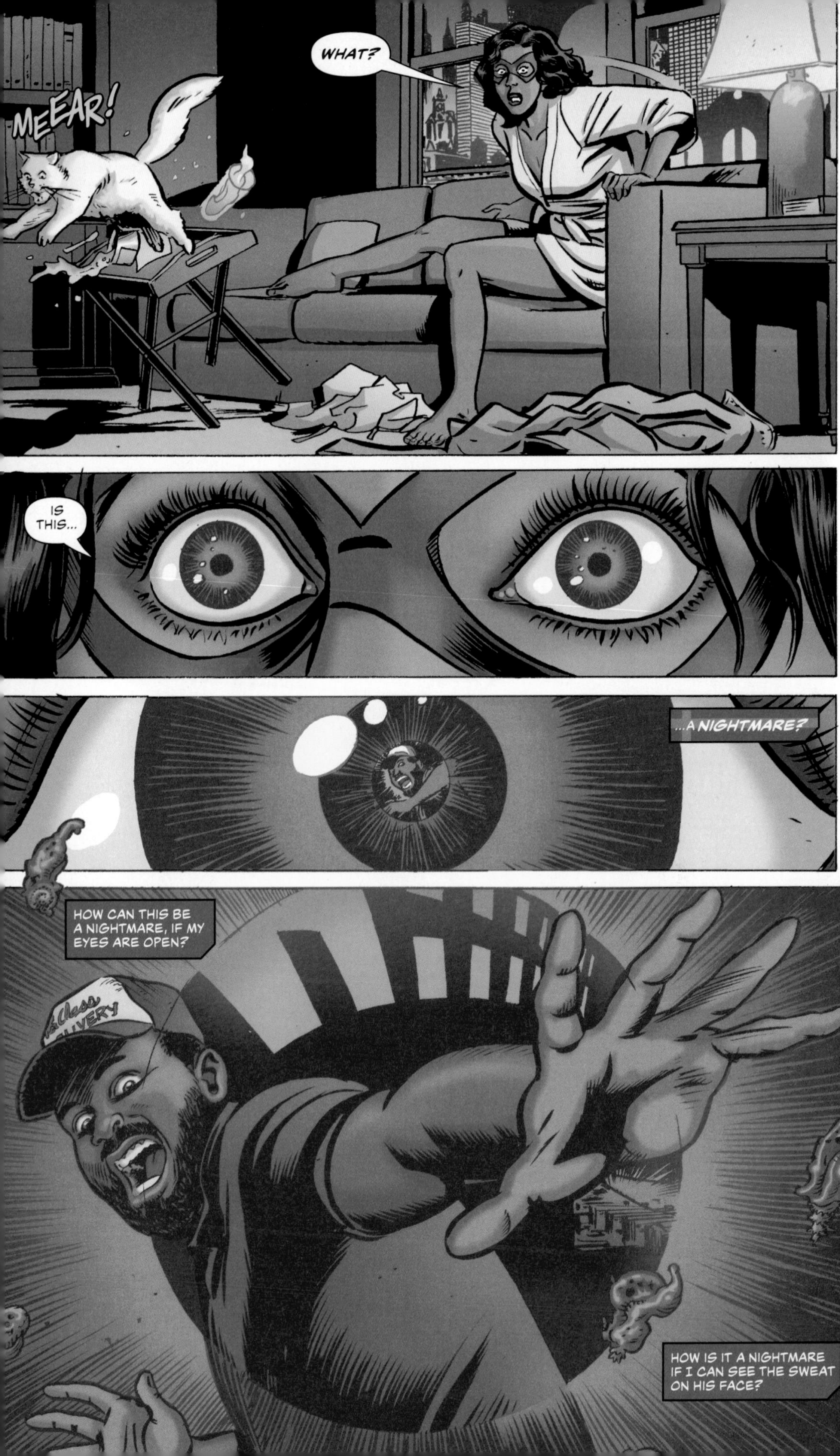
MEEAR!
WHAT?
IS THIS...
...A NIGHTMARE?
HOW CAN THIS BE A NIGHTMARE, IF MY EYES ARE OPEN?
HOW IS IT A NIGHTMARE IF I CAN SEE THE SWEAT ON HIS FACE?

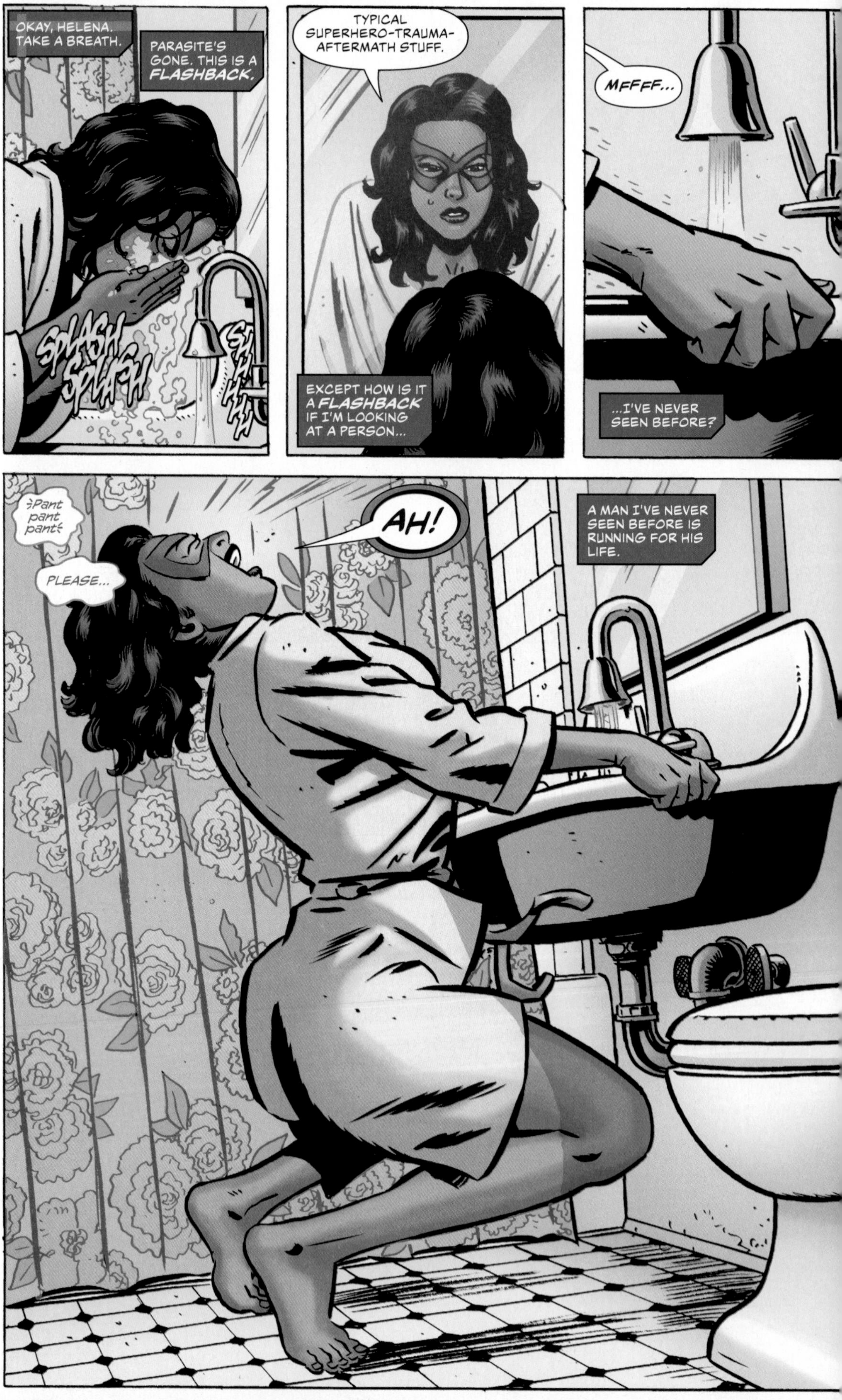
OKAY, HELENA. TAKE A BREATH.
PARASITE'S GONE. THIS IS A FLASHBACK.
SPLASH SPLASH
TYPICAL SUPERHERO-TRAUMA-AFTERMATH STUFF.
EXCEPT HOW IS IT A FLASHBACK IF I'M LOOKING AT A PERSON...
MFFFF...
...I'VE NEVER SEEN BEFORE?
Pant pant pant
PLEASE...
AH!
A MAN I'VE NEVER SEEN BEFORE IS RUNNING FOR HIS LIFE.

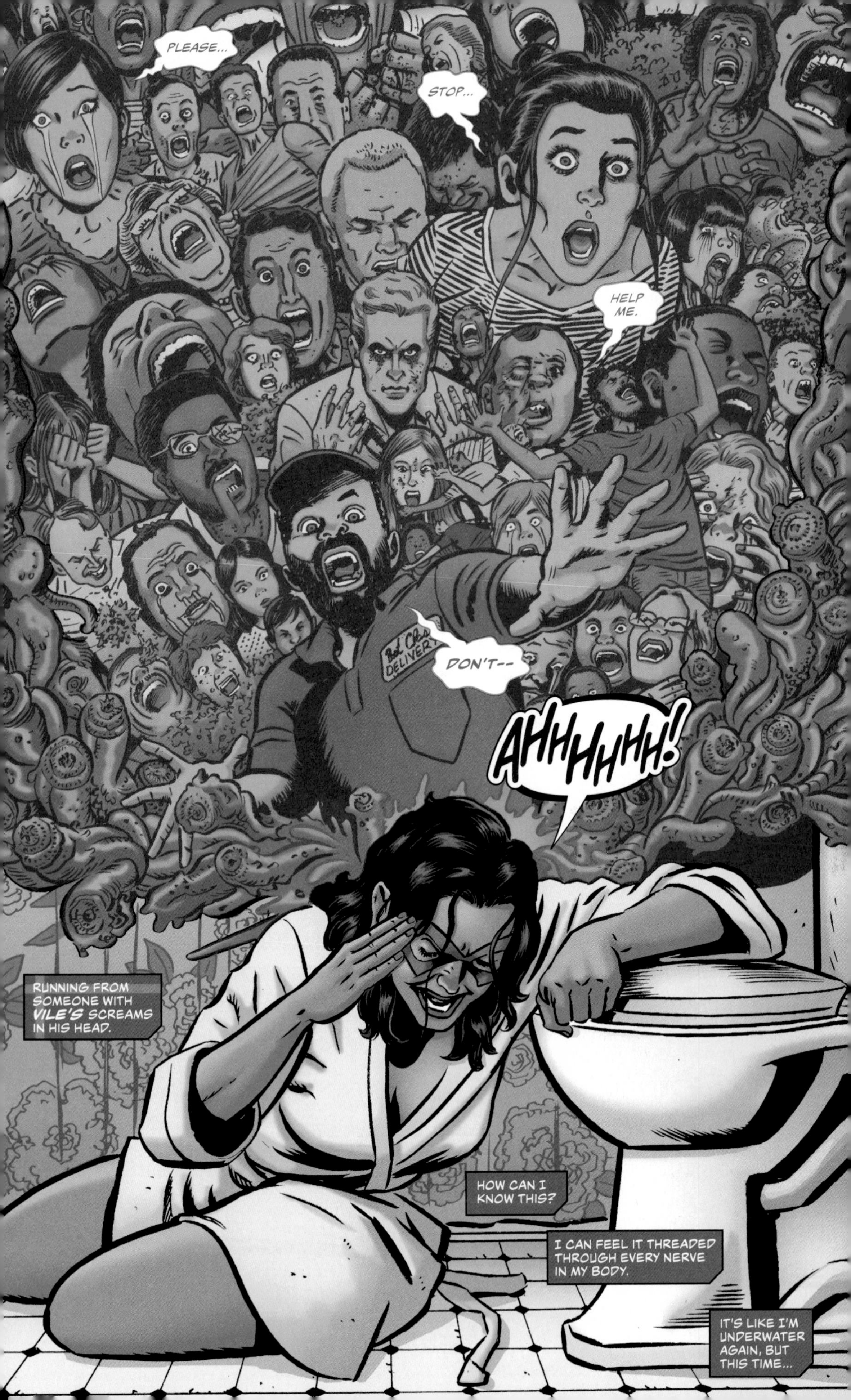
PLEASE...
STOP...
HELP ME.
DON'T--
AHHHHHHH!
RUNNING FROM SOMEONE WITH VILE'S SCREAMS IN HIS HEAD.
HOW CAN I KNOW THIS?
I CAN FEEL IT THREADED THROUGH EVERY NERVE IN MY BODY.
IT'S LIKE I'M UNDERWATER AGAIN, BUT THIS TIME...

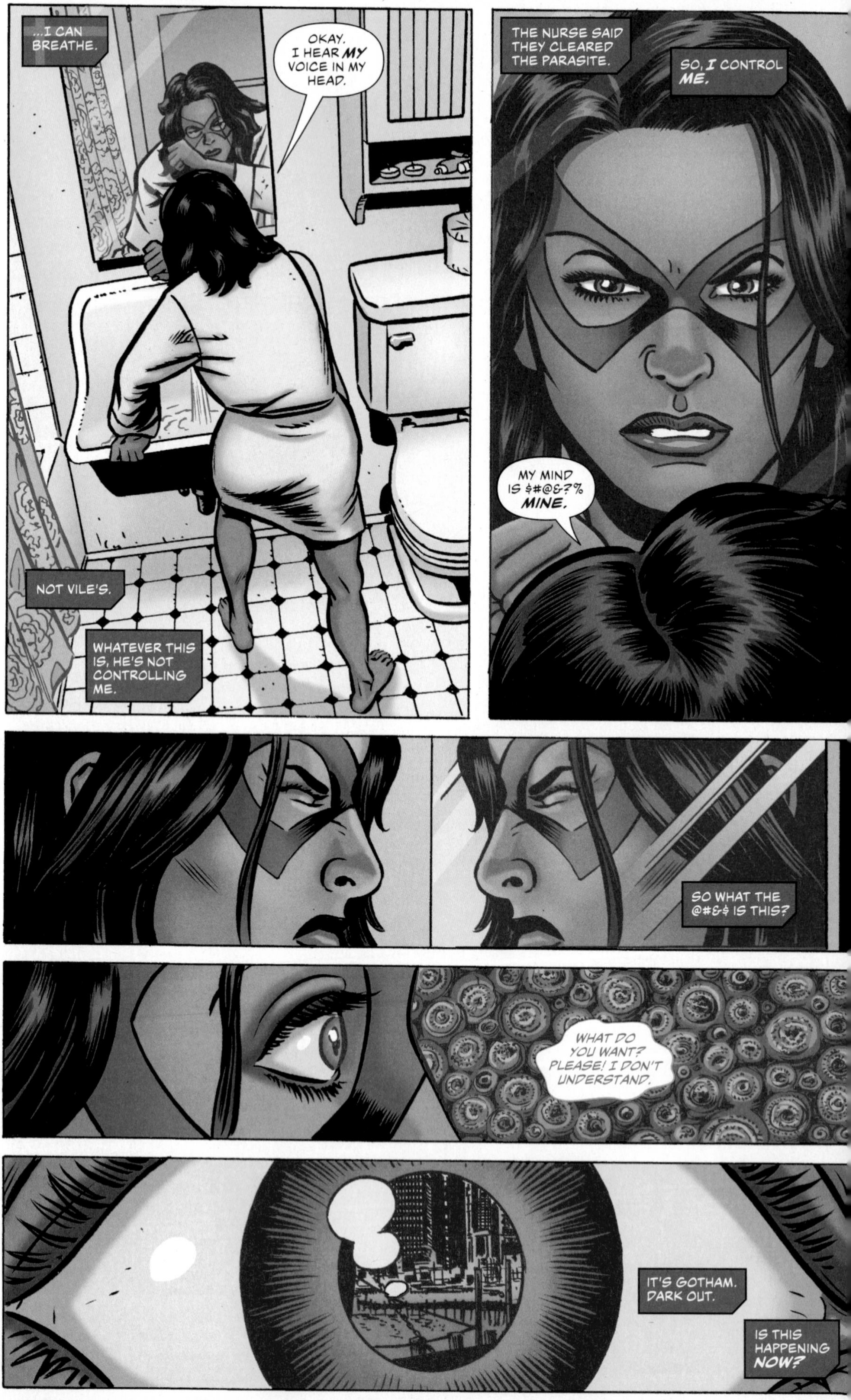
...I CAN BREATHE.
OKAY. I HEAR MY VOICE IN MY HEAD.
NOT VILE'S.
WHATEVER THIS IS, HE'S NOT CONTROLLING ME.
THE NURSE SAID THEY CLEARED THE PARASITE.
SO, I CONTROL ME.
MY MIND IS $#@&?% MINE.
SO WHAT THE @#&$ IS THIS?
WHAT DO YOU WANT? PLEASE! I DON'T UNDERSTAND.
IT'S GOTHAM. DARK OUT.
IS THIS HAPPENING NOW?

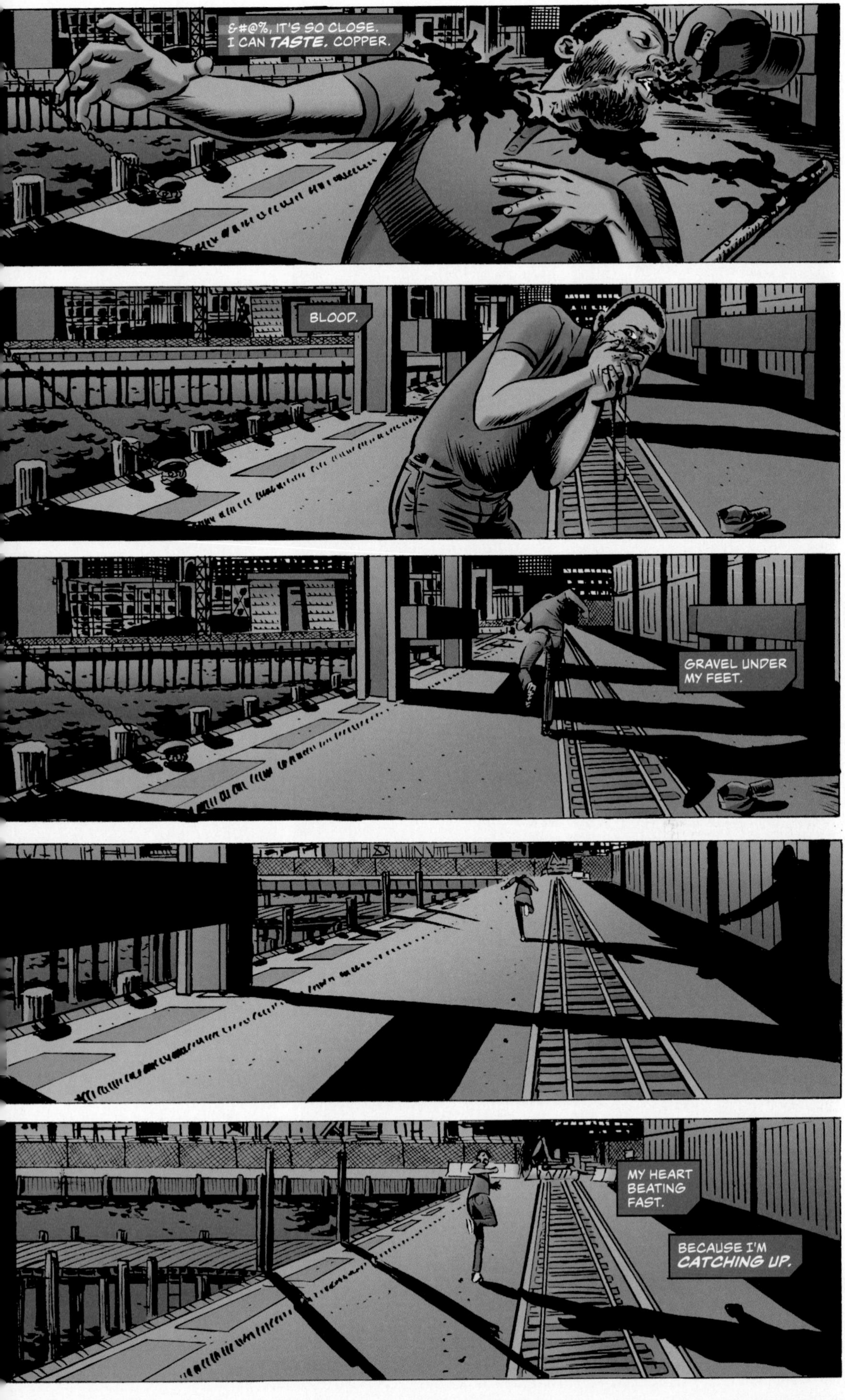
&#@%, IT'S SO CLOSE. I CAN TASTE. COPPER.
BLOOD.
GRAVEL UNDER MY FEET.
MY HEART BEATING FAST.
BECAUSE I'M CATCHING UP.

$#&@!
$#&@!

I KNOW IT'S NOT VILE. I REMEMBER STABBING HIM DEEP ENOUGH THAT HE WASN'T RUNNING OFF ANYWHERE AFTERWARD.*

*IT'S TRUE, SHE DID. DTC #1039 AGAIN. --PAUL

THIS IS PROBABLY-- THIS COULD BE NOTHING.

CAUTION
CONSTRUCTION ZONE
UNAUTHORIZED PERSONNEL
KEEP OUT

I MEAN, I WAS JUST INFECTED BY A *BLOOD-LUSTING* PARASITE.

I SHOULD BE IN BED, OR, AT THE VERY LEAST, NOT GEARING UP.

I'LL GO OUT THERE. PROVE TO MYSELF THAT THIS IS...WHAT? A GHOST.

CAU
CONSTR
UNAUTHOR
KEE

A MEDICAL HALLUCINATION.

$#&@!

‹Pant pant›

$#@!

THEN I'LL COME BACK HOME AND ORDER A PIZZA. FINE.

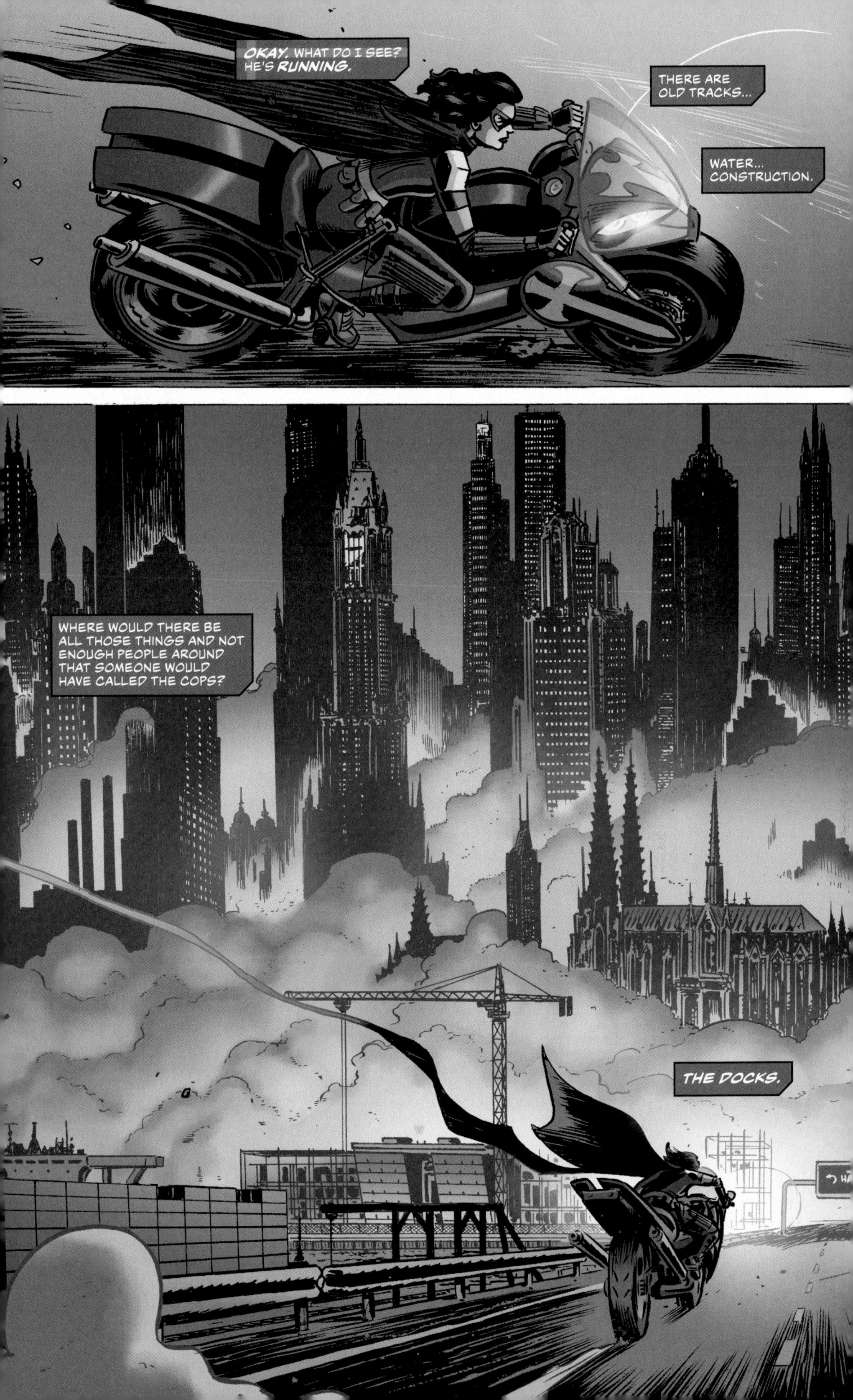
OKAY. WHAT DO I SEE? HE'S RUNNING.
THERE ARE OLD TRACKS...
WATER... CONSTRUCTION.
WHERE WOULD THERE BE ALL THOSE THINGS AND NOT ENOUGH PEOPLE AROUND THAT SOMEONE WOULD HAVE CALLED THE COPS?
THE DOCKS.

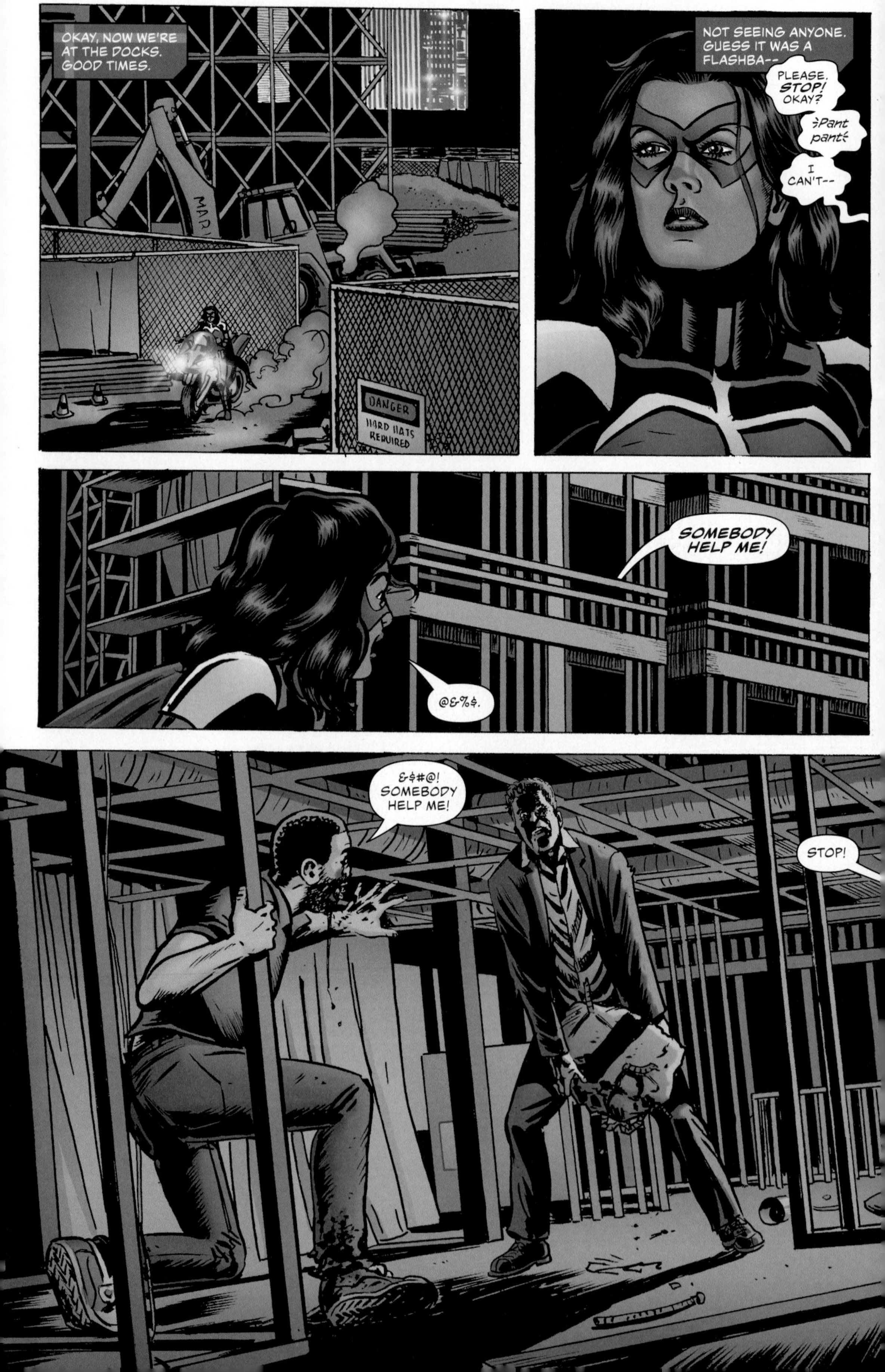
OKAY, NOW WE'RE AT THE DOCKS. GOOD TIMES.
DANGER
HARD HATS REQUIRED
NOT SEEING ANYONE. GUESS IT WAS A FLASHBA--
PLEASE. STOP! OKAY?
Pant pant
I CAN'T--
SOMEBODY HELP ME!
@&%$.
&$#@! SOMEBODY HELP ME!
STOP!

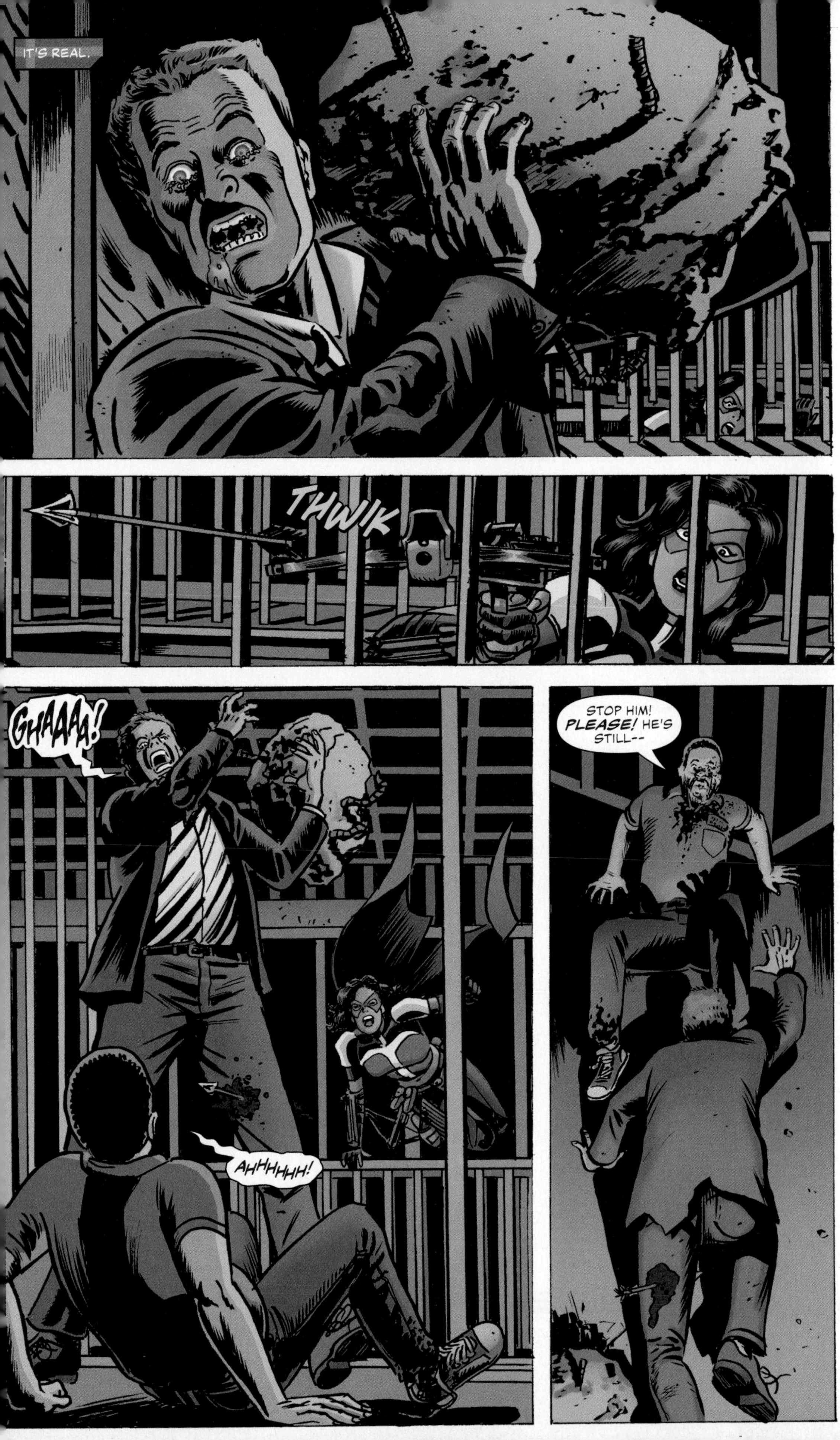
IT'S REAL.
THWIK
GHAAAA!
AHHHHHH!
STOP HIM! PLEASE! HE'S STILL--

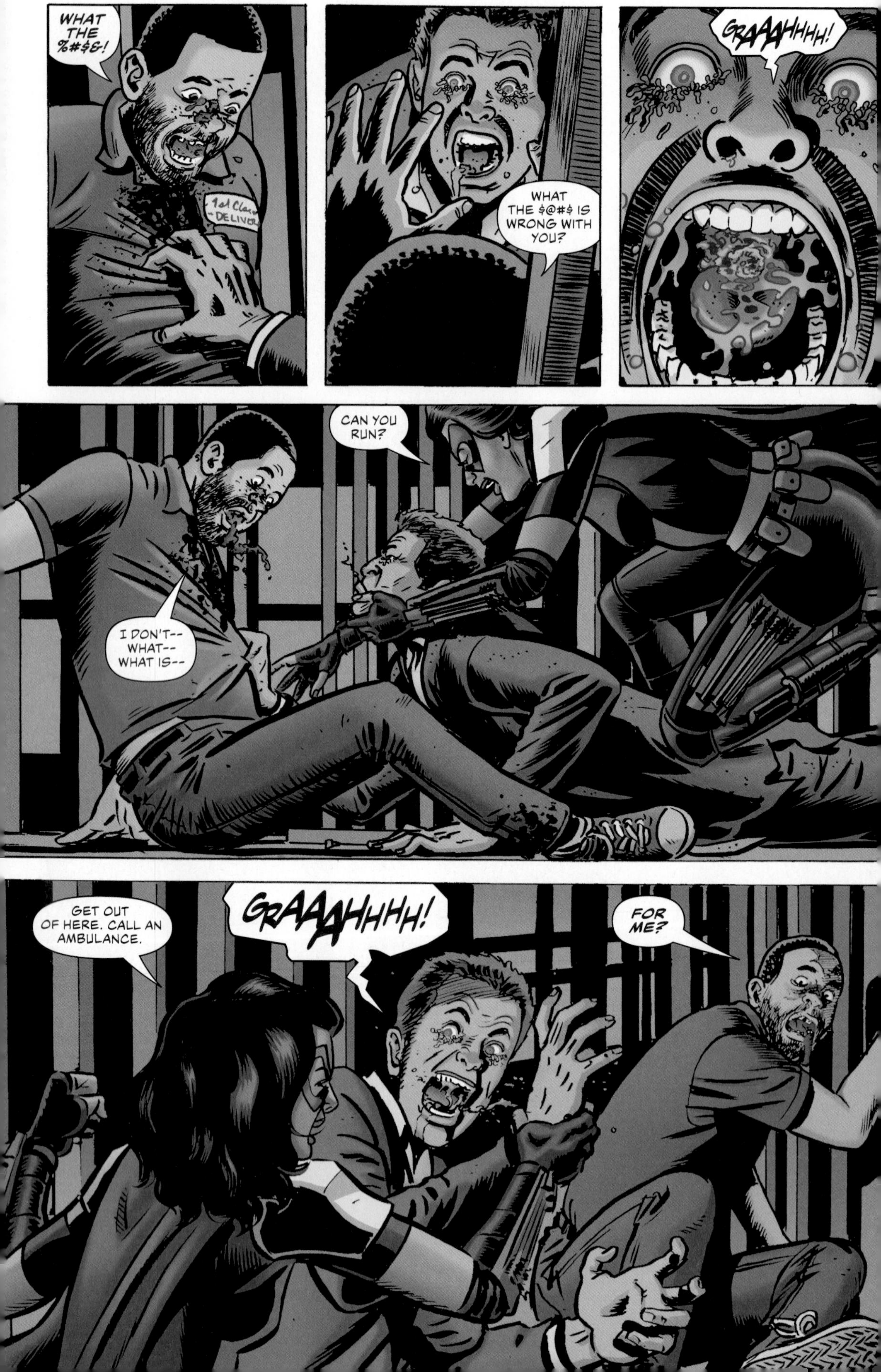
WHAT THE %#$&!
WHAT THE $@#$ IS WRONG WITH YOU?
GRAAAHHHH!
CAN YOU RUN?
I DON'T-- WHAT-- WHAT IS--
GET OUT OF HERE. CALL AN AMBULANCE.
GRAAAHHHH!
FOR ME?

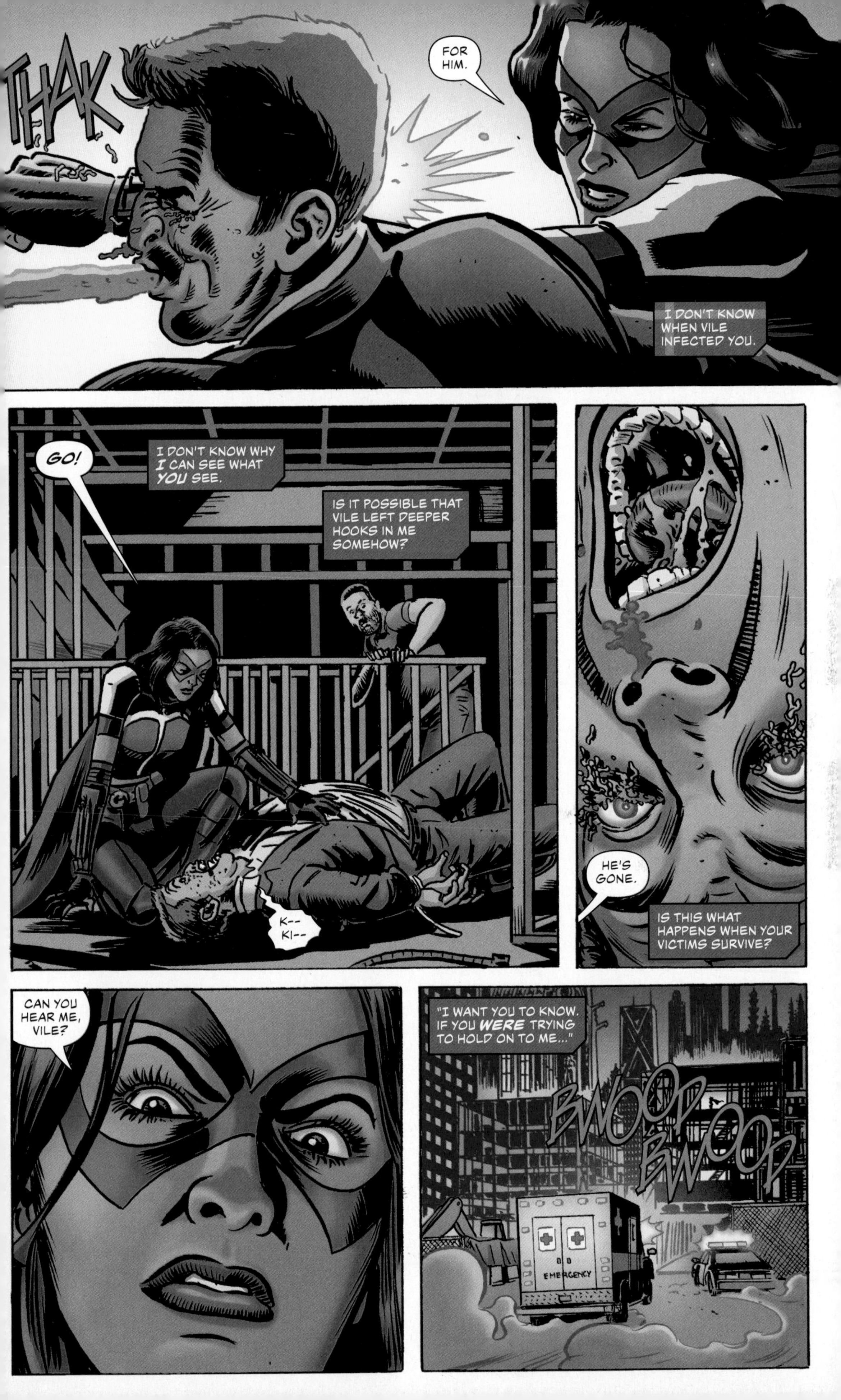
THAK
FOR HIM.
I DON'T KNOW WHEN VILE INFECTED YOU.
GO!
I DON'T KNOW WHY I CAN SEE WHAT YOU SEE.
IS IT POSSIBLE THAT VILE LEFT DEEPER HOOKS IN ME SOMEHOW?
K-- KI--
HE'S GONE.
IS THIS WHAT HAPPENS WHEN YOUR VICTIMS SURVIVE?
CAN YOU HEAR ME, VILE?
"I WANT YOU TO KNOW. IF YOU WERE TRYING TO HOLD ON TO ME..."
BWOOD BWOOD
EMERGENCY

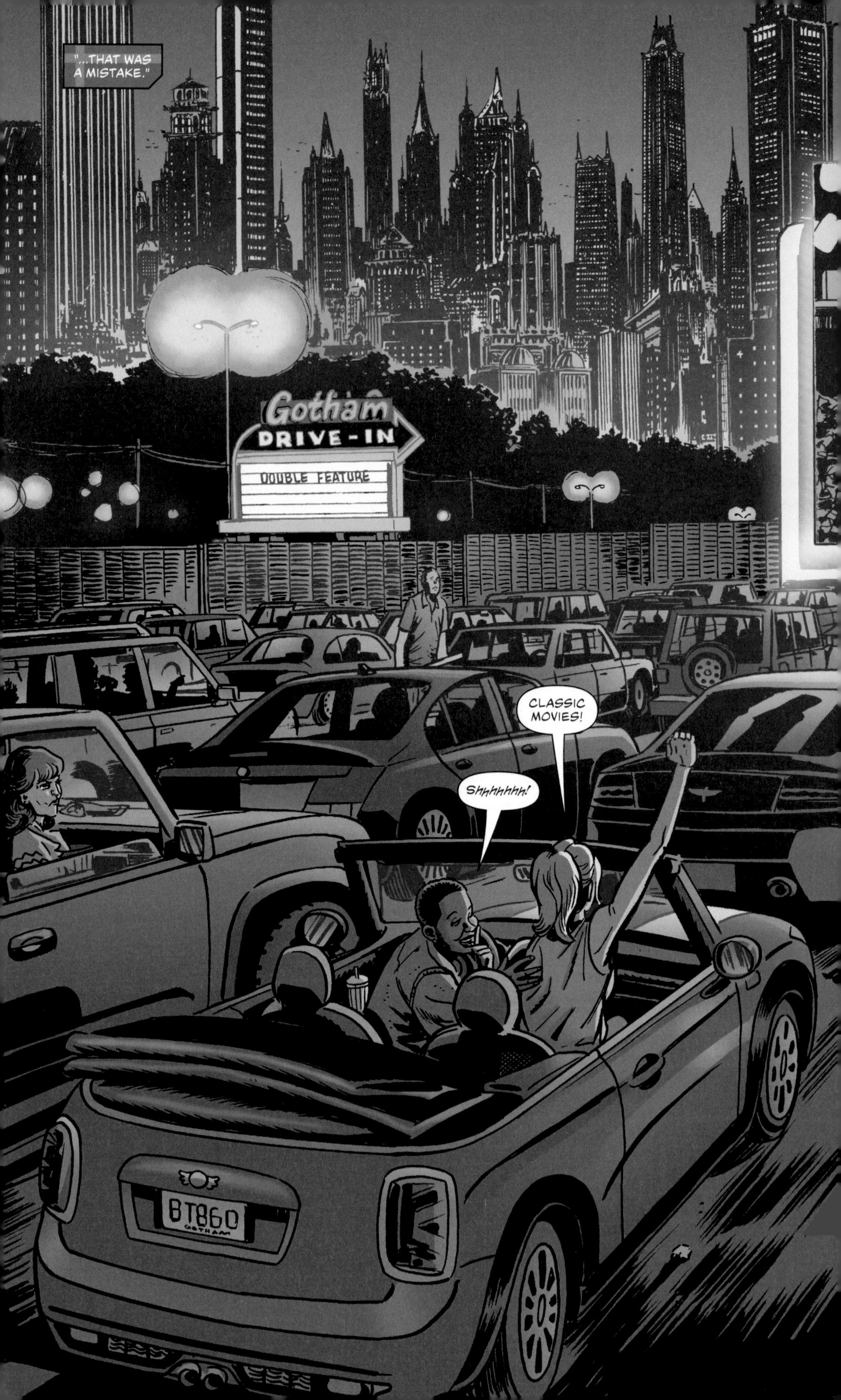
"...THAT WAS A MISTAKE."
Gotham
DRIVE-IN
DOUBLE FEATURE
CLASSIC MOVIES!
Shhhhhhh!
BT860
GOTHAM

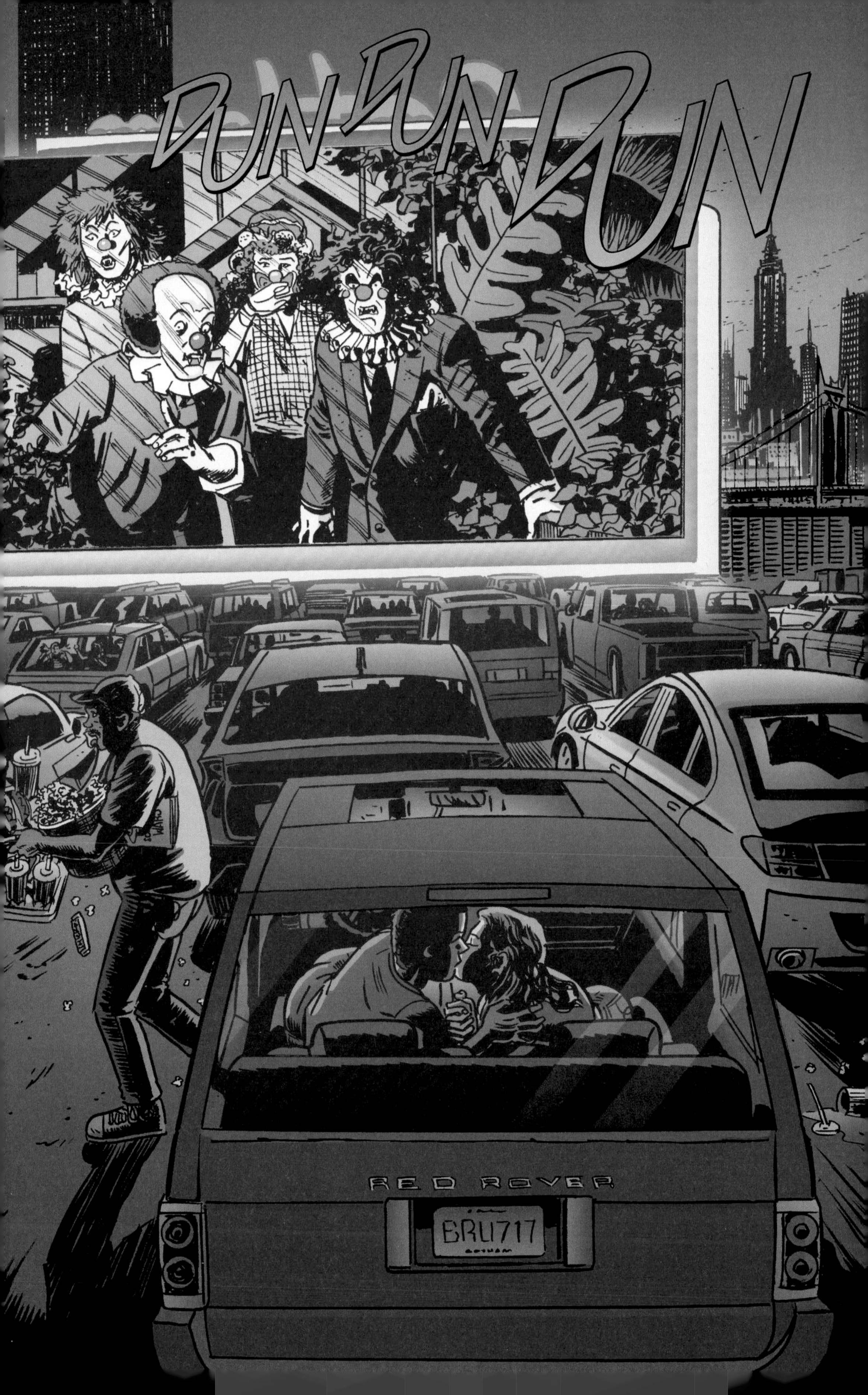
DUN DUN DUN DUN
RED ROVER
BRU717

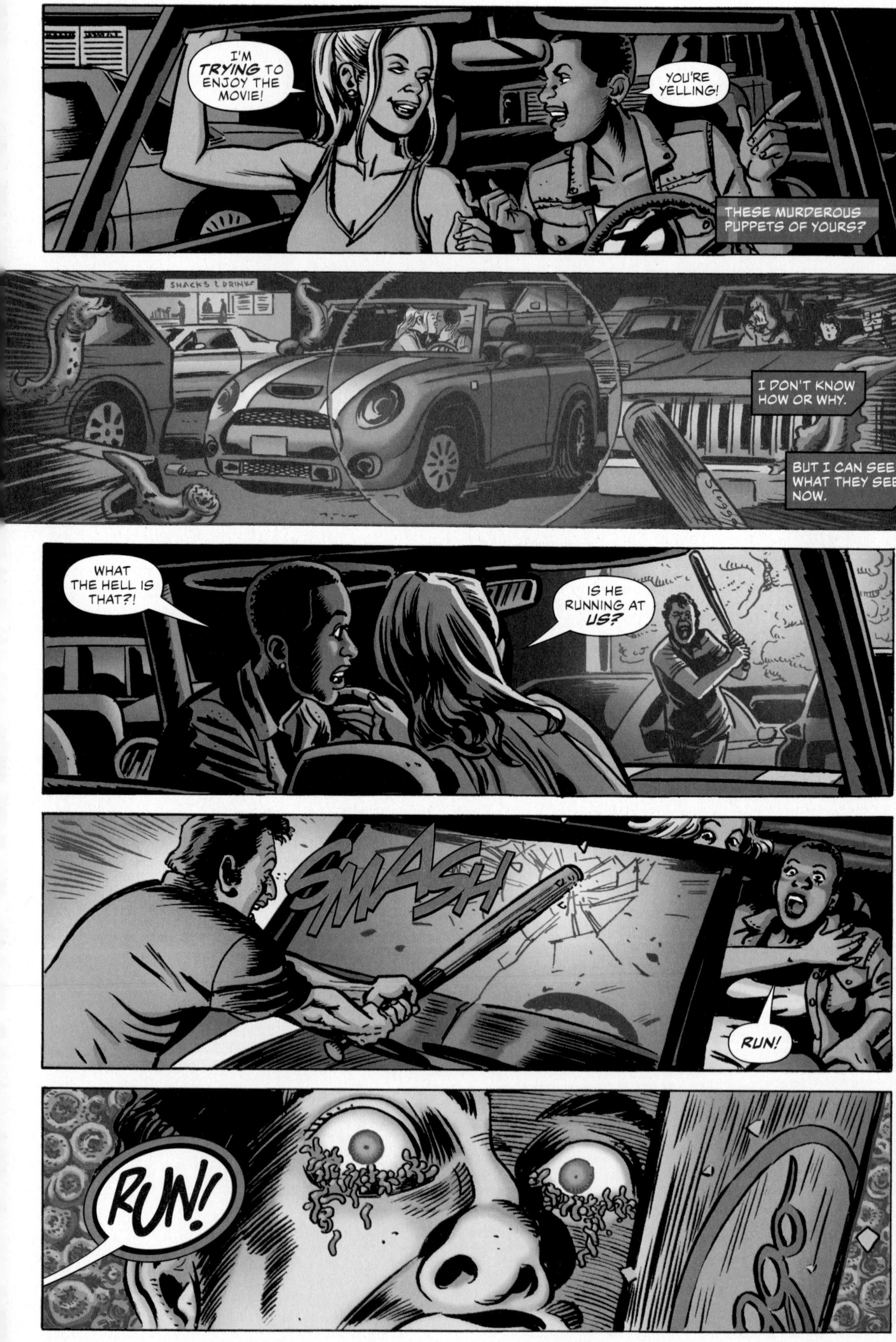
I'M TRYING TO ENJOY THE MOVIE!
YOU'RE YELLING!
THESE MURDEROUS PUPPETS OF YOURS?
SNACKS & DRINKS
I DON'T KNOW HOW OR WHY.
BUT I CAN SEE WHAT THEY SEE NOW.
WHAT THE HELL IS THAT?!
IS HE RUNNING AT US?
SMASH
RUN!
RUN!

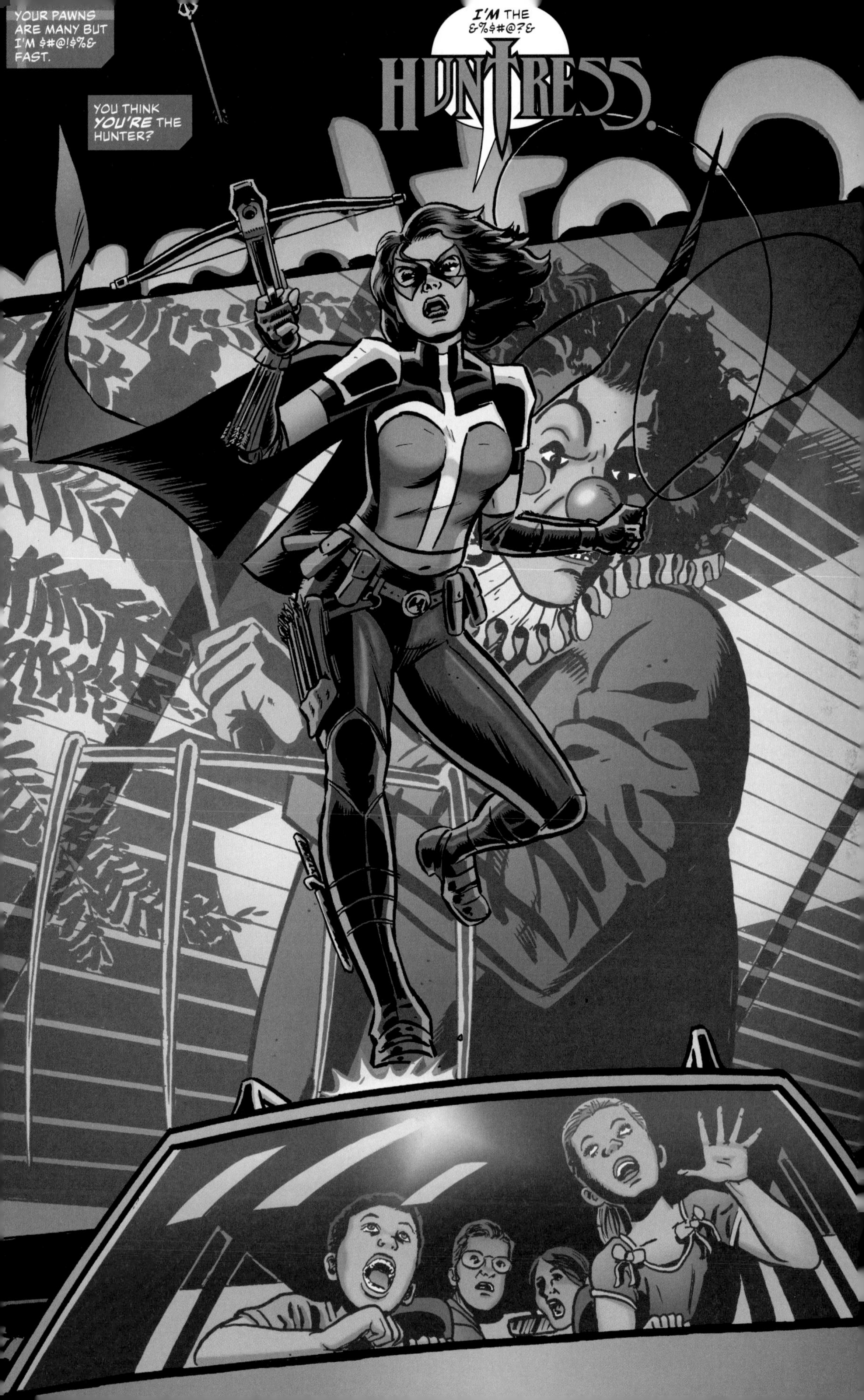
YOUR PAWNS ARE MANY BUT I'M $#@!$%& FAST.
YOU THINK YOU'RE THE HUNTER?
I'M THE &%$#@?& HUNTRESS.

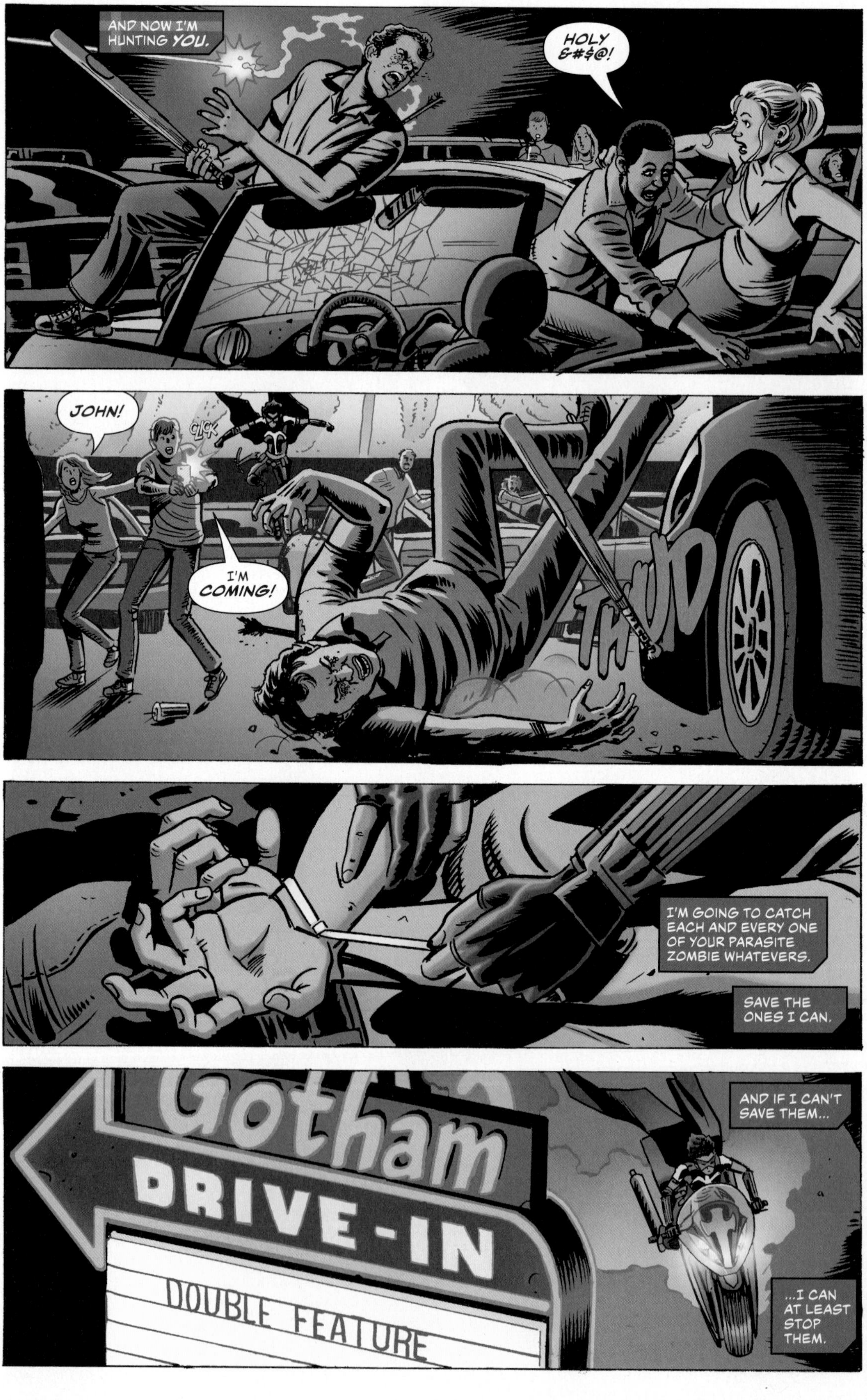
AND NOW I'M HUNTING YOU.
HOLY &#$@!
JOHN!
CLICK
I'M COMING!
THUD
I'M GOING TO CATCH EACH AND EVERY ONE OF YOUR PARASITE ZOMBIE WHATEVERS.
SAVE THE ONES I CAN.
Gotham
DRIVE-IN
DOUBLE FEATURE
AND IF I CAN'T SAVE THEM...
...I CAN AT LEAST STOP THEM.

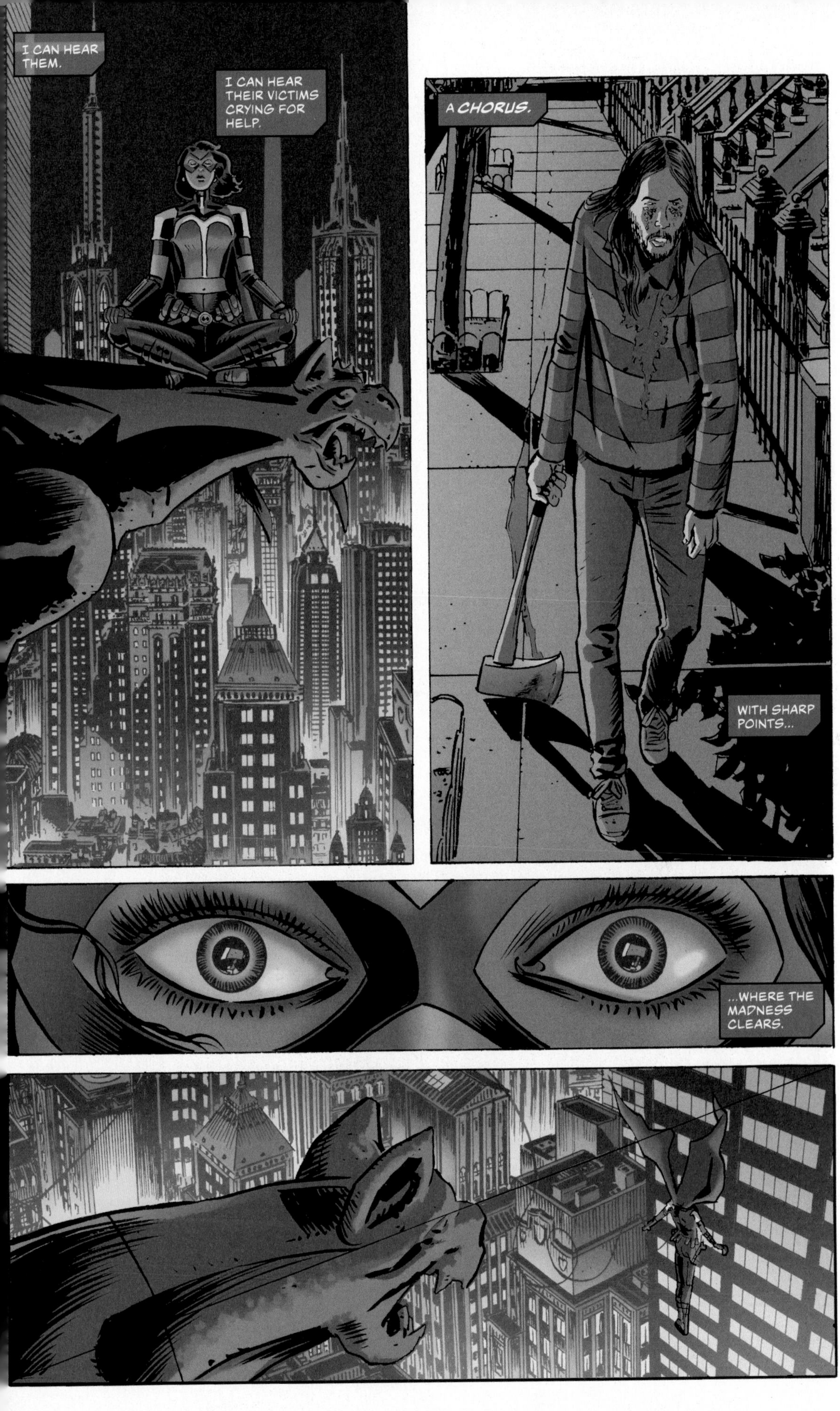
I CAN HEAR THEM.
I CAN HEAR THEIR VICTIMS CRYING FOR HELP.
A CHORUS.
WITH SHARP POINTS...
...WHERE THE MADNESS CLEARS.

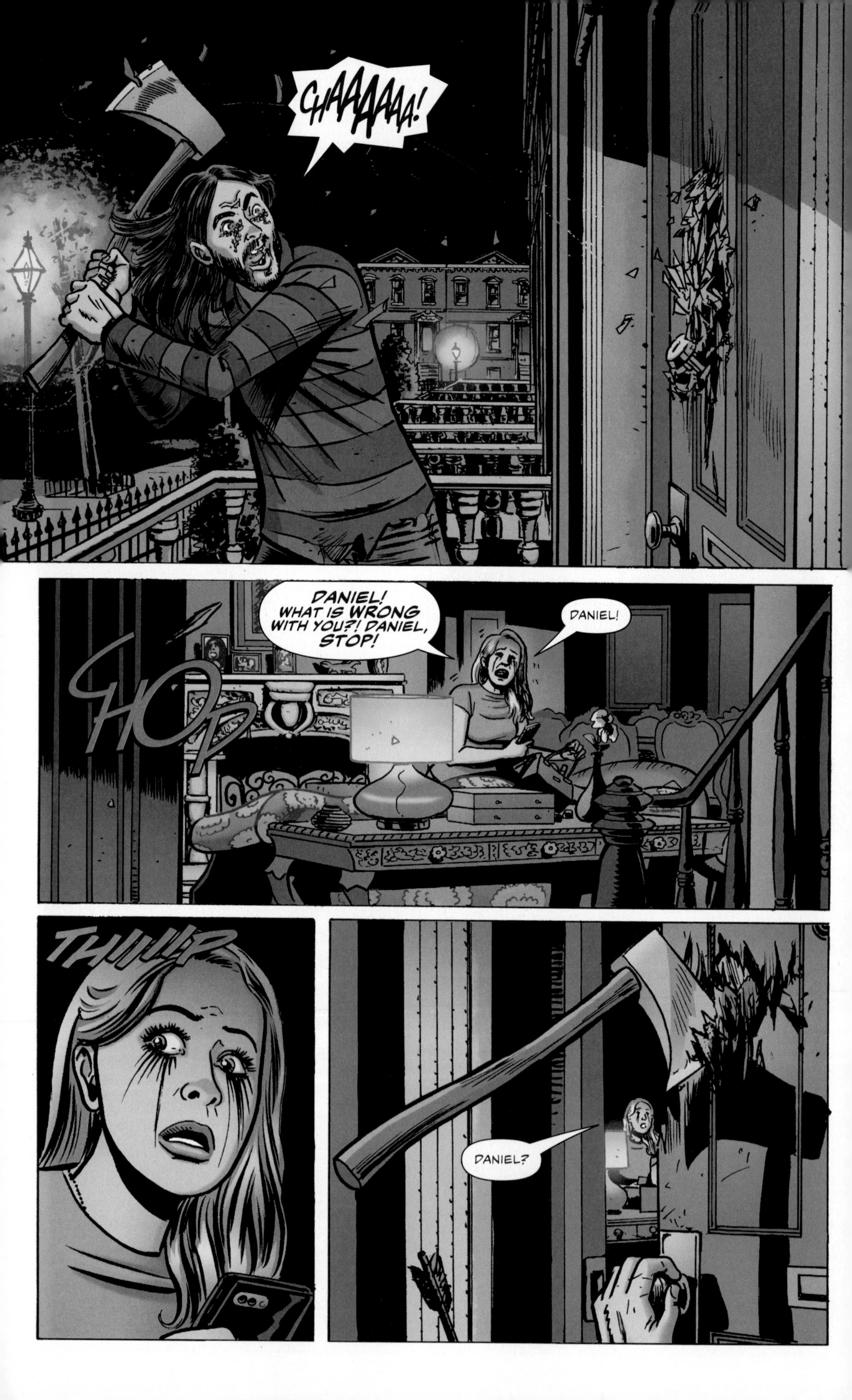
CHAAAAAA!
SHOP
DANIEL! WHAT IS WRONG WITH YOU?! DANIEL, STOP!
DANIEL!
THUUUP
DANIEL?

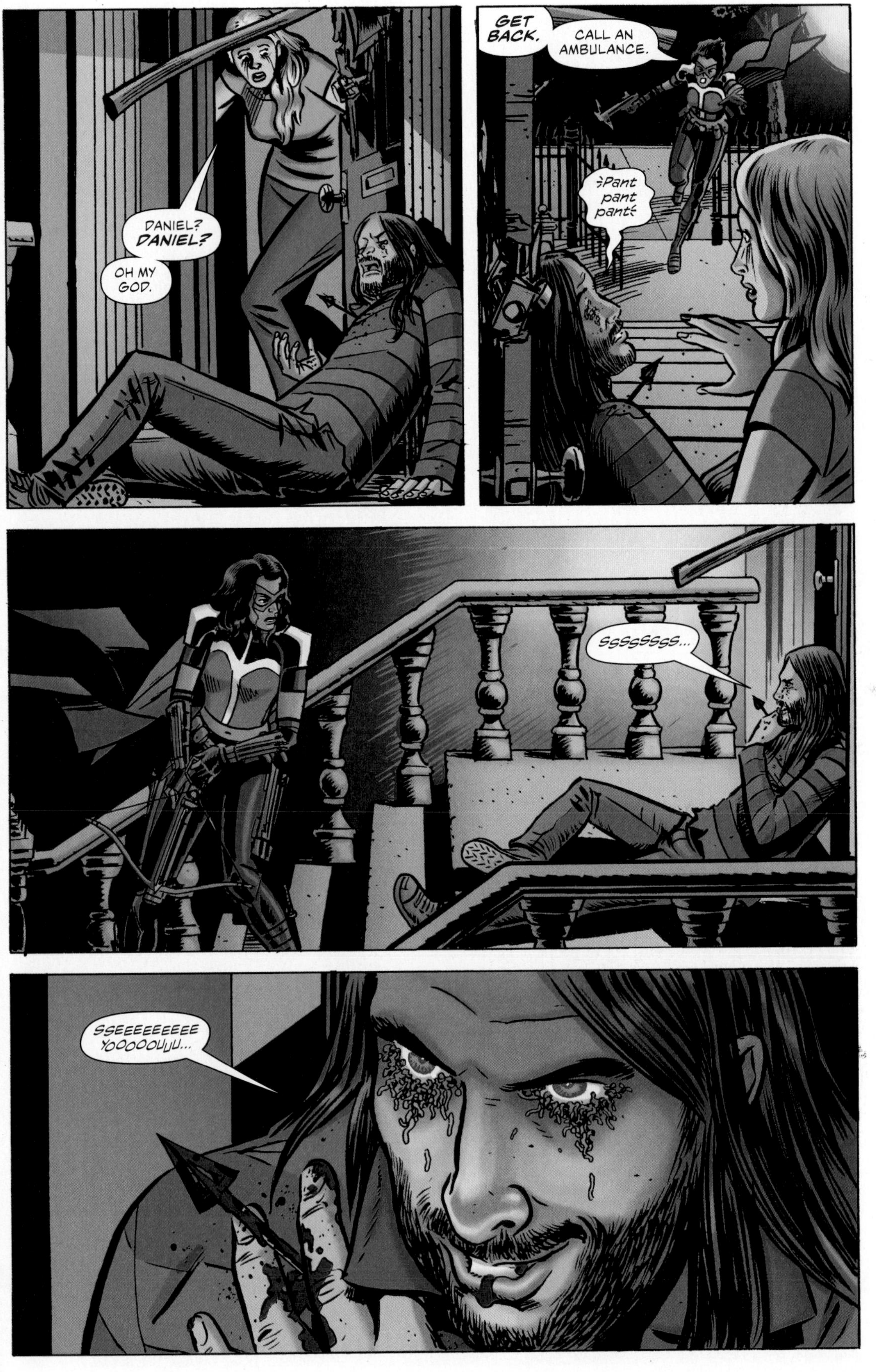
DANIEL? DANIEL?
OH MY GOD.
GET BACK.
CALL AN AMBULANCE.
Pant pant pant
SSSSSSSS...
SSEEEEEEEEE YOOOOUUU...

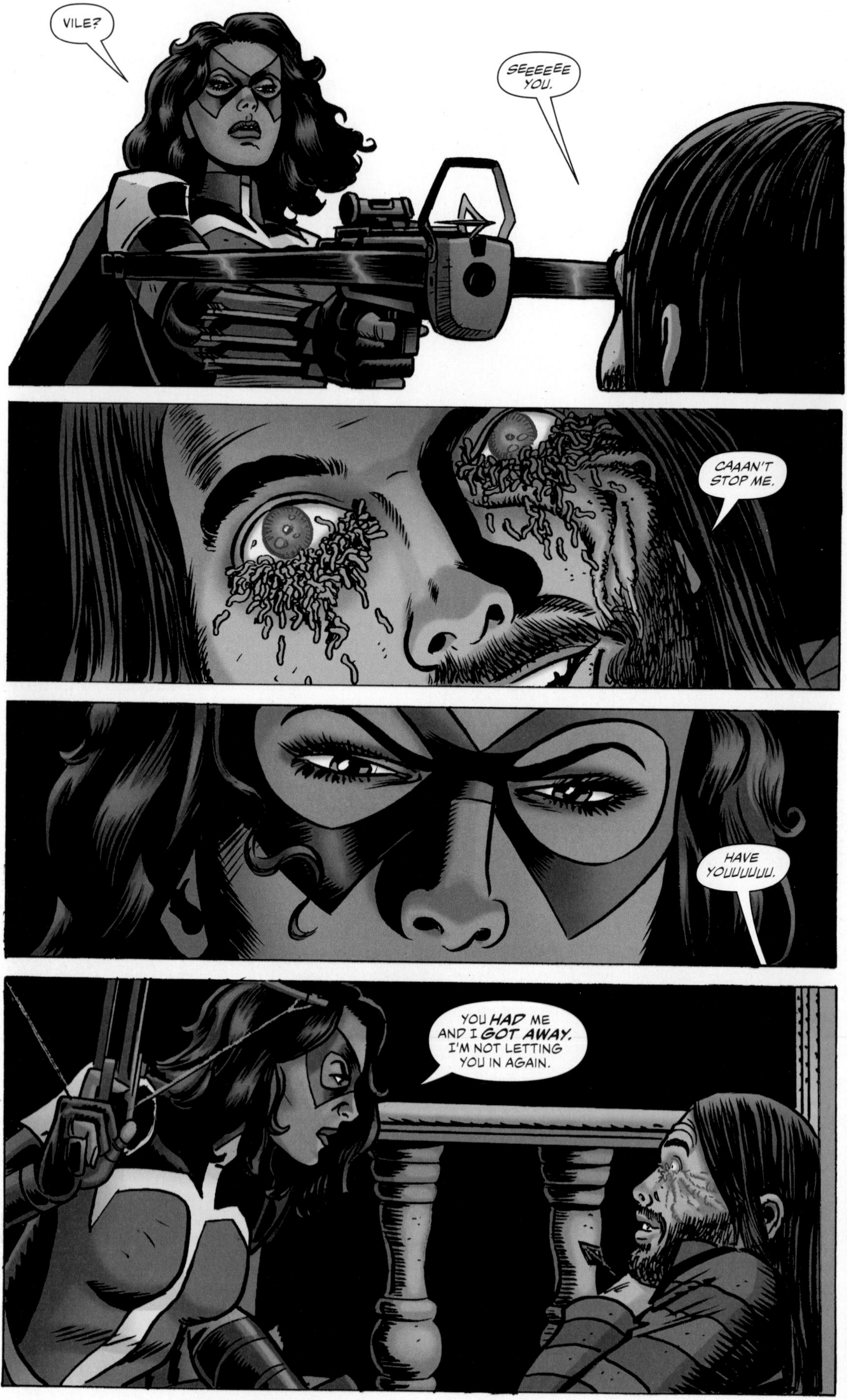
VILE?
SEEEEEEE YOU.
CAAAN'T STOP ME.
HAVE YOUUUUUU.
YOU HAD ME AND I GOT AWAY. I'M NOT LETTING YOU IN AGAIN.

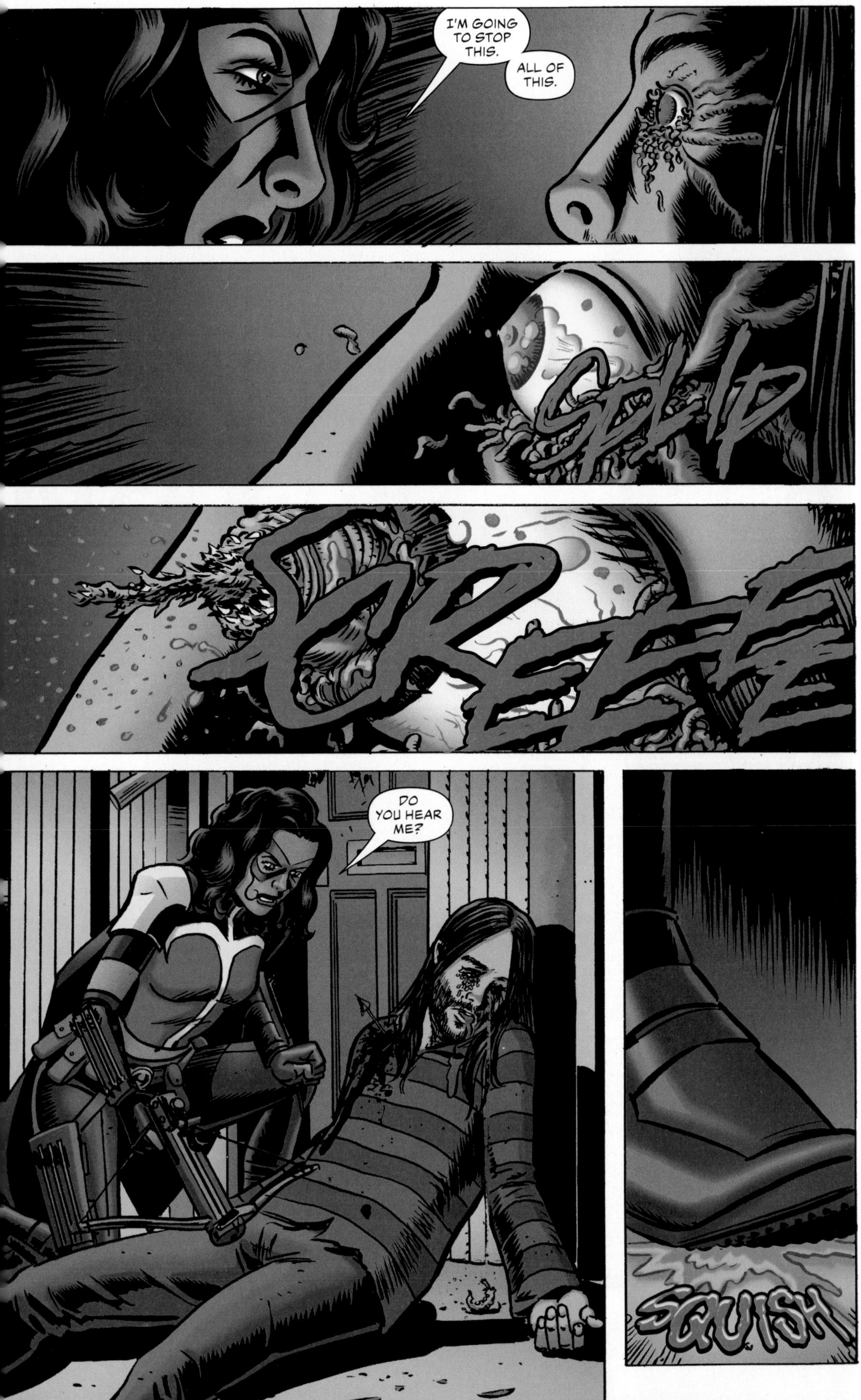

I'M GOING TO STOP THIS.
ALL OF THIS.
DO YOU HEAR ME?
SQUISH

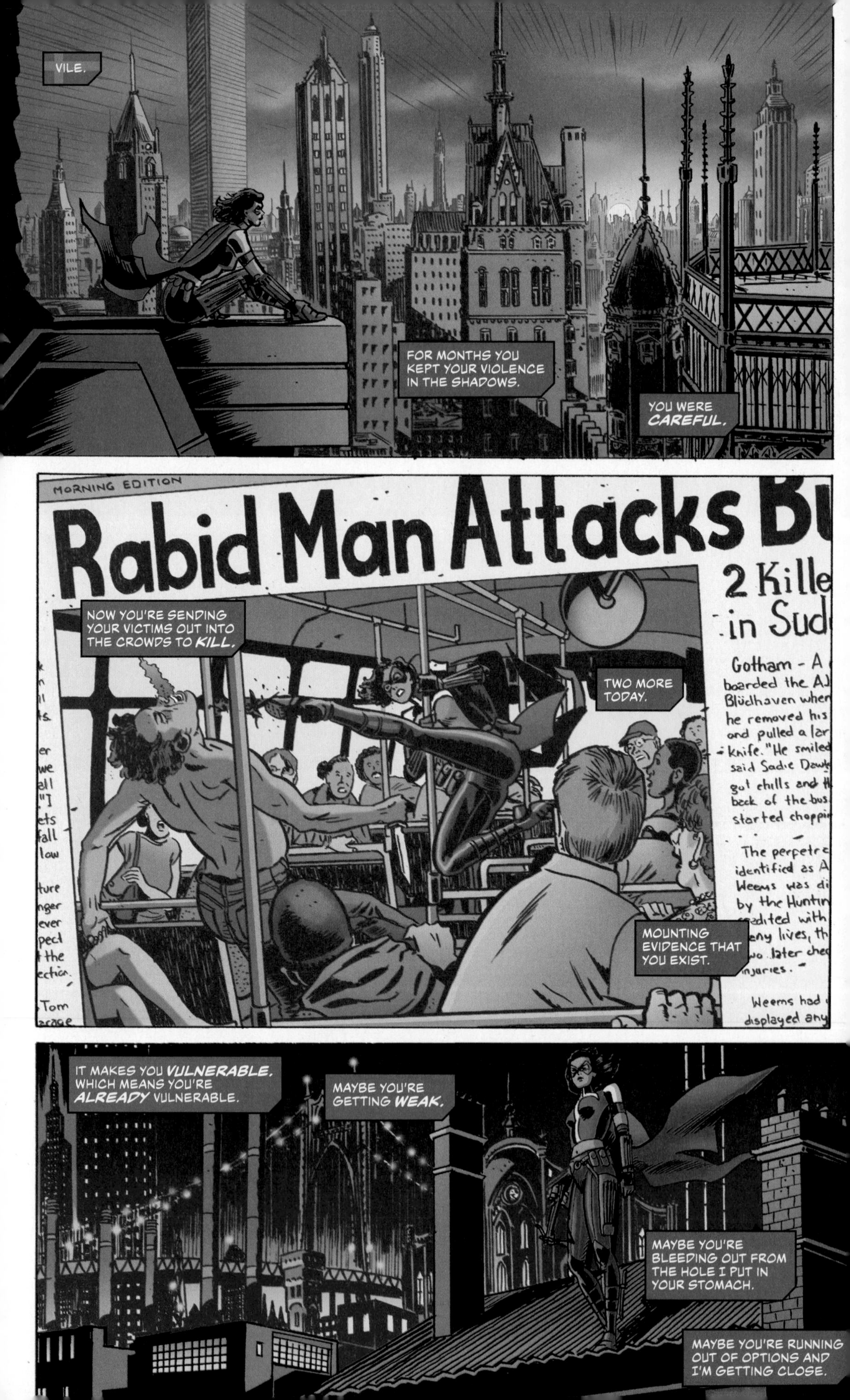
VILE.
FOR MONTHS YOU KEPT YOUR VIOLENCE IN THE SHADOWS.
YOU WERE CAREFUL.
MORNING EDITION
Rabid Man Attacks Bu
2 Kille
in Sud
Gotham - A
boarded the AJ
Blüdhaven when
he removed his
and pulled a lar
knife. "He smiled
said Sadie Dawg
got chills and th
back of the bus
started choppi
The perpetr
identified as A
Weems was di
by the Huntin
credited with
eny lives, th
two later chec
injuries.
Weems had
displayed any
NOW YOU'RE SENDING YOUR VICTIMS OUT INTO THE CROWDS TO KILL.
TWO MORE TODAY.
MOUNTING EVIDENCE THAT YOU EXIST.
IT MAKES YOU VULNERABLE. WHICH MEANS YOU'RE ALREADY VULNERABLE.
MAYBE YOU'RE GETTING WEAK.
MAYBE YOU'RE BLEEDING OUT FROM THE HOLE I PUT IN YOUR STOMACH.
MAYBE YOU'RE RUNNING OUT OF OPTIONS AND I'M GETTING CLOSE.

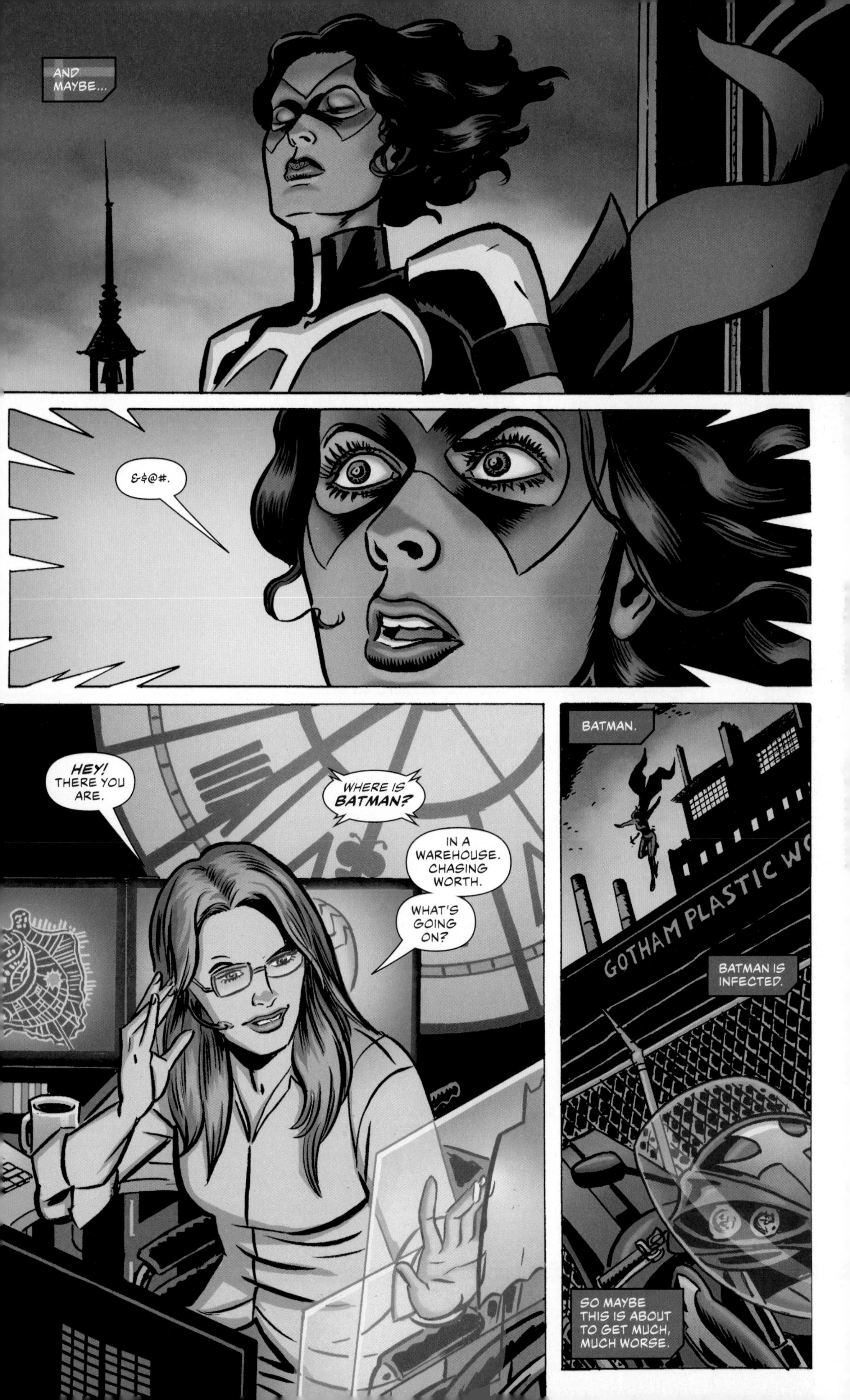
AND MAYBE...
&$@#.
HEY! THERE YOU ARE.
WHERE IS BATMAN?
IN A WAREHOUSE. CHASING WORTH.
WHAT'S GOING ON?
BATMAN.
GOTHAM PLASTIC WO
BATMAN IS INFECTED.
SO MAYBE THIS IS ABOUT TO GET MUCH, MUCH WORSE.

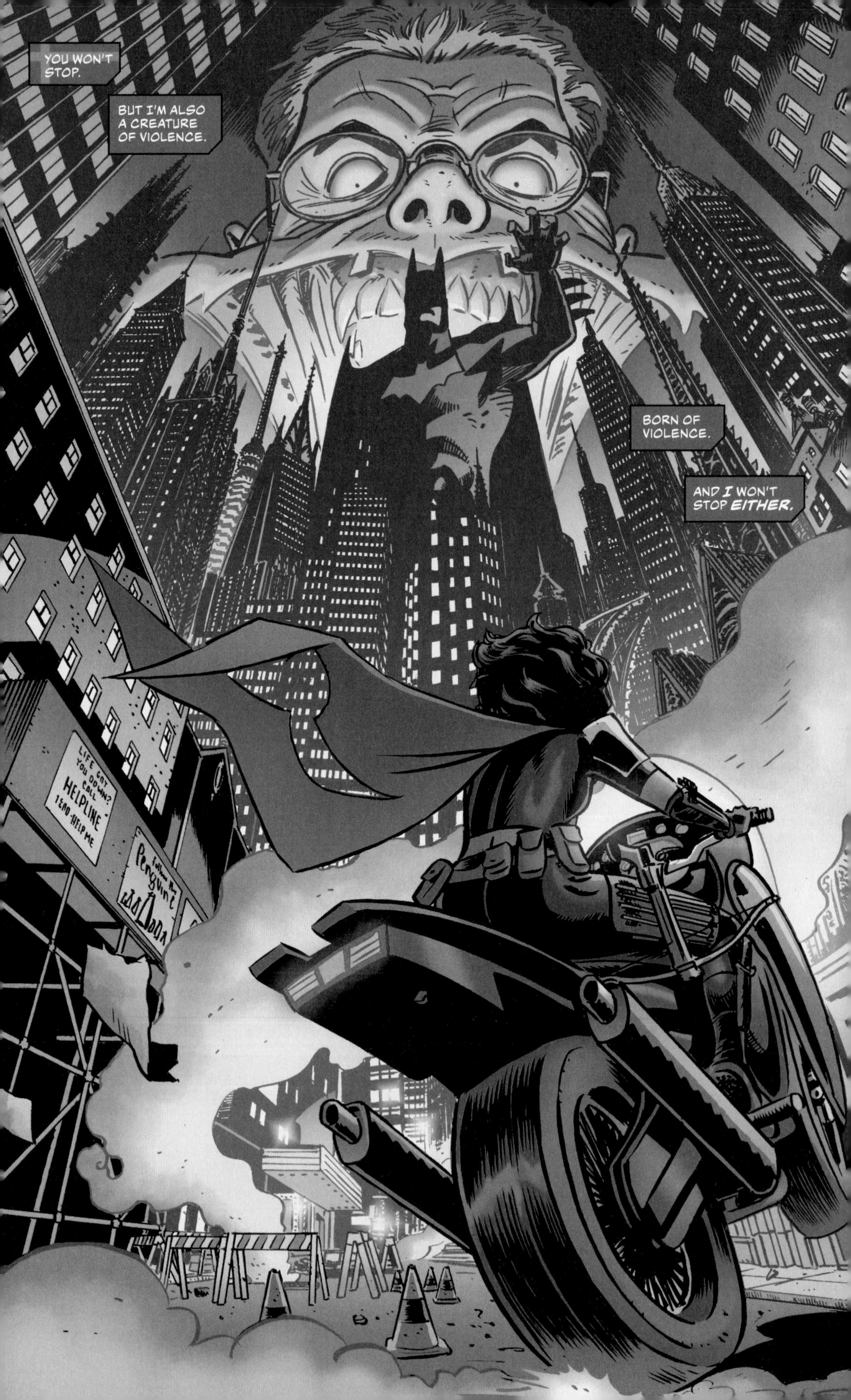
YOU WON'T STOP.
BUT I'M ALSO A CREATURE OF VIOLENCE.
BORN OF VIOLENCE.
AND *I* WON'T STOP ***EITHER.***
LIFE GOT YOU DOWN? CALL HELPLINE 1800-HELP ME
Follow the Penguin

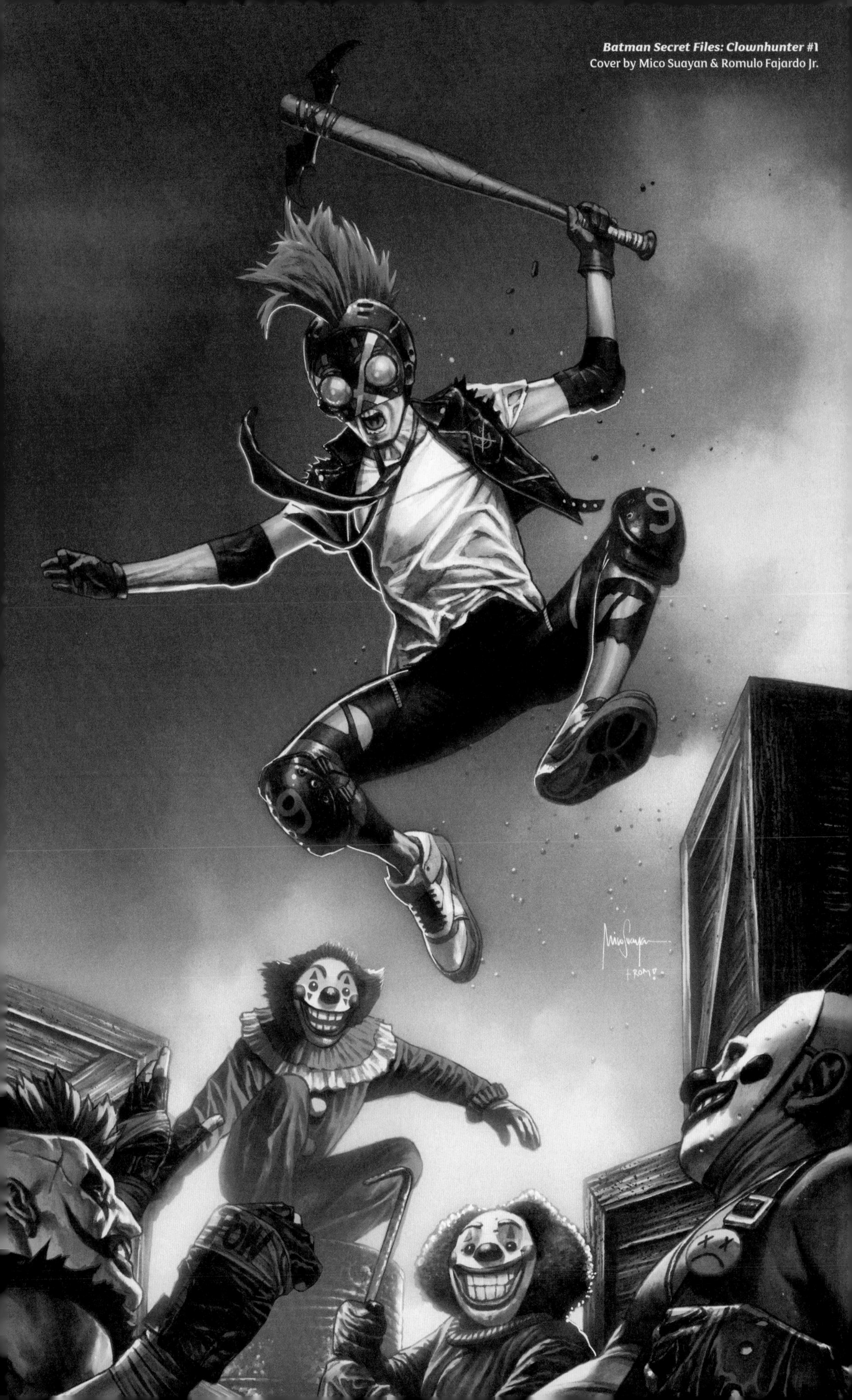

Batman Secret Files: Clownhunter #1
Cover by Mico Suayan & Romulo Fajardo Jr.

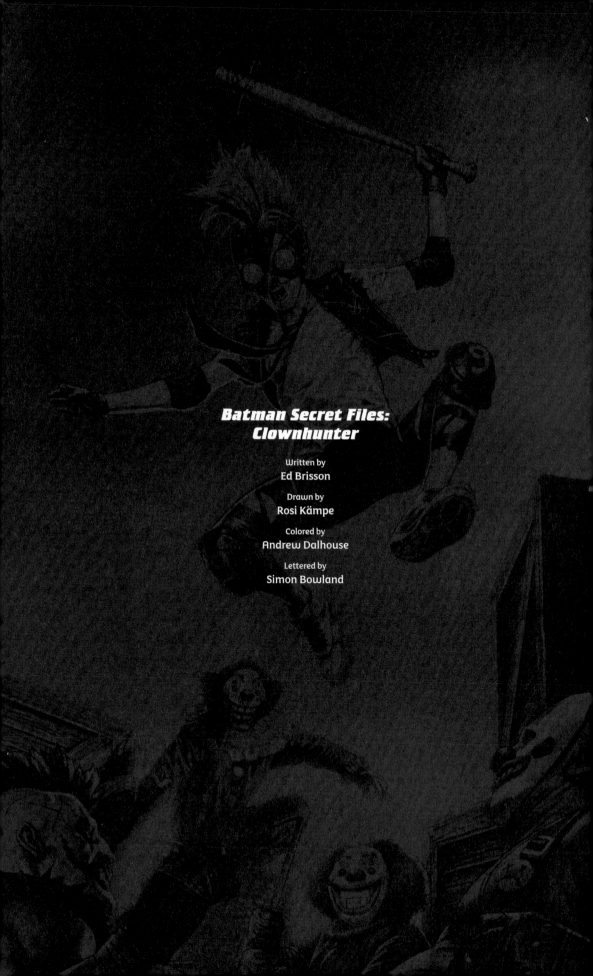

Batman Secret Files:
Clownhunter

Written by
Ed Brisson

Drawn by
Rosi Kämpe

Colored by
Andrew Dalhouse

Lettered by
Simon Bowland

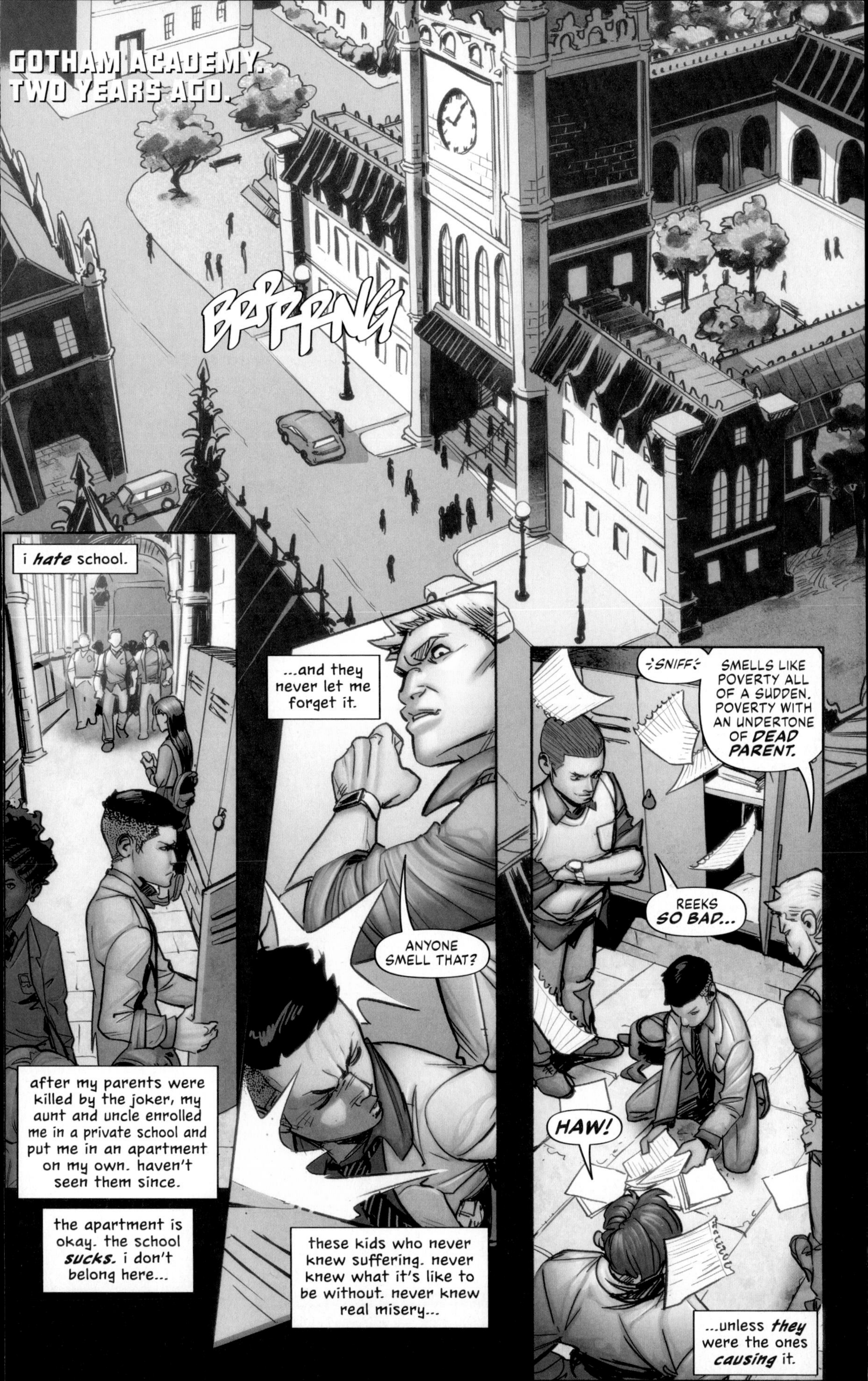
GOTHAM ACADEMY. TWO YEARS AGO.
BRRRRNG
i hate school.
after my parents were killed by the joker, my aunt and uncle enrolled me in a private school and put me in an apartment on my own. haven't seen them since.
the apartment is okay. the school sucks. i don't belong here...
...and they never let me forget it.
ANYONE SMELL THAT?
these kids who never knew suffering. never knew what it's like to be without. never knew real misery...
SNIFF
SMELLS LIKE POVERTY ALL OF A SUDDEN. POVERTY WITH AN UNDERTONE OF DEAD PARENT.
REEKS SO BAD...
HAW!
...unless they were the ones causing it.

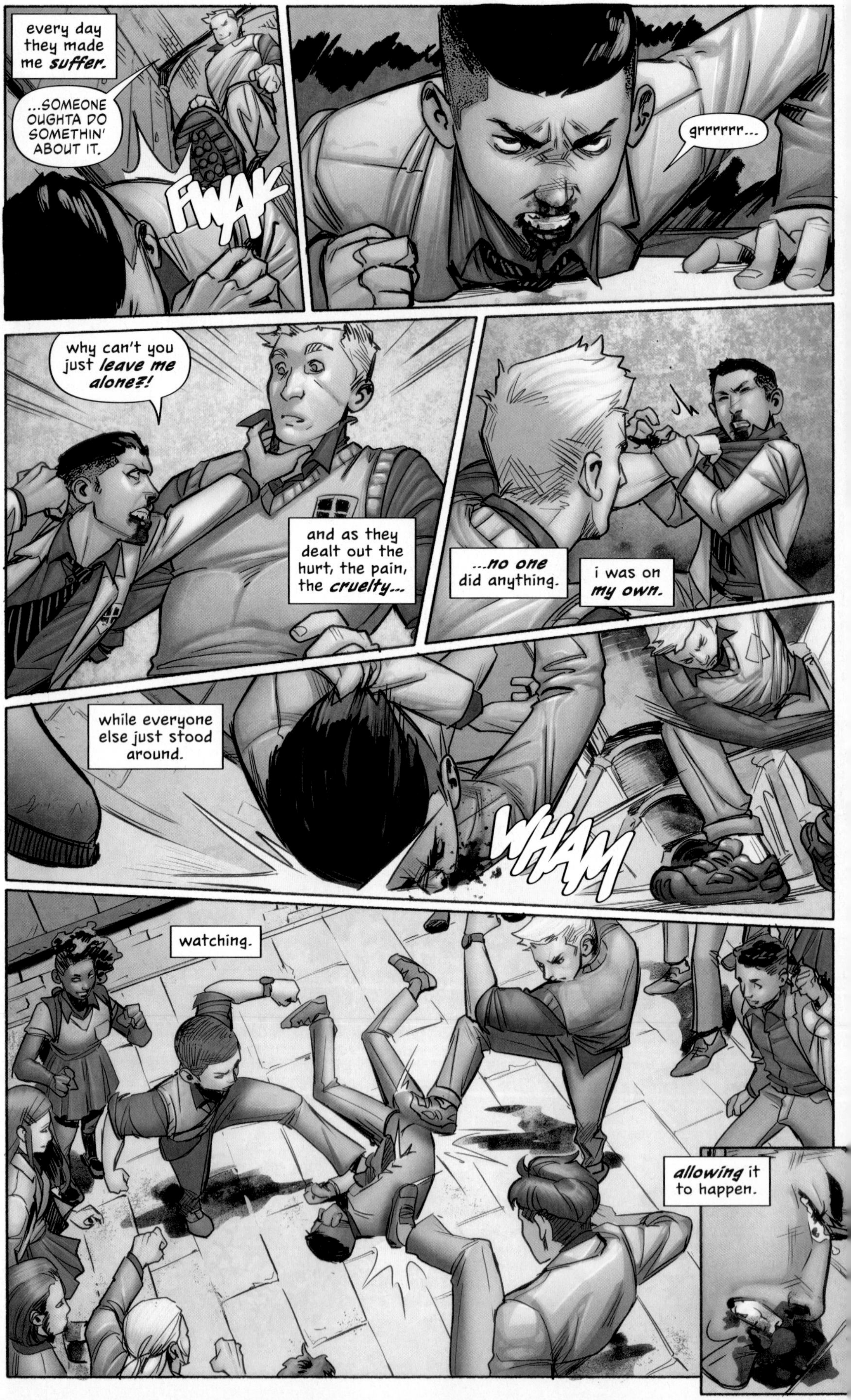
every day they made me suffer.
...SOMEONE OUGHTA DO SOMETHIN' ABOUT IT.
FWAK
grrrrrr...
why can't you just leave me alone?!
and as they dealt out the hurt, the pain, the cruelty...
...no one did anything.
i was on my own.
while everyone else just stood around.
WHAM
watching.
allowing it to happen.

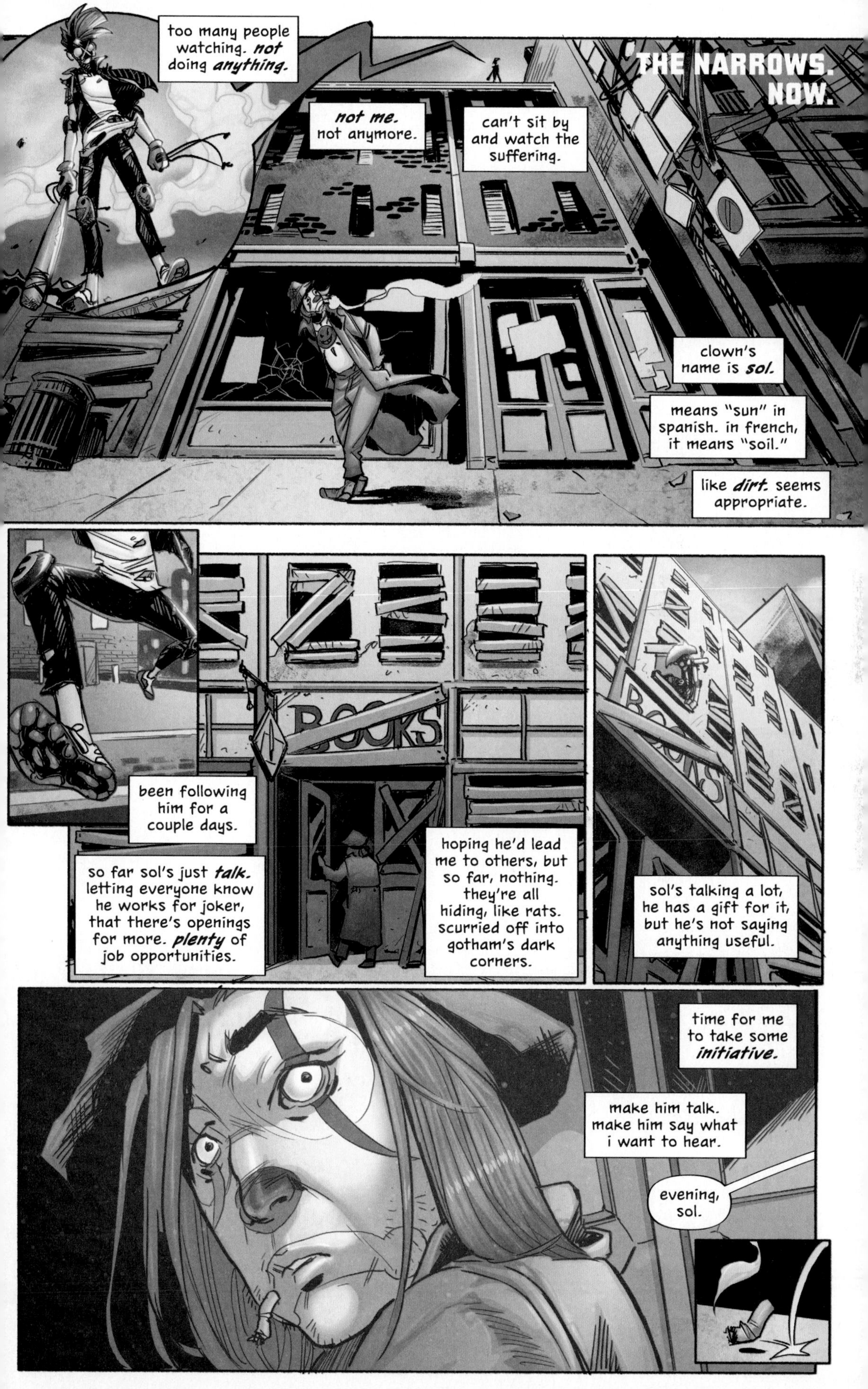
too many people watching. not doing anything.
THE NARROWS. NOW.
not me. not anymore.
can't sit by and watch the suffering.
clown's name is sol.
means "sun" in spanish. in french, it means "soil."
like dirt. seems appropriate.
BOOKS
been following him for a couple days.
so far sol's just talk. letting everyone know he works for joker, that there's openings for more. plenty of job opportunities.
hoping he'd lead me to others, but so far, nothing. they're all hiding, like rats. scurried off into gotham's dark corners.
sol's talking a lot, he has a gift for it, but he's not saying anything useful.
time for me to take some initiative.
make him talk. make him say what i want to hear.
evening, sol.

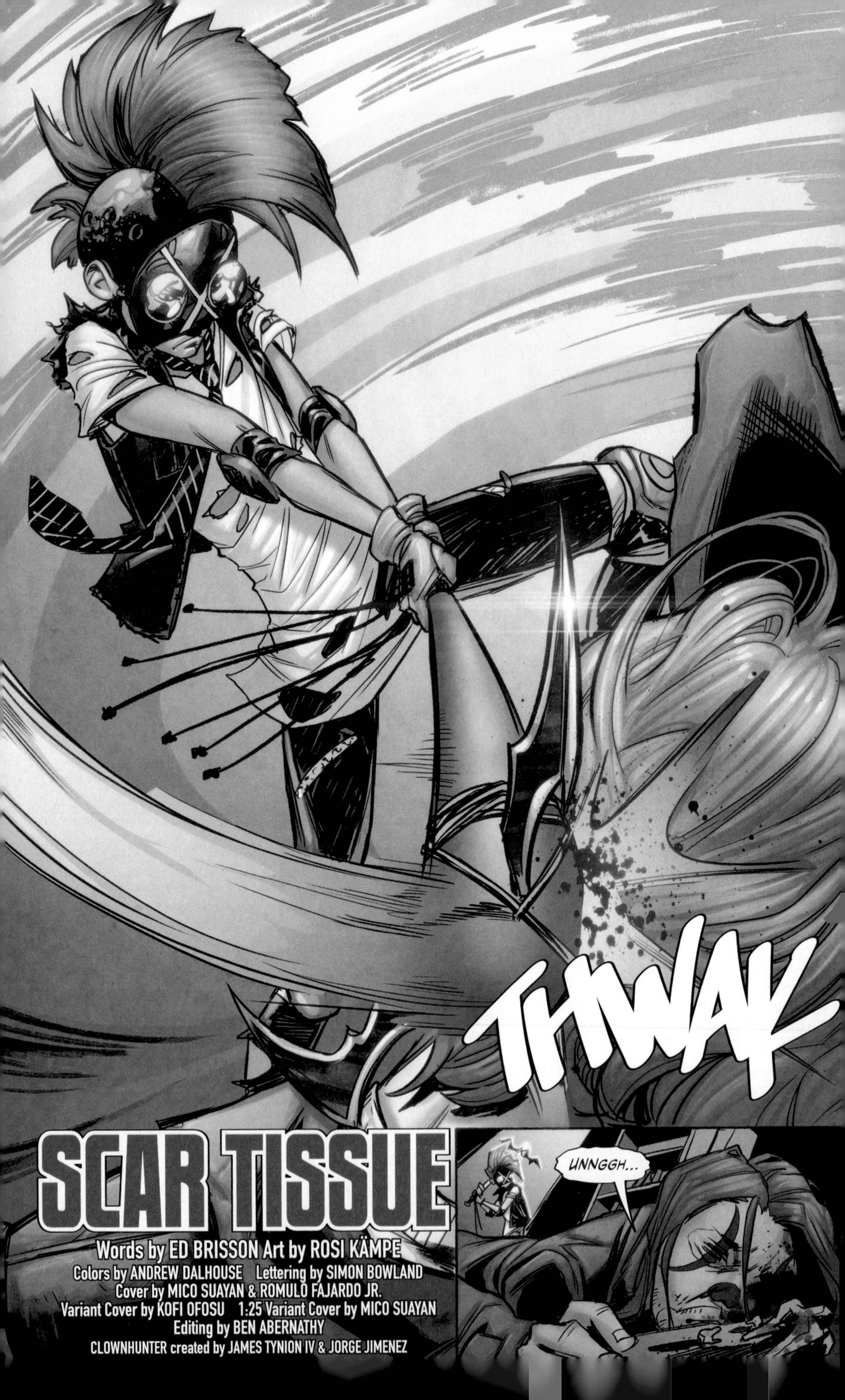
THWAK
UNNGGH...

SCAR TISSUE

Words by ED BRISSON Art by ROSI KÄMPE
Colors by ANDREW DALHOUSE Lettering by SIMON BOWLAND
Cover by MICO SUAYAN & ROMULO FAJARDO JR.
Variant Cover by KOFI OFOSU 1:25 Variant Cover by MICO SUAYAN
Editing by BEN ABERNATHY
CLOWNHUNTER created by JAMES TYNION IV & JORGE JIMENEZ

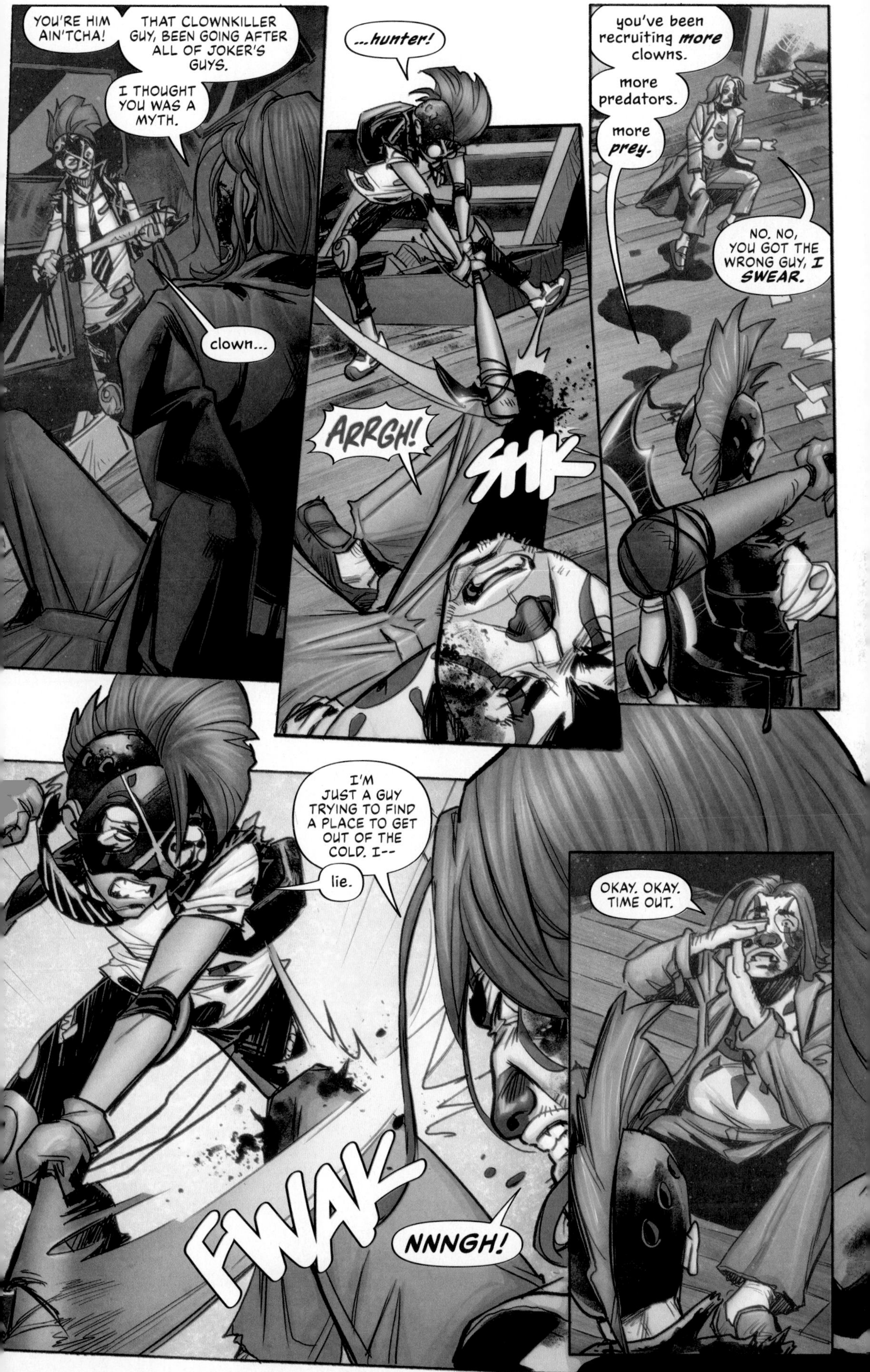
YOU'RE HIM AIN'TCHA!
THAT CLOWNKILLER GUY, BEEN GOING AFTER ALL OF JOKER'S GUYS.
I THOUGHT YOU WAS A MYTH.
clown...
...hunter!
ARRGH!
SHK
you've been recruiting more clowns.
more predators.
more prey.
NO. NO, YOU GOT THE WRONG GUY, I SWEAR.
I'M JUST A GUY TRYING TO FIND A PLACE TO GET OUT OF THE COLD. I--
lie.
FWAK
NNNGH!
OKAY. OKAY. TIME OUT.

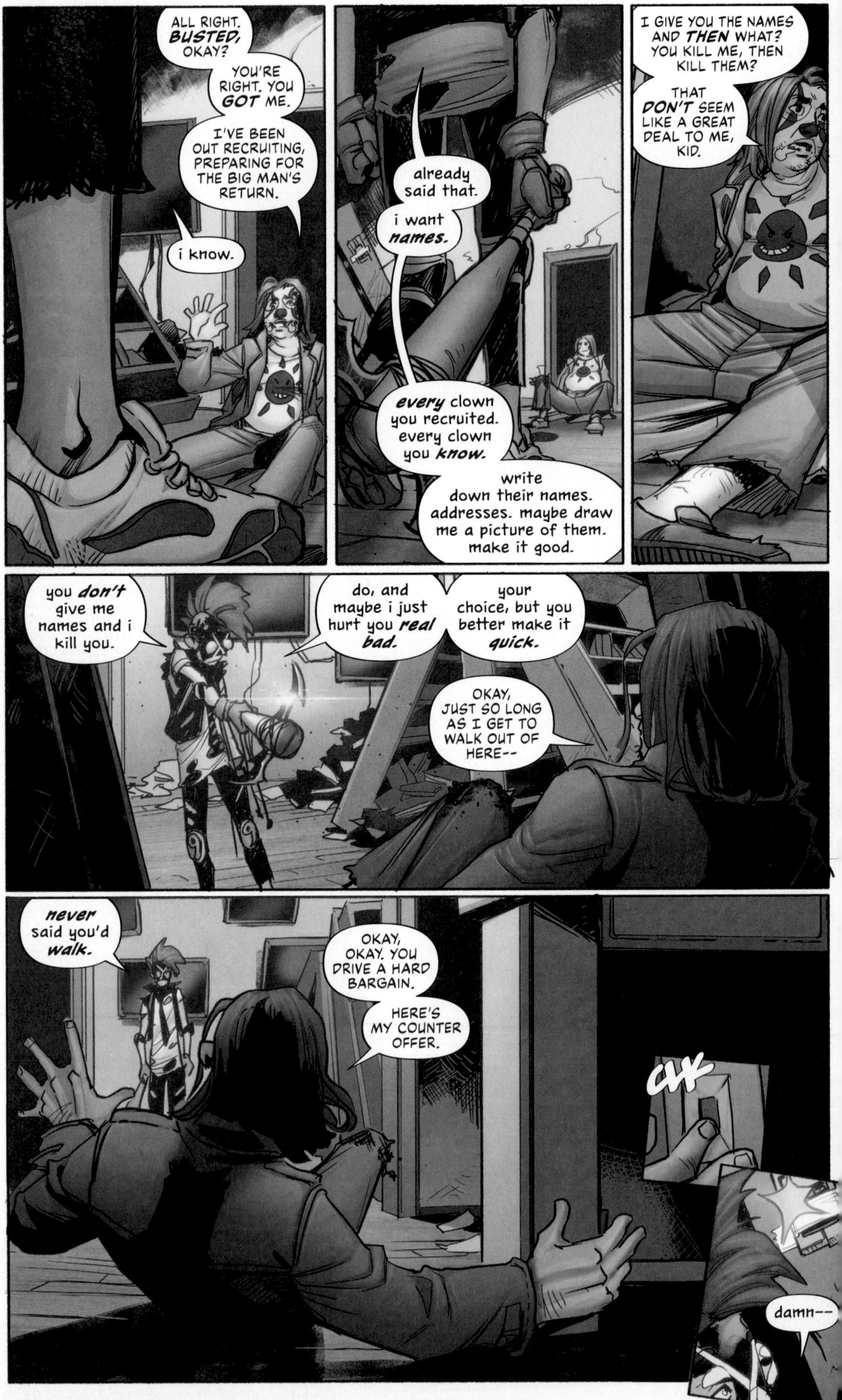
ALL RIGHT. BUSTED, OKAY?
YOU'RE RIGHT. YOU GOT ME.
I'VE BEEN OUT RECRUITING, PREPARING FOR THE BIG MAN'S RETURN.
i know.
already said that.
i want names.
every clown you recruited. every clown you know.
write down their names. addresses. maybe draw me a picture of them. make it good.
I GIVE YOU THE NAMES AND THEN WHAT? YOU KILL ME, THEN KILL THEM?
THAT DON'T SEEM LIKE A GREAT DEAL TO ME, KID.
you don't give me names and i kill you.
do, and maybe i just hurt you real bad.
your choice, but you better make it quick.
OKAY, JUST SO LONG AS I GET TO WALK OUT OF HERE--
never said you'd walk.
OKAY, OKAY. YOU DRIVE A HARD BARGAIN.
HERE'S MY COUNTER OFFER.
CLIK
damn--

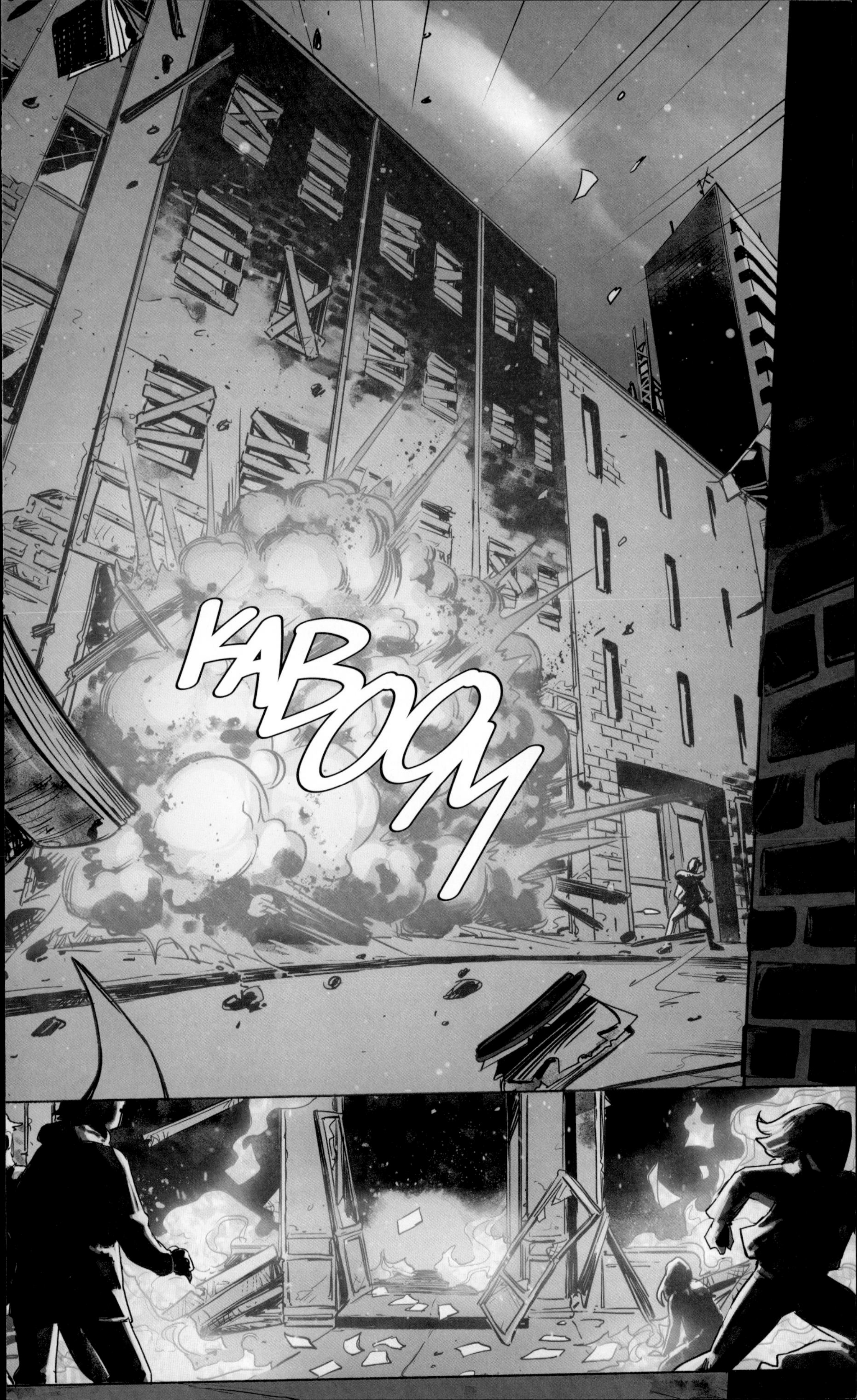
KABOOM

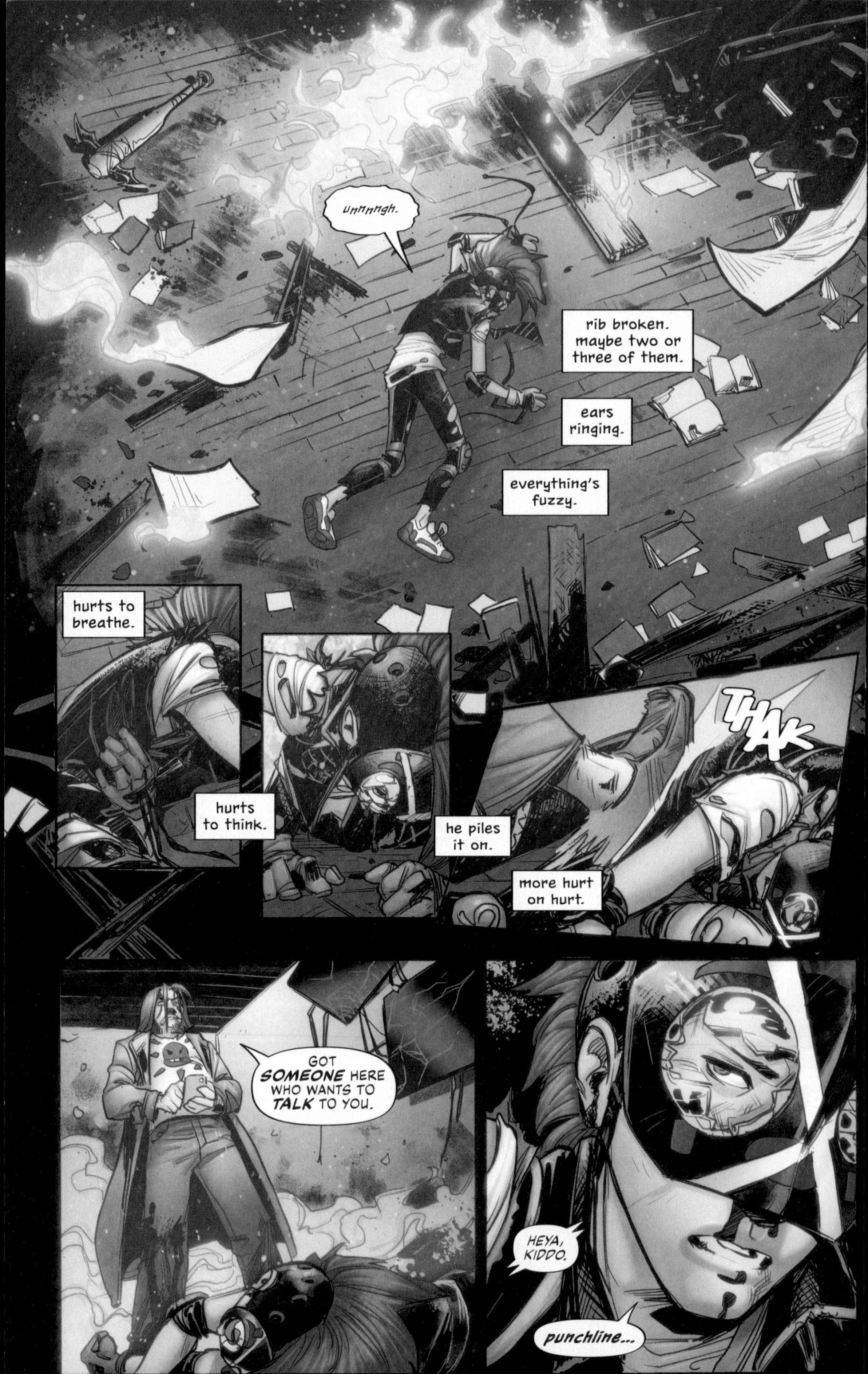
unnnngh.
rib broken. maybe two or three of them.
ears ringing.
everything's fuzzy.
hurts to breathe.
hurts to think.
he piles it on.
THAK
more hurt on hurt.
GOT *SOMEONE* HERE WHO WANTS TO *TALK* TO YOU.
HEYA, KIDDO.
punchline...

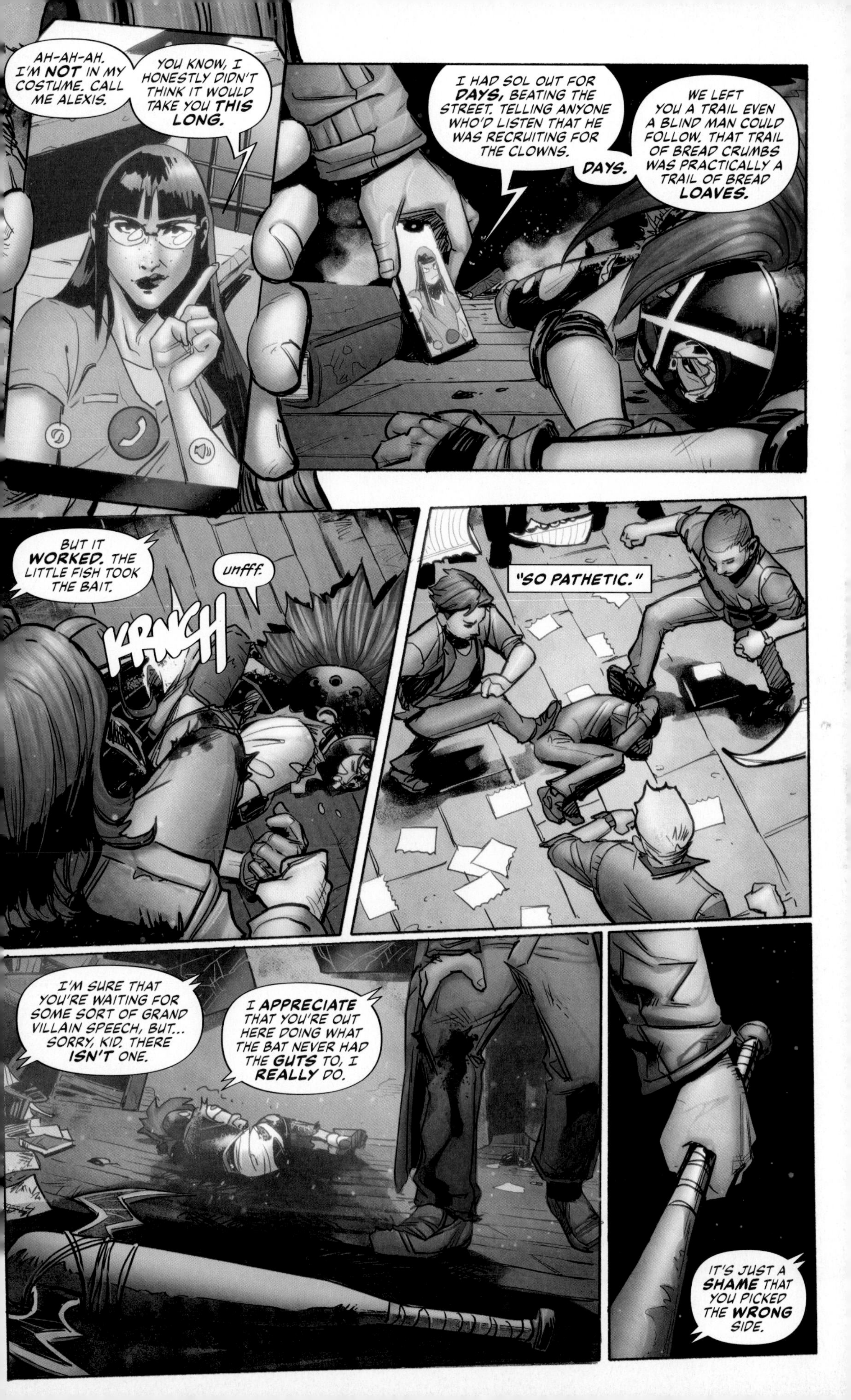
AH-AH-AH. I'M NOT IN MY COSTUME. CALL ME ALEXIS.
YOU KNOW, I HONESTLY DIDN'T THINK IT WOULD TAKE YOU THIS LONG.
I HAD SOL OUT FOR DAYS, BEATING THE STREET. TELLING ANYONE WHO'D LISTEN THAT HE WAS RECRUITING FOR THE CLOWNS.
DAYS.
WE LEFT YOU A TRAIL EVEN A BLIND MAN COULD FOLLOW. THAT TRAIL OF BREAD CRUMBS WAS PRACTICALLY A TRAIL OF BREAD LOAVES.
BUT IT WORKED. THE LITTLE FISH TOOK THE BAIT.
unfff.
KRNCH
"SO PATHETIC."
I'M SURE THAT YOU'RE WAITING FOR SOME SORT OF GRAND VILLAIN SPEECH, BUT... SORRY, KID. THERE ISN'T ONE.
I APPRECIATE THAT YOU'RE OUT HERE DOING WHAT THE BAT NEVER HAD THE GUTS TO, I REALLY DO.
IT'S JUST A SHAME THAT YOU PICKED THE WRONG SIDE.

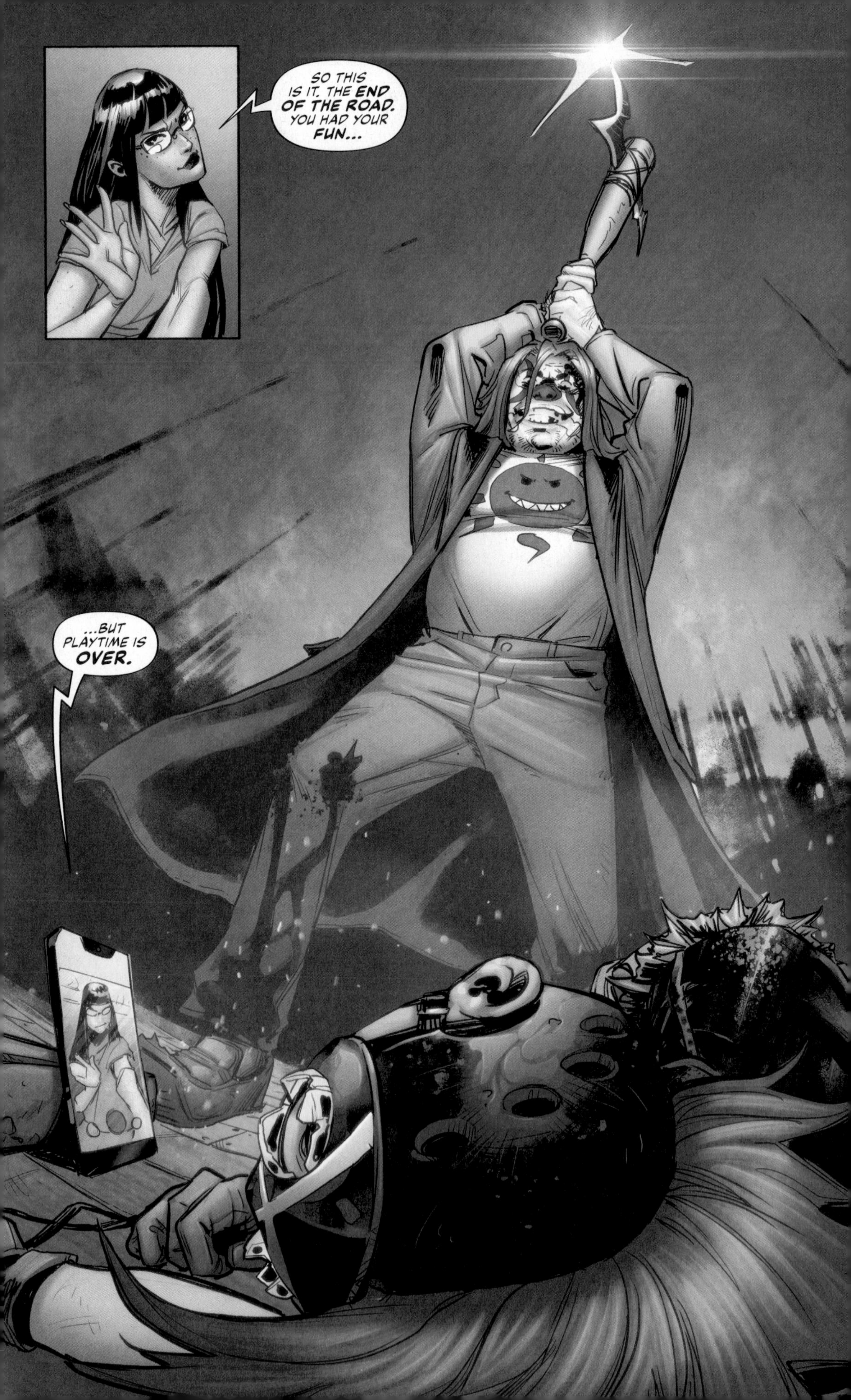
SO THIS IS IT. THE END OF THE ROAD. YOU HAD YOUR FUN...
...BUT PLAYTIME IS OVER.

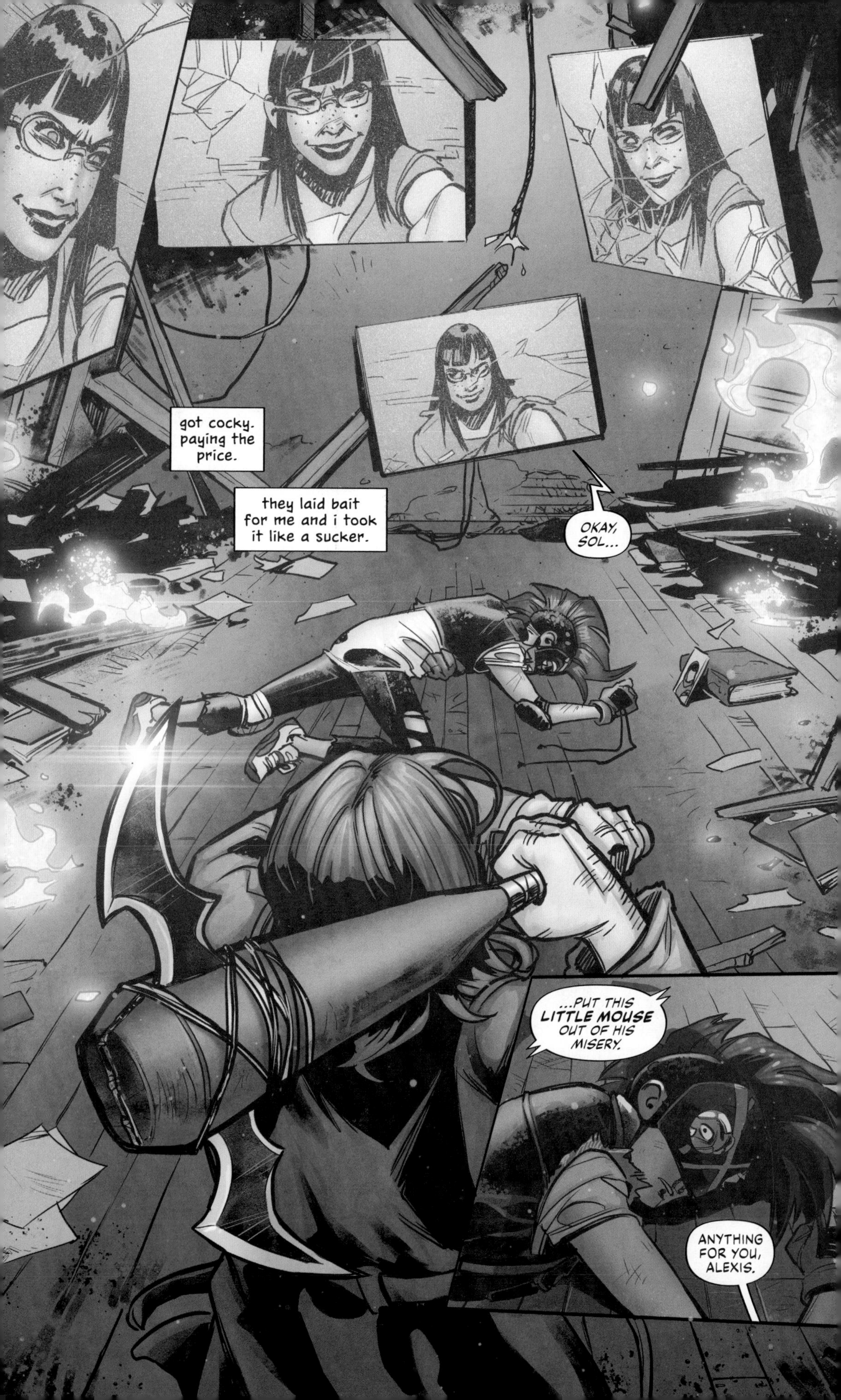
got cocky. paying the price.
they laid bait for me and i took it like a sucker.
OKAY, SOL...
...PUT THIS LITTLE MOUSE OUT OF HIS MISERY.
ANYTHING FOR YOU, ALEXIS.

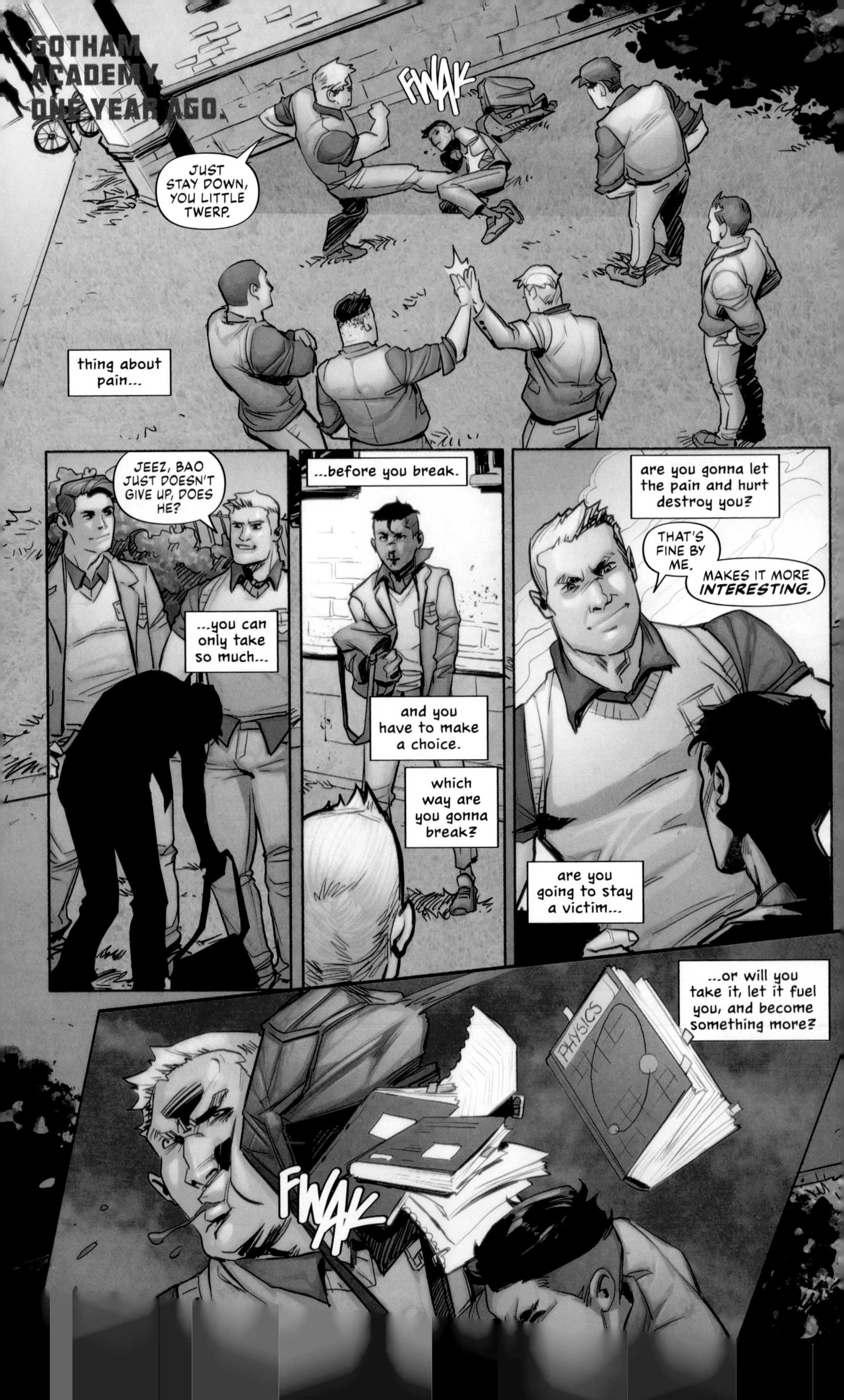
GOTHAM ACADEMY. ONE YEAR AGO.
FWAK
JUST STAY DOWN, YOU LITTLE TWERP.
thing about pain...
JEEZ, BAO JUST DOESN'T GIVE UP, DOES HE?
...you can only take so much...
...before you break.
and you have to make a choice.
which way are you gonna break?
are you gonna let the pain and hurt destroy you?
THAT'S FINE BY ME.
MAKES IT MORE INTERESTING.
are you going to stay a victim...
...or will you take it, let it fuel you, and become something more?
PHYSICS
FWAK

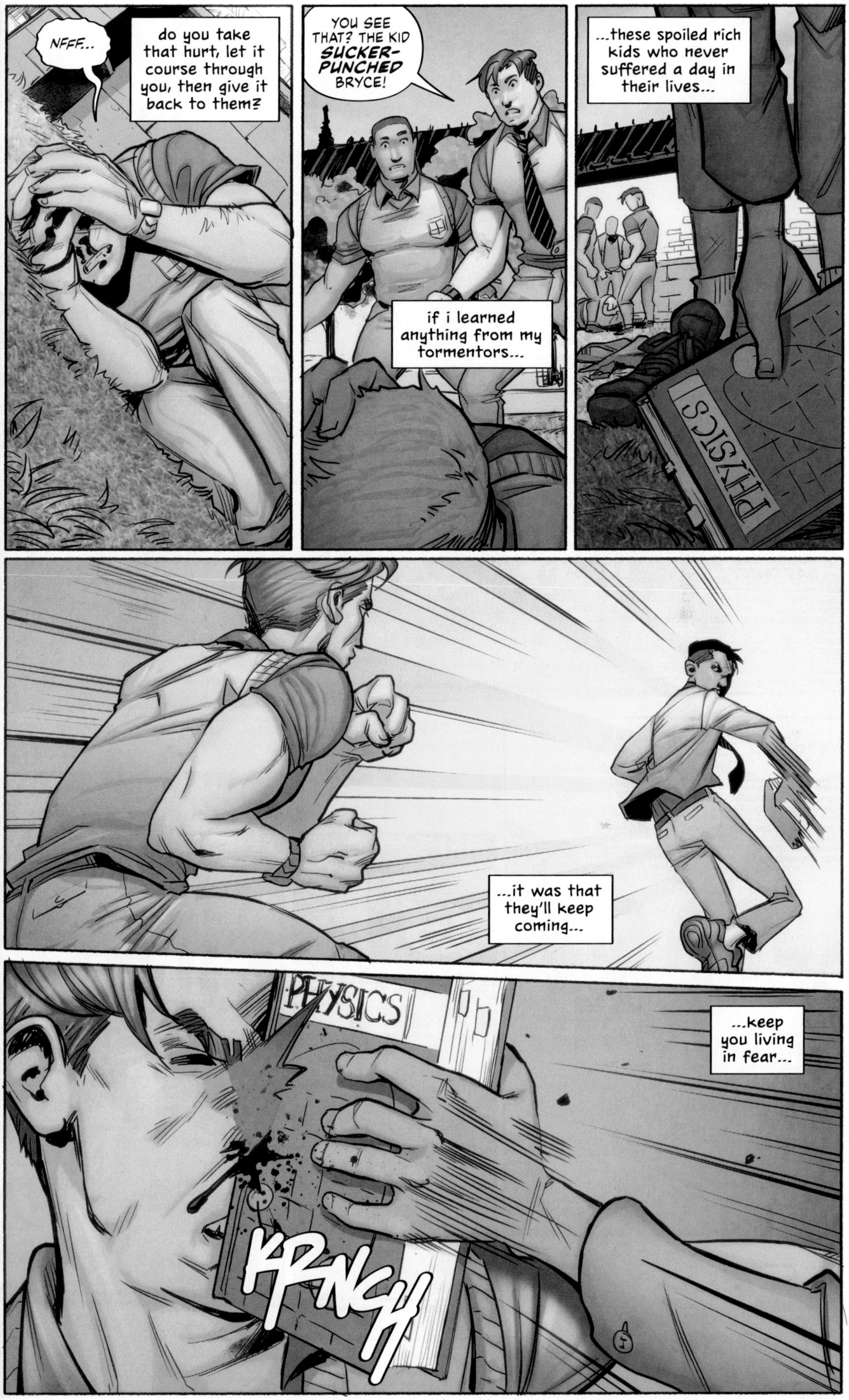
NFFF...
do you take that hurt, let it course through you, then give it back to them?
YOU SEE THAT? THE KID SUCKER-PUNCHED BRYCE!
if i learned anything from my tormentors...
...these spoiled rich kids who never suffered a day in their lives...
PHYSICS
...it was that they'll keep coming...
PHYSICS
...keep you living in fear...
KRNCH

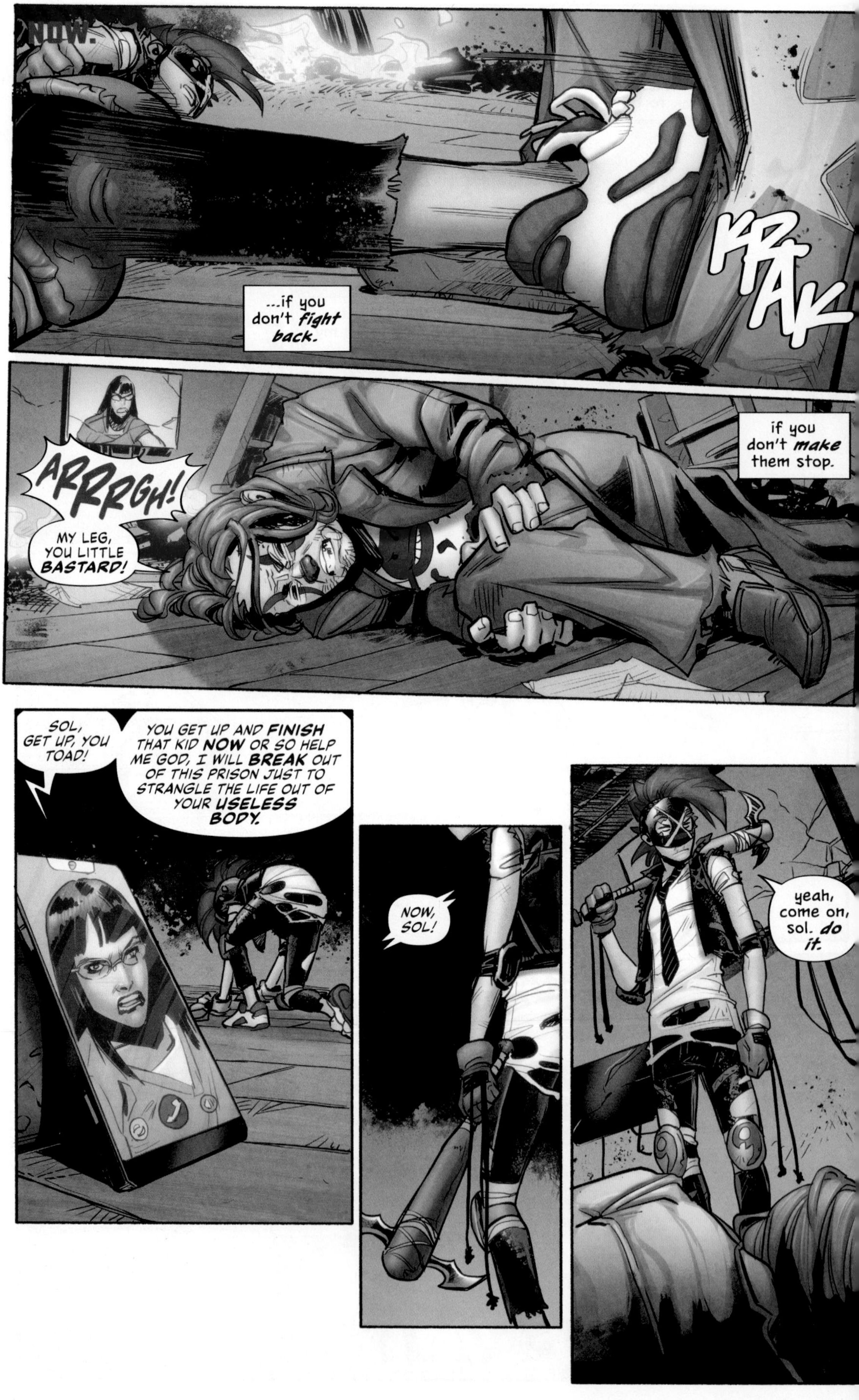
NOW.
...if you don't *fight back.*
KRAK
ARRRGH!
MY LEG, YOU LITTLE **BASTARD!**
if you don't *make* them stop.
SOL, GET UP, YOU TOAD!
YOU GET UP AND **FINISH** THAT KID **NOW** OR SO HELP ME GOD, I WILL **BREAK** OUT OF THIS PRISON JUST TO STRANGLE THE LIFE OUT OF YOUR **USELESS BODY.**
NOW, SOL!
yeah, come on, sol. *do it.*

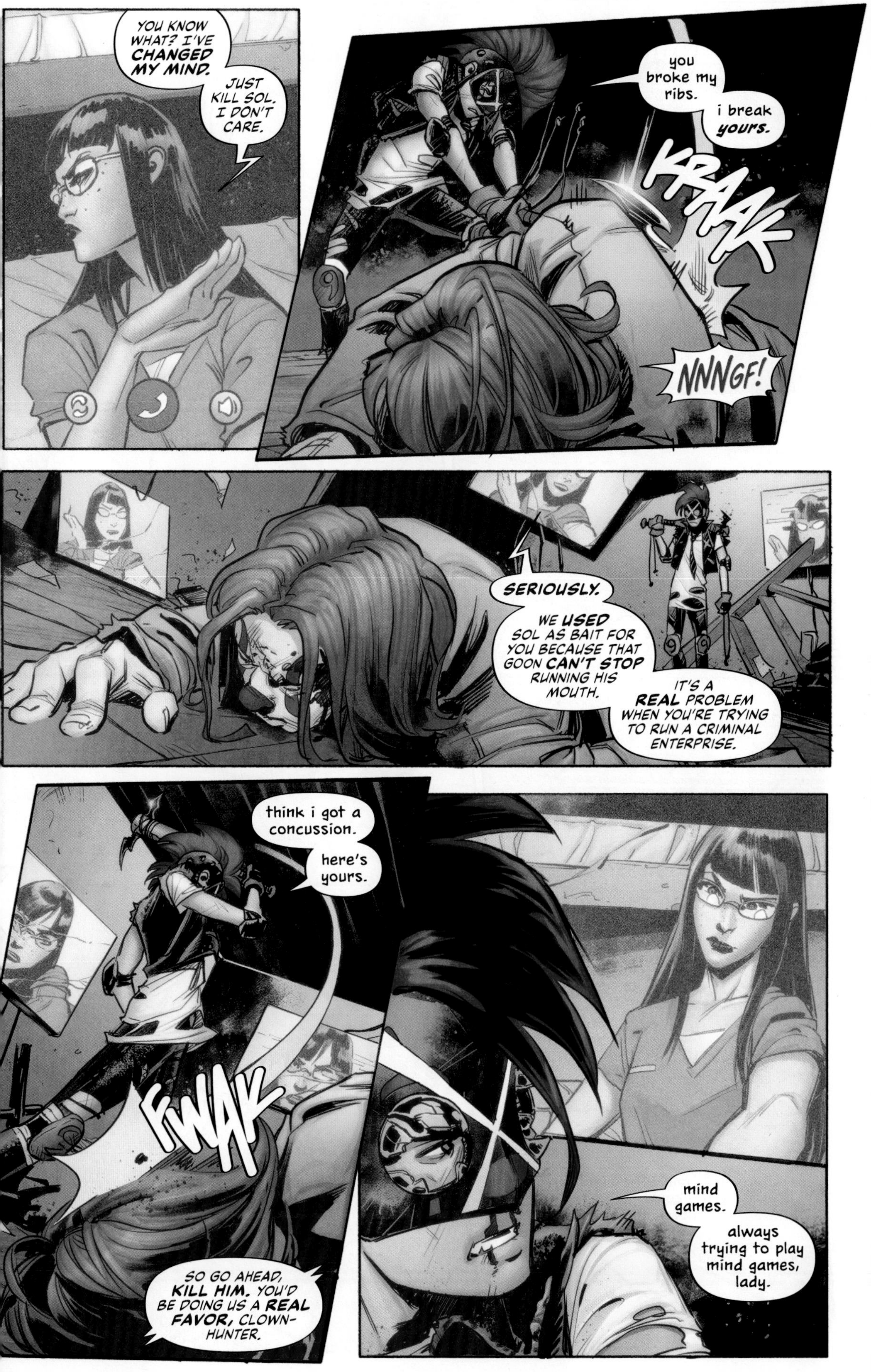
YOU KNOW WHAT? I'VE CHANGED MY MIND.
JUST KILL SOL. I DON'T CARE.
you broke my ribs.
i break yours.
KRAAK
NNNGF!
SERIOUSLY.
WE USED SOL AS BAIT FOR YOU BECAUSE THAT GOON CAN'T STOP RUNNING HIS MOUTH.
IT'S A REAL PROBLEM WHEN YOU'RE TRYING TO RUN A CRIMINAL ENTERPRISE.
think i got a concussion.
here's yours.
FWAK
SO GO AHEAD, KILL HIM. YOU'D BE DOING US A REAL FAVOR, CLOWN-HUNTER.
mind games.
always trying to play mind games, lady.

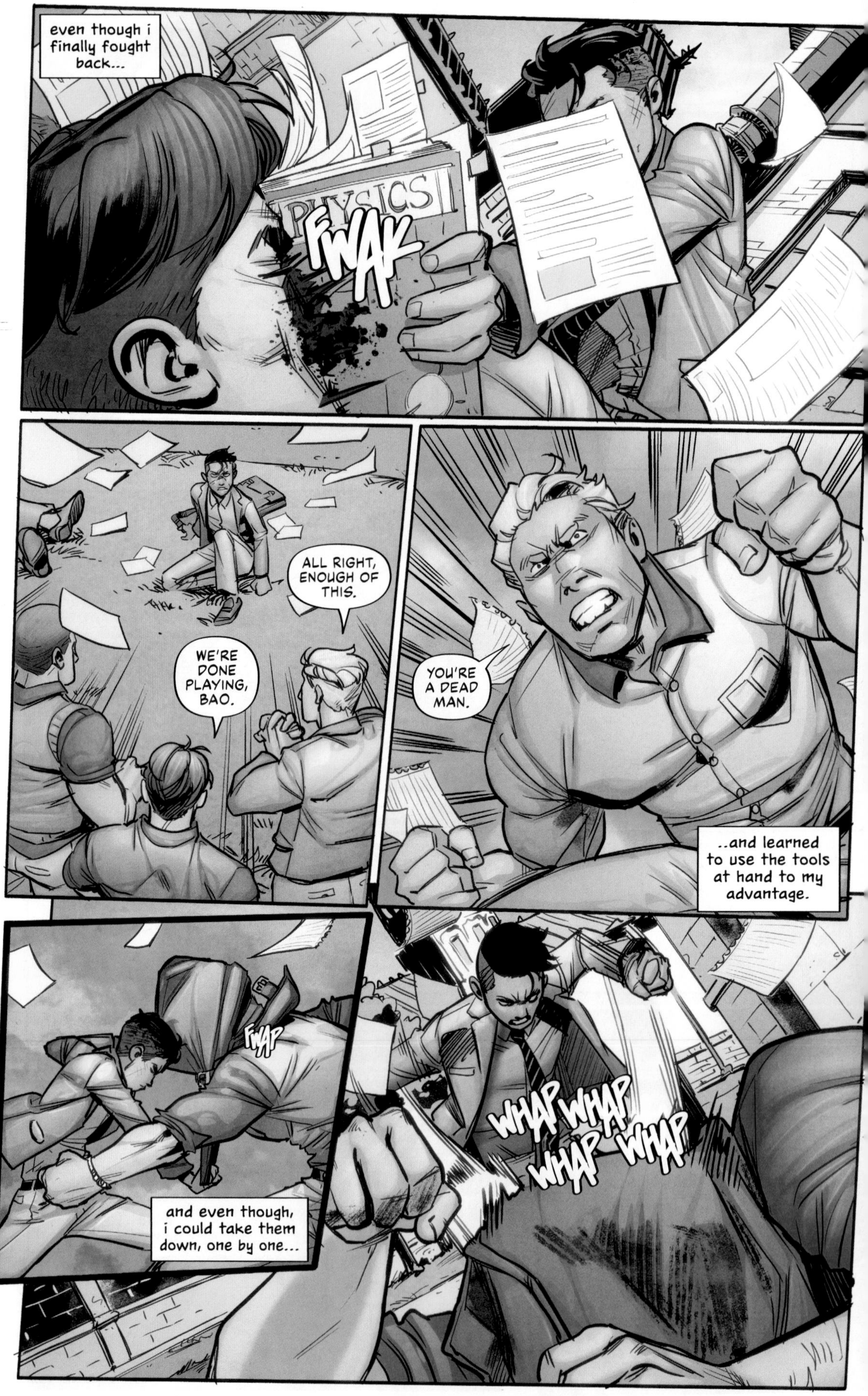

even though i finally fought back...
PHYSICS II
FWAK
ALL RIGHT, ENOUGH OF THIS.
WE'RE DONE PLAYING, BAO.
YOU'RE A DEAD MAN.
..and learned to use the tools at hand to my advantage.
FWAP
and even though, i could take them down, one by one...
WHAP WHAP WHAP WHAP

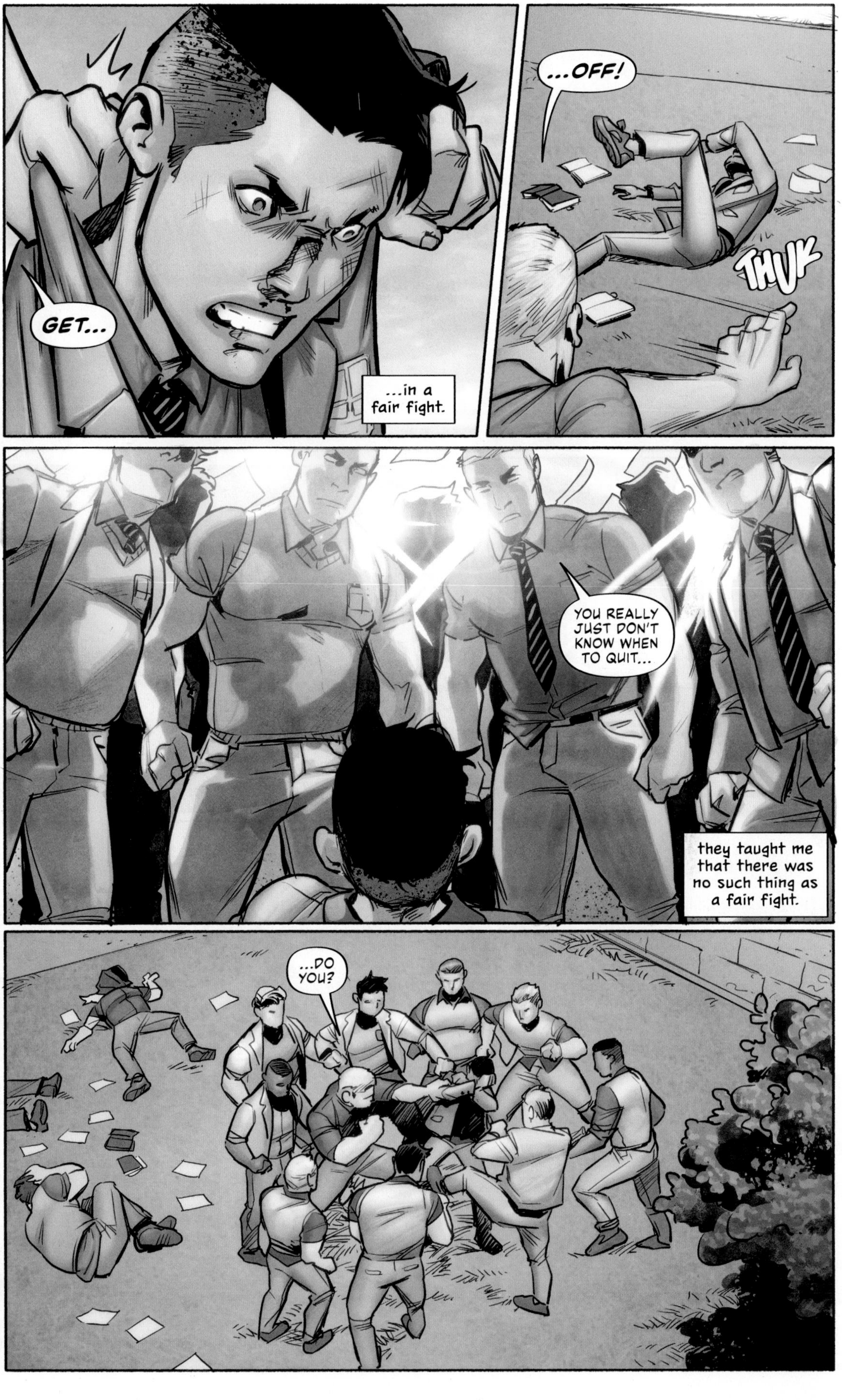
GET...
...in a fair fight.
...OFF!
THUK
YOU REALLY JUST DON'T KNOW WHEN TO QUIT...
they taught me that there was no such thing as a fair fight.
...DO YOU?

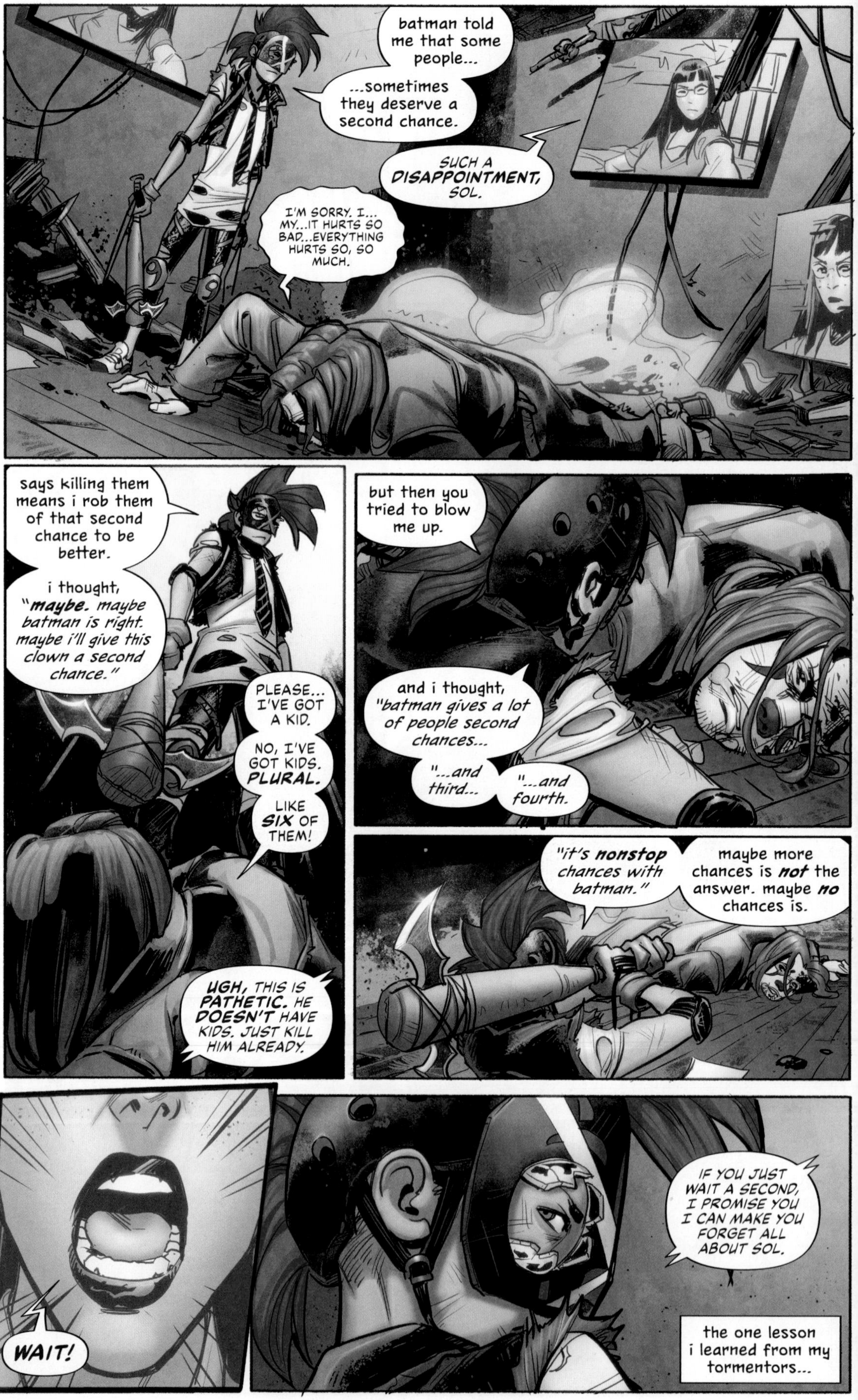

batman told me that some people...
...sometimes they deserve a second chance.
SUCH A **DISAPPOINTMENT,** SOL.
I'M SORRY. I... MY...IT HURTS SO BAD...EVERYTHING HURTS SO, SO MUCH.
says killing them means i rob them of that second chance to be better.
i thought, "***maybe.*** *maybe batman is right. maybe i'll give this clown a second chance."*
PLEASE... I'VE GOT A KID.
NO, I'VE GOT KIDS. **PLURAL.**
LIKE ***SIX*** OF THEM!
UGH, THIS IS **PATHETIC.** HE **DOESN'T** HAVE KIDS. JUST KILL HIM ALREADY.
but then you tried to blow me up.
and i thought, *"batman gives a lot of people second chances...*
"...and third...
"...and fourth.
*"it's **nonstop** chances with batman."*
maybe more chances is ***not*** the answer. maybe ***no*** chances is.
WAIT!
IF YOU JUST WAIT A SECOND, I PROMISE YOU I CAN MAKE YOU FORGET ALL ABOUT SOL.
the one lesson i learned from my tormentors...

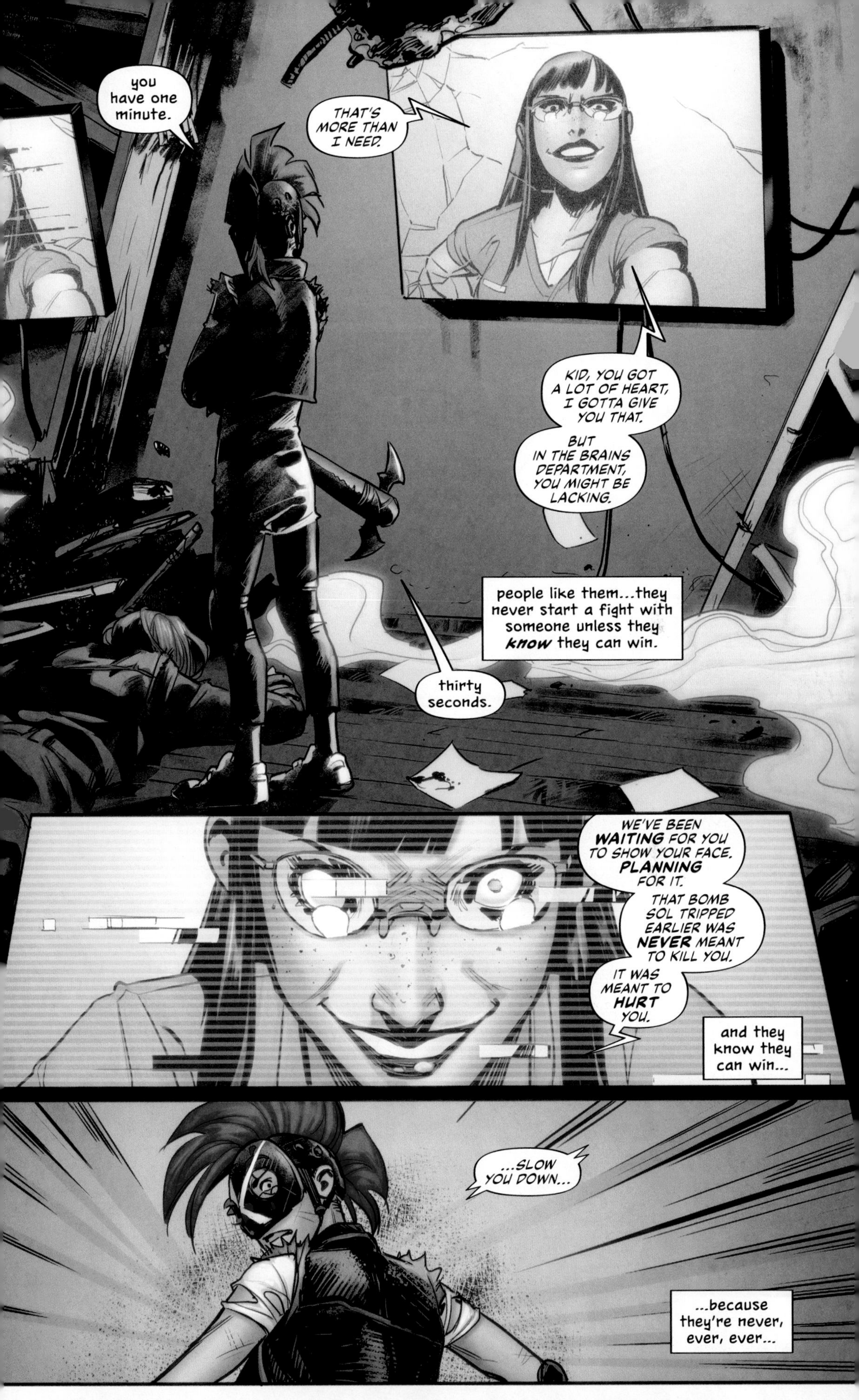

you have one minute.
THAT'S MORE THAN I NEED.
KID, YOU GOT A LOT OF HEART, I GOTTA GIVE YOU THAT.
BUT IN THE BRAINS DEPARTMENT, YOU MIGHT BE LACKING.
people like them...they never start a fight with someone unless they **know** they can win.
thirty seconds.
WE'VE BEEN **WAITING** FOR YOU TO SHOW YOUR FACE. **PLANNING** FOR IT.
THAT BOMB SOL TRIPPED EARLIER WAS **NEVER** MEANT TO KILL YOU.
IT WAS MEANT TO **HURT** YOU.
and they know they can win...
...SLOW YOU DOWN...
...because they're never, ever, ever...

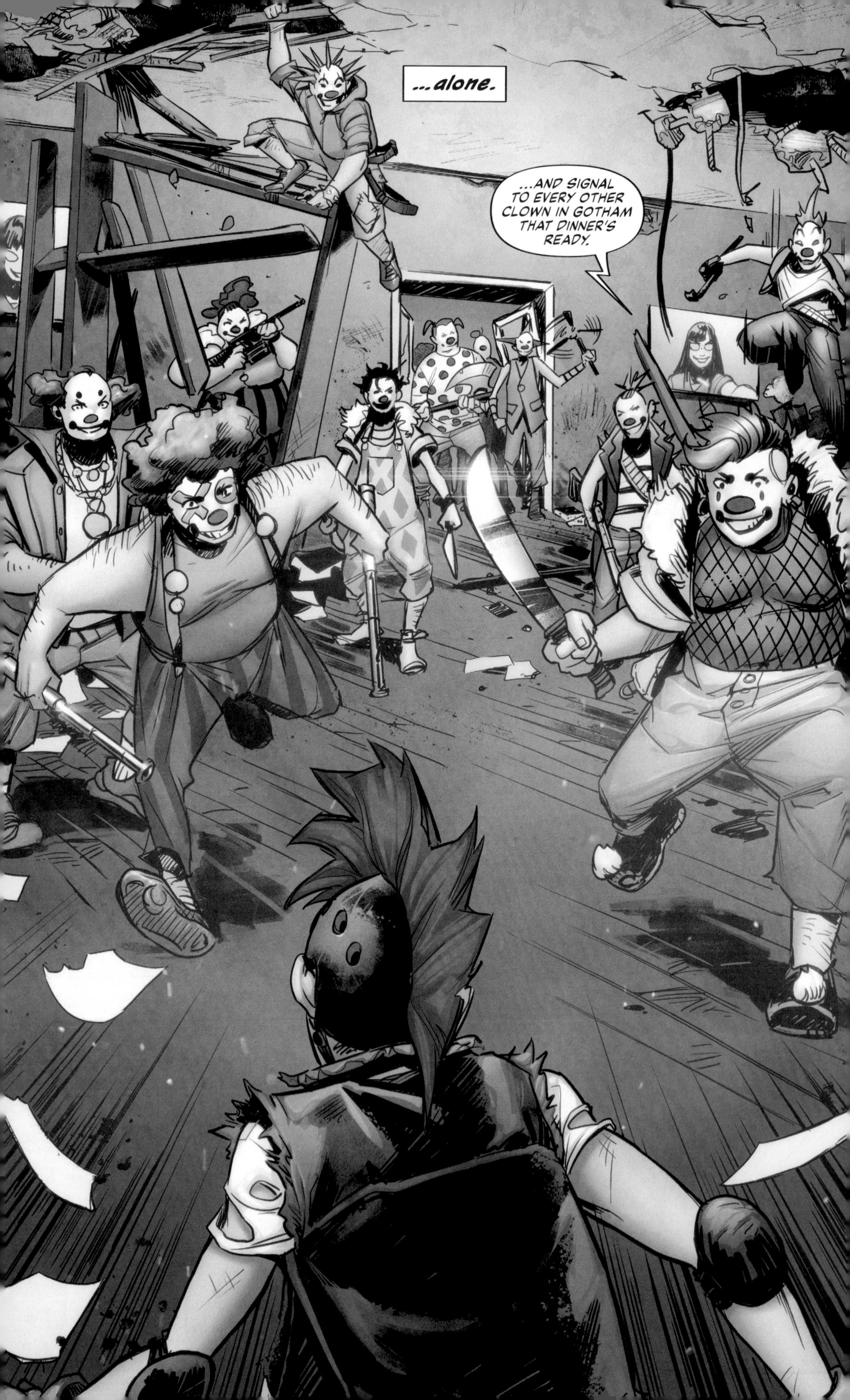
...alone.
...AND SIGNAL TO EVERY OTHER CLOWN IN GOTHAM THAT DINNER'S READY.

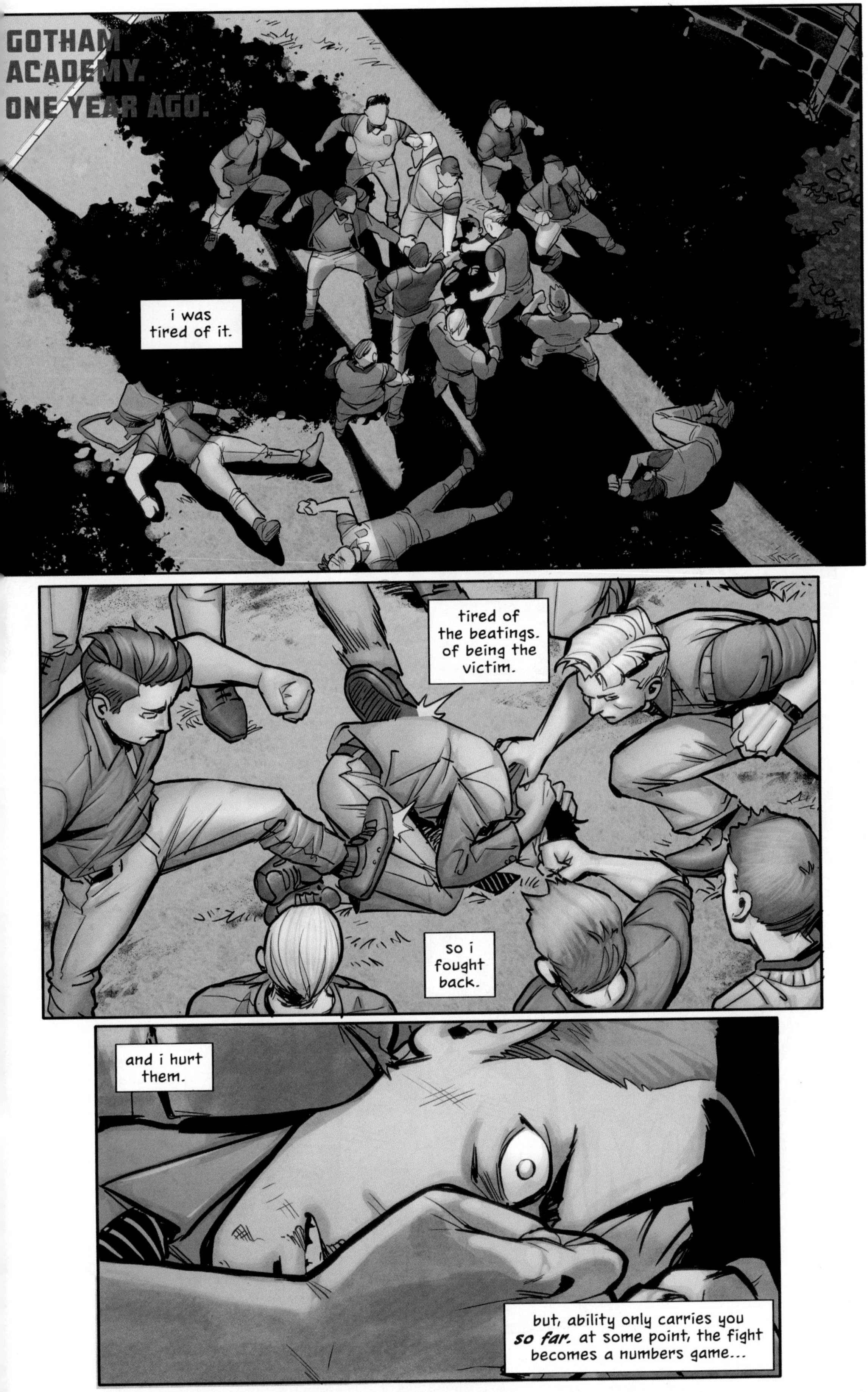
GOTHAM ACADEMY. ONE YEAR AGO.
i was tired of it.
tired of the beatings. of being the victim.
so i fought back.
and i hurt them.
but, ability only carries you *so far.* at some point, the fight becomes a numbers game...

...and they *always* seem to have the numbers.

because they're *afraid* to be alone.

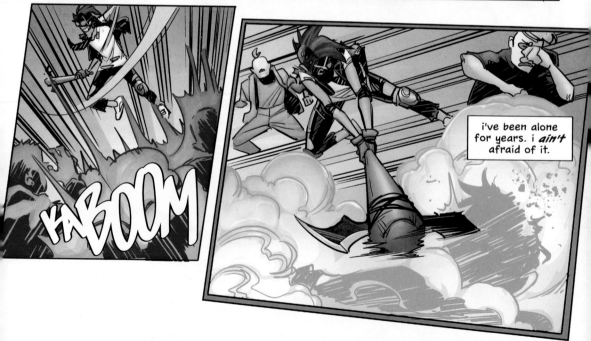

KABOOM

i've been alone for years. i *ain't* afraid of it.

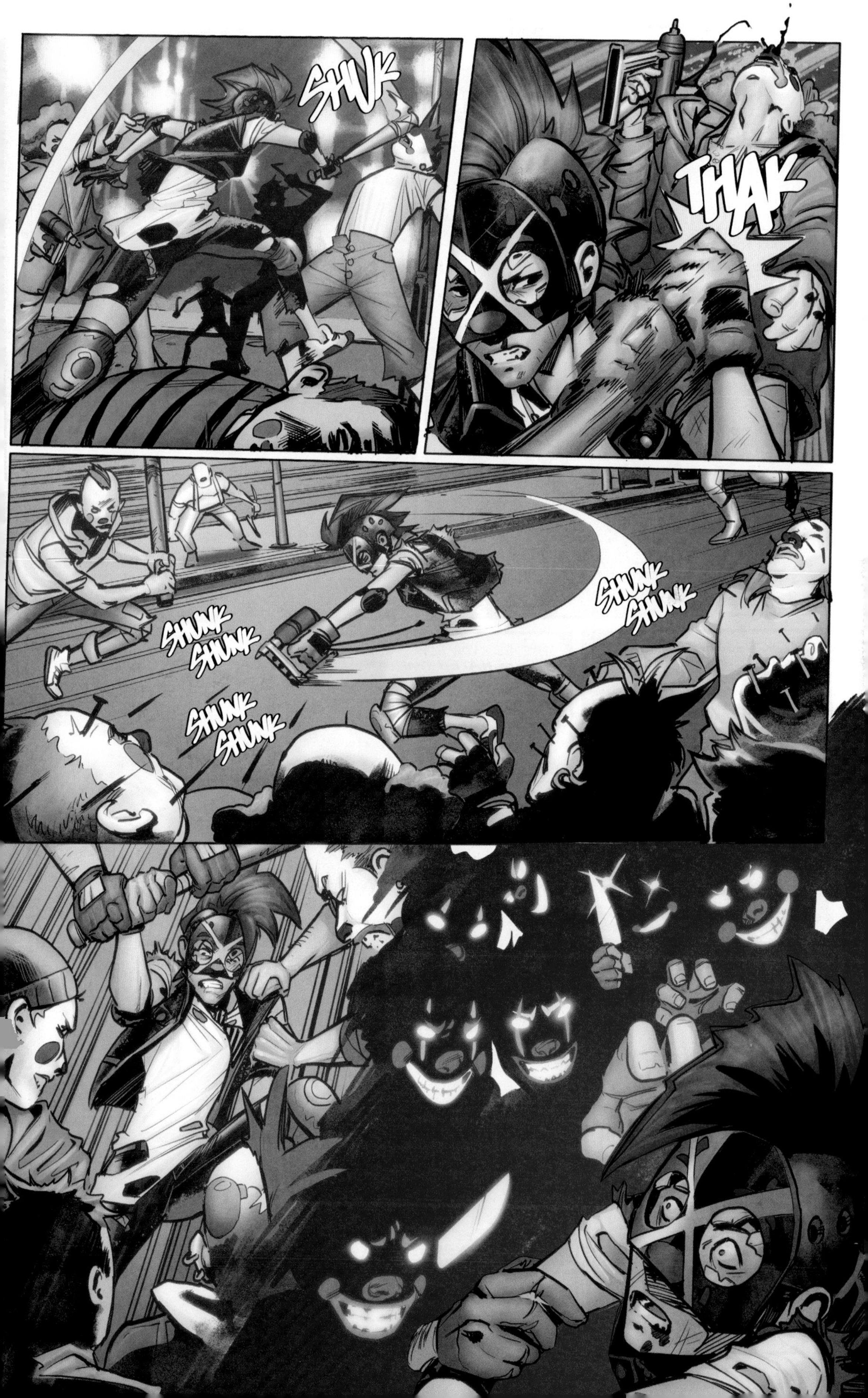
SHUK
THAK
SHUNK
SHUNK
SHUNK
SHUNK
SHUNK
SHUNK

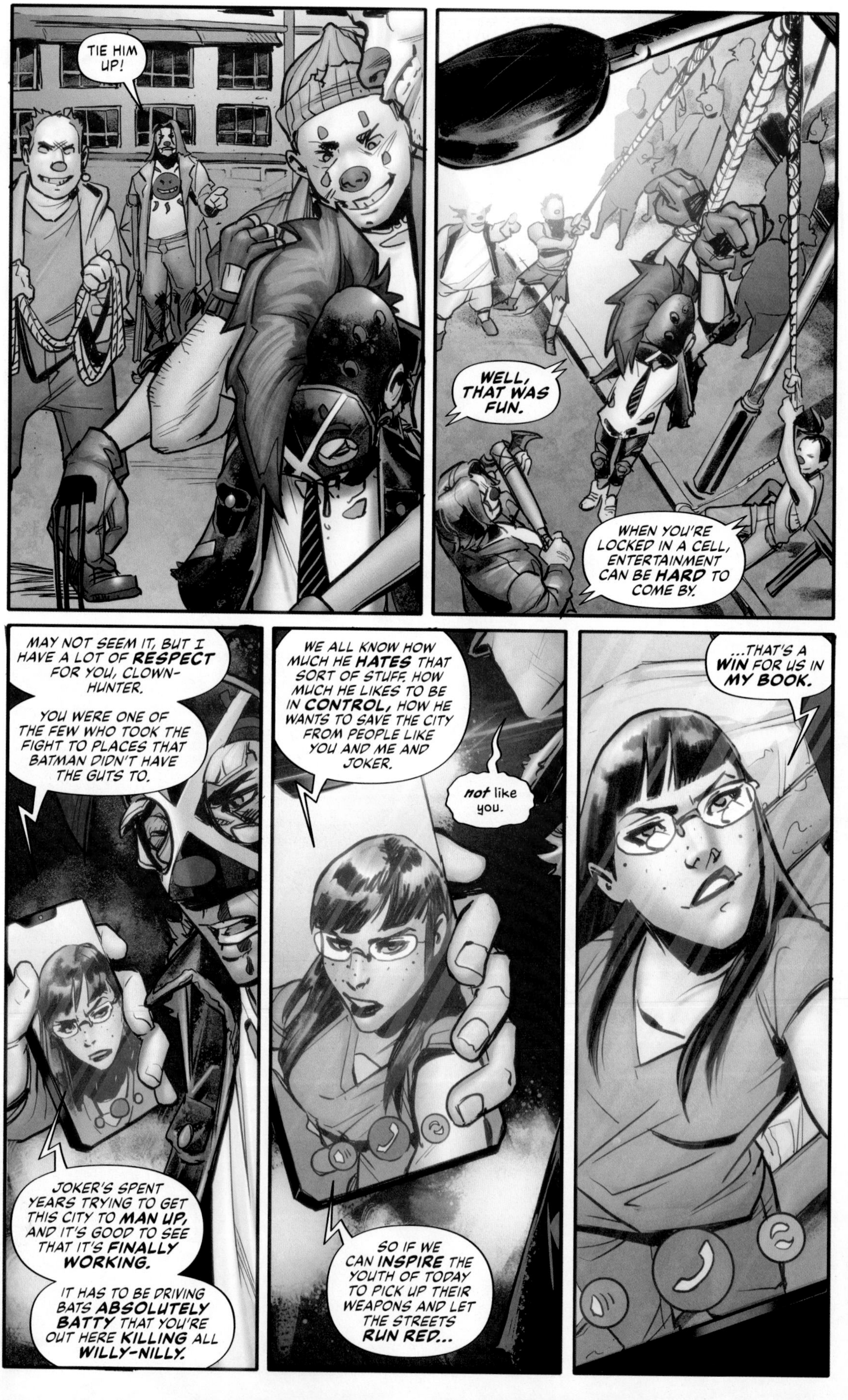
TIE HIM UP!
WELL, THAT WAS FUN.
WHEN YOU'RE LOCKED IN A CELL, ENTERTAINMENT CAN BE HARD TO COME BY.
MAY NOT SEEM IT, BUT I HAVE A LOT OF RESPECT FOR YOU, CLOWN-HUNTER.
YOU WERE ONE OF THE FEW WHO TOOK THE FIGHT TO PLACES THAT BATMAN DIDN'T HAVE THE GUTS TO.
JOKER'S SPENT YEARS TRYING TO GET THIS CITY TO MAN UP, AND IT'S GOOD TO SEE THAT IT'S FINALLY WORKING.
IT HAS TO BE DRIVING BATS ABSOLUTELY BATTY THAT YOU'RE OUT HERE KILLING ALL WILLY-NILLY.
WE ALL KNOW HOW MUCH HE HATES THAT SORT OF STUFF. HOW MUCH HE LIKES TO BE IN CONTROL, HOW HE WANTS TO SAVE THE CITY FROM PEOPLE LIKE YOU AND ME AND JOKER.
not like you.
SO IF WE CAN INSPIRE THE YOUTH OF TODAY TO PICK UP THEIR WEAPONS AND LET THE STREETS RUN RED...
...THAT'S A WIN FOR US IN MY BOOK.

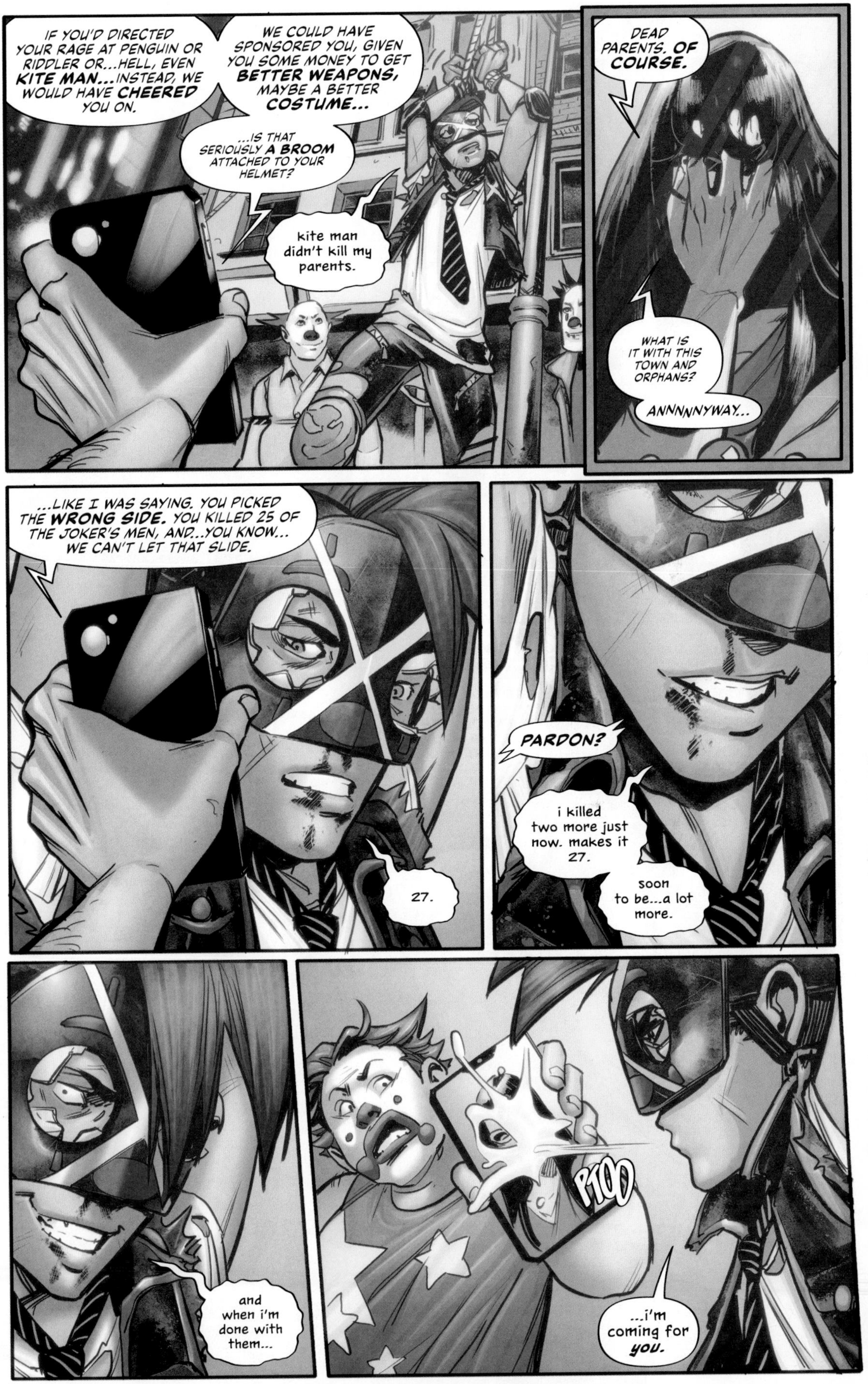
IF YOU'D DIRECTED YOUR RAGE AT PENGUIN OR RIDDLER OR...HELL, EVEN KITE MAN...INSTEAD, WE WOULD HAVE CHEERED YOU ON.
WE COULD HAVE SPONSORED YOU, GIVEN YOU SOME MONEY TO GET BETTER WEAPONS, MAYBE A BETTER COSTUME...
...IS THAT SERIOUSLY A BROOM ATTACHED TO YOUR HELMET?
kite man didn't kill my parents.
DEAD PARENTS. OF COURSE.
WHAT IS IT WITH THIS TOWN AND ORPHANS?
ANNNNNYWAY...
...LIKE I WAS SAYING. YOU PICKED THE WRONG SIDE. YOU KILLED 25 OF THE JOKER'S MEN, AND...YOU KNOW... WE CAN'T LET THAT SLIDE.
27.
PARDON?
i killed two more just now. makes it 27.
soon to be...a lot more.
and when i'm done with them...
PTOO
...i'm coming for you.

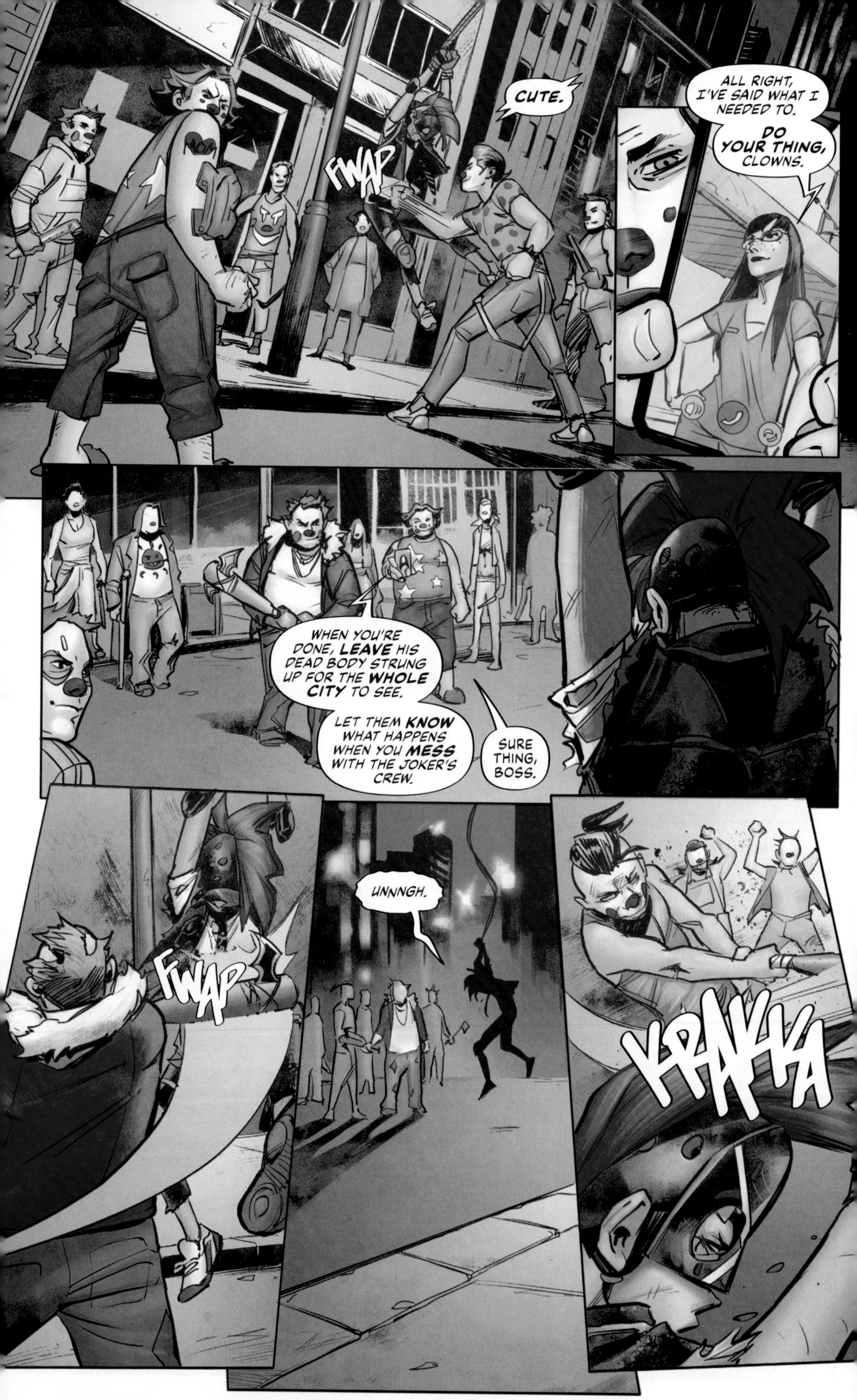
FWAP
CUTE.
ALL RIGHT, I'VE SAID WHAT I NEEDED TO.
DO YOUR THING, CLOWNS.
WHEN YOU'RE DONE, LEAVE HIS DEAD BODY STRUNG UP FOR THE WHOLE CITY TO SEE.
LET THEM KNOW WHAT HAPPENS WHEN YOU MESS WITH THE JOKER'S CREW.
SURE THING, BOSS.
FWAP
UNNNGH.
KRAKKA

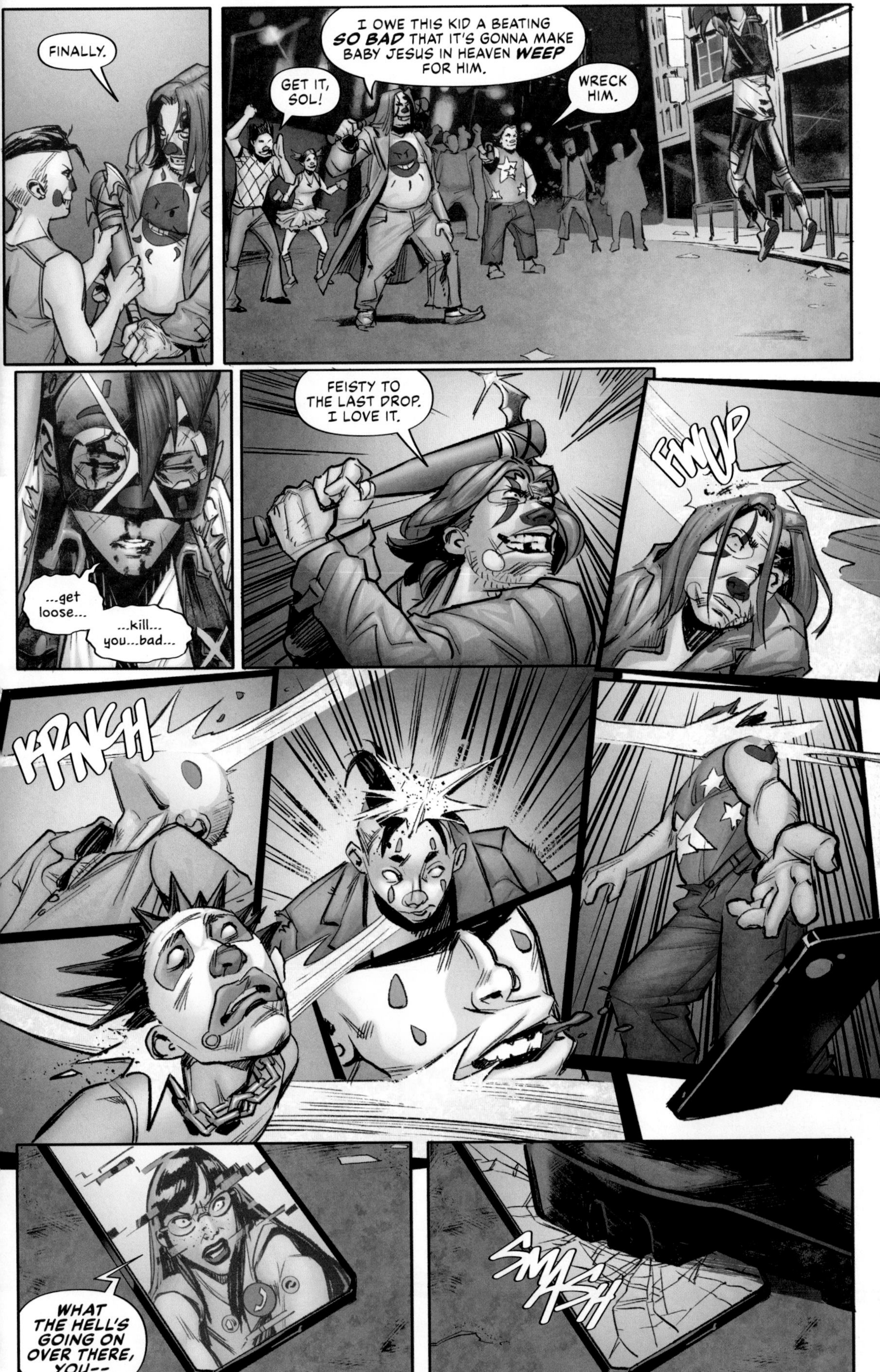
FINALLY.
I OWE THIS KID A BEATING SO BAD THAT IT'S GONNA MAKE BABY JESUS IN HEAVEN WEEP FOR HIM.
GET IT, SOL!
WRECK HIM.
...get loose...
...kill... you...bad...
FEISTY TO THE LAST DROP. I LOVE IT.
FWUP
KRNCH
SMASH
WHAT THE HELL'S GOING ON OVER THERE, YOU--

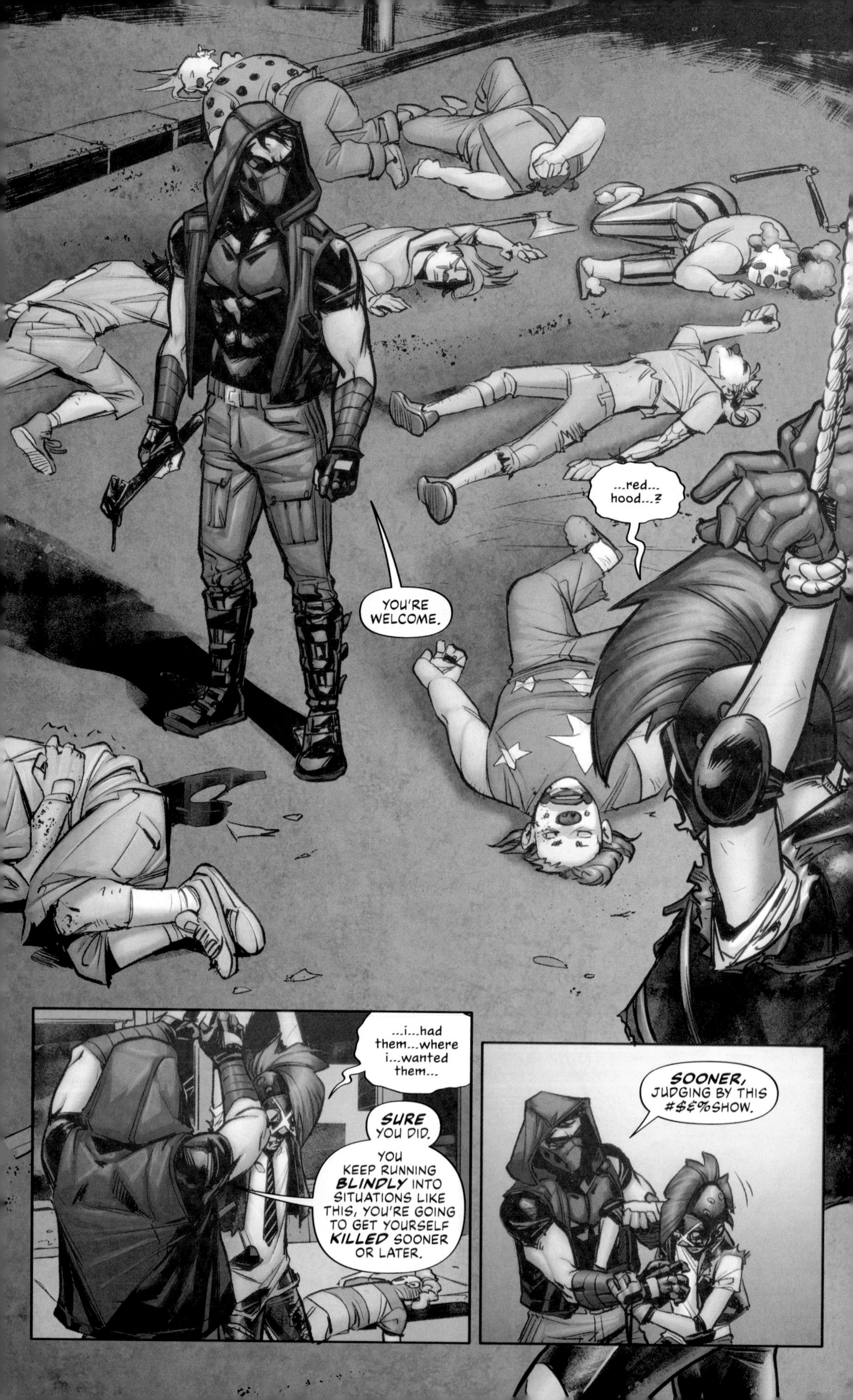
YOU'RE WELCOME.
...red... hood...?
...i...had them...where i...wanted them...
SURE YOU DID.
YOU KEEP RUNNING BLINDLY INTO SITUATIONS LIKE THIS, YOU'RE GOING TO GET YOURSELF KILLED SOONER OR LATER.
SOONER, JUDGING BY THIS #$&%SHOW.

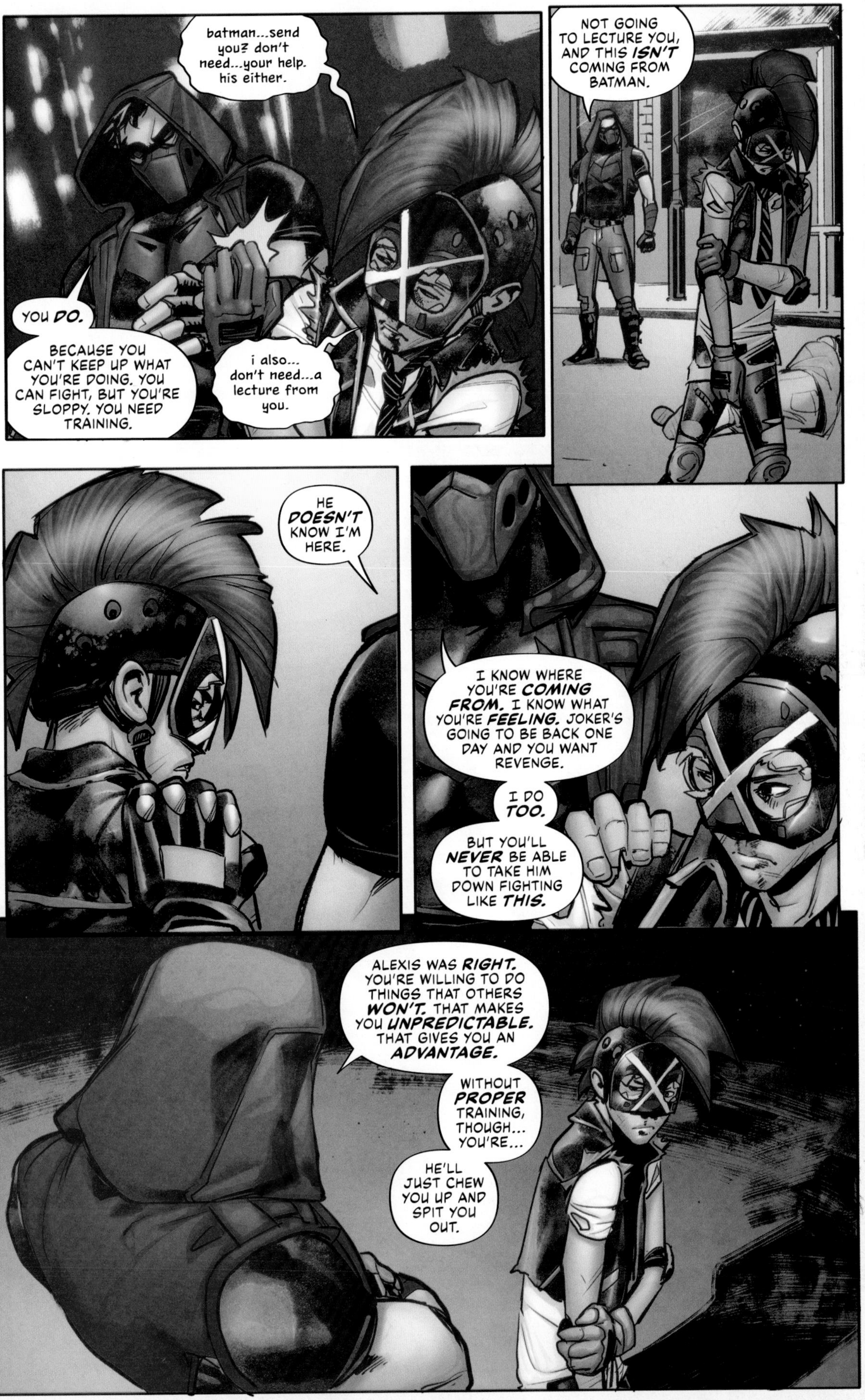
batman...send you? don't need...your help. his either.
YOU DO.
BECAUSE YOU CAN'T KEEP UP WHAT YOU'RE DOING. YOU CAN FIGHT, BUT YOU'RE SLOPPY. YOU NEED TRAINING.
i also... don't need...a lecture from you.
NOT GOING TO LECTURE YOU, AND THIS ISN'T COMING FROM BATMAN.
HE DOESN'T KNOW I'M HERE.
I KNOW WHERE YOU'RE COMING FROM. I KNOW WHAT YOU'RE FEELING. JOKER'S GOING TO BE BACK ONE DAY AND YOU WANT REVENGE.
I DO TOO.
BUT YOU'LL NEVER BE ABLE TO TAKE HIM DOWN FIGHTING LIKE THIS.
ALEXIS WAS RIGHT. YOU'RE WILLING TO DO THINGS THAT OTHERS WON'T. THAT MAKES YOU UNPREDICTABLE. THAT GIVES YOU AN ADVANTAGE.
WITHOUT PROPER TRAINING, THOUGH... YOU'RE...
HE'LL JUST CHEW YOU UP AND SPIT YOU OUT.

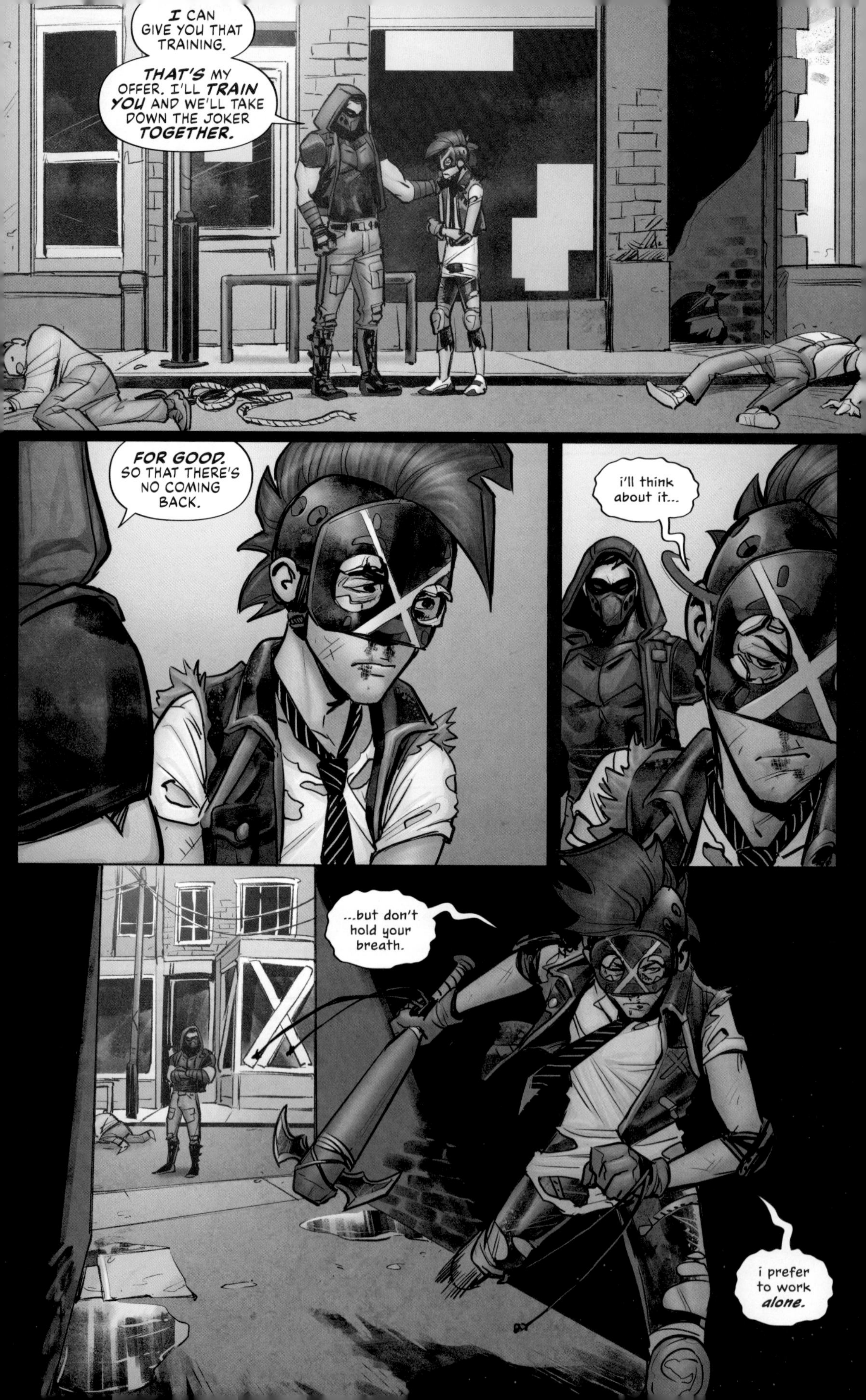
I CAN GIVE YOU THAT TRAINING.
THAT'S MY OFFER. I'LL TRAIN YOU AND WE'LL TAKE DOWN THE JOKER TOGETHER.
FOR GOOD. SO THAT THERE'S NO COMING BACK.
i'll think about it...
...but don't hold your breath.
i prefer to work alone.

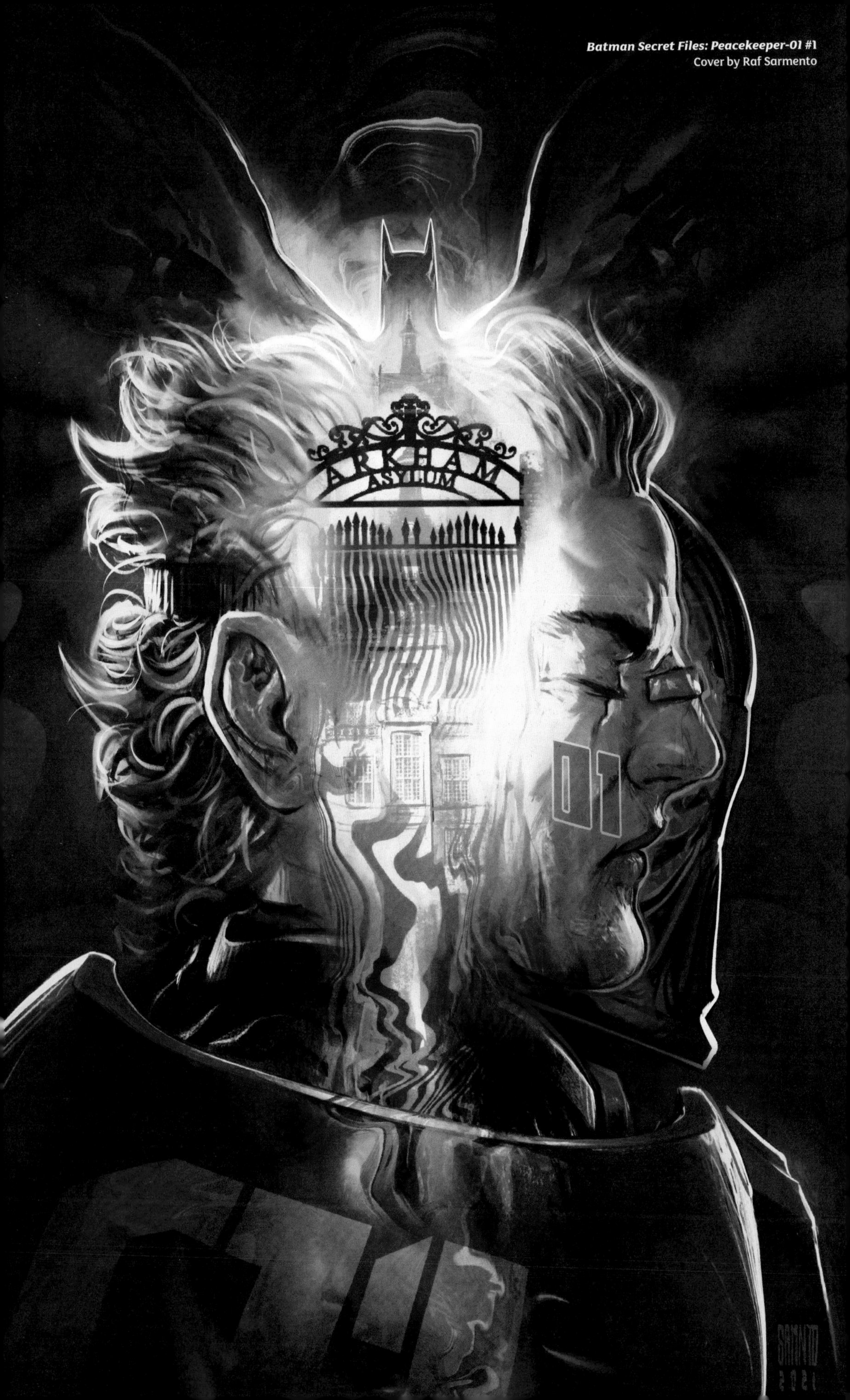
ARKHAM
ASYLUM
01

Batman Secret Files: Peacekeeper-01 #1
Cover by Raf Sarmento

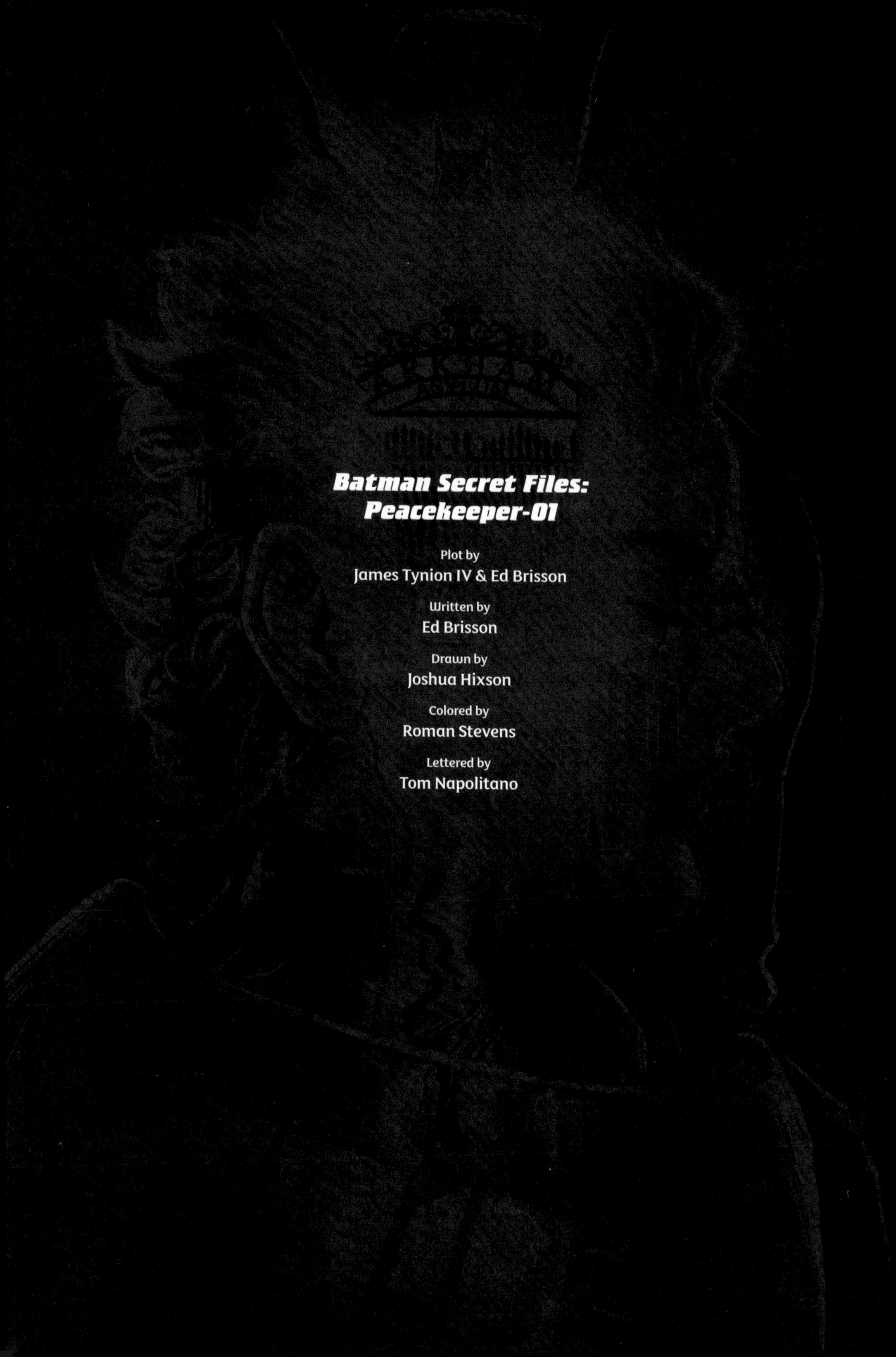

Batman Secret Files: Peacekeeper-01

Plot by
James Tynion IV & Ed Brisson

Written by
Ed Brisson

Drawn by
Joshua Hixson

Colored by
Roman Stevens

Lettered by
Tom Napolitano

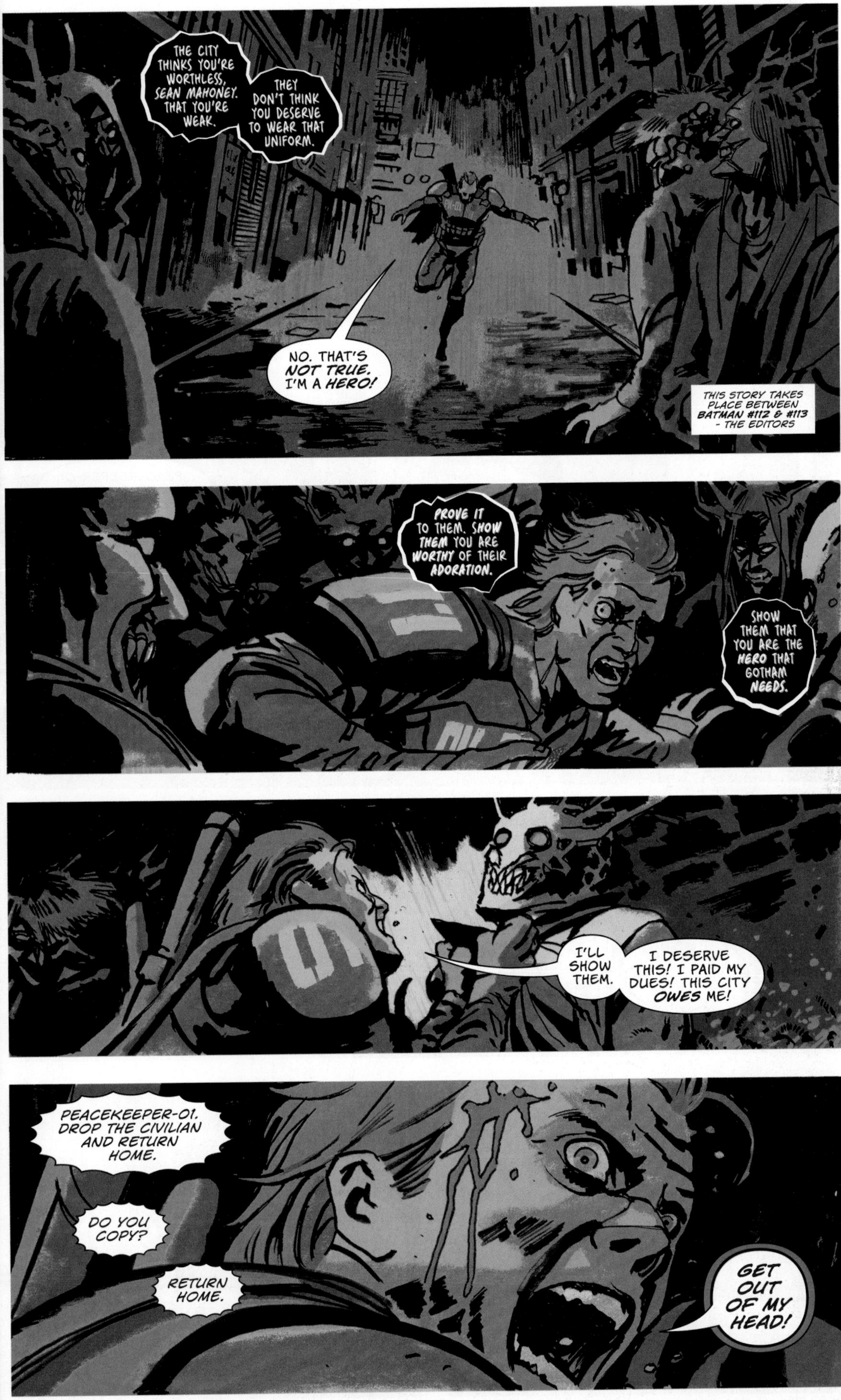
THE CITY THINKS YOU'RE WORTHLESS, SEAN MAHONEY. THAT YOU'RE WEAK.
THEY DON'T THINK YOU DESERVE TO WEAR THAT UNIFORM.
NO. THAT'S NOT TRUE. I'M A HERO!
THIS STORY TAKES PLACE BETWEEN BATMAN #112 & #113 - THE EDITORS
PROVE IT TO THEM. SHOW THEM YOU ARE WORTHY OF THEIR ADORATION.
SHOW THEM THAT YOU ARE THE HERO THAT GOTHAM NEEDS.
I'LL SHOW THEM.
I DESERVE THIS! I PAID MY DUES! THIS CITY OWES ME!
PEACEKEEPER-01. DROP THE CIVILIAN AND RETURN HOME.
DO YOU COPY?
RETURN HOME.
GET OUT OF MY HEAD!

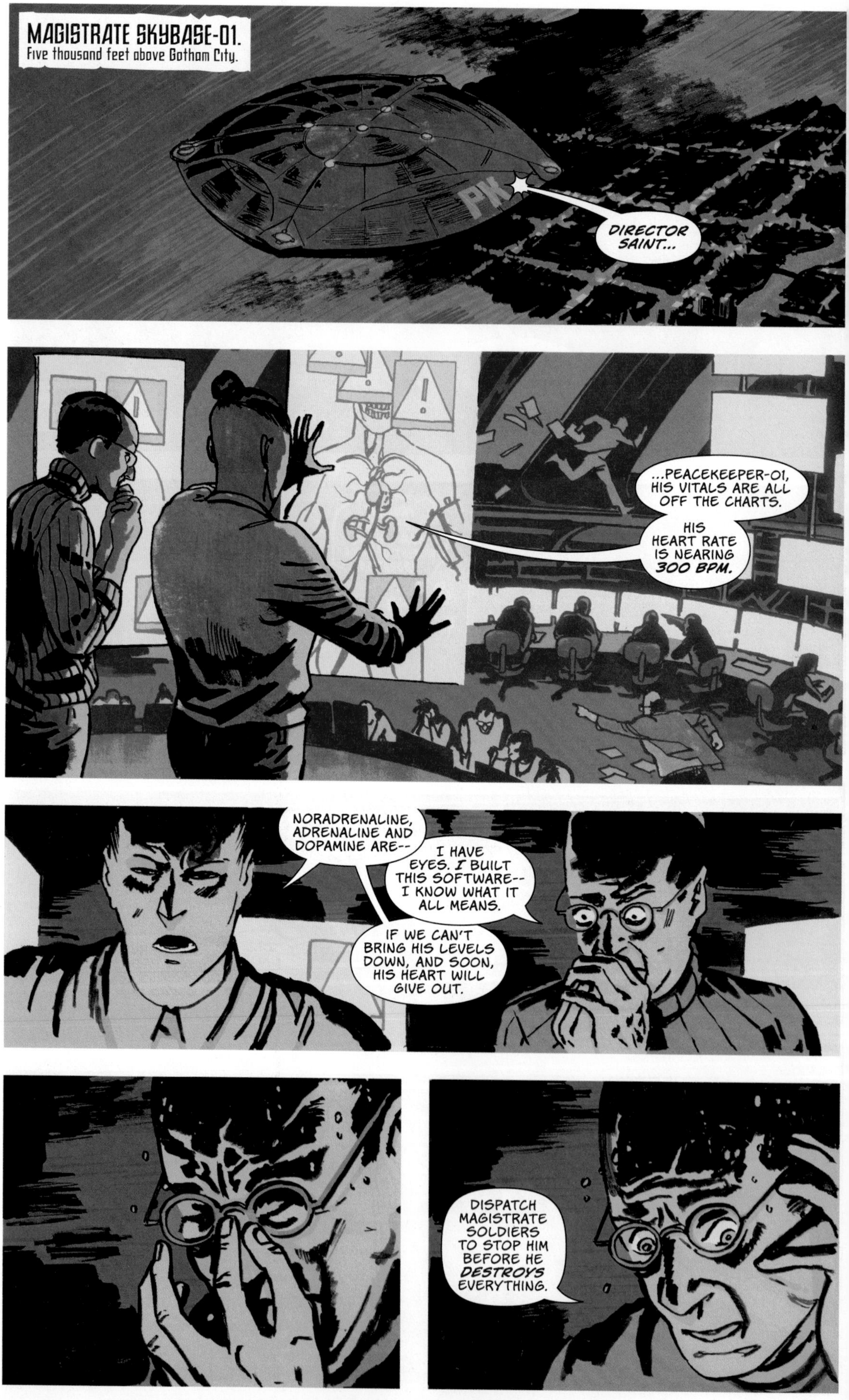
MAGISTRATE SKYBASE-01.
Five thousand feet above Gotham City.
DIRECTOR SAINT...
...PEACEKEEPER-01, HIS VITALS ARE ALL OFF THE CHARTS.
HIS HEART RATE IS NEARING 300 BPM.
NORADRENALINE, ADRENALINE AND DOPAMINE ARE--
I HAVE EYES. I BUILT THIS SOFTWARE-- I KNOW WHAT IT ALL MEANS.
IF WE CAN'T BRING HIS LEVELS DOWN, AND SOON, HIS HEART WILL GIVE OUT.
DISPATCH MAGISTRATE SOLDIERS TO STOP HIM BEFORE HE DESTROYS EVERYTHING.

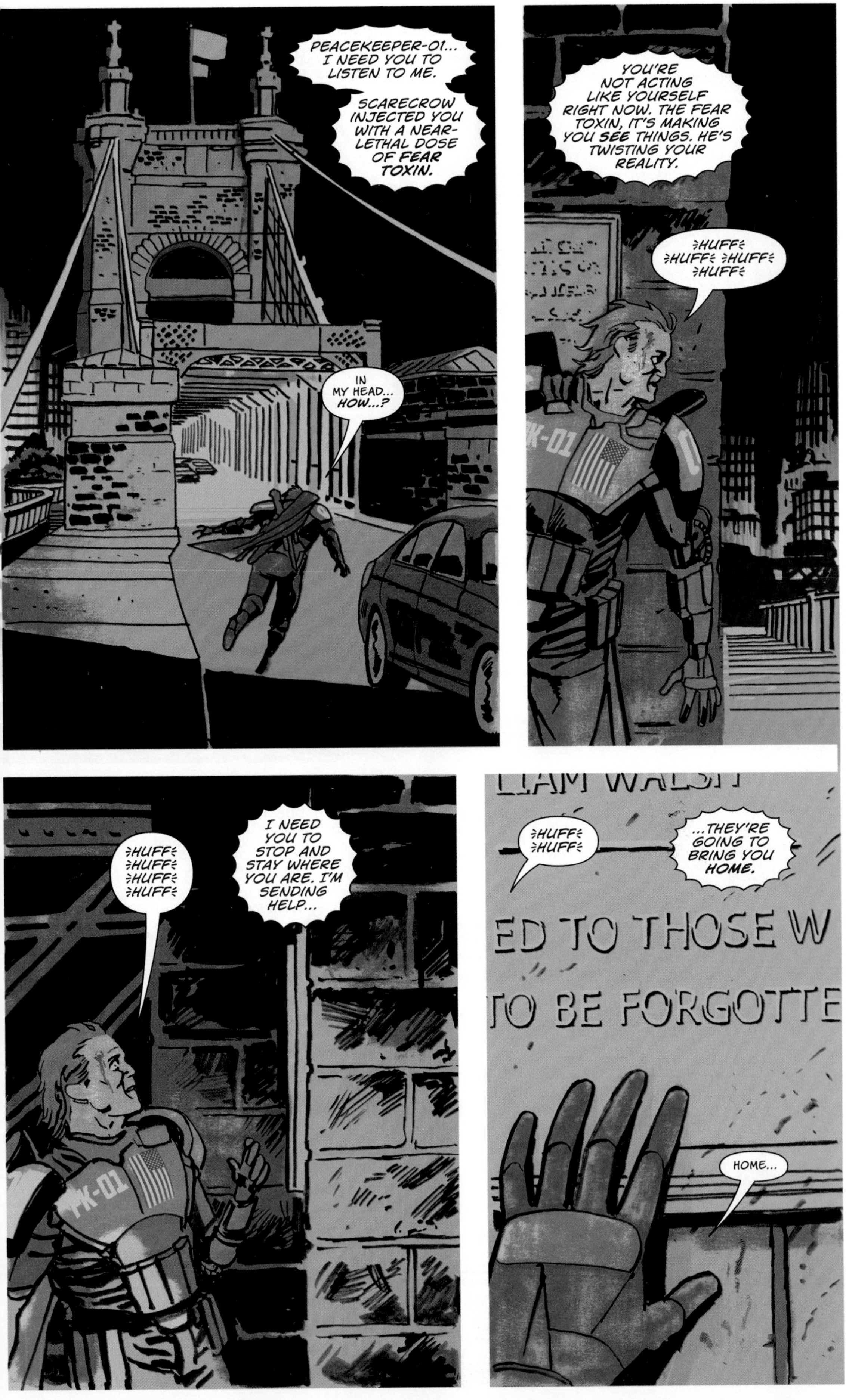
PEACEKEEPER-01... I NEED YOU TO LISTEN TO ME.
SCARECROW INJECTED YOU WITH A NEAR-LETHAL DOSE OF FEAR TOXIN.
IN MY HEAD... HOW...?
YOU'RE NOT ACTING LIKE YOURSELF RIGHT NOW. THE FEAR TOXIN, IT'S MAKING YOU SEE THINGS. HE'S TWISTING YOUR REALITY.
HUFF HUFF HUFF HUFF
HUFF HUFF HUFF HUFF
I NEED YOU TO STOP AND STAY WHERE YOU ARE. I'M SENDING HELP...
LIAM WALSH
HUFF HUFF
...THEY'RE GOING TO BRING YOU HOME.
ED TO THOSE W
TO BE FORGOTTE
HOME...

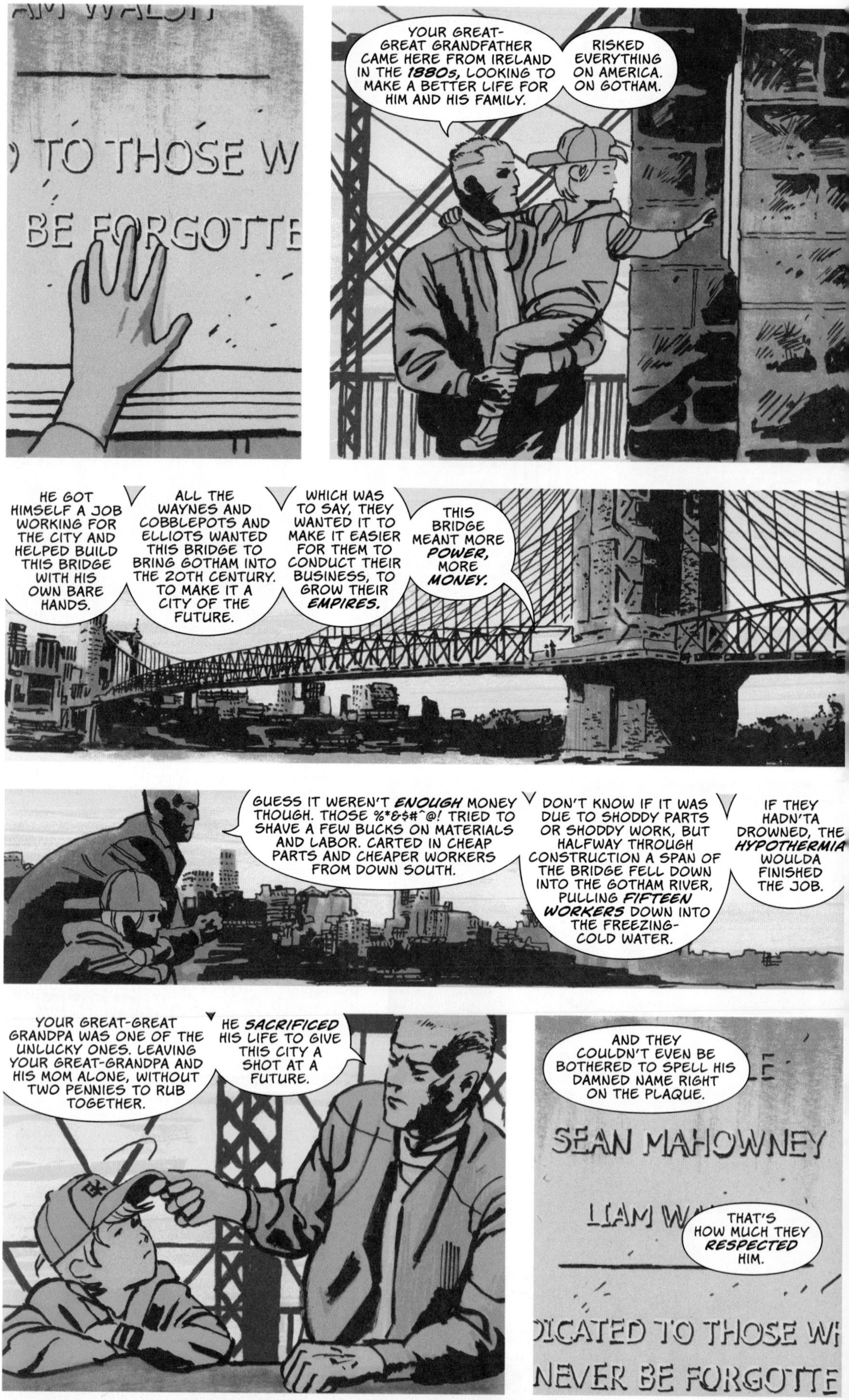

TO THOSE W
BE FORGOTTE
YOUR GREAT-GREAT GRANDFATHER CAME HERE FROM IRELAND IN THE *1880s,* LOOKING TO MAKE A BETTER LIFE FOR HIM AND HIS FAMILY.
RISKED EVERYTHING ON AMERICA. ON GOTHAM.
HE GOT HIMSELF A JOB WORKING FOR THE CITY AND HELPED BUILD THIS BRIDGE WITH HIS OWN BARE HANDS.
ALL THE WAYNES AND COBBLEPOTS AND ELLIOTS WANTED THIS BRIDGE TO BRING GOTHAM INTO THE 20TH CENTURY. TO MAKE IT A CITY OF THE FUTURE.
WHICH WAS TO SAY, THEY WANTED IT TO MAKE IT EASIER FOR THEM TO CONDUCT THEIR BUSINESS, TO GROW THEIR *EMPIRES.*
THIS BRIDGE MEANT MORE *POWER,* MORE *MONEY.*
GUESS IT WEREN'T *ENOUGH* MONEY THOUGH. THOSE %*&$#^@! TRIED TO SHAVE A FEW BUCKS ON MATERIALS AND LABOR. CARTED IN CHEAP PARTS AND CHEAPER WORKERS FROM DOWN SOUTH.
DON'T KNOW IF IT WAS DUE TO SHODDY PARTS OR SHODDY WORK, BUT HALFWAY THROUGH CONSTRUCTION A SPAN OF THE BRIDGE FELL DOWN INTO THE GOTHAM RIVER, PULLING *FIFTEEN WORKERS* DOWN INTO THE FREEZING-COLD WATER.
IF THEY HADN'TA DROWNED, THE *HYPOTHERMIA* WOULDA FINISHED THE JOB.
YOUR GREAT-GREAT GRANDPA WAS ONE OF THE UNLUCKY ONES. LEAVING YOUR GREAT-GRANDPA AND HIS MOM ALONE, WITHOUT TWO PENNIES TO RUB TOGETHER.
HE *SACRIFICED* HIS LIFE TO GIVE THIS CITY A SHOT AT A FUTURE.
AND THEY COULDN'T EVEN BE BOTHERED TO SPELL HIS DAMNED NAME RIGHT ON THE PLAQUE.
SEAN MAHOWNEY
THAT'S HOW MUCH THEY *RESPECTED* HIM.
DICATED TO THOSE W
NEVER BE FORGOTTE

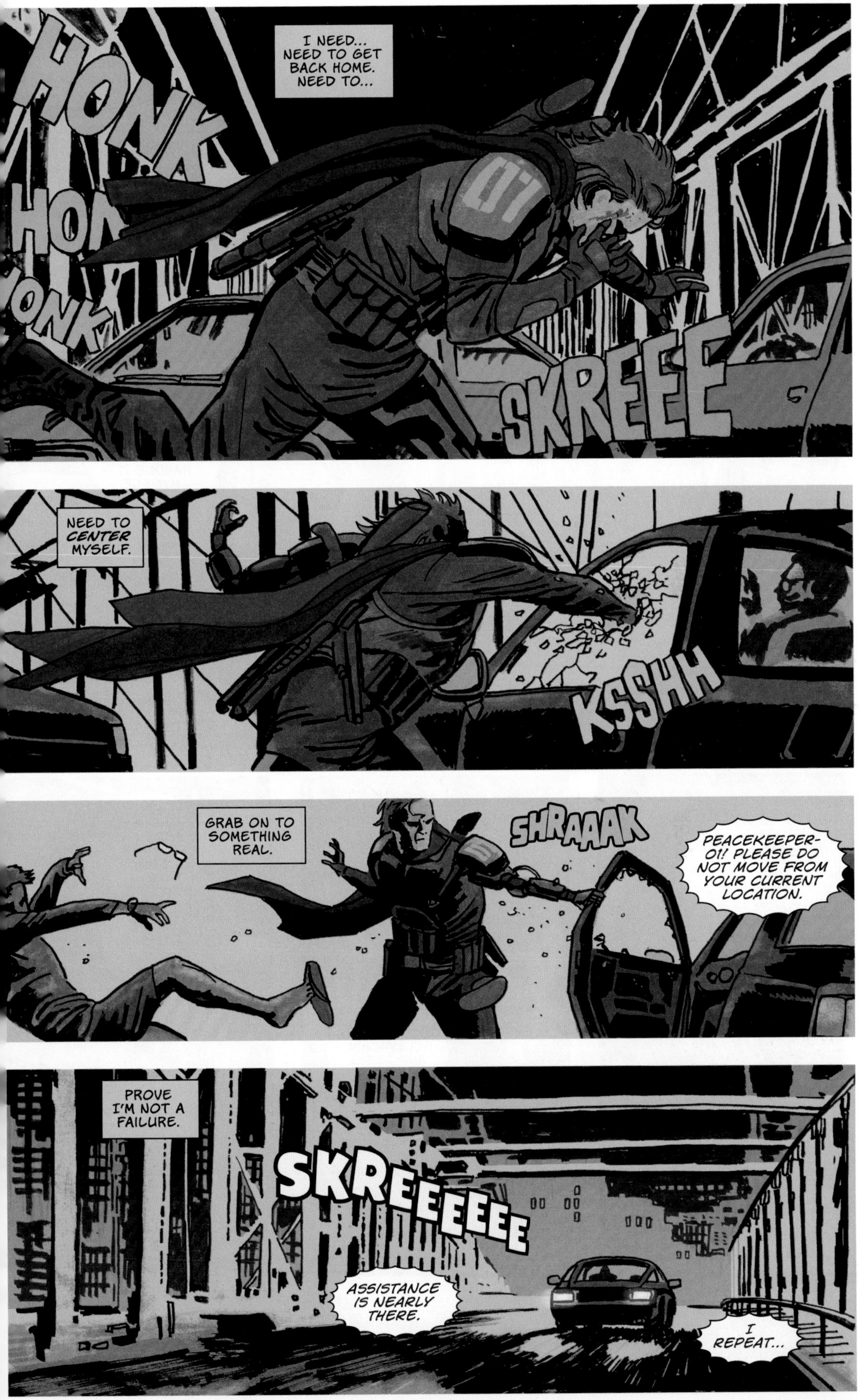
HONK
I NEED... NEED TO GET BACK HOME. NEED TO...
SKREEE
NEED TO *CENTER* MYSELF.
KSSHH
GRAB ON TO SOMETHING REAL.
SHRAAAK
PEACEKEEPER-01! PLEASE DO NOT MOVE FROM YOUR CURRENT LOCATION.
PROVE I'M NOT A FAILURE.
SKREEEEEEE
ASSISTANCE IS NEARLY THERE.
I REPEAT...

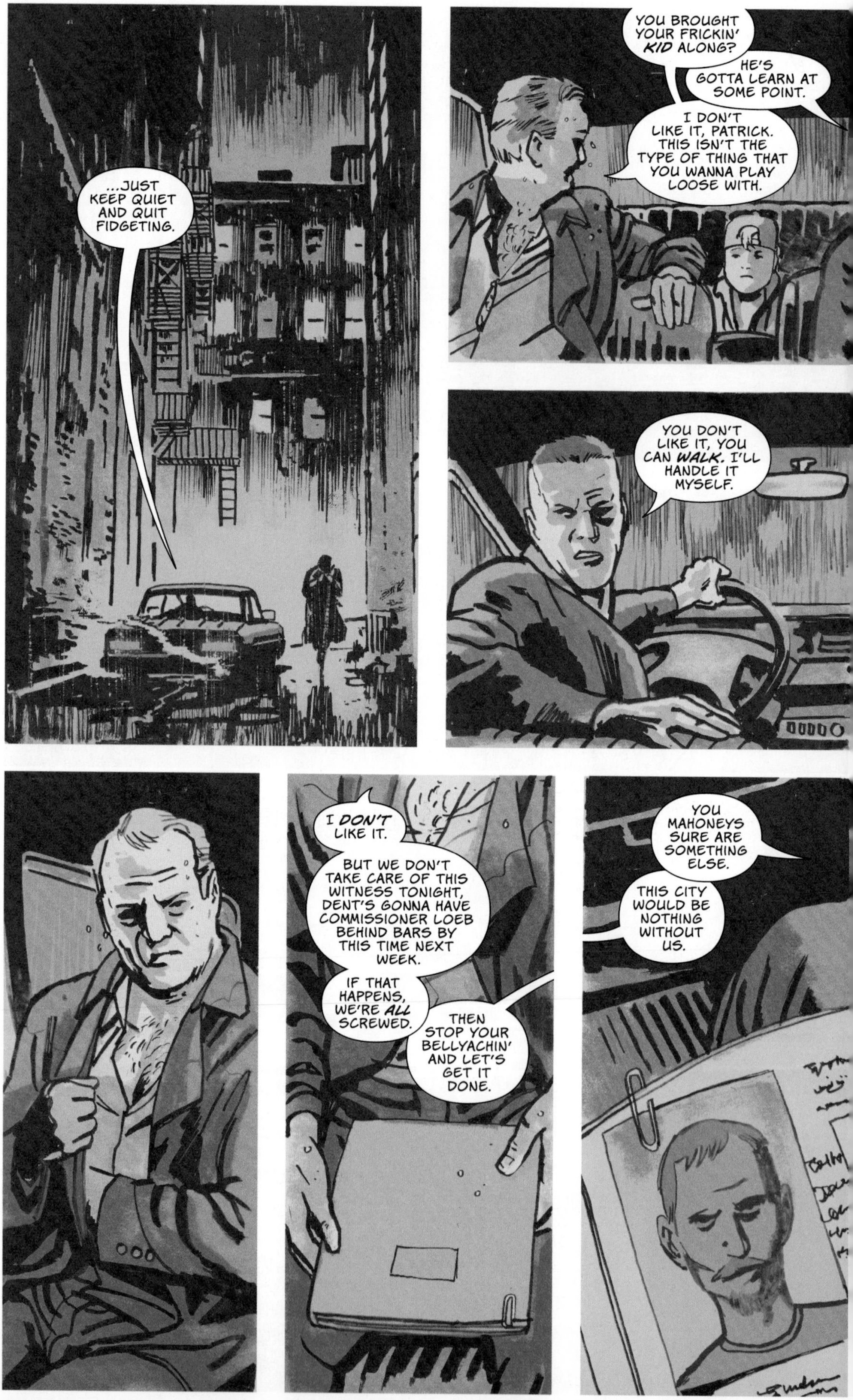
...JUST KEEP QUIET AND QUIT FIDGETING.
YOU BROUGHT YOUR FRICKIN' *KID* ALONG?
HE'S GOTTA LEARN AT SOME POINT.
I DON'T LIKE IT, PATRICK. THIS ISN'T THE TYPE OF THING THAT YOU WANNA PLAY LOOSE WITH.
YOU DON'T LIKE IT, YOU CAN *WALK.* I'LL HANDLE IT MYSELF.
I *DON'T* LIKE IT.
BUT WE DON'T TAKE CARE OF THIS WITNESS TONIGHT, DENT'S GONNA HAVE COMMISSIONER LOEB BEHIND BARS BY THIS TIME NEXT WEEK.
IF THAT HAPPENS, WE'RE *ALL* SCREWED.
THEN STOP YOUR BELLYACHIN' AND LET'S GET IT DONE.
YOU MAHONEYS SURE ARE SOMETHING ELSE.
THIS CITY WOULD BE NOTHING WITHOUT US.

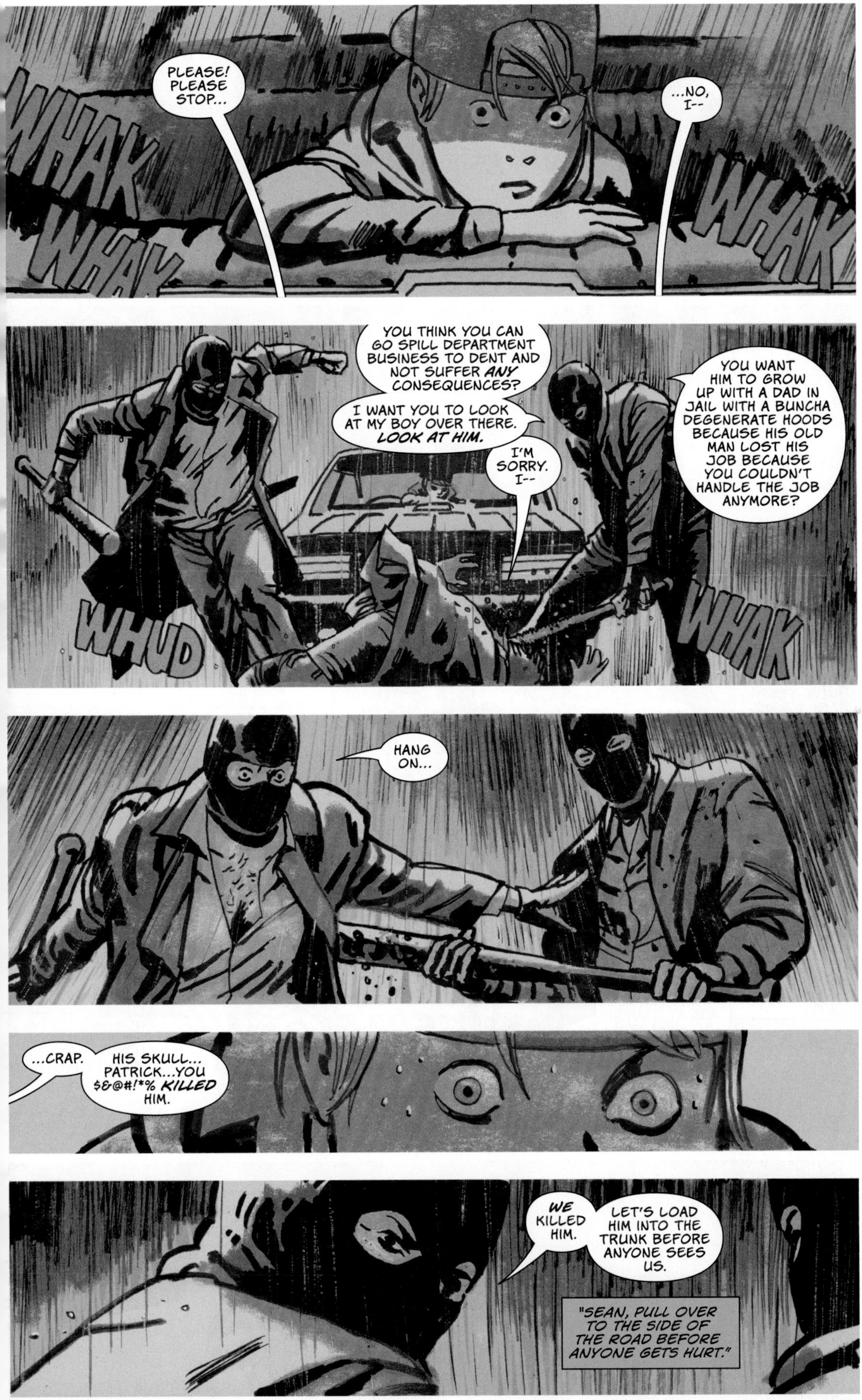
WHAK
WHAK
PLEASE! PLEASE STOP...
...NO, I--
WHAK
YOU THINK YOU CAN GO SPILL DEPARTMENT BUSINESS TO DENT AND NOT SUFFER ANY CONSEQUENCES?
I WANT YOU TO LOOK AT MY BOY OVER THERE. LOOK AT HIM.
I'M SORRY. I--
YOU WANT HIM TO GROW UP WITH A DAD IN JAIL WITH A BUNCHA DEGENERATE HOODS BECAUSE HIS OLD MAN LOST HIS JOB BECAUSE YOU COULDN'T HANDLE THE JOB ANYMORE?
WHUD
WHAK
HANG ON...
...CRAP.
HIS SKULL... PATRICK...YOU $&@#!*% KILLED HIM.
WE KILLED HIM.
LET'S LOAD HIM INTO THE TRUNK BEFORE ANYONE SEES US.
"SEAN, PULL OVER TO THE SIDE OF THE ROAD BEFORE ANYONE GETS HURT."

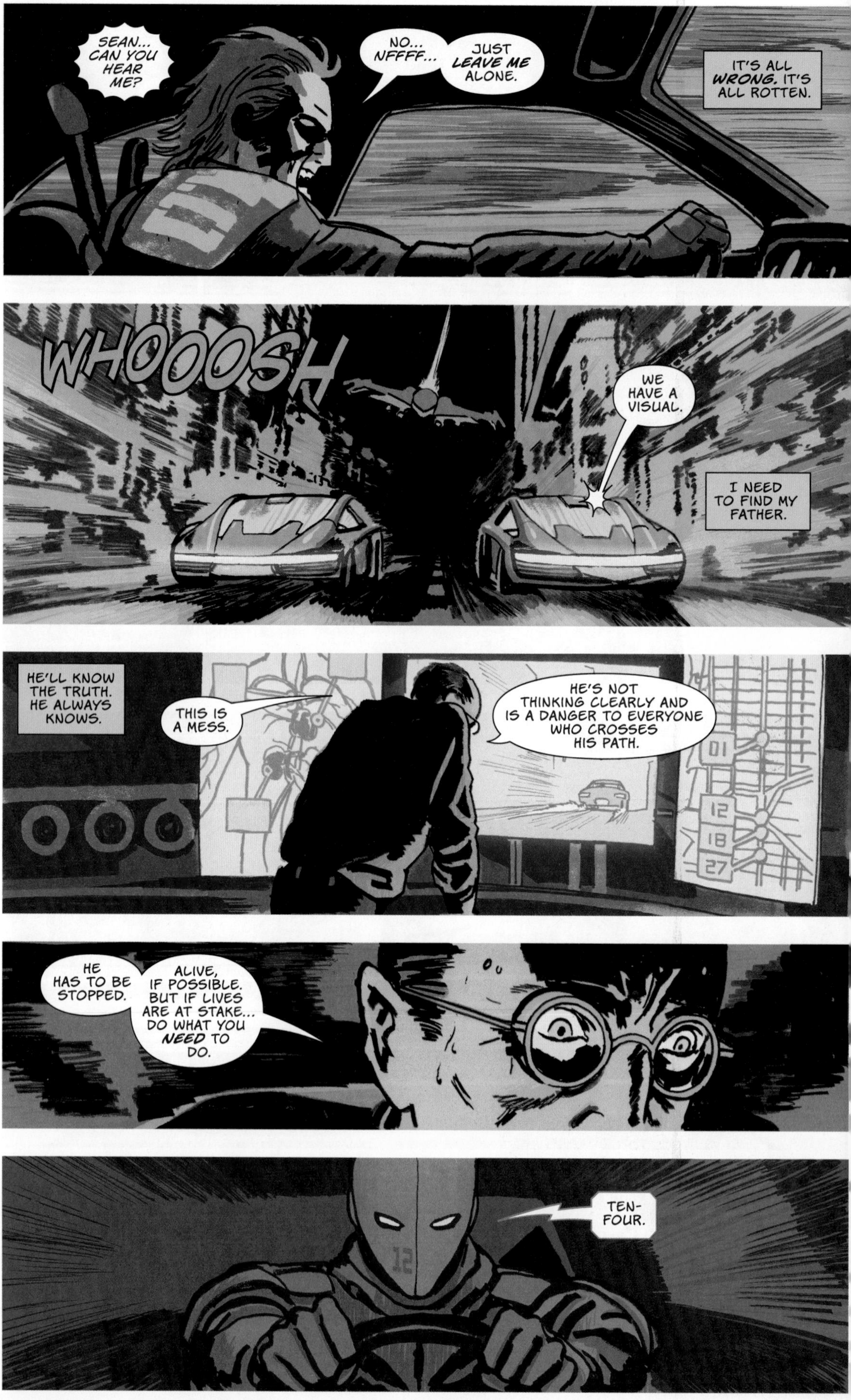
SEAN... CAN YOU HEAR ME?
NO... NFFFF...
JUST LEAVE ME ALONE.
IT'S ALL WRONG. IT'S ALL ROTTEN.
WHOOOSH
WE HAVE A VISUAL.
I NEED TO FIND MY FATHER.
HE'LL KNOW THE TRUTH. HE ALWAYS KNOWS.
THIS IS A MESS.
HE'S NOT THINKING CLEARLY AND IS A DANGER TO EVERYONE WHO CROSSES HIS PATH.
01
12
18
27
HE HAS TO BE STOPPED.
ALIVE, IF POSSIBLE. BUT IF LIVES ARE AT STAKE... DO WHAT YOU NEED TO DO.
TEN-FOUR.

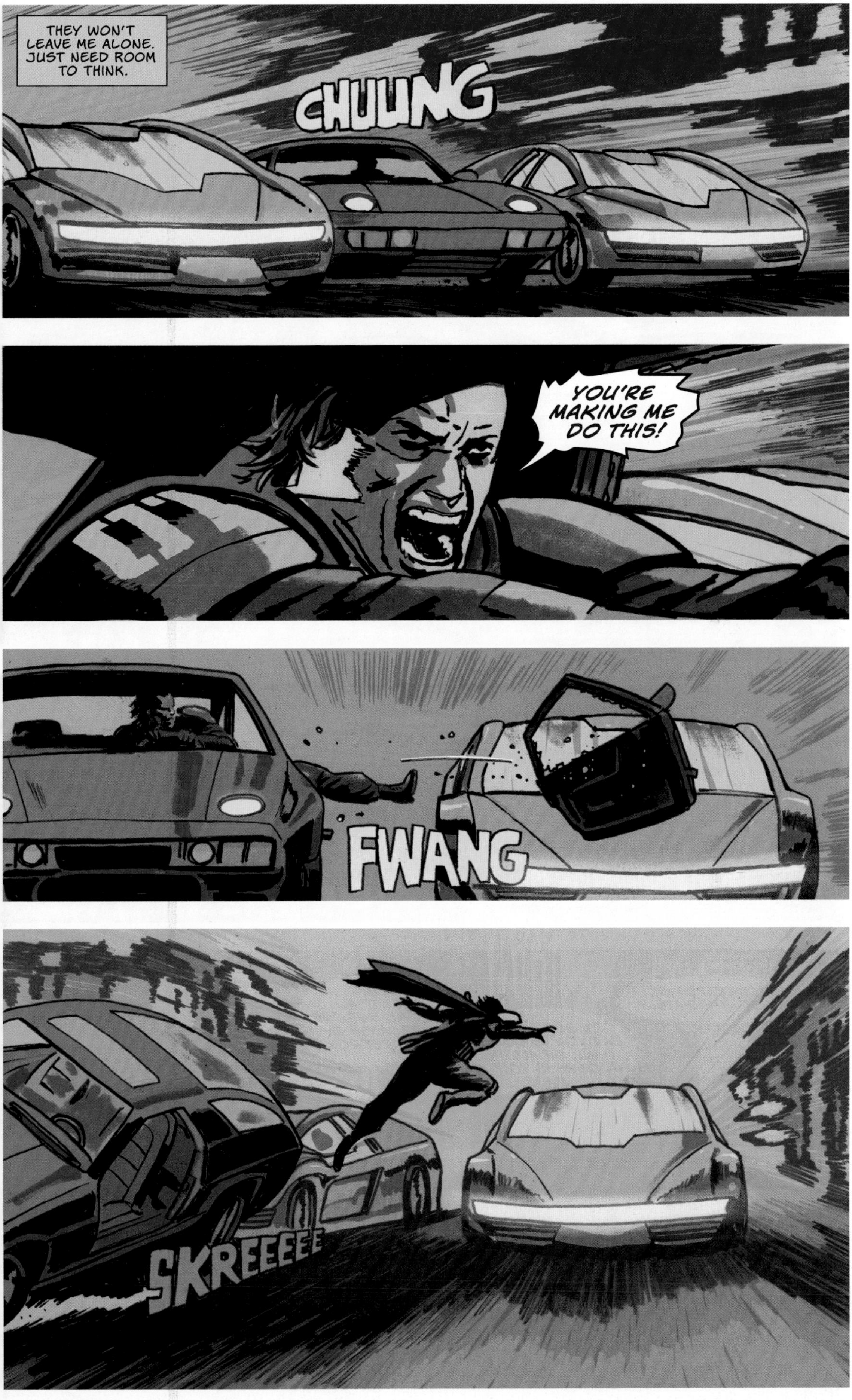

THEY WON'T LEAVE ME ALONE. JUST NEED ROOM TO THINK.
CHUUNG
YOU'RE MAKING ME DO THIS!
FWANG
SKREEEEE

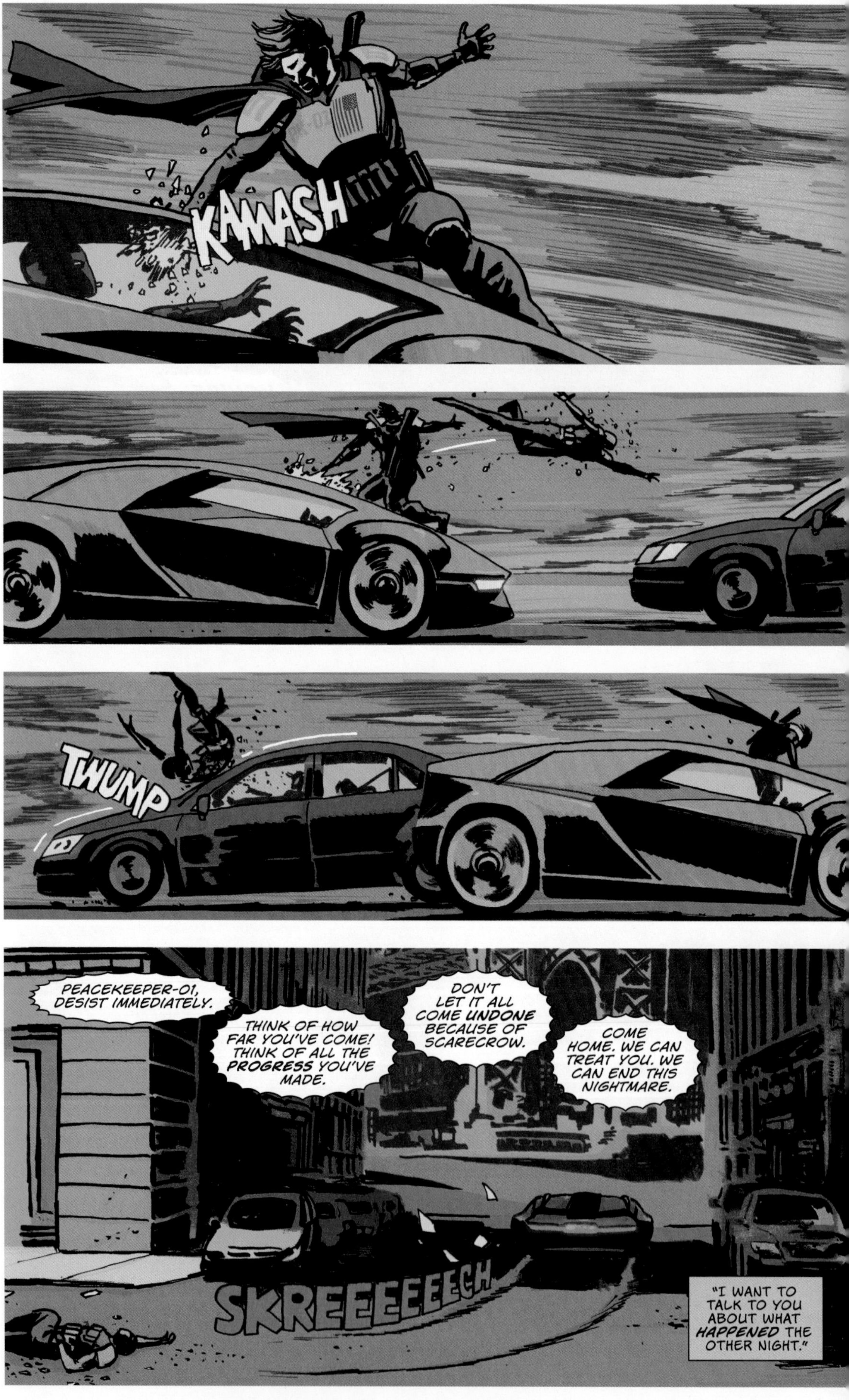
KAWASH
TWUMP
PEACEKEEPER-01, DESIST IMMEDIATELY.
THINK OF HOW FAR YOU'VE COME! THINK OF ALL THE PROGRESS YOU'VE MADE.
DON'T LET IT ALL COME UNDONE BECAUSE OF SCARECROW.
COME HOME. WE CAN TREAT YOU. WE CAN END THIS NIGHTMARE.
SKREEEEEEEECH
"I WANT TO TALK TO YOU ABOUT WHAT HAPPENED THE OTHER NIGHT."

S'OKAY. I'M NOT GONNA SAY ANYTHING.

THAT'S GOOD, BUT STILL... YOU'RE *OWED* AN EXPLANATION.

HENRY MAHONEY, YOUR GREAT-GRANDPA... HE WAS ONE OF THE *FIRST* OFFICERS IN THE GOTHAM CITY POLICE DEPARTMENT.

THIS WAS BACK...DAMN, MORE THAN *A HUNDRED YEARS AGO* NOW.

HE REALIZED THAT IN ORDER TO SURVIVE IN GOTHAM, YOU NEEDED TO HAVE *POWER,* AND SINCE HE WASN'T RICH, JOINING THE FORCE WAS THE WAY TO GET IT.

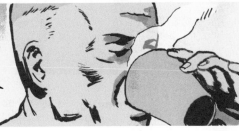

EVERYONE *LOVED* HIM. HE ENDED UP BEING THE HEAD OF THE UNION AND HELPED SHAPE THE GCPD INTO WHAT IT IS TODAY.

WHEN HE DIED, *EVERY SINGLE COP* SHOWED UP TO HIS FUNERAL. THE MAYOR WAS THERE, GAVE HIS EULOGY.

FOR A WEEK, EVERY FLAG IN THE CITY WAS AT HALF-MAST.

THAT'S HOW MUCH HE *MEANT* TO GOTHAM.

YOUR GRANDFATHER FOLLOWED HIM ONTO THE FORCE, JUST LIKE I FOLLOWED YOUR GRANDFATHER.

THIS CITY NEEDS MEN LIKE *US.*

BECAUSE WE KNOW HOW THIS CITY *REALLY* OPERATES AND WE AREN'T AFRAID TO GET A LITTLE DIRT UNDER OUR FINGERNAILS WHEN THE TIME COMES.

THAT MAN... THE OTHER NIGHT, THE ONE IN THE TRUNK... WAS HE A COP TOO?

HE WAS.

BUT HE WAS THE *OTHER* KIND.

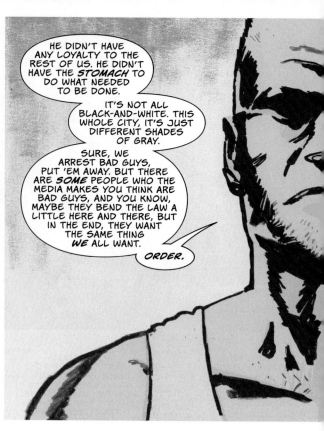

HE DIDN'T HAVE ANY LOYALTY TO THE REST OF US. HE DIDN'T HAVE THE *STOMACH* TO DO WHAT NEEDED TO BE DONE.

IT'S NOT ALL BLACK-AND-WHITE. THIS WHOLE CITY, IT'S JUST DIFFERENT SHADES OF GRAY.

SURE, WE ARREST BAD GUYS, PUT 'EM AWAY. BUT THERE ARE *SOME* PEOPLE WHO THE MEDIA MAKES YOU THINK ARE BAD GUYS, AND YOU KNOW, MAYBE THEY BEND THE LAW A LITTLE HERE AND THERE, BUT IN THE END, THEY WANT THE SAME THING *WE* ALL WANT.

ORDER.

SOMETIMES, YOU LET ONE OR TWO OF THESE GUYS...YOU KNOW, YOU LET THEM OPERATE THEIR GAMBLING OR... *OTHER THINGS,* BECAUSE NO MATTER HOW HARD YOU TRY, YOU'LL NEVER STOMP IT OUT.

BUT WHAT THEY DO IS THEY KEEP IT SMALL. THEY KEEP IT *CONTROLLED.* THEY DON'T LIKE ATTENTION. THEY DON'T LIKE WHEN THINGS GET MESSY.

THEY DON'T LIKE IT WHEN YOU HAVE THUGS OUT ON THE STREET KILLING ONE ANOTHER.

SO THEY KEEP IT *CLEAN.* THEY KEEP OUT THE COMPETITION AND LET OTHER BAD GUYS KNOW THAT THEY'RE NOT WELCOME HERE IN GOTHAM.

AND SOMETIMES THEY NEED A LITTLE HELP.

AND SO WE HELP THEM IF IT MAKES GOTHAM SAFER.

PLUS, THE *EXTRA* MONEY, IT DOESN'T HURT. I WON'T LIE.

THAT MAN, THE OTHER NIGHT...

...IF HE HAD HIS WAY, ALL THOSE PEOPLE I WAS TELLING YOU ABOUT WOULD BE IN JAIL. SO WOULD ME AND YOUR GRANDPA.

IT'S A DELICATE ECOSYSTEM...

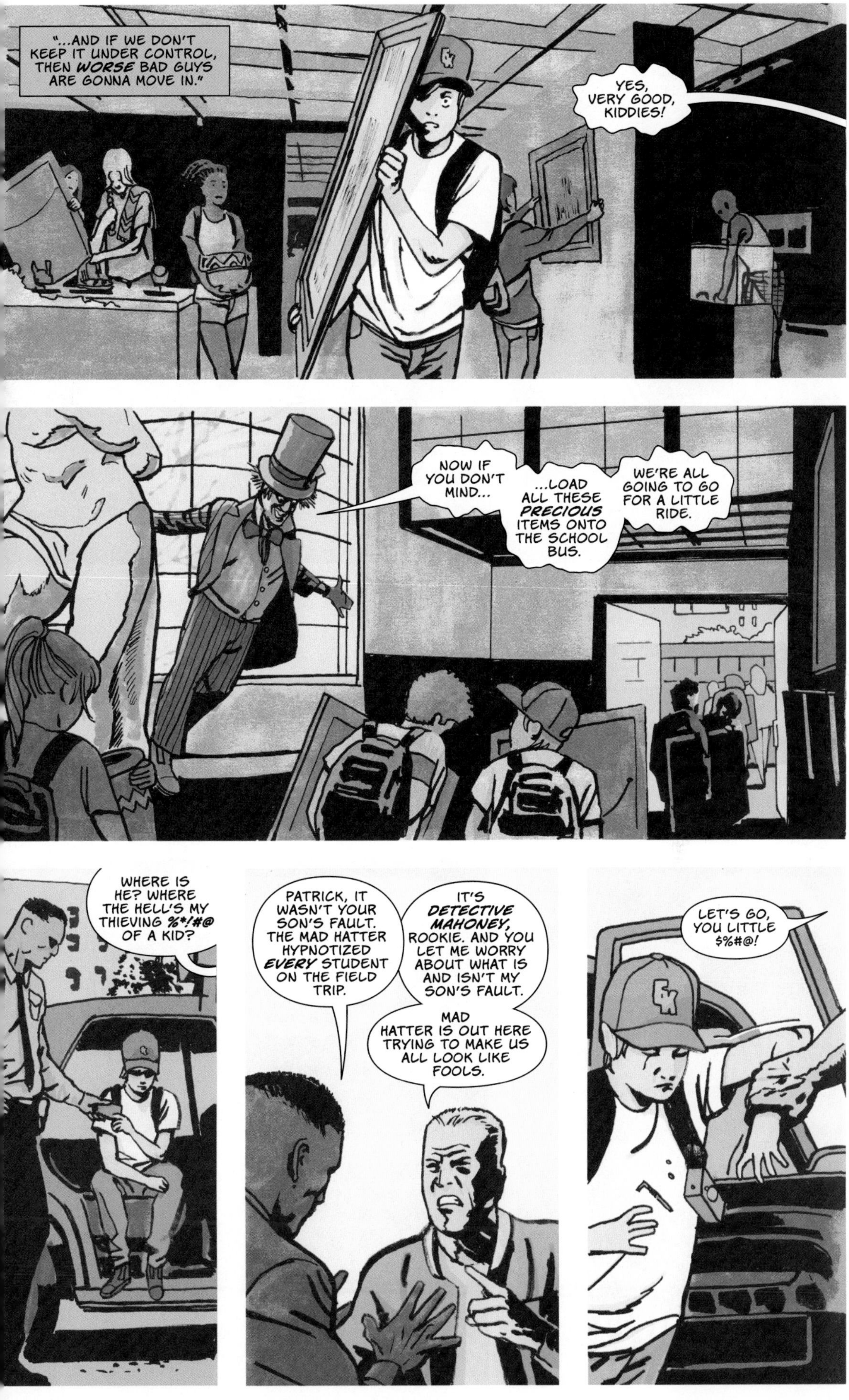
"...AND IF WE DON'T KEEP IT UNDER CONTROL, THEN WORSE BAD GUYS ARE GONNA MOVE IN."
YES, VERY GOOD, KIDDIES!
NOW IF YOU DON'T MIND...
...LOAD ALL THESE PRECIOUS ITEMS ONTO THE SCHOOL BUS.
WE'RE ALL GOING TO GO FOR A LITTLE RIDE.
WHERE IS HE? WHERE THE HELL'S MY THIEVING %*!#@ OF A KID?
PATRICK, IT WASN'T YOUR SON'S FAULT. THE MAD HATTER HYPNOTIZED EVERY STUDENT ON THE FIELD TRIP.
IT'S DETECTIVE MAHONEY, ROOKIE. AND YOU LET ME WORRY ABOUT WHAT IS AND ISN'T MY SON'S FAULT.
MAD HATTER IS OUT HERE TRYING TO MAKE US ALL LOOK LIKE FOOLS.
LET'S GO, YOU LITTLE $%#@!

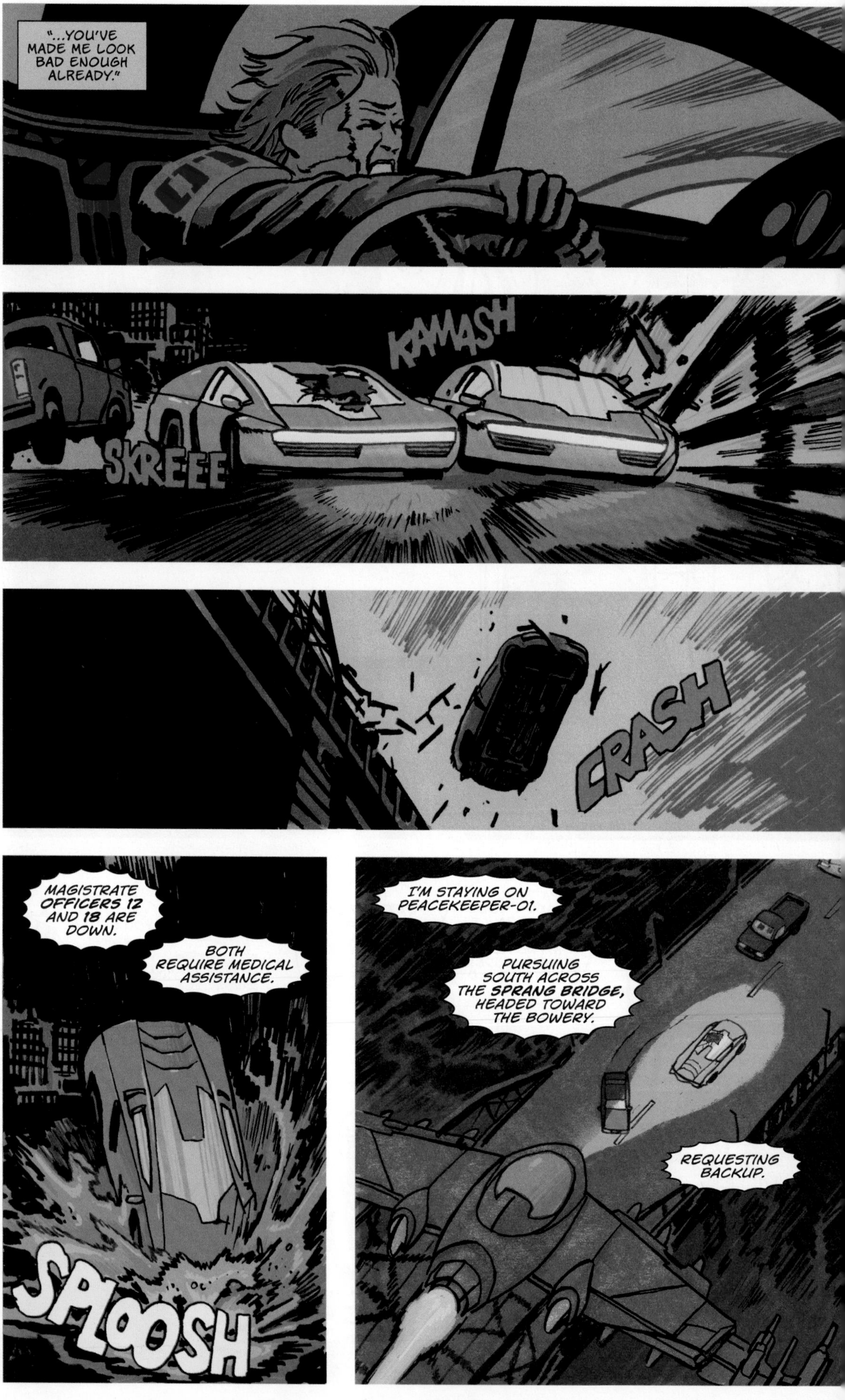
"...YOU'VE MADE ME LOOK BAD ENOUGH ALREADY."
KAMASH
SKREEEE
CRASH
MAGISTRATE OFFICERS 12 AND 18 ARE DOWN.
BOTH REQUIRE MEDICAL ASSISTANCE.
SPLOOSH
I'M STAYING ON PEACEKEEPER-01.
PURSUING SOUTH ACROSS THE SPRANG BRIDGE, HEADED TOWARD THE BOWERY.
REQUESTING BACKUP.

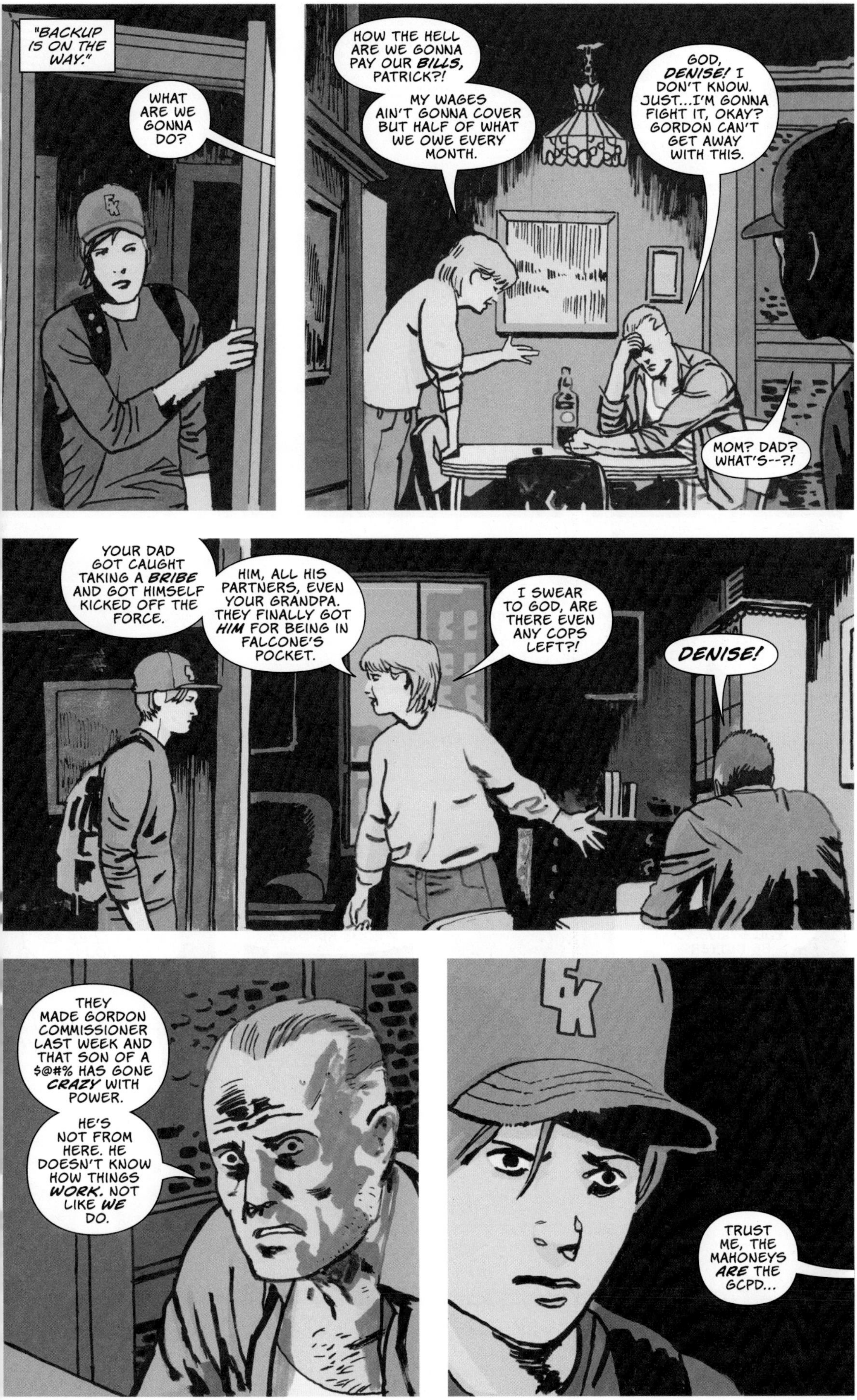
"BACKUP IS ON THE WAY."
WHAT ARE WE GONNA DO?
HOW THE HELL ARE WE GONNA PAY OUR BILLS, PATRICK?!
MY WAGES AIN'T GONNA COVER BUT HALF OF WHAT WE OWE EVERY MONTH.
GOD, DENISE! I DON'T KNOW. JUST...I'M GONNA FIGHT IT, OKAY? GORDON CAN'T GET AWAY WITH THIS.
MOM? DAD? WHAT'S--?!
YOUR DAD GOT CAUGHT TAKING A BRIBE AND GOT HIMSELF KICKED OFF THE FORCE.
HIM, ALL HIS PARTNERS, EVEN YOUR GRANDPA. THEY FINALLY GOT HIM FOR BEING IN FALCONE'S POCKET.
I SWEAR TO GOD, ARE THERE EVEN ANY COPS LEFT?!
DENISE!
THEY MADE GORDON COMMISSIONER LAST WEEK AND THAT SON OF A $@#% HAS GONE CRAZY WITH POWER.
HE'S NOT FROM HERE. HE DOESN'T KNOW HOW THINGS WORK. NOT LIKE WE DO.
TRUST ME, THE MAHONEYS ARE THE GCPD...

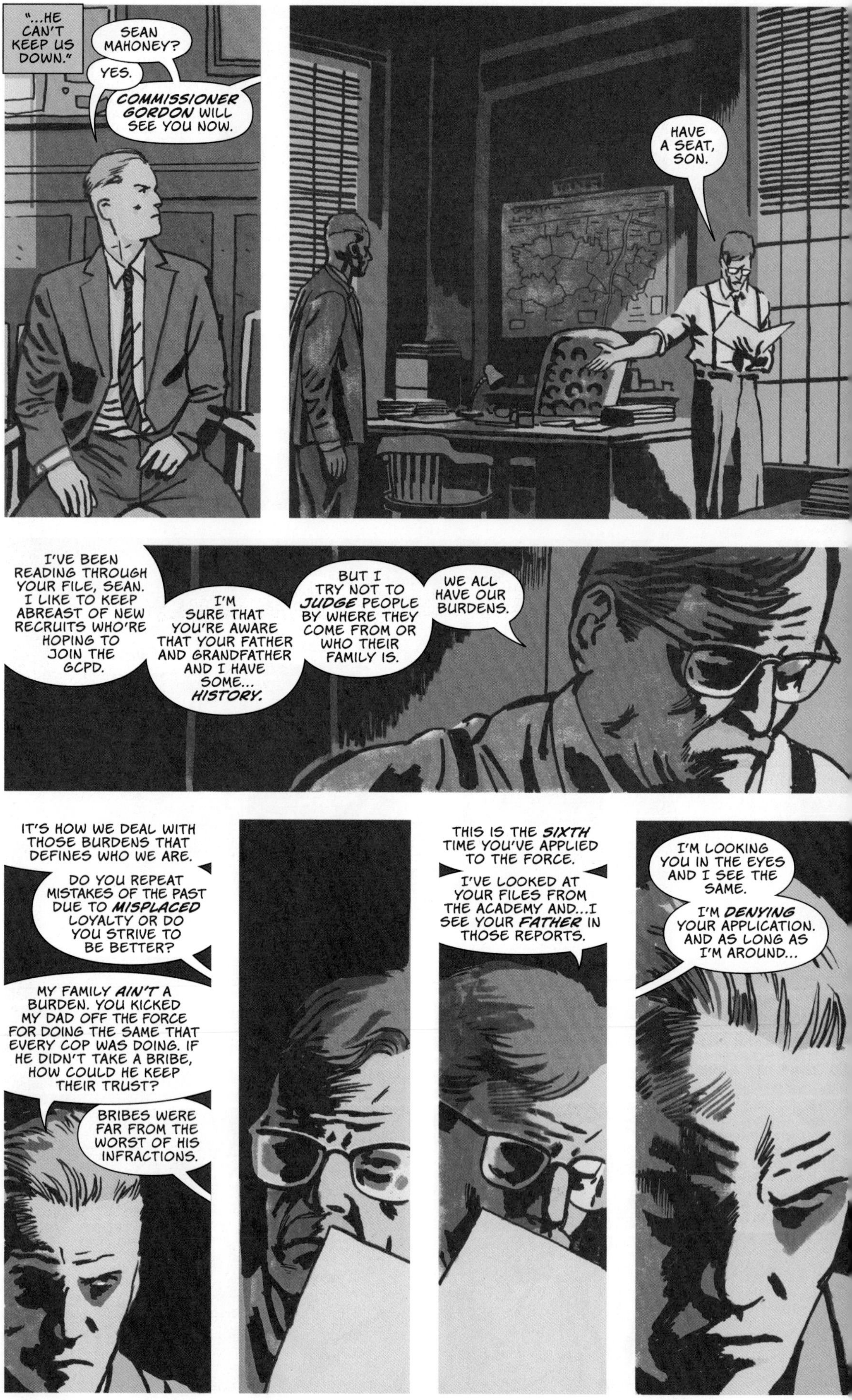
"...HE CAN'T KEEP US DOWN."
SEAN MAHONEY?
YES.
COMMISSIONER GORDON WILL SEE YOU NOW.
HAVE A SEAT, SON.
I'VE BEEN READING THROUGH YOUR FILE, SEAN. I LIKE TO KEEP ABREAST OF NEW RECRUITS WHO'RE HOPING TO JOIN THE GCPD.
I'M SURE THAT YOU'RE AWARE THAT YOUR FATHER AND GRANDFATHER AND I HAVE SOME... HISTORY.
BUT I TRY NOT TO JUDGE PEOPLE BY WHERE THEY COME FROM OR WHO THEIR FAMILY IS.
WE ALL HAVE OUR BURDENS.
IT'S HOW WE DEAL WITH THOSE BURDENS THAT DEFINES WHO WE ARE.
DO YOU REPEAT MISTAKES OF THE PAST DUE TO MISPLACED LOYALTY OR DO YOU STRIVE TO BE BETTER?
MY FAMILY AIN'T A BURDEN. YOU KICKED MY DAD OFF THE FORCE FOR DOING THE SAME THAT EVERY COP WAS DOING. IF HE DIDN'T TAKE A BRIBE, HOW COULD HE KEEP THEIR TRUST?
BRIBES WERE FAR FROM THE WORST OF HIS INFRACTIONS.
THIS IS THE SIXTH TIME YOU'VE APPLIED TO THE FORCE.
I'VE LOOKED AT YOUR FILES FROM THE ACADEMY AND...I SEE YOUR FATHER IN THOSE REPORTS.
I'M LOOKING YOU IN THE EYES AND I SEE THE SAME.
I'M DENYING YOUR APPLICATION. AND AS LONG AS I'M AROUND...

"...THERE WILL *NEVER* BE A PLACE FOR YOU IN THE GCPD."

WHERE'S THAT BACKUP?

THREE MINUTES OUT.

I DON'T KNOW THAT I CAN WAIT THAT LONG.

WHY...WHY ARE THEY ALWAYS TRYING TO *STOP* ME?

PEACEKEEPER-01 IS ALL OVER THE PLACE.

SOMEONE'S GOING TO GET HURT.

I SEE YOU OUT THERE. I. SEE. YOU.

THIS CITY NEEDS TO BE SAVED.

SKYBASE... PEACEKEEPER-01 IS STOPPING. HE'S...

SKRRREEEEEEEE

AND I CAN'T SAVE IT IF THEY'RE *ALWAYS* IN THE WAY.

...CRAP!

HE'S--

BRAKABRA BRAKABRA BRAKABRA BRAKABRA BRAKABRA

KABOOM

WE'VE LOST EYES ON PEACEKEEPER-01. REPEAT...

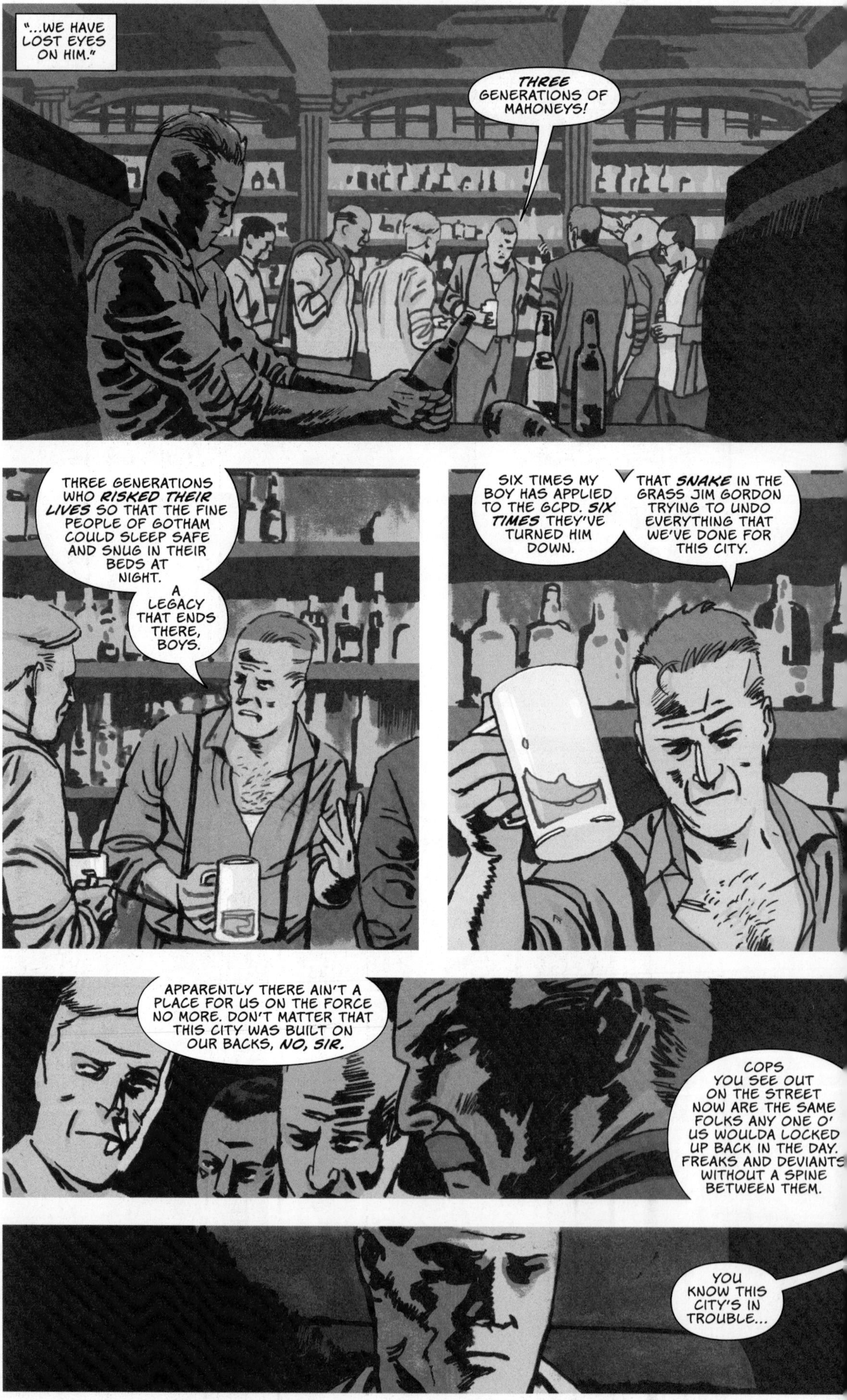
"...WE HAVE LOST EYES ON HIM."
THREE GENERATIONS OF MAHONEYS!
THREE GENERATIONS WHO *RISKED THEIR LIVES* SO THAT THE FINE PEOPLE OF GOTHAM COULD SLEEP SAFE AND SNUG IN THEIR BEDS AT NIGHT.
A LEGACY THAT ENDS THERE, BOYS.
SIX TIMES MY BOY HAS APPLIED TO THE GCPD. *SIX TIMES* THEY'VE TURNED HIM DOWN.
THAT *SNAKE* IN THE GRASS JIM GORDON TRYING TO UNDO EVERYTHING THAT WE'VE DONE FOR THIS CITY.
APPARENTLY THERE AIN'T A PLACE FOR US ON THE FORCE NO MORE. DON'T MATTER THAT THIS CITY WAS BUILT ON OUR BACKS, *NO, SIR.*
COPS YOU SEE OUT ON THE STREET NOW ARE THE SAME FOLKS ANY ONE O' US WOULDA LOCKED UP BACK IN THE DAY. FREAKS AND DEVIANTS WITHOUT A SPINE BETWEEN THEM.
YOU KNOW THIS CITY'S IN TROUBLE...

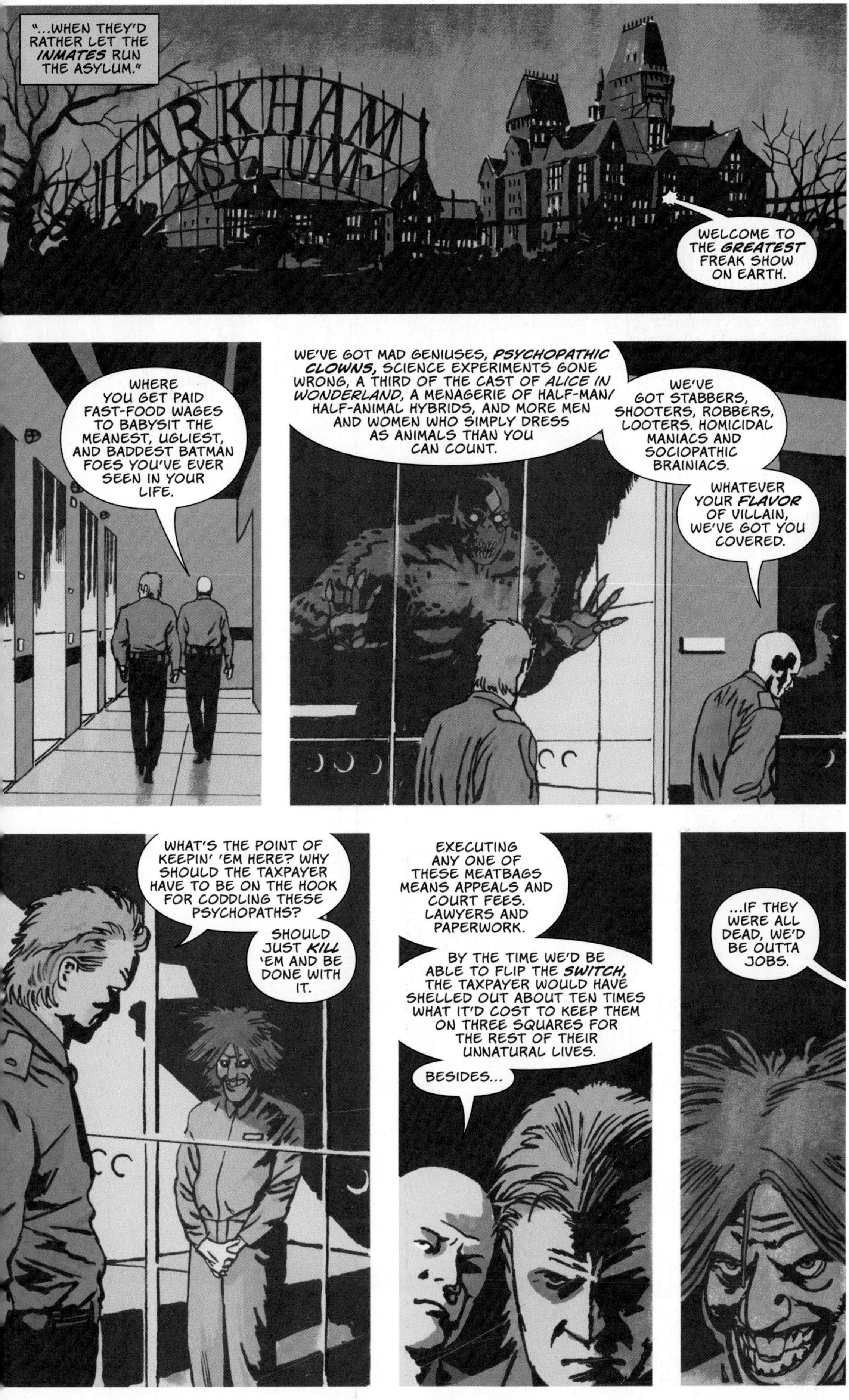
"...WHEN THEY'D RATHER LET THE *INMATES* RUN THE ASYLUM."
ARKHAM ASYLUM
WELCOME TO THE *GREATEST* FREAK SHOW ON EARTH.
WHERE YOU GET PAID FAST-FOOD WAGES TO BABYSIT THE MEANEST, UGLIEST, AND BADDEST BATMAN FOES YOU'VE EVER SEEN IN YOUR LIFE.
WE'VE GOT MAD GENIUSES, *PSYCHOPATHIC CLOWNS,* SCIENCE EXPERIMENTS GONE WRONG, A THIRD OF THE CAST OF *ALICE IN WONDERLAND,* A MENAGERIE OF HALF-MAN/HALF-ANIMAL HYBRIDS, AND MORE MEN AND WOMEN WHO SIMPLY DRESS AS ANIMALS THAN YOU CAN COUNT.
WE'VE GOT STABBERS, SHOOTERS, ROBBERS, LOOTERS. HOMICIDAL MANIACS AND SOCIOPATHIC BRAINIACS.
WHATEVER YOUR *FLAVOR* OF VILLAIN, WE'VE GOT YOU COVERED.
WHAT'S THE POINT OF KEEPIN' 'EM HERE? WHY SHOULD THE TAXPAYER HAVE TO BE ON THE HOOK FOR CODDLING THESE PSYCHOPATHS?
SHOULD JUST *KILL* 'EM AND BE DONE WITH IT.
EXECUTING ANY ONE OF THESE MEATBAGS MEANS APPEALS AND COURT FEES. LAWYERS AND PAPERWORK.
BY THE TIME WE'D BE ABLE TO FLIP THE *SWITCH,* THE TAXPAYER WOULD HAVE SHELLED OUT ABOUT TEN TIMES WHAT IT'D COST TO KEEP THEM ON THREE SQUARES FOR THE REST OF THEIR UNNATURAL LIVES.
BESIDES...
...IF THEY WERE ALL DEAD, WE'D BE OUTTA JOBS.

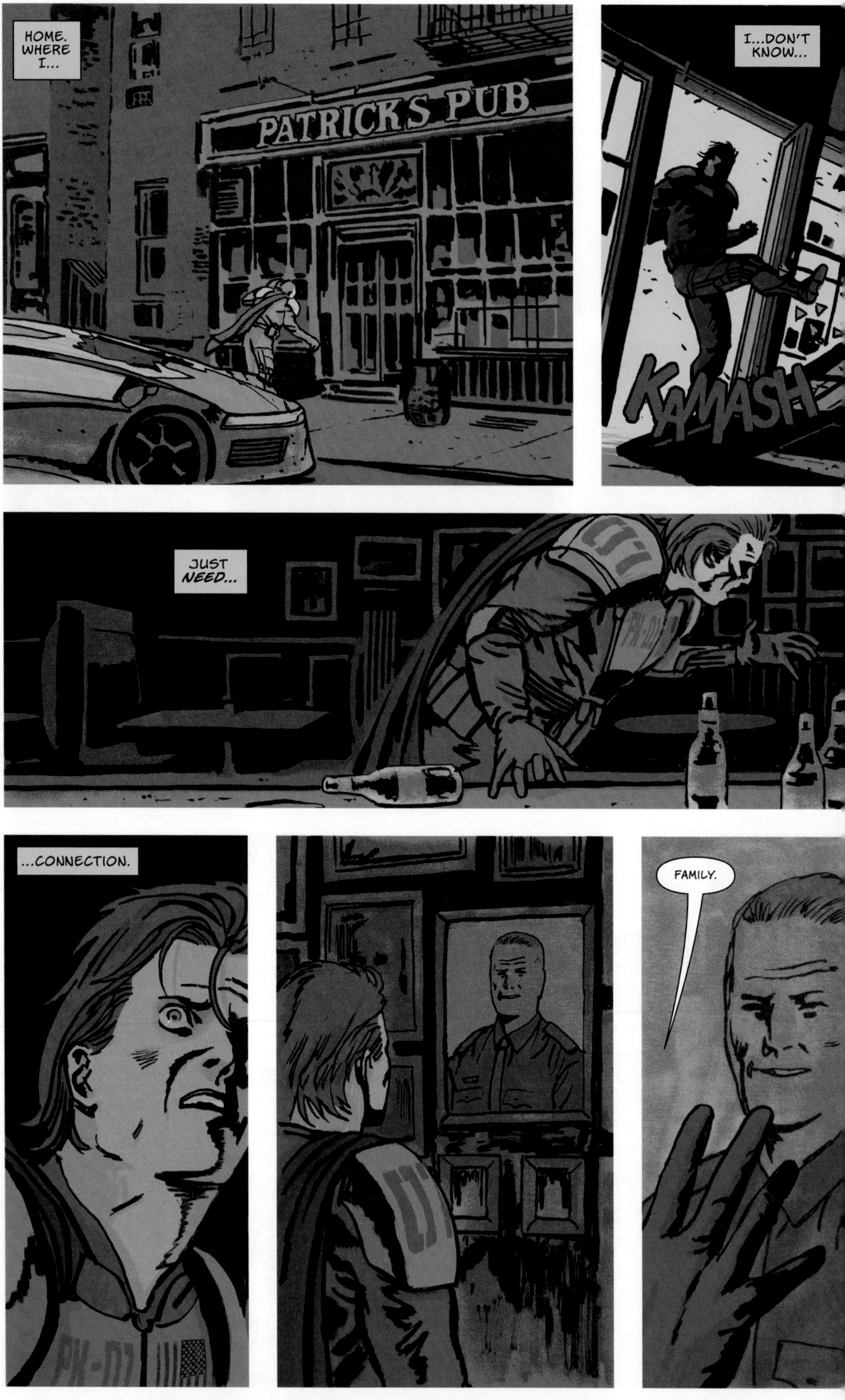
HOME. WHERE I...
PATRICKS PUB
I...DON'T KNOW...
KAMASH
JUST NEED...
...CONNECTION.
FAMILY.

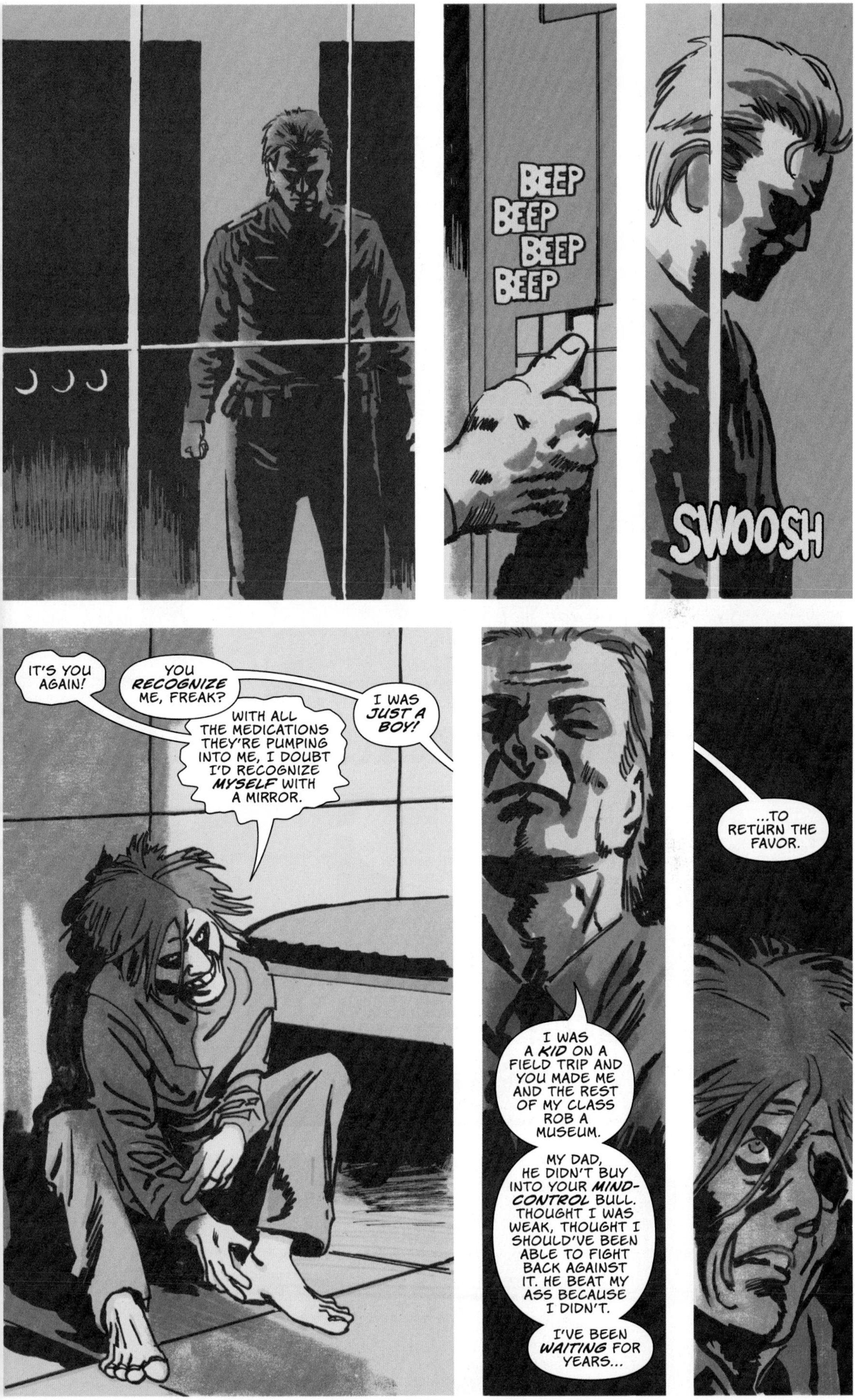
BEEP
BEEP
BEEP
BEEP
SWOOSH
IT'S YOU AGAIN!
YOU RECOGNIZE ME, FREAK?
WITH ALL THE MEDICATIONS THEY'RE PUMPING INTO ME, I DOUBT I'D RECOGNIZE MYSELF WITH A MIRROR.
I WAS JUST A BOY!
I WAS A KID ON A FIELD TRIP AND YOU MADE ME AND THE REST OF MY CLASS ROB A MUSEUM.
MY DAD, HE DIDN'T BUY INTO YOUR MIND-CONTROL BULL. THOUGHT I WAS WEAK, THOUGHT I SHOULD'VE BEEN ABLE TO FIGHT BACK AGAINST IT. HE BEAT MY ASS BECAUSE I DIDN'T.
I'VE BEEN WAITING FOR YEARS...
...TO RETURN THE FAVOR.

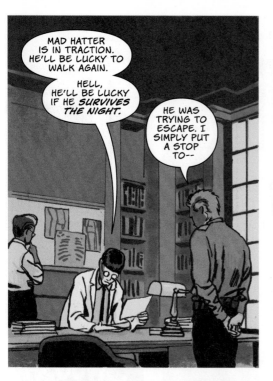

MAD HATTER IS IN TRACTION. HE'LL BE LUCKY TO WALK AGAIN.

HELL, HE'LL BE LUCKY IF HE *SURVIVES THE NIGHT.*

HE WAS TRYING TO ESCAPE. I SIMPLY PUT A STOP TO--

THE *INCIDENT* WAS CAUGHT ON CAMERA, MR. MAHONEY. THERE IS NO USE IN OBFUSCATING THE TRUTH.

I'M AWARE OF YOUR HISTORY WITH MR. TETCH. THE FIELD TRIP, THE ATTEMPTED ROBBERY. YOU HAVE MY SYMPATHY.

MY GOAL HERE IS TO WORK WITH PATIENTS LIKE MR. TETCH TO *ENSURE* THAT WHAT HAPPENED TO YOU DOESN'T HAPPEN TO OTHERS. YOUR ACTIONS HAVE SET MY WORK BACK BY--

HA!

WHAT A CROCK! HOW MANY TIMES HAS HE BEEN *REHABILITATED?* HOW MANY TIMES HAS HE BEEN LET LOOSE TO ROB AND KILL?

AND YET YOU'RE TREATING ME LIKE THE LUNATIC!

WE *DO NOT* USE THAT TERM--

DR. JOY, PLEASE. I HAVE A HANDLE ON THIS.

THIS IS NOT THE FIRST TIME YOU'VE DONE SOMETHING LIKE THIS, SEAN. FAR FROM IT.

THIS ISN'T A *DAY CARE* FOR THESE ANIMALS. THEY'RE *KILLERS.* IF THEY ACT OUT, THEY'RE GOING TO GET PUT DOWN. THAT'S WHAT WE--

THAT'S *NOT* WHAT WE DO HERE.

EFFECTIVE IMMEDIATELY, YOU'RE ON PROBATION. ONE MORE INFRACTION AND YOU'RE FINISHED HERE.

PROBATION? FOR HOW LONG?!

UNTIL THE END OF YOUR CONTRACT.

WHICH, UNLESS THINGS IMPROVE DRASTICALLY, WE WILL *NOT* BE RENEWING.

NOW IF YOU DON'T MIND...

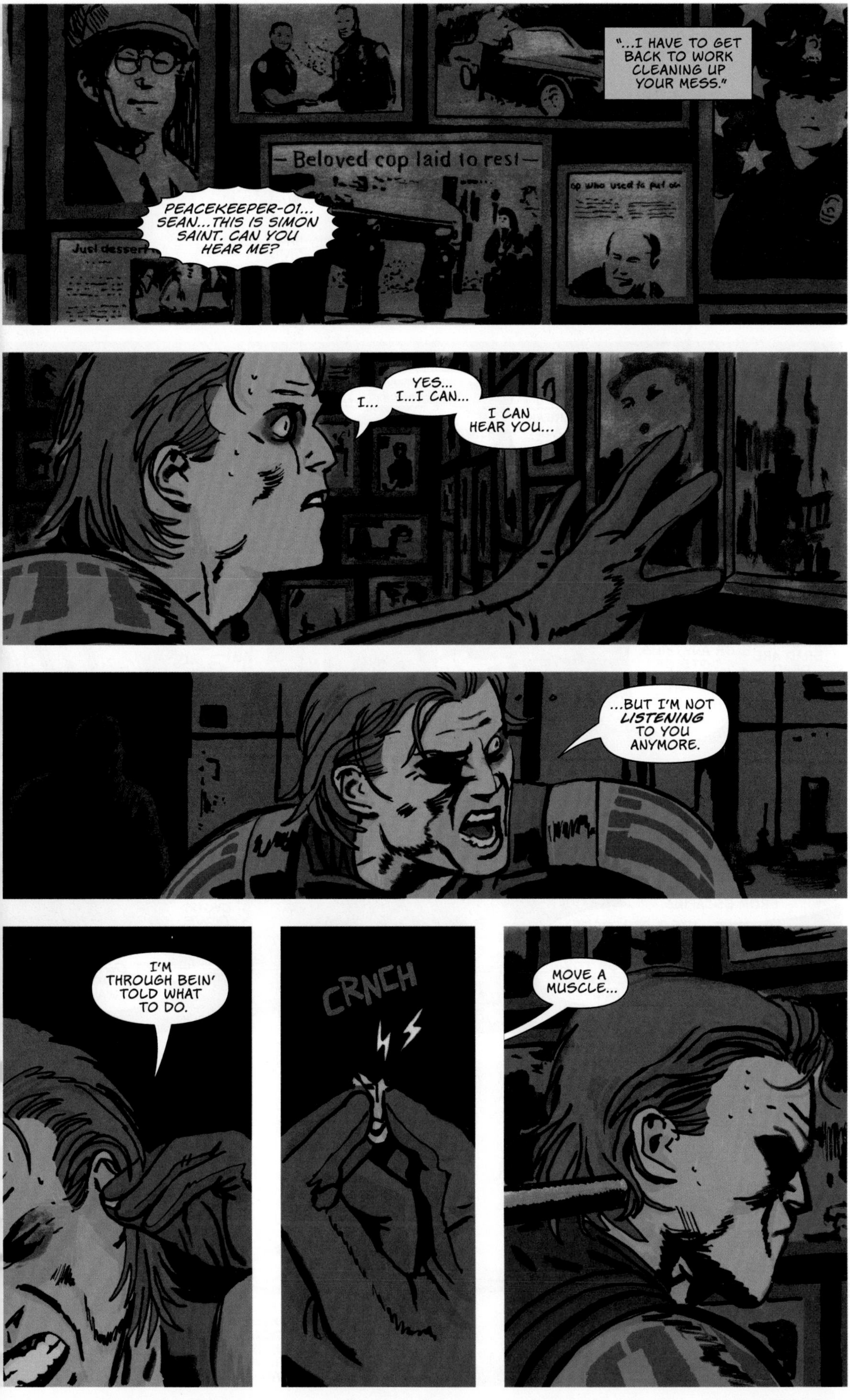
"...I HAVE TO GET BACK TO WORK CLEANING UP YOUR MESS."
— Beloved cop laid to rest —
PEACEKEEPER-01... SEAN...THIS IS SIMON SAINT. CAN YOU HEAR ME?
I...
YES... I...I CAN...
I CAN HEAR YOU...
...BUT I'M NOT *LISTENING* TO YOU ANYMORE.
I'M THROUGH BEIN' TOLD WHAT TO DO.
CRNCH
MOVE A MUSCLE...

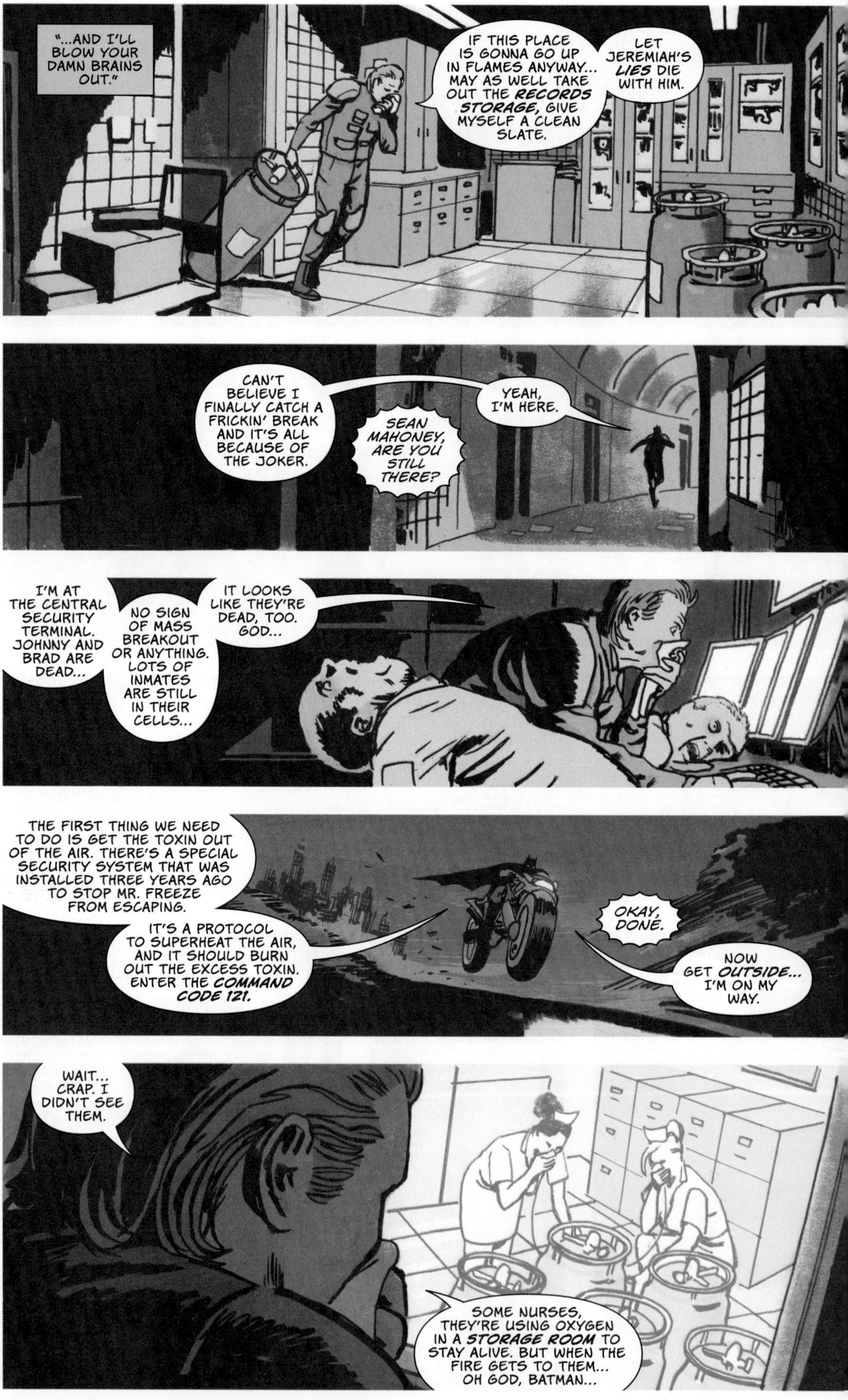
"...AND I'LL BLOW YOUR DAMN BRAINS OUT."
IF THIS PLACE IS GONNA GO UP IN FLAMES ANYWAY... MAY AS WELL TAKE OUT THE **RECORDS STORAGE,** GIVE MYSELF A CLEAN SLATE.
LET JEREMIAH'S **LIES** DIE WITH HIM.
CAN'T BELIEVE I FINALLY CATCH A FRICKIN' BREAK AND IT'S ALL BECAUSE OF THE JOKER.
SEAN MAHONEY, ARE YOU STILL THERE?
YEAH, I'M HERE.
I'M AT THE CENTRAL SECURITY TERMINAL. JOHNNY AND BRAD ARE DEAD...
NO SIGN OF MASS BREAKOUT OR ANYTHING. LOTS OF INMATES ARE STILL IN THEIR CELLS...
IT LOOKS LIKE THEY'RE DEAD, TOO. GOD...
THE FIRST THING WE NEED TO DO IS GET THE TOXIN OUT OF THE AIR. THERE'S A SPECIAL SECURITY SYSTEM THAT WAS INSTALLED THREE YEARS AGO TO STOP MR. FREEZE FROM ESCAPING.
IT'S A PROTOCOL TO SUPERHEAT THE AIR, AND IT SHOULD BURN OUT THE EXCESS TOXIN. ENTER THE **COMMAND CODE 121.**
OKAY, DONE.
NOW GET **OUTSIDE...** I'M ON MY WAY.
WAIT... CRAP. I DIDN'T SEE THEM.
SOME NURSES, THEY'RE USING OXYGEN IN A **STORAGE ROOM** TO STAY ALIVE. BUT WHEN THE FIRE GETS TO THEM... OH GOD, BATMAN...

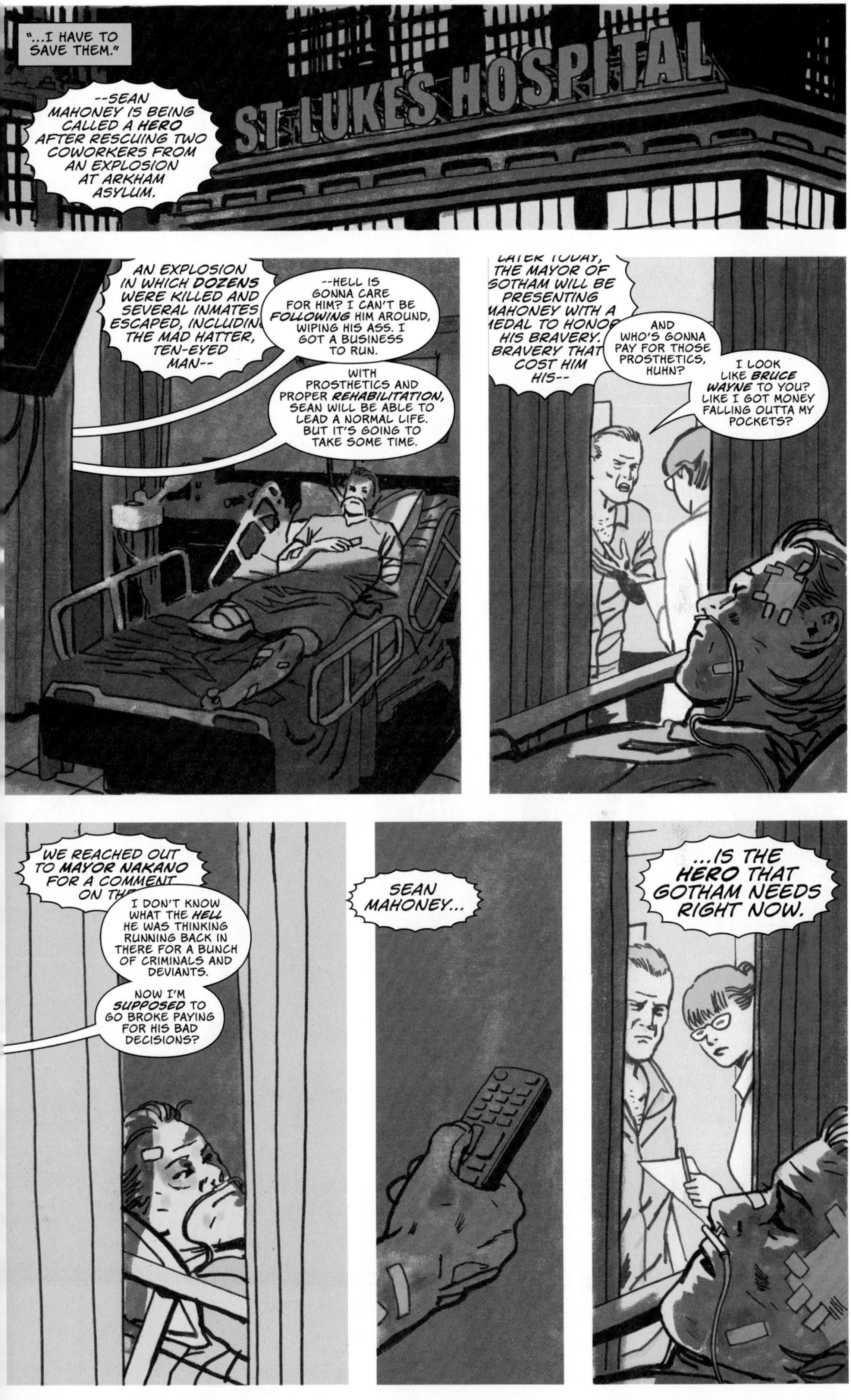
"...I HAVE TO SAVE THEM."
ST. LUKE'S HOSPITAL
--SEAN MAHONEY IS BEING CALLED A HERO AFTER RESCUING TWO COWORKERS FROM AN EXPLOSION AT ARKHAM ASYLUM.
AN EXPLOSION IN WHICH DOZENS WERE KILLED AND SEVERAL INMATES ESCAPED, INCLUDING THE MAD HATTER, TEN-EYED MAN--
--HELL IS GONNA CARE FOR HIM? I CAN'T BE FOLLOWING HIM AROUND, WIPING HIS ASS. I GOT A BUSINESS TO RUN.
WITH PROSTHETICS AND PROPER REHABILITATION, SEAN WILL BE ABLE TO LEAD A NORMAL LIFE. BUT IT'S GOING TO TAKE SOME TIME.
LATER TODAY, THE MAYOR OF GOTHAM WILL BE PRESENTING MAHONEY WITH A MEDAL TO HONOR HIS BRAVERY. BRAVERY THAT COST HIM HIS--
AND WHO'S GONNA PAY FOR THOSE PROSTHETICS, HUHN?
I LOOK LIKE BRUCE WAYNE TO YOU? LIKE I GOT MONEY FALLING OUTTA MY POCKETS?
WE REACHED OUT TO MAYOR NAKANO FOR A COMMENT ON TH
I DON'T KNOW WHAT THE HELL HE WAS THINKING RUNNING BACK IN THERE FOR A BUNCH OF CRIMINALS AND DEVIANTS.
NOW I'M SUPPOSED TO GO BROKE PAYING FOR HIS BAD DECISIONS?
SEAN MAHONEY...
...IS THE HERO THAT GOTHAM NEEDS RIGHT NOW.

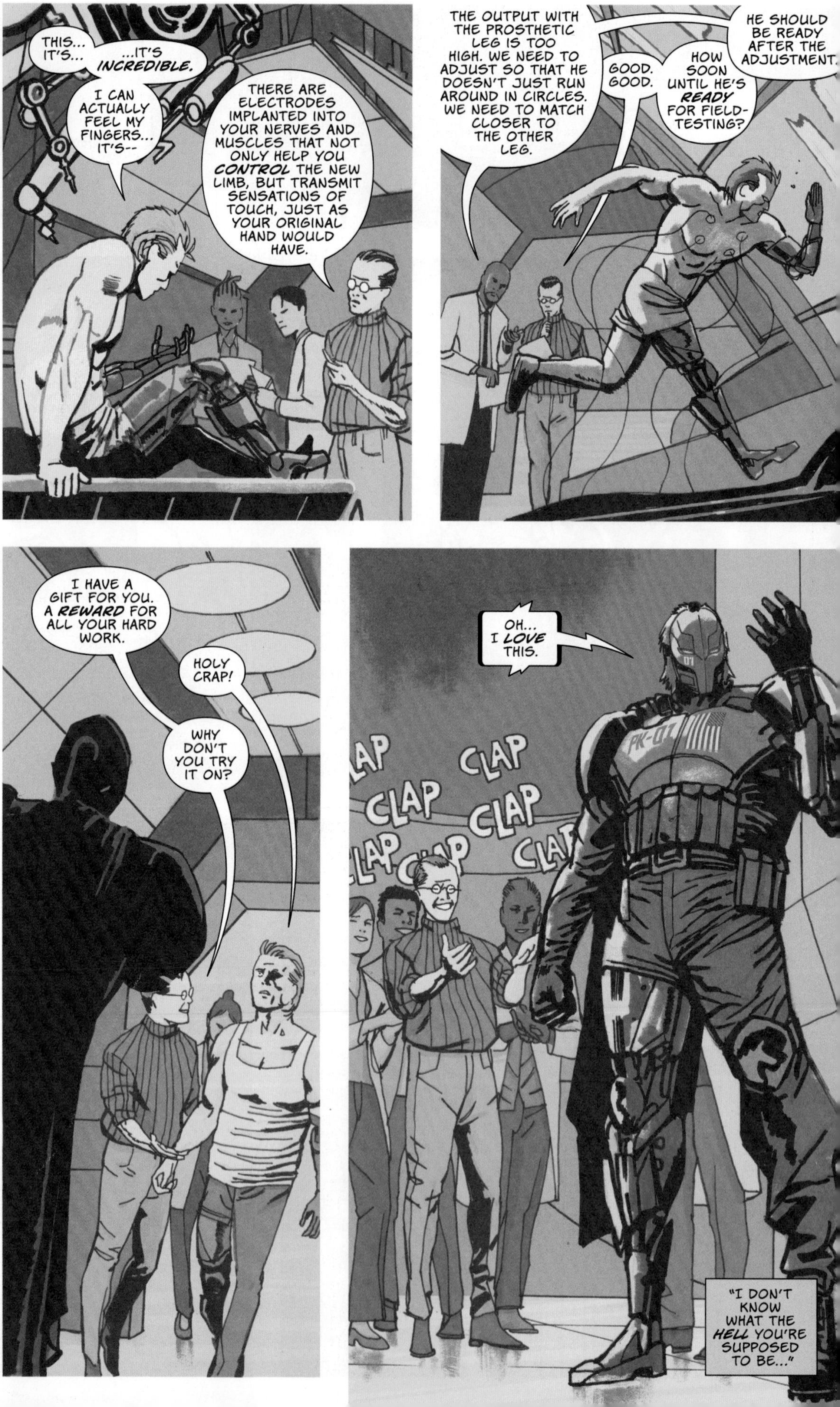
THIS... IT'S...
...IT'S *INCREDIBLE.*
I CAN ACTUALLY FEEL MY FINGERS... IT'S--
THERE ARE ELECTRODES IMPLANTED INTO YOUR NERVES AND MUSCLES THAT NOT ONLY HELP YOU *CONTROL* THE NEW LIMB, BUT TRANSMIT SENSATIONS OF TOUCH, JUST AS YOUR ORIGINAL HAND WOULD HAVE.
THE OUTPUT WITH THE PROSTHETIC LEG IS TOO HIGH. WE NEED TO ADJUST SO THAT HE DOESN'T JUST RUN AROUND IN CIRCLES. WE NEED TO MATCH CLOSER TO THE OTHER LEG.
GOOD. GOOD.
HOW SOON UNTIL HE'S *READY* FOR FIELD-TESTING?
HE SHOULD BE READY AFTER THE ADJUSTMENT.
I HAVE A GIFT FOR YOU. A *REWARD* FOR ALL YOUR HARD WORK.
HOLY CRAP!
WHY DON'T YOU TRY IT ON?
OH... I *LOVE* THIS.
PK-07
CLAP CLAP CLAP CLAP CLAP CLAP CLAP
"I DON'T KNOW WHAT THE *HELL* YOU'RE SUPPOSED TO BE..."

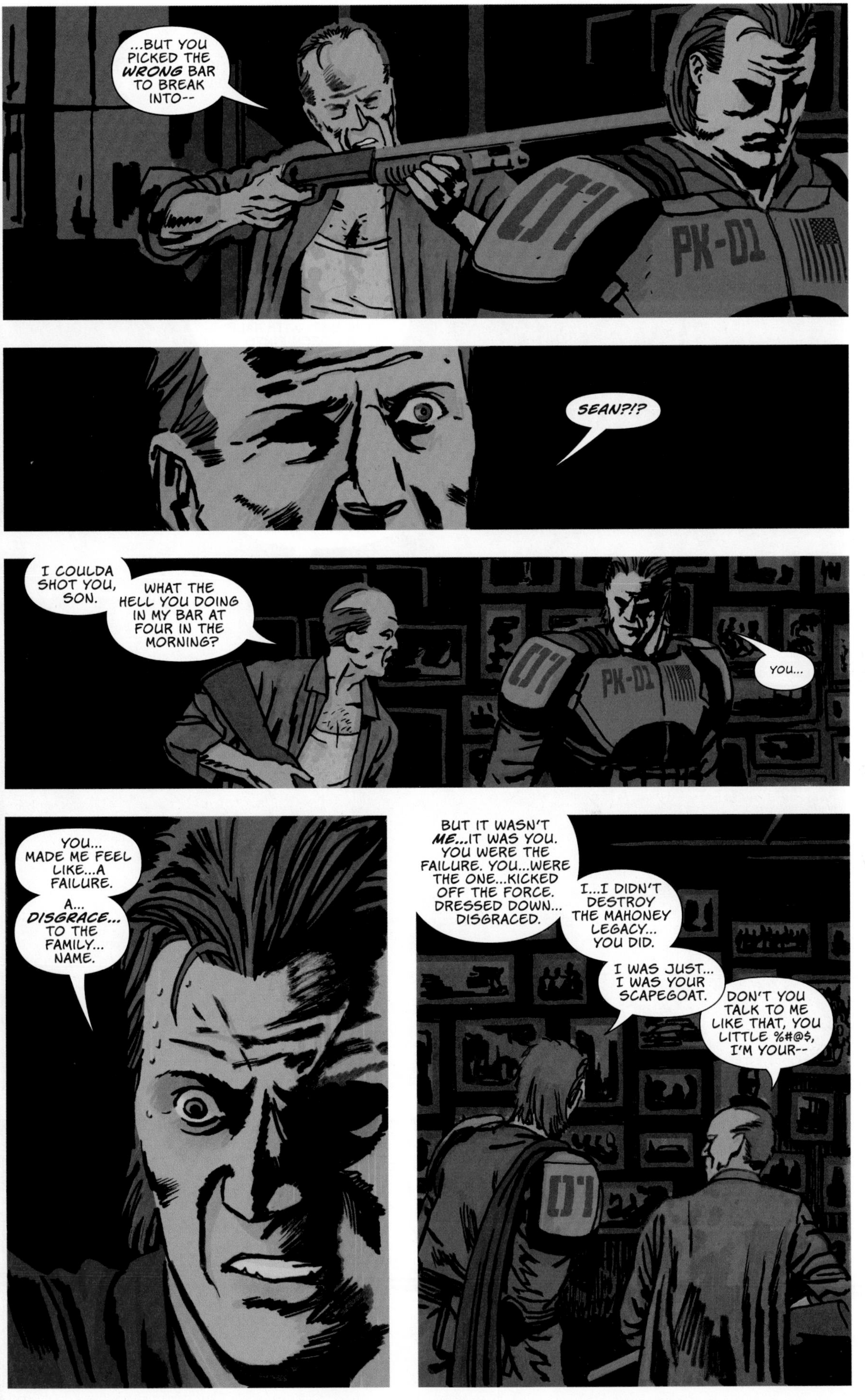
...BUT YOU PICKED THE WRONG BAR TO BREAK INTO--
PK-01
SEAN?!?
I COULDA SHOT YOU, SON.
WHAT THE HELL YOU DOING IN MY BAR AT FOUR IN THE MORNING?
YOU...
YOU... MADE ME FEEL LIKE...A FAILURE.
A... DISGRACE... TO THE FAMILY... NAME.
BUT IT WASN'T ME...IT WAS YOU. YOU WERE THE FAILURE. YOU...WERE THE ONE...KICKED OFF THE FORCE. DRESSED DOWN... DISGRACED.
I...I DIDN'T DESTROY THE MAHONEY LEGACY... YOU DID.
I WAS JUST... I WAS YOUR SCAPEGOAT.
DON'T YOU TALK TO ME LIKE THAT, YOU LITTLE %#@$, I'M YOUR--

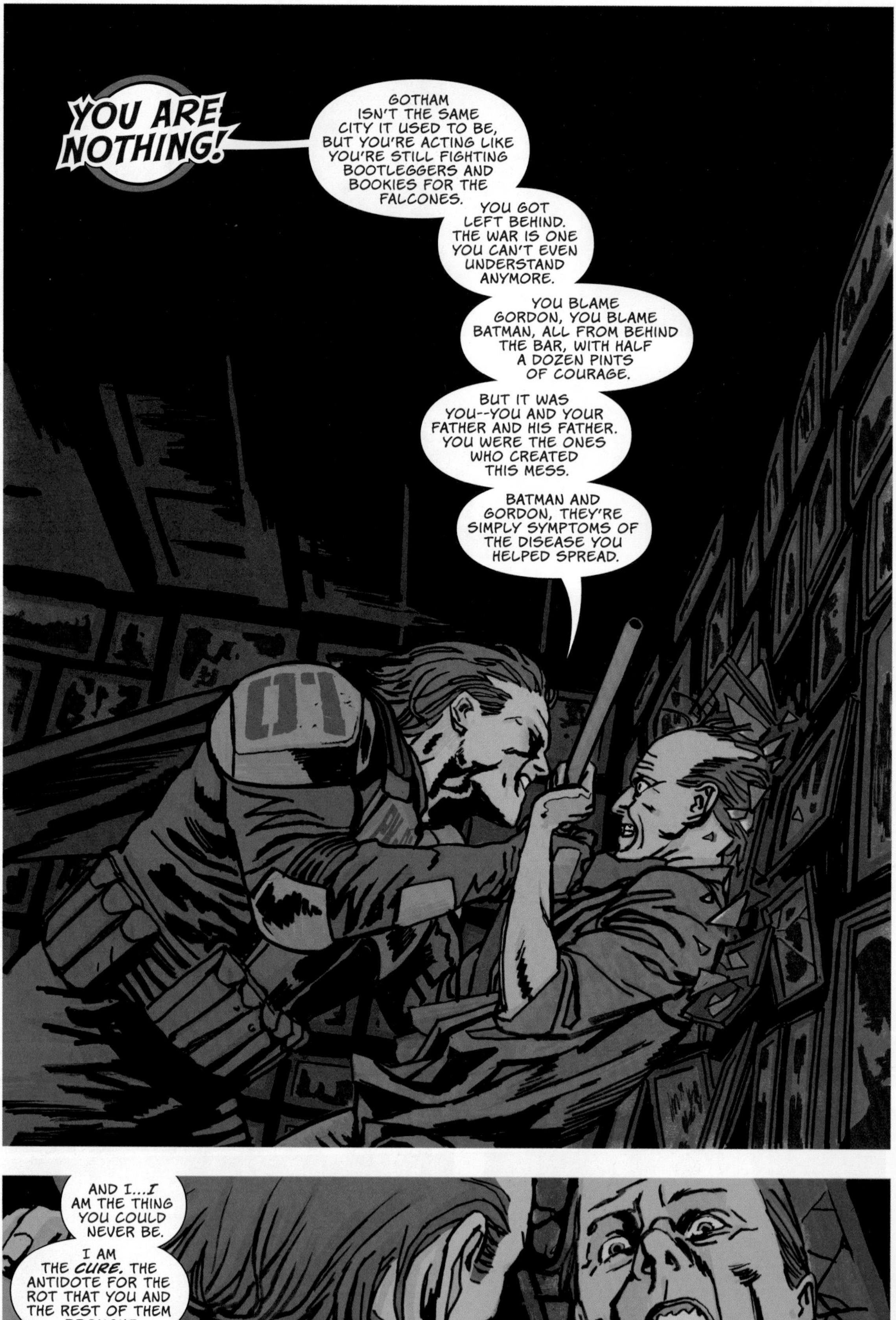
YOU ARE NOTHING!
GOTHAM ISN'T THE SAME CITY IT USED TO BE, BUT YOU'RE ACTING LIKE YOU'RE STILL FIGHTING BOOTLEGGERS AND BOOKIES FOR THE FALCONES.
YOU GOT LEFT BEHIND. THE WAR IS ONE YOU CAN'T EVEN UNDERSTAND ANYMORE.
YOU BLAME GORDON, YOU BLAME BATMAN, ALL FROM BEHIND THE BAR, WITH HALF A DOZEN PINTS OF COURAGE.
BUT IT WAS YOU--YOU AND YOUR FATHER AND HIS FATHER. YOU WERE THE ONES WHO CREATED THIS MESS.
BATMAN AND GORDON, THEY'RE SIMPLY SYMPTOMS OF THE DISEASE YOU HELPED SPREAD.

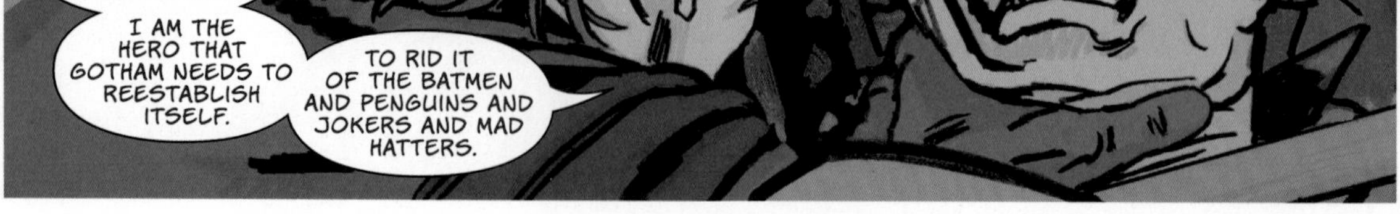
AND I...*I* AM THE THING YOU COULD NEVER BE.
I AM THE ***CURE.*** THE ANTIDOTE FOR THE ROT THAT YOU AND THE REST OF THEM BROUGHT.
I AM THE HERO THAT GOTHAM NEEDS TO REESTABLISH ITSELF.
TO RID IT OF THE BATMEN AND PENGUINS AND JOKERS AND MAD HATTERS.

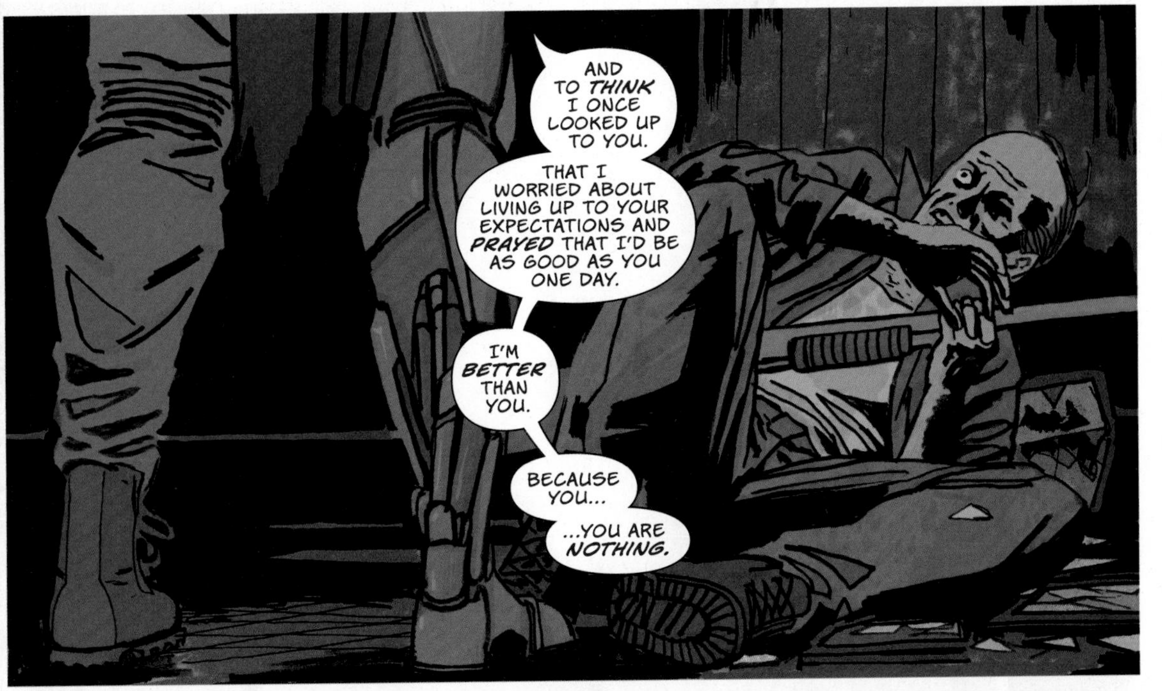
AND TO *THINK* I ONCE LOOKED UP TO YOU.
THAT I WORRIED ABOUT LIVING UP TO YOUR EXPECTATIONS AND *PRAYED* THAT I'D BE AS GOOD AS YOU ONE DAY.
I'M *BETTER* THAN YOU.
BECAUSE YOU...
...YOU ARE *NOTHING.*

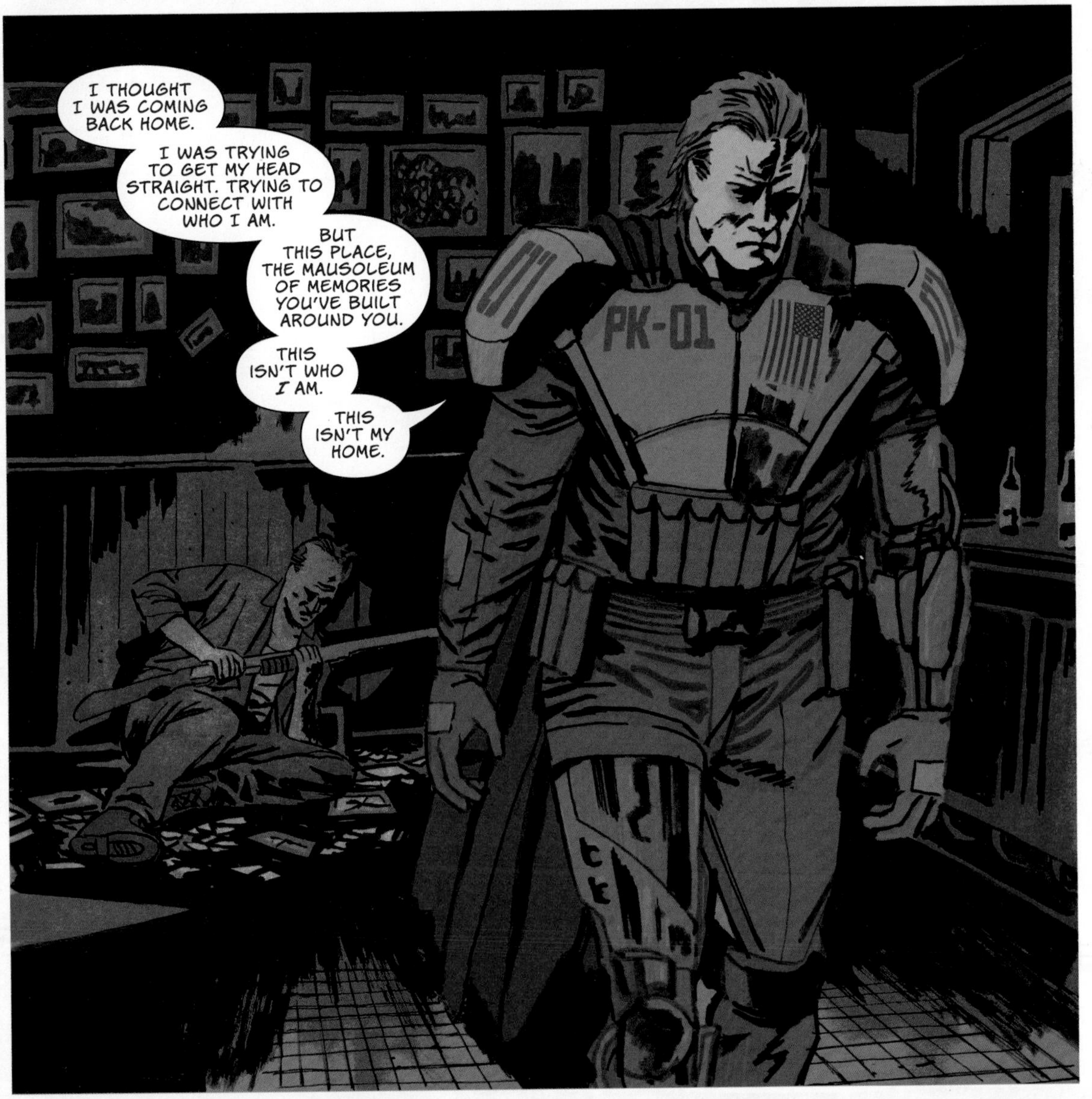
I THOUGHT I WAS COMING BACK HOME.
I WAS TRYING TO GET MY HEAD STRAIGHT. TRYING TO CONNECT WITH WHO I AM.
BUT THIS PLACE, THE MAUSOLEUM OF MEMORIES YOU'VE BUILT AROUND YOU.
THIS ISN'T WHO *I* AM.
THIS ISN'T MY HOME.
PK-01

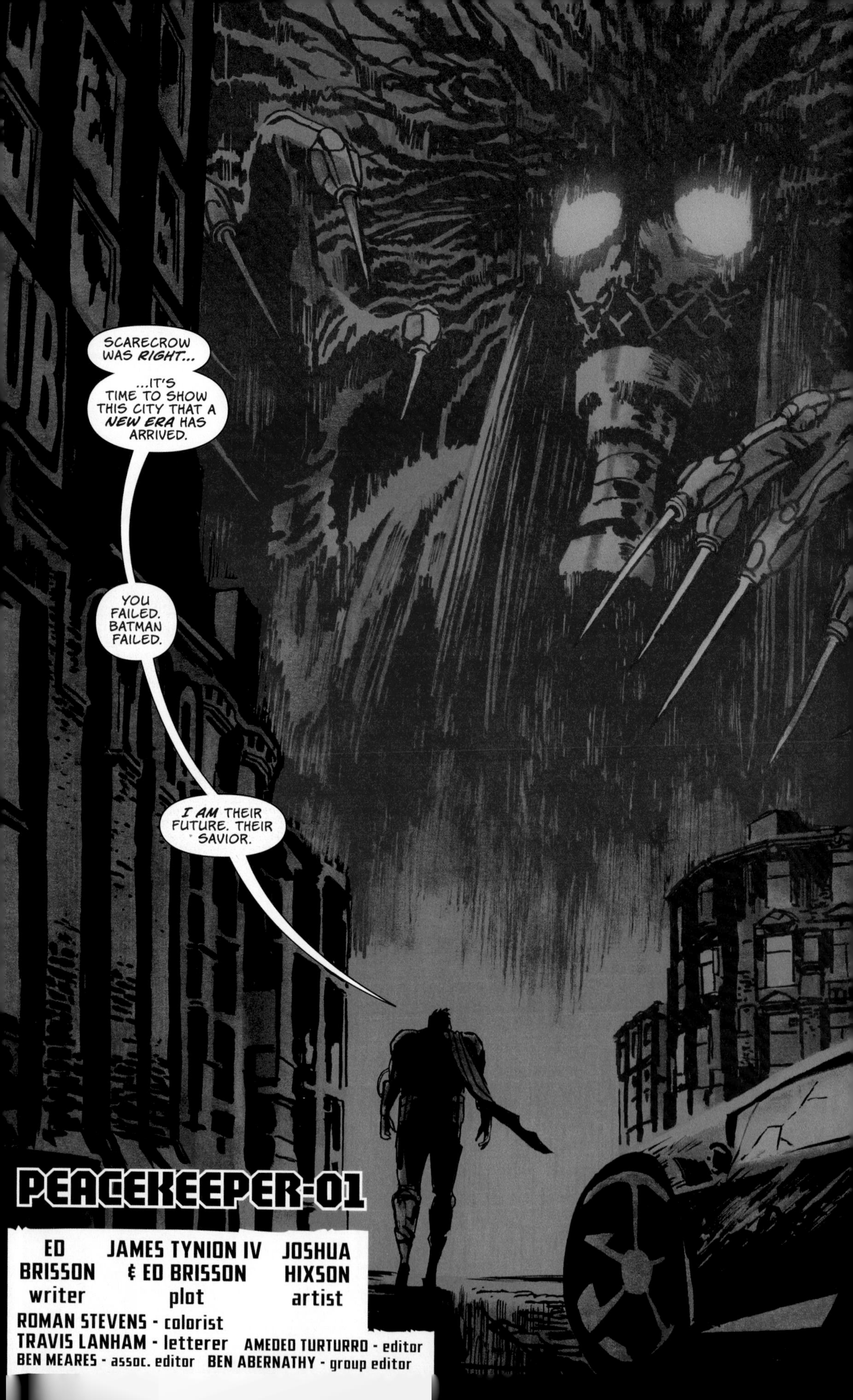
SCARECROW WAS *RIGHT*...
...IT'S TIME TO SHOW THIS CITY THAT A *NEW ERA* HAS ARRIVED.
YOU FAILED. BATMAN FAILED.
I AM THEIR FUTURE. THEIR SAVIOR.

PEACEKEEPER-01

ED BRISSON writer
JAMES TYNION IV & ED BRISSON plot
JOSHUA HIXSON artist
ROMAN STEVENS - colorist
TRAVIS LANHAM - letterer
AMEDEO TURTURRO - editor
BEN MEARES - assoc. editor
BEN ABERNATHY - group editor

***Batman Secret Files: Miracle Molly* #1**
Cover by Little Thunder

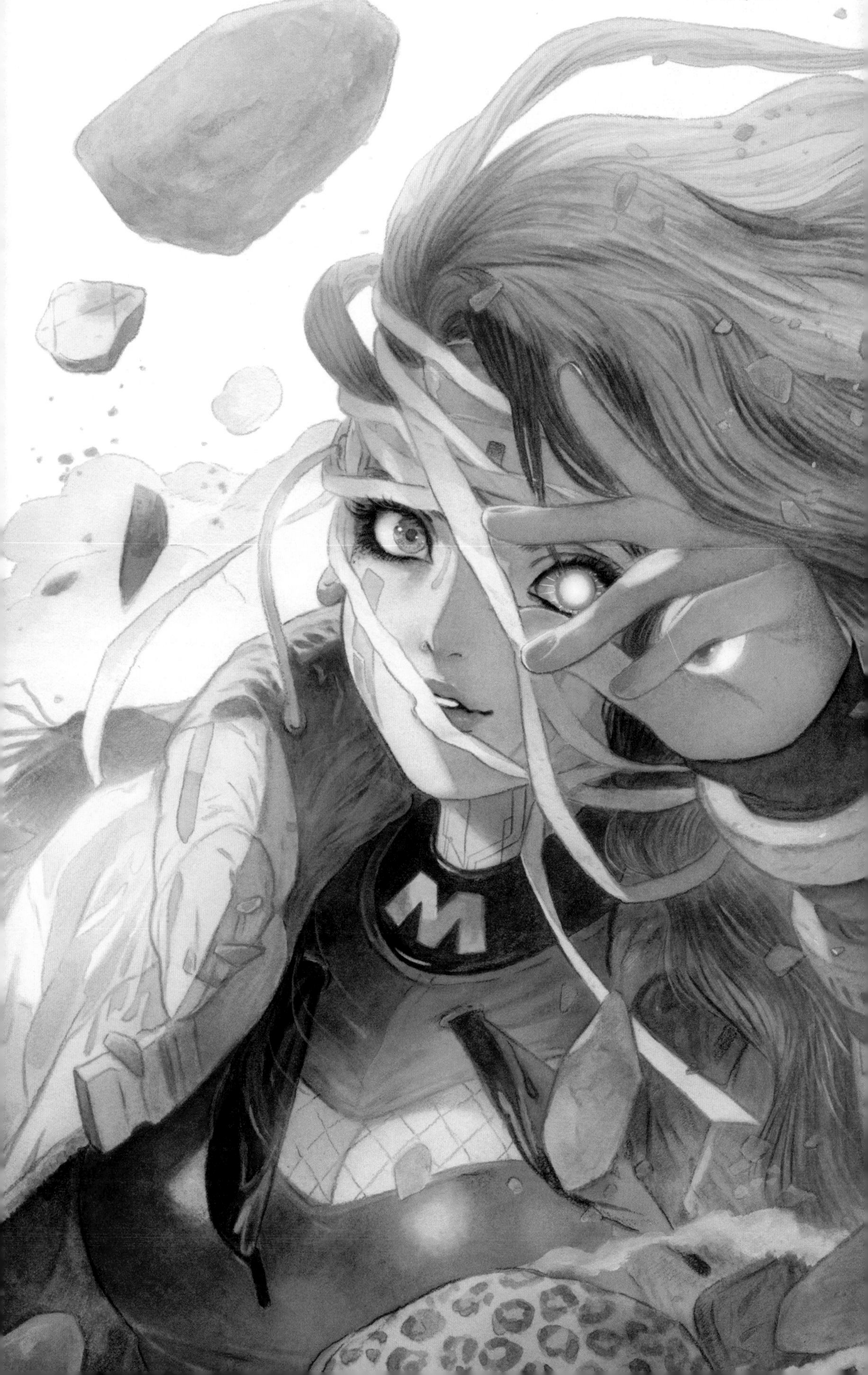
M

Batman Secret Files:
Miracle Molly

Written by
James Tynion IV

Drawn by
DaNi

Colored by
Lee Loughridge

Lettered by
Tom Napolitano

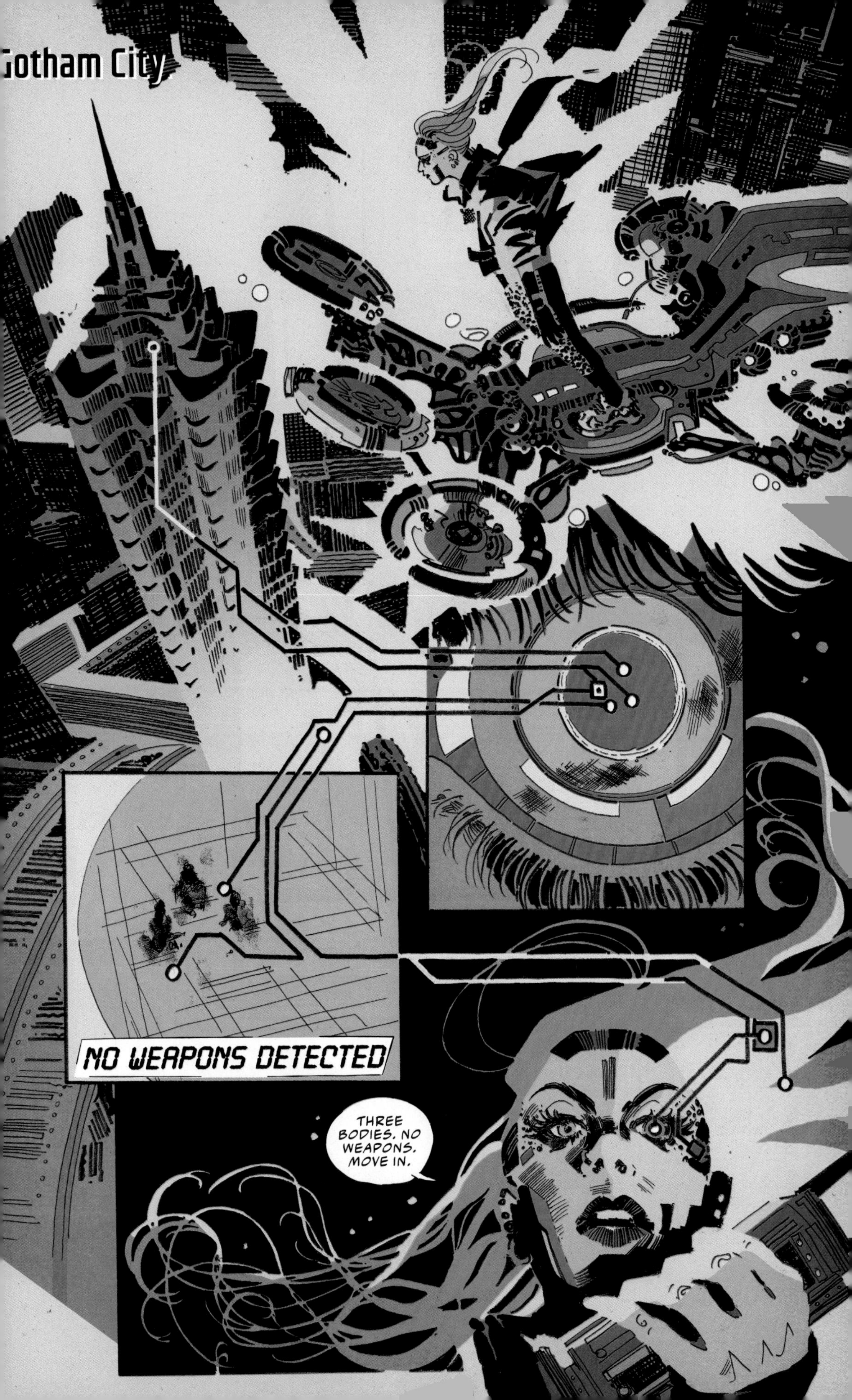
Gotham City.
NO WEAPONS DETECTED
THREE BODIES. NO WEAPONS. MOVE IN.

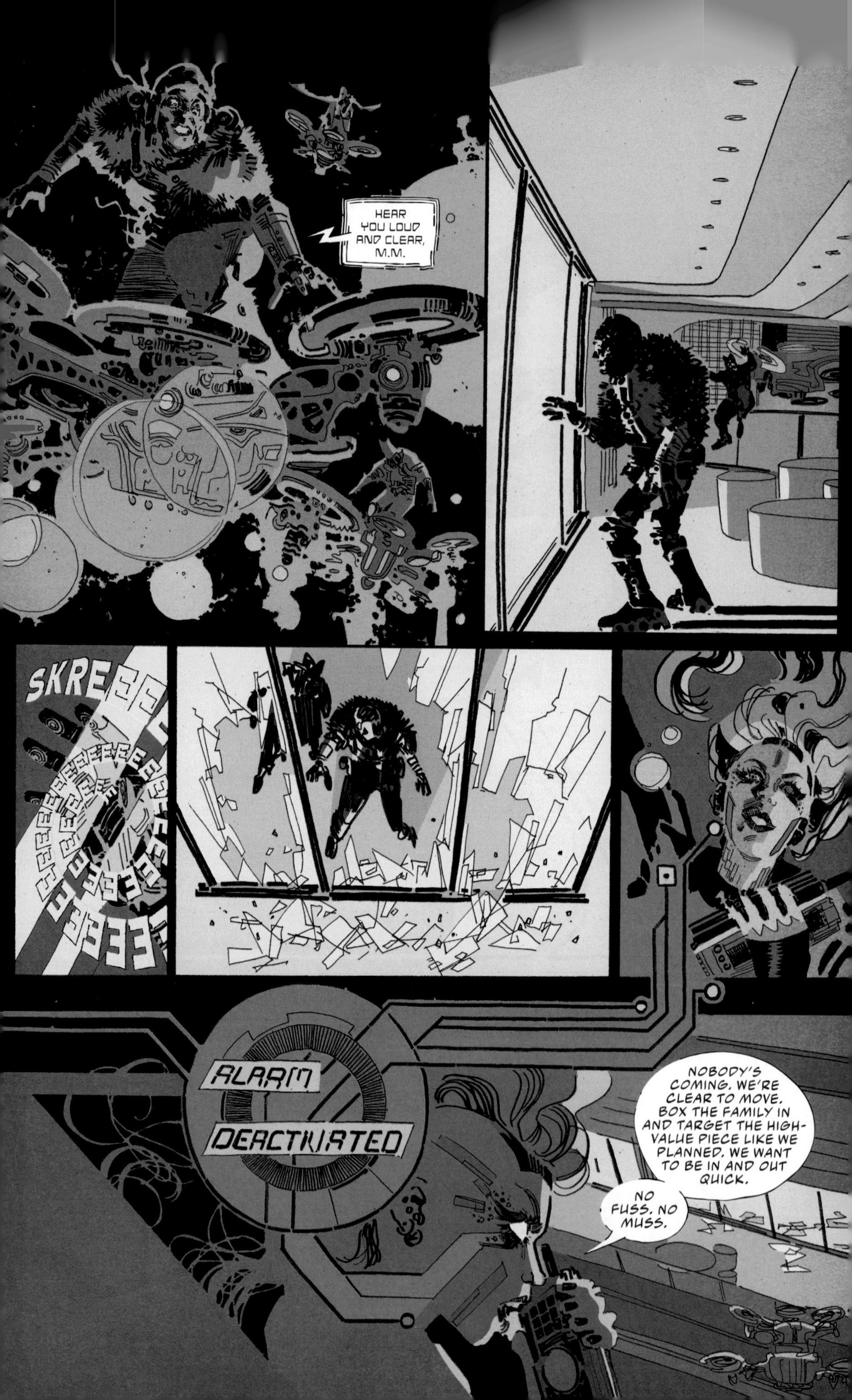
HEAR YOU LOUD AND CLEAR, M.M.
SKREEEEEEEEEEEEEEEEEEEEEEEE
ALARM
DEACTIVATED
NOBODY'S COMING. WE'RE CLEAR TO MOVE. BOX THE FAMILY IN AND TARGET THE HIGH-VALUE PIECE LIKE WE PLANNED. WE WANT TO BE IN AND OUT QUICK.
NO FUSS. NO MUSS.

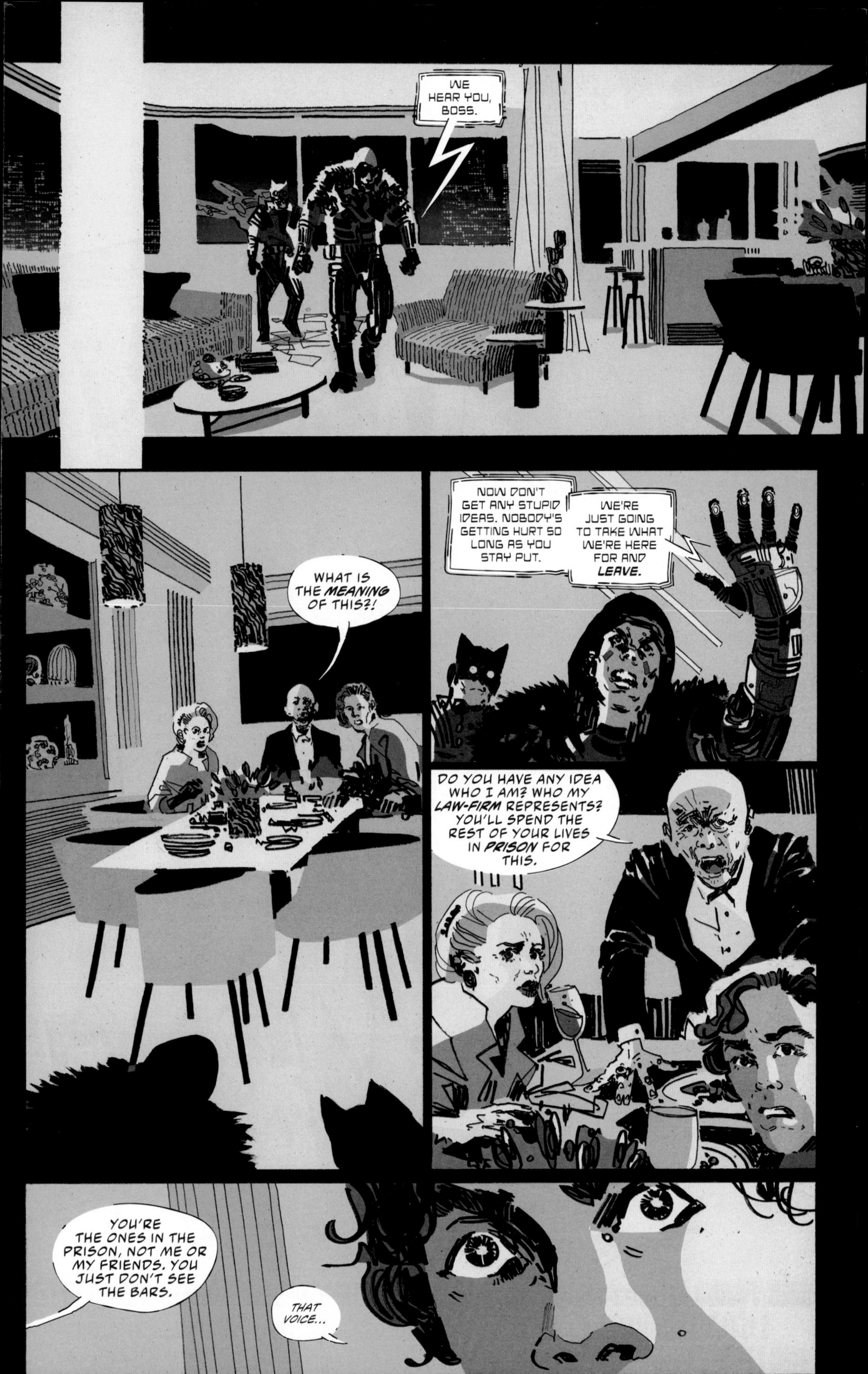
WE HEAR YOU, BOSS.
WHAT IS THE MEANING OF THIS?!
NOW DON'T GET ANY STUPID IDEAS. NOBODY'S GETTING HURT SO LONG AS YOU STAY PUT.
WE'RE JUST GOING TO TAKE WHAT WE'RE HERE FOR AND LEAVE.
DO YOU HAVE ANY IDEA WHO I AM? WHO MY LAW-FIRM REPRESENTS? YOU'LL SPEND THE REST OF YOUR LIVES IN PRISON FOR THIS.
YOU'RE THE ONES IN THE PRISON, NOT ME OR MY FRIENDS. YOU JUST DON'T SEE THE BARS.
THAT VOICE...

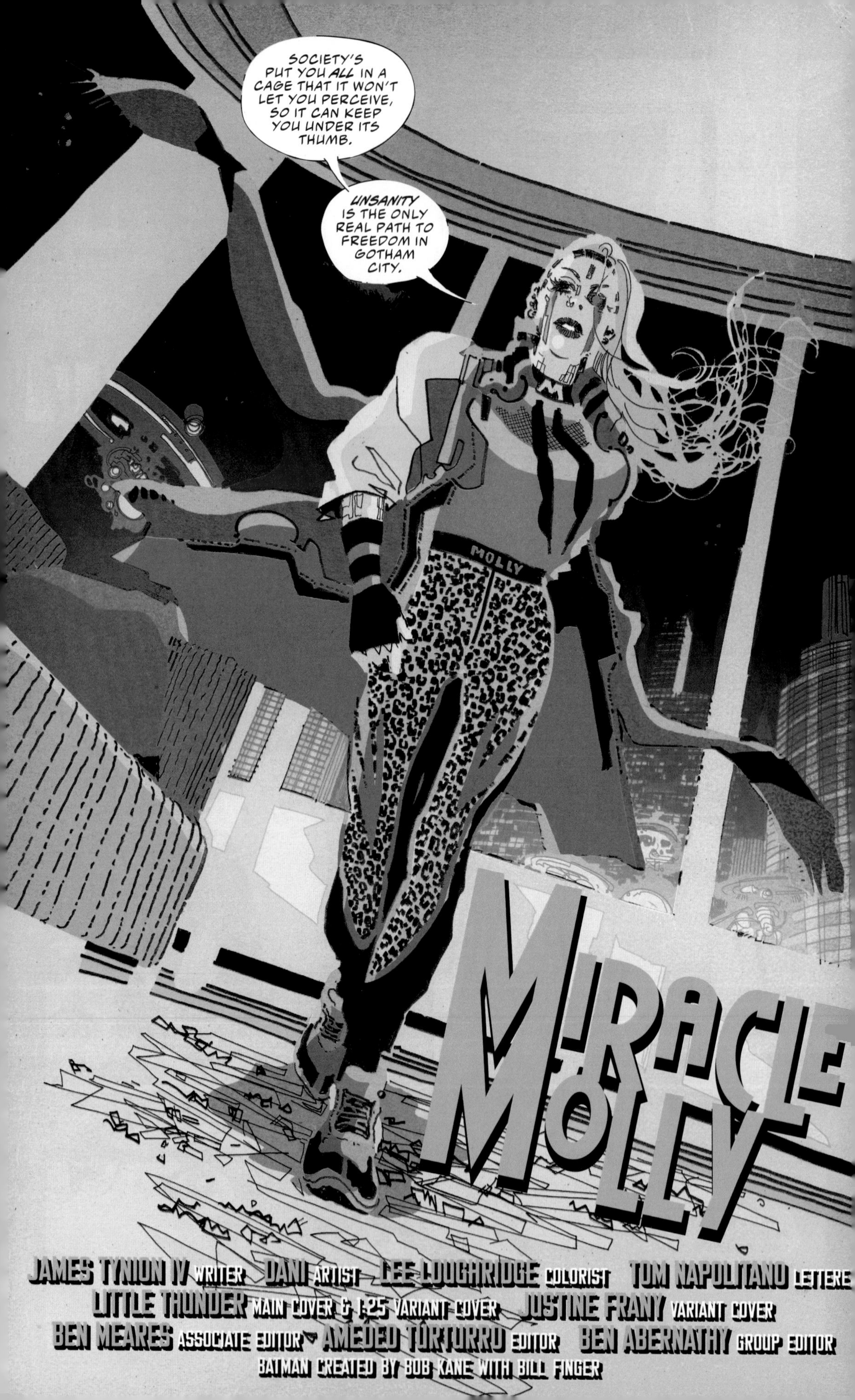
SOCIETY'S PUT YOU *ALL* IN A CAGE THAT IT WON'T LET YOU PERCEIVE, SO IT CAN KEEP YOU UNDER ITS THUMB.
UNSANITY IS THE ONLY REAL PATH TO FREEDOM IN GOTHAM CITY.
MIRACLE MOLLY
JAMES TYNION IV WRITER DANI ARTIST LEE LOUGHRIDGE COLORIST TOM NAPOLITANO LETTERE
LITTLE THUNDER MAIN COVER & 1:25 VARIANT COVER JUSTINE FRANY VARIANT COVER
BEN MEARES ASSOCIATE EDITOR AMEDEO TURTURRO EDITOR BEN ABERNATHY GROUP EDITOR
BATMAN CREATED BY BOB KANE WITH BILL FINGER

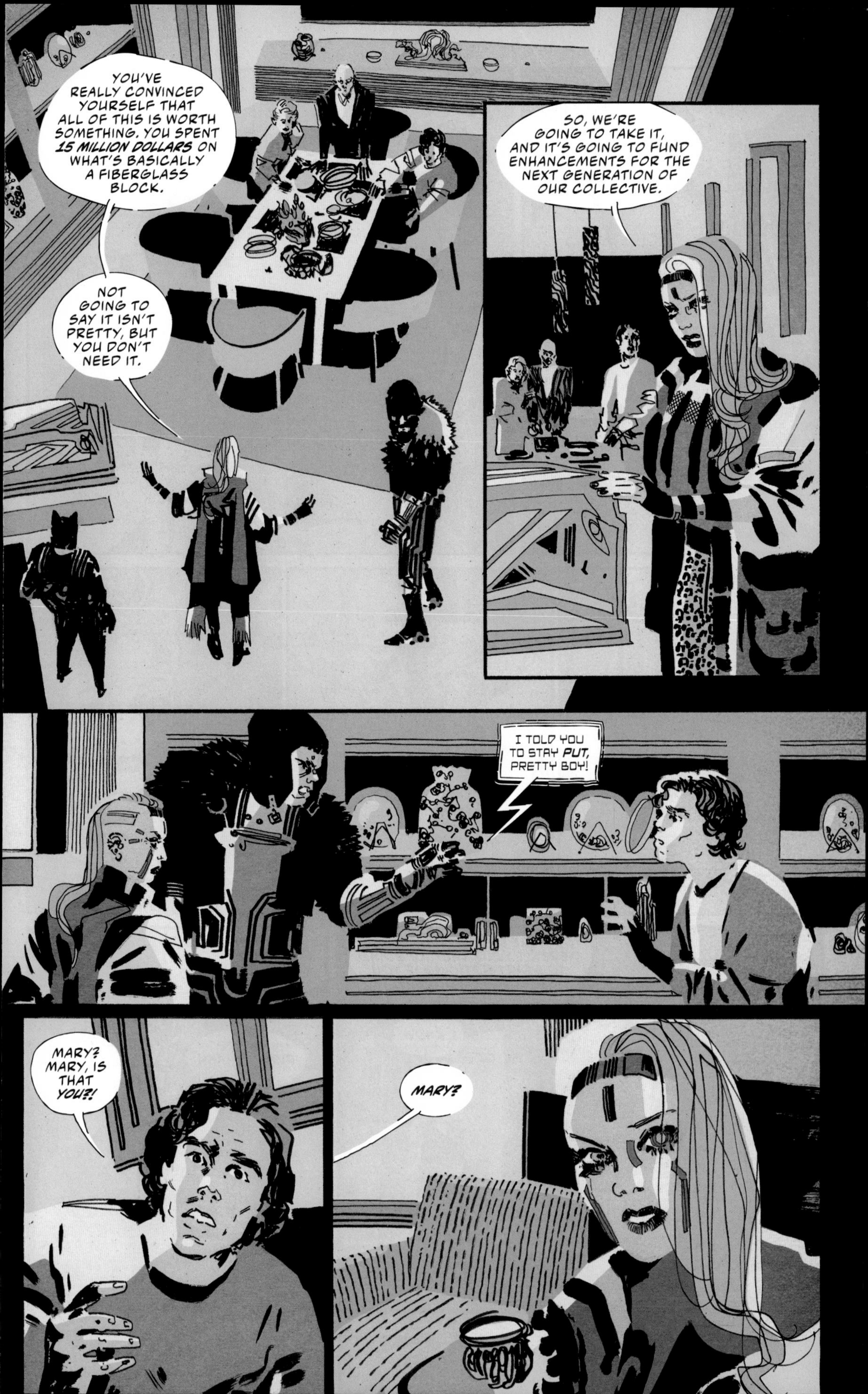
YOU'VE REALLY CONVINCED YOURSELF THAT ALL OF THIS IS WORTH SOMETHING. YOU SPENT *15 MILLION DOLLARS* ON WHAT'S BASICALLY A FIBERGLASS BLOCK.
NOT GOING TO SAY IT ISN'T PRETTY, BUT YOU DON'T NEED IT.
SO, WE'RE GOING TO TAKE IT, AND IT'S GOING TO FUND ENHANCEMENTS FOR THE NEXT GENERATION OF OUR COLLECTIVE.
I TOLD YOU TO STAY *PUT*, PRETTY BOY!
MARY? MARY, IS THAT *YOU?!*
MARY?

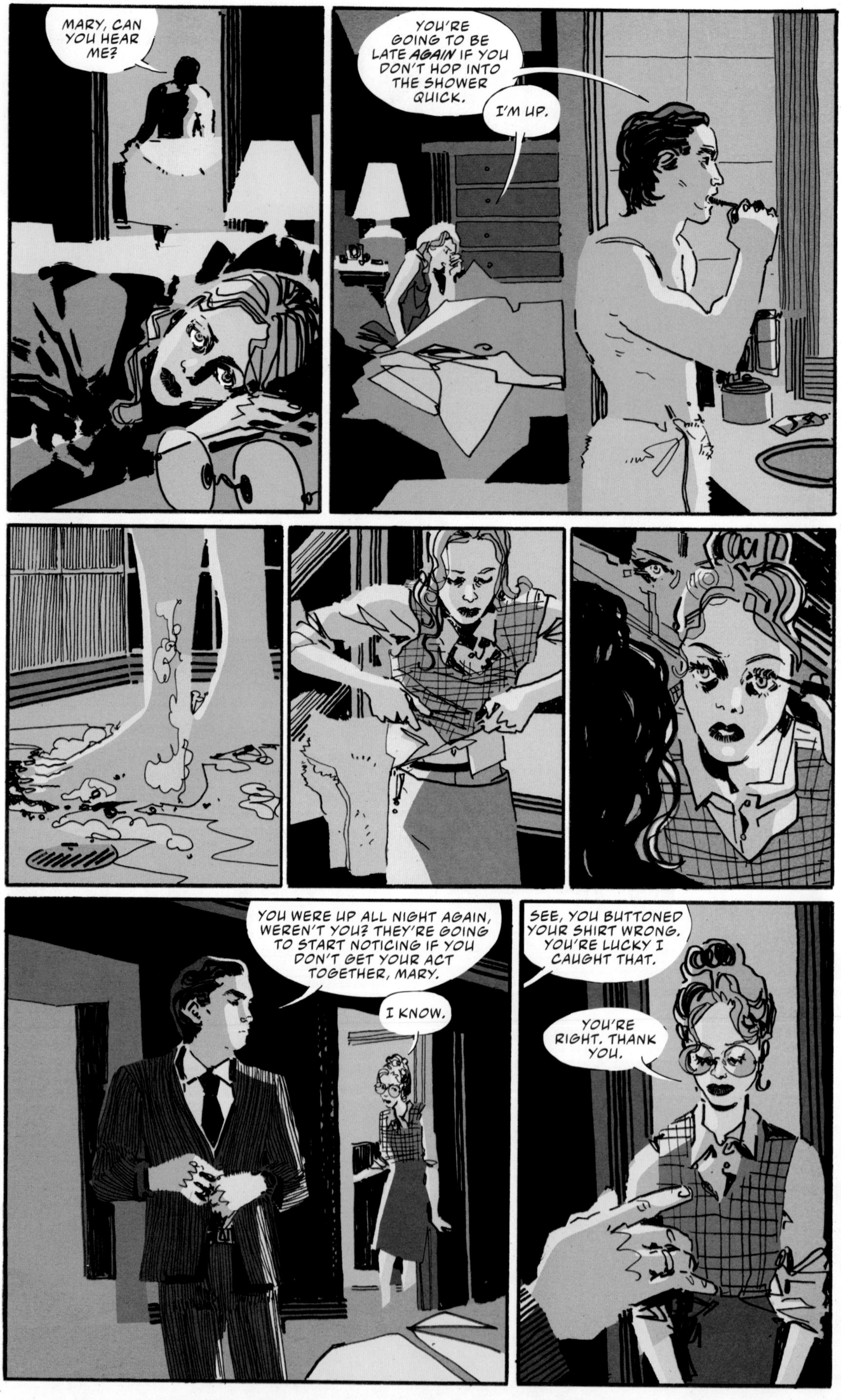
MARY, CAN YOU HEAR ME?
YOU'RE GOING TO BE LATE *AGAIN* IF YOU DON'T HOP INTO THE SHOWER QUICK.
I'M UP.
YOU WERE UP ALL NIGHT AGAIN, WEREN'T YOU? THEY'RE GOING TO START NOTICING IF YOU DON'T GET YOUR ACT TOGETHER, MARY.
I KNOW.
SEE, YOU BUTTONED YOUR SHIRT WRONG. YOU'RE LUCKY I CAUGHT THAT.
YOU'RE RIGHT. THANK YOU.

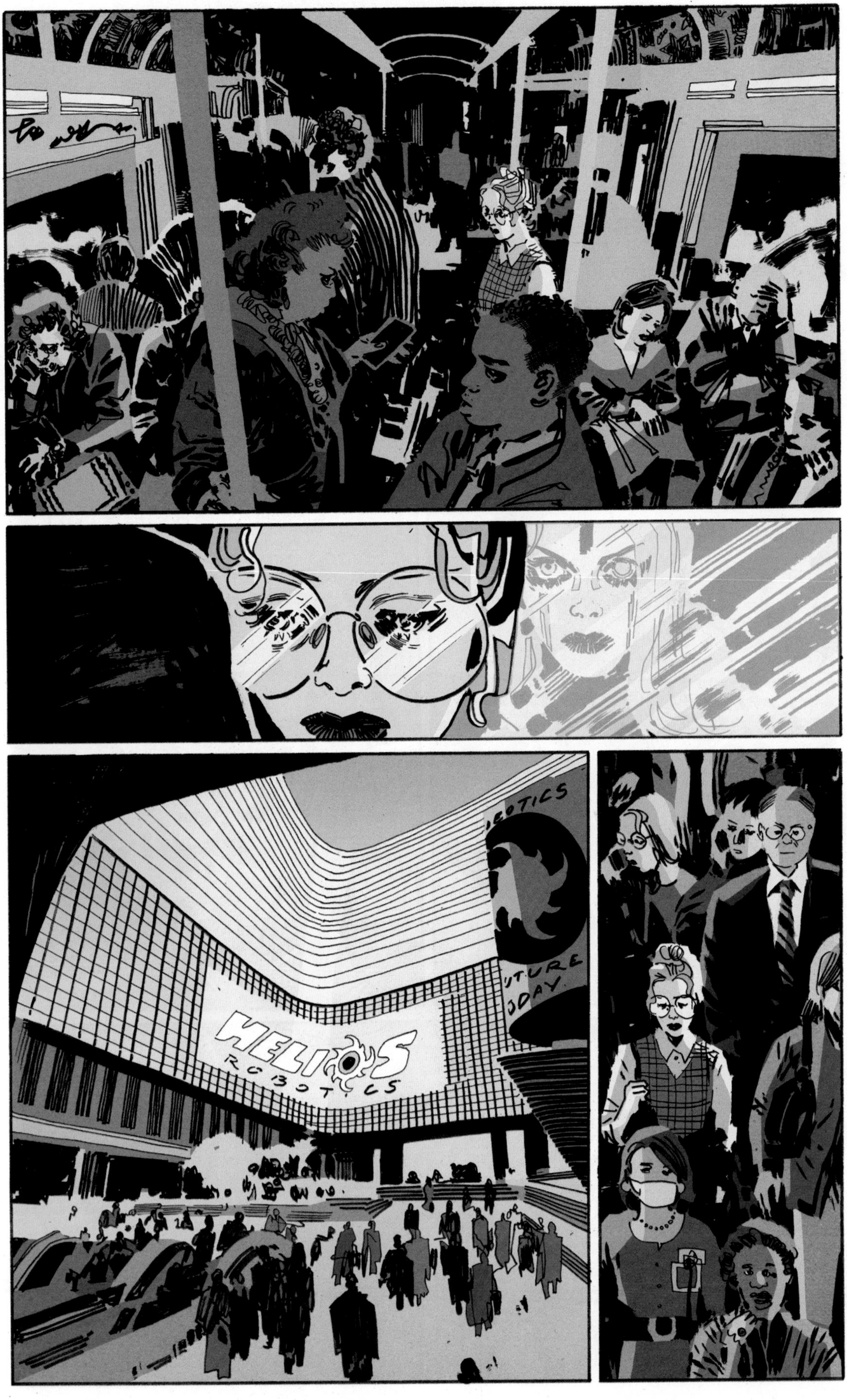
HELIOS
ROBOTICS

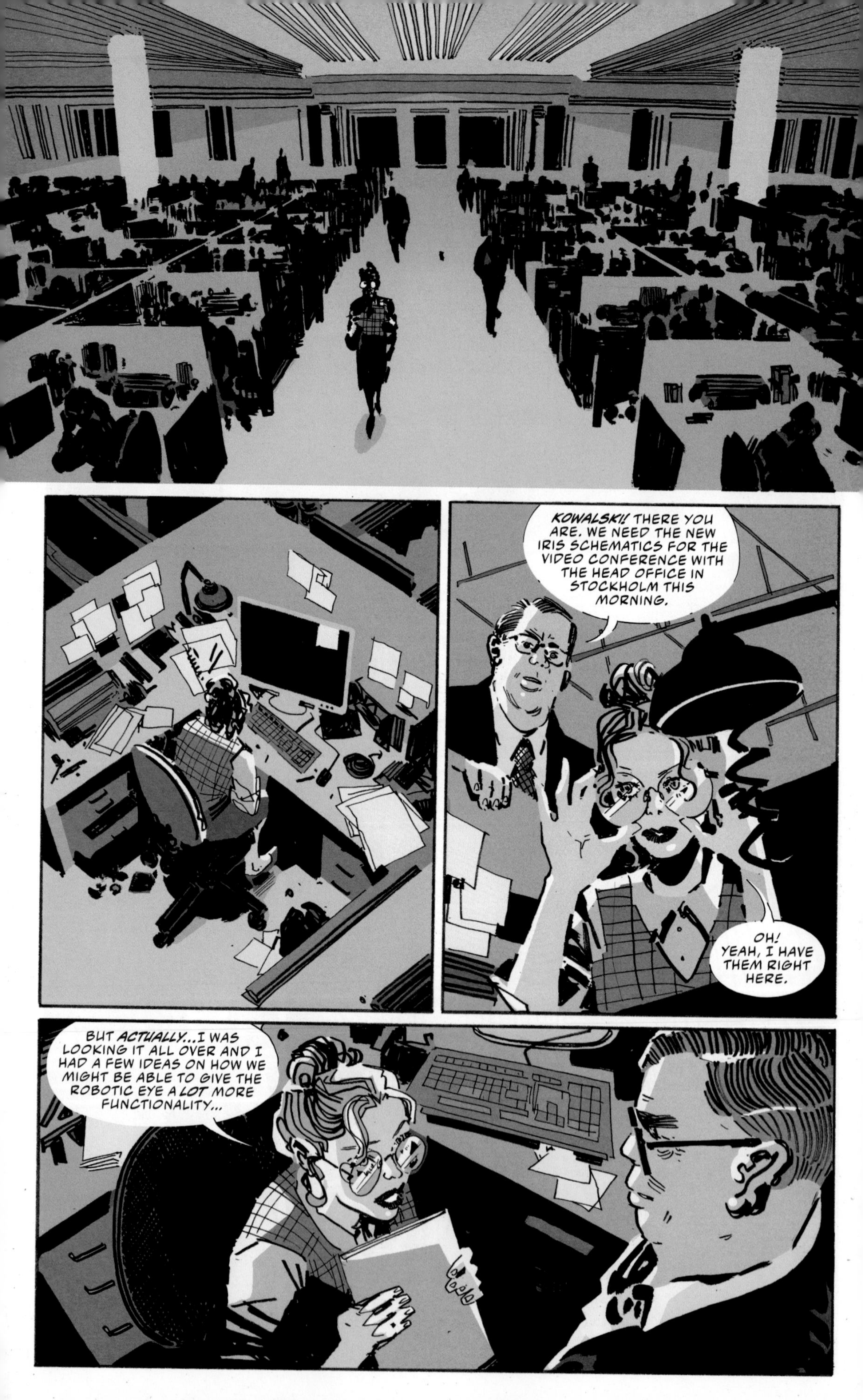

KOWALSKI! THERE YOU ARE. WE NEED THE NEW IRIS SCHEMATICS FOR THE VIDEO CONFERENCE WITH THE HEAD OFFICE IN STOCKHOLM THIS MORNING.
OH! YEAH, I HAVE THEM RIGHT HERE.
BUT ACTUALLY...I WAS LOOKING IT ALL OVER AND I HAD A FEW IDEAS ON HOW WE MIGHT BE ABLE TO GIVE THE ROBOTIC EYE A LOT MORE FUNCTIONALITY...

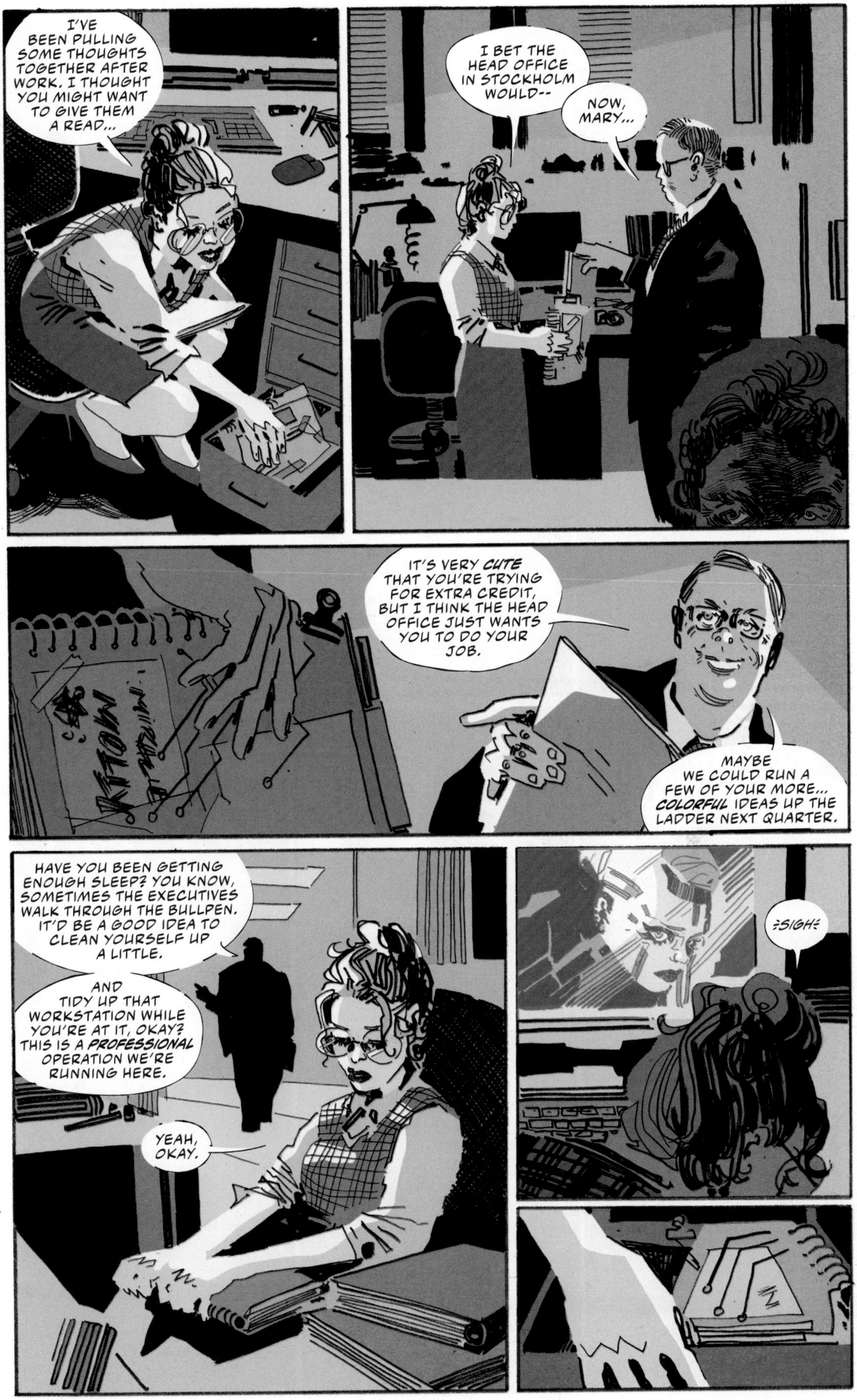
I'VE BEEN PULLING SOME THOUGHTS TOGETHER AFTER WORK. I THOUGHT YOU MIGHT WANT TO GIVE THEM A READ...
I BET THE HEAD OFFICE IN STOCKHOLM WOULD--
NOW, MARY...
IT'S VERY *CUTE* THAT YOU'RE TRYING FOR EXTRA CREDIT, BUT I THINK THE HEAD OFFICE JUST WANTS YOU TO DO YOUR JOB.
MAYBE WE COULD RUN A FEW OF YOUR MORE... ***COLORFUL*** IDEAS UP THE LADDER NEXT QUARTER.
HAVE YOU BEEN GETTING ENOUGH SLEEP? YOU KNOW, SOMETIMES THE EXECUTIVES WALK THROUGH THE BULLPEN. IT'D BE A GOOD IDEA TO CLEAN YOURSELF UP A LITTLE.
AND TIDY UP THAT WORKSTATION WHILE YOU'RE AT IT, OKAY? THIS IS A ***PROFESSIONAL*** OPERATION WE'RE RUNNING HERE.
YEAH, OKAY.
SIGH

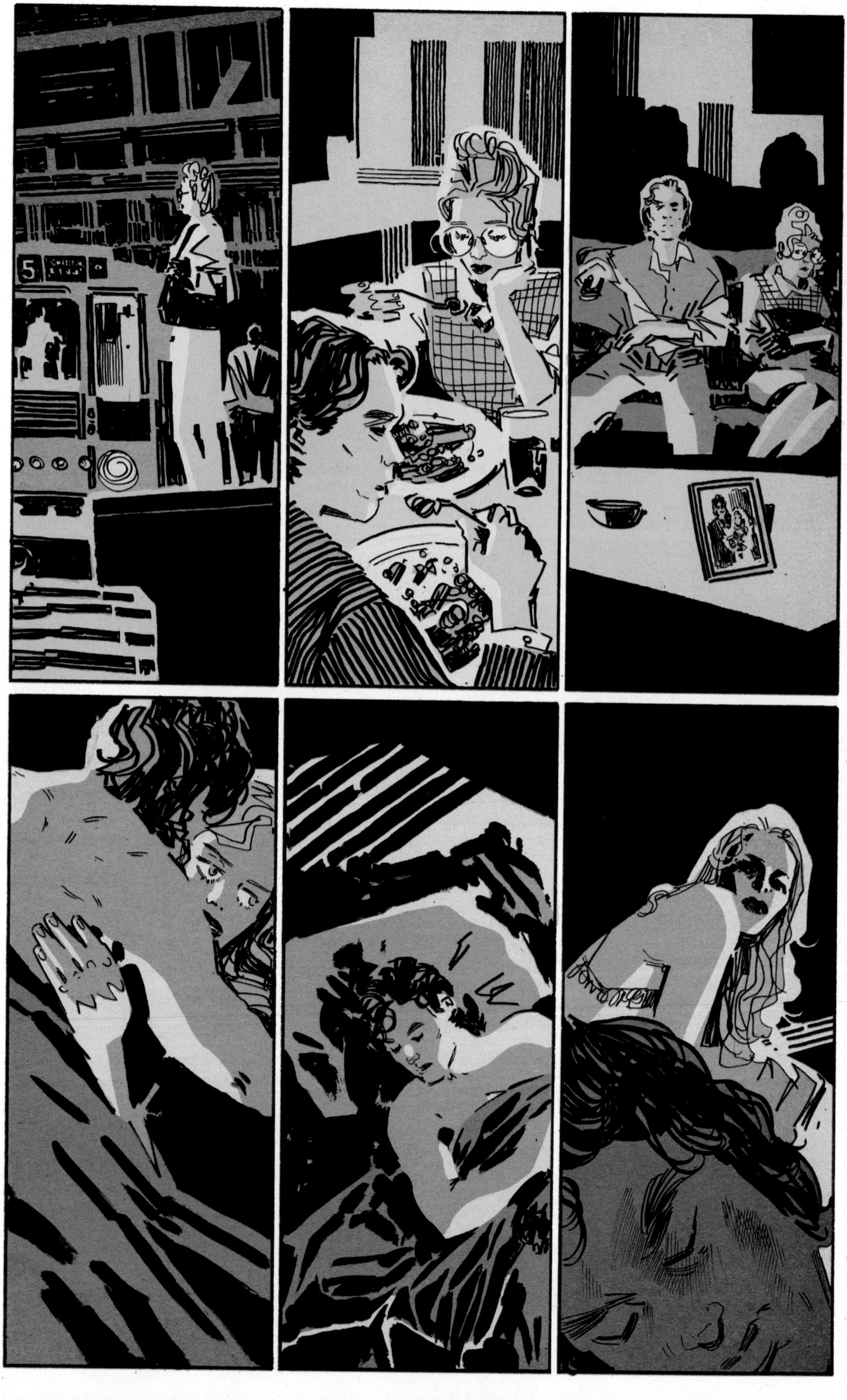

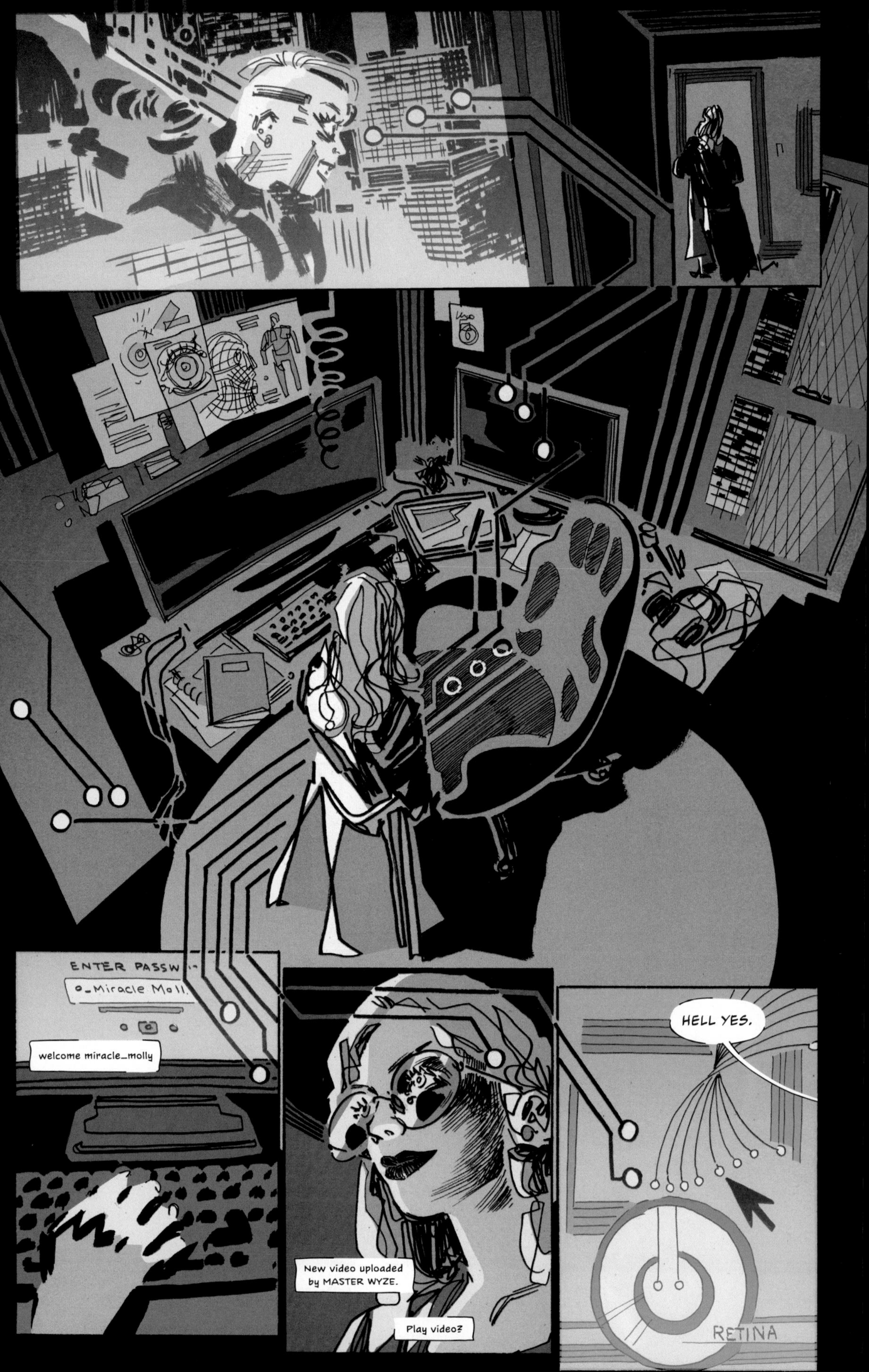
ENTER PASSW
o_Miracle Moll
welcome miracle_molly
New video uploaded by MASTER WYZE.
Play video?
HELL YES.
RETINA

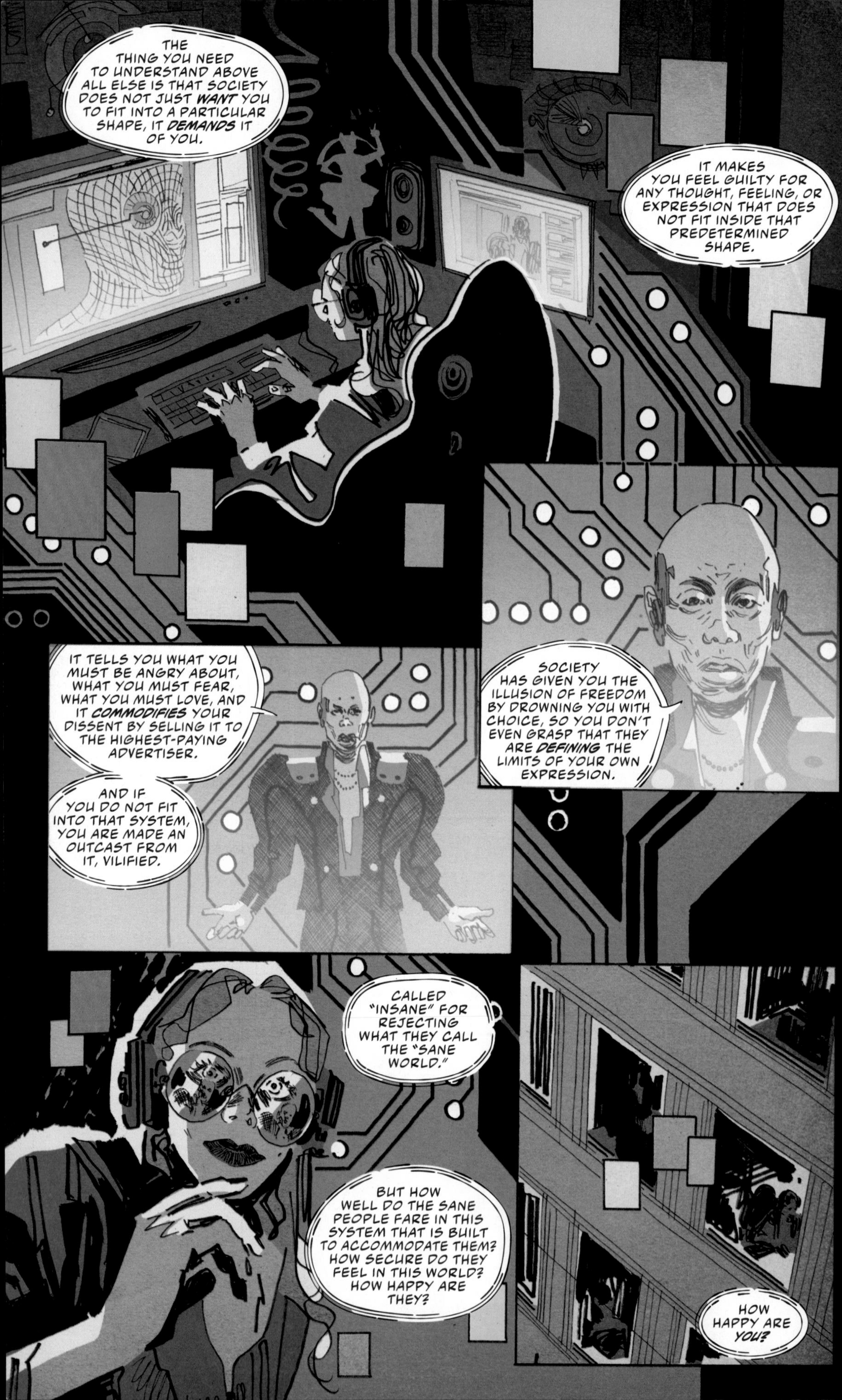
THE THING YOU NEED TO UNDERSTAND ABOVE ALL ELSE IS THAT SOCIETY DOES NOT JUST *WANT* YOU TO FIT INTO A PARTICULAR SHAPE, IT *DEMANDS* IT OF YOU.
IT MAKES YOU FEEL GUILTY FOR ANY THOUGHT, FEELING, OR EXPRESSION THAT DOES NOT FIT INSIDE THAT PREDETERMINED SHAPE.
SOCIETY HAS GIVEN YOU THE ILLUSION OF FREEDOM BY DROWNING YOU WITH CHOICE, SO YOU DON'T EVEN GRASP THAT THEY ARE *DEFINING* THE LIMITS OF YOUR OWN EXPRESSION.
IT TELLS YOU WHAT YOU MUST BE ANGRY ABOUT, WHAT YOU MUST FEAR, WHAT YOU MUST LOVE, AND IT *COMMODIFIES* YOUR DISSENT BY SELLING IT TO THE HIGHEST-PAYING ADVERTISER.
AND IF YOU DO NOT FIT INTO THAT SYSTEM, YOU ARE MADE AN OUTCAST FROM IT, VILIFIED.
CALLED "INSANE" FOR REJECTING WHAT THEY CALL THE "SANE WORLD."
BUT HOW WELL DO THE SANE PEOPLE FARE IN THIS SYSTEM THAT IS BUILT TO ACCOMMODATE THEM? HOW SECURE DO THEY FEEL IN THIS WORLD? HOW HAPPY ARE THEY?
HOW HAPPY ARE *YOU?*

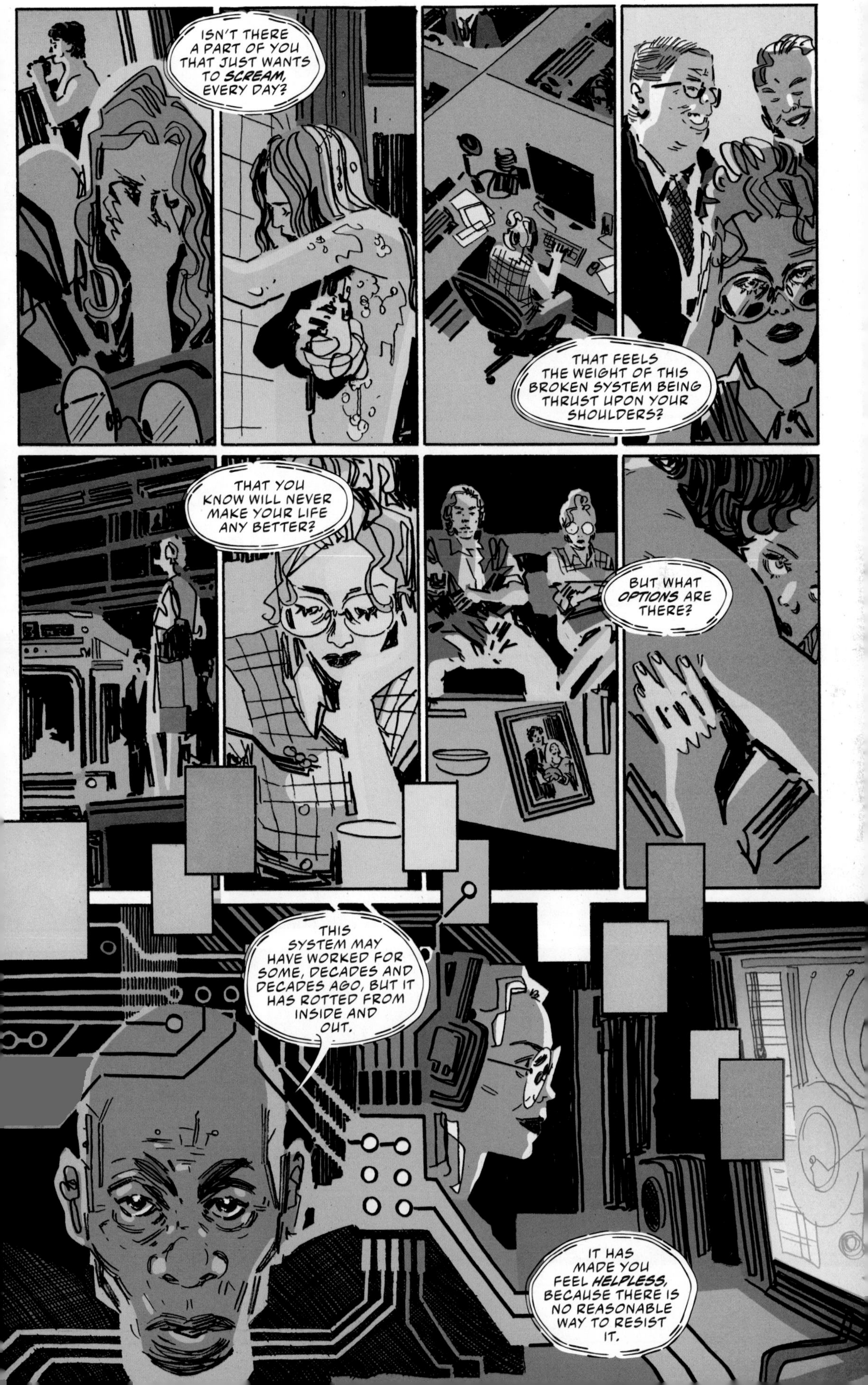
ISN'T THERE A PART OF YOU THAT JUST WANTS TO SCREAM, EVERY DAY?
THAT FEELS THE WEIGHT OF THIS BROKEN SYSTEM BEING THRUST UPON YOUR SHOULDERS?
THAT YOU KNOW WILL NEVER MAKE YOUR LIFE ANY BETTER?
BUT WHAT OPTIONS ARE THERE?
THIS SYSTEM MAY HAVE WORKED FOR SOME, DECADES AND DECADES AGO, BUT IT HAS ROTTED FROM INSIDE AND OUT.
IT HAS MADE YOU FEEL HELPLESS, BECAUSE THERE IS NO REASONABLE WAY TO RESIST IT.

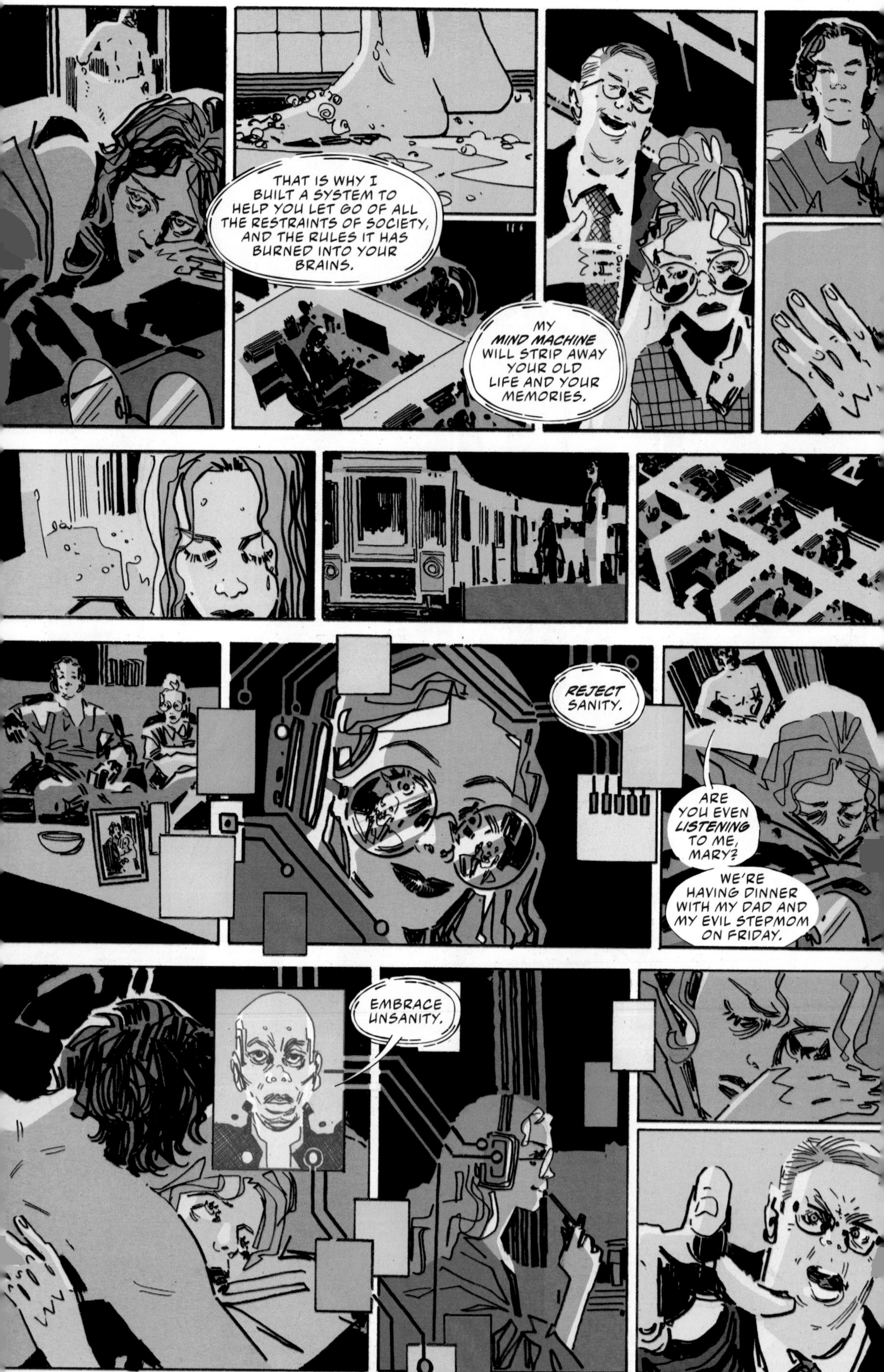
THAT IS WHY I BUILT A SYSTEM TO HELP YOU LET GO OF ALL THE RESTRAINTS OF SOCIETY, AND THE RULES IT HAS BURNED INTO YOUR BRAINS.
MY *MIND MACHINE* WILL STRIP AWAY YOUR OLD LIFE AND YOUR MEMORIES.
REJECT SANITY.
ARE YOU EVEN *LISTENING* TO ME, MARY?
WE'RE HAVING DINNER WITH MY DAD AND MY EVIL STEPMOM ON FRIDAY.
EMBRACE UNSANITY.

AND WITH THEM THE STRICTURES THAT HAVE KEPT YOU CONFORMED TO REALITY'S DEFINITION OF SANITY.

I AM INVITING ANYONE AND EVERYONE TO GO THROUGH THIS PROCESS AND JOIN MY COLLECTIVE.

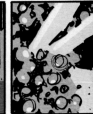

MAYBE YOU DON'T NEED TO STAY UP ALL NIGHT THURSDAY? IT'D BE NICE TO ACTUALLY HAVE YOU *PRESENT* AT THE DINNER.

YEAH...OF COURSE. I'M SORRY.

I'M SORRY, DID YOU SAY *KIDS?*

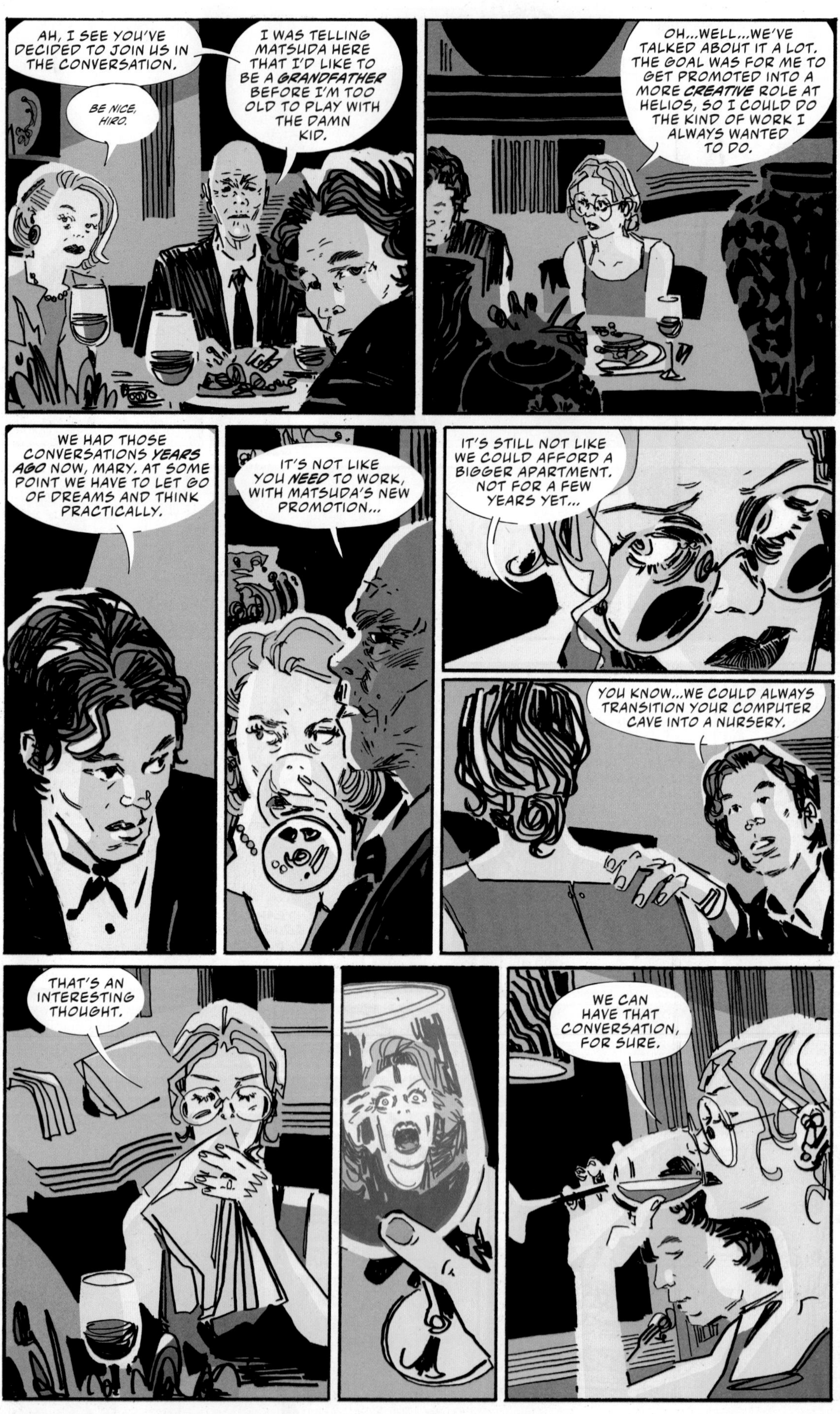
AH, I SEE YOU'VE DECIDED TO JOIN US IN THE CONVERSATION.
BE NICE, HIRO.
I WAS TELLING MATSUDA HERE THAT I'D LIKE TO BE A GRANDFATHER BEFORE I'M TOO OLD TO PLAY WITH THE DAMN KID.
OH...WELL...WE'VE TALKED ABOUT IT A LOT. THE GOAL WAS FOR ME TO GET PROMOTED INTO A MORE CREATIVE ROLE AT HELIOS, SO I COULD DO THE KIND OF WORK I ALWAYS WANTED TO DO.
WE HAD THOSE CONVERSATIONS YEARS AGO NOW, MARY. AT SOME POINT WE HAVE TO LET GO OF DREAMS AND THINK PRACTICALLY.
IT'S NOT LIKE YOU NEED TO WORK, WITH MATSUDA'S NEW PROMOTION...
IT'S STILL NOT LIKE WE COULD AFFORD A BIGGER APARTMENT. NOT FOR A FEW YEARS YET...
YOU KNOW...WE COULD ALWAYS TRANSITION YOUR COMPUTER CAVE INTO A NURSERY.
THAT'S AN INTERESTING THOUGHT.
WE CAN HAVE THAT CONVERSATION, FOR SURE.

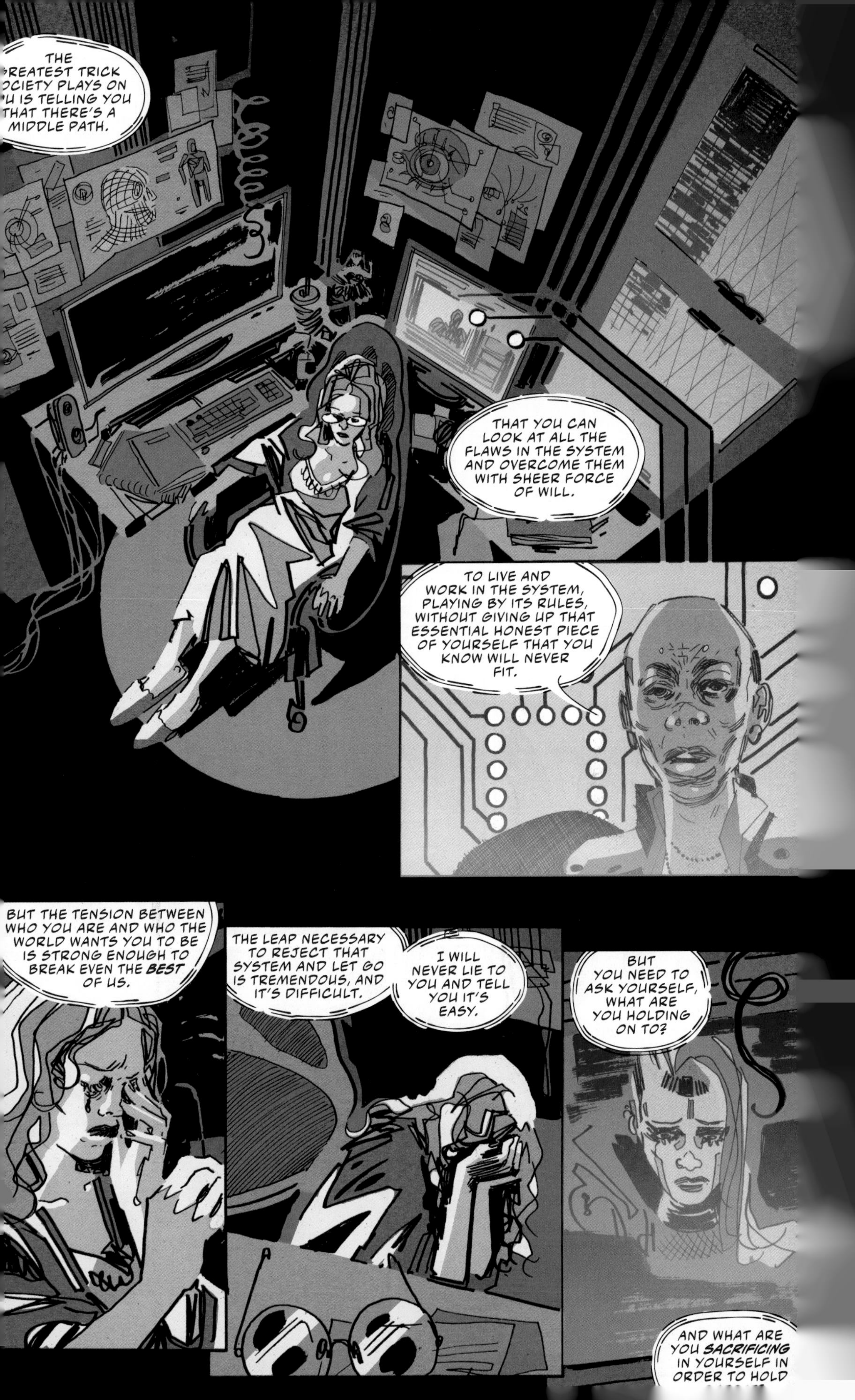
THE REATEST TRICK OCIETY PLAYS ON U IS TELLING YOU THAT THERE'S A MIDDLE PATH.
THAT YOU CAN LOOK AT ALL THE FLAWS IN THE SYSTEM AND OVERCOME THEM WITH SHEER FORCE OF WILL.
TO LIVE AND WORK IN THE SYSTEM, PLAYING BY ITS RULES, WITHOUT GIVING UP THAT ESSENTIAL HONEST PIECE OF YOURSELF THAT YOU KNOW WILL NEVER FIT.
BUT THE TENSION BETWEEN WHO YOU ARE AND WHO THE WORLD WANTS YOU TO BE IS STRONG ENOUGH TO BREAK EVEN THE *BEST* OF US.
THE LEAP NECESSARY TO REJECT THAT SYSTEM AND LET GO IS TREMENDOUS, AND IT'S DIFFICULT.
I WILL NEVER LIE TO YOU AND TELL YOU IT'S EASY.
BUT YOU NEED TO ASK YOURSELF, WHAT ARE YOU HOLDING ON TO?
AND WHAT ARE YOU *SACRIFICING* IN YOURSELF IN ORDER TO HOLD

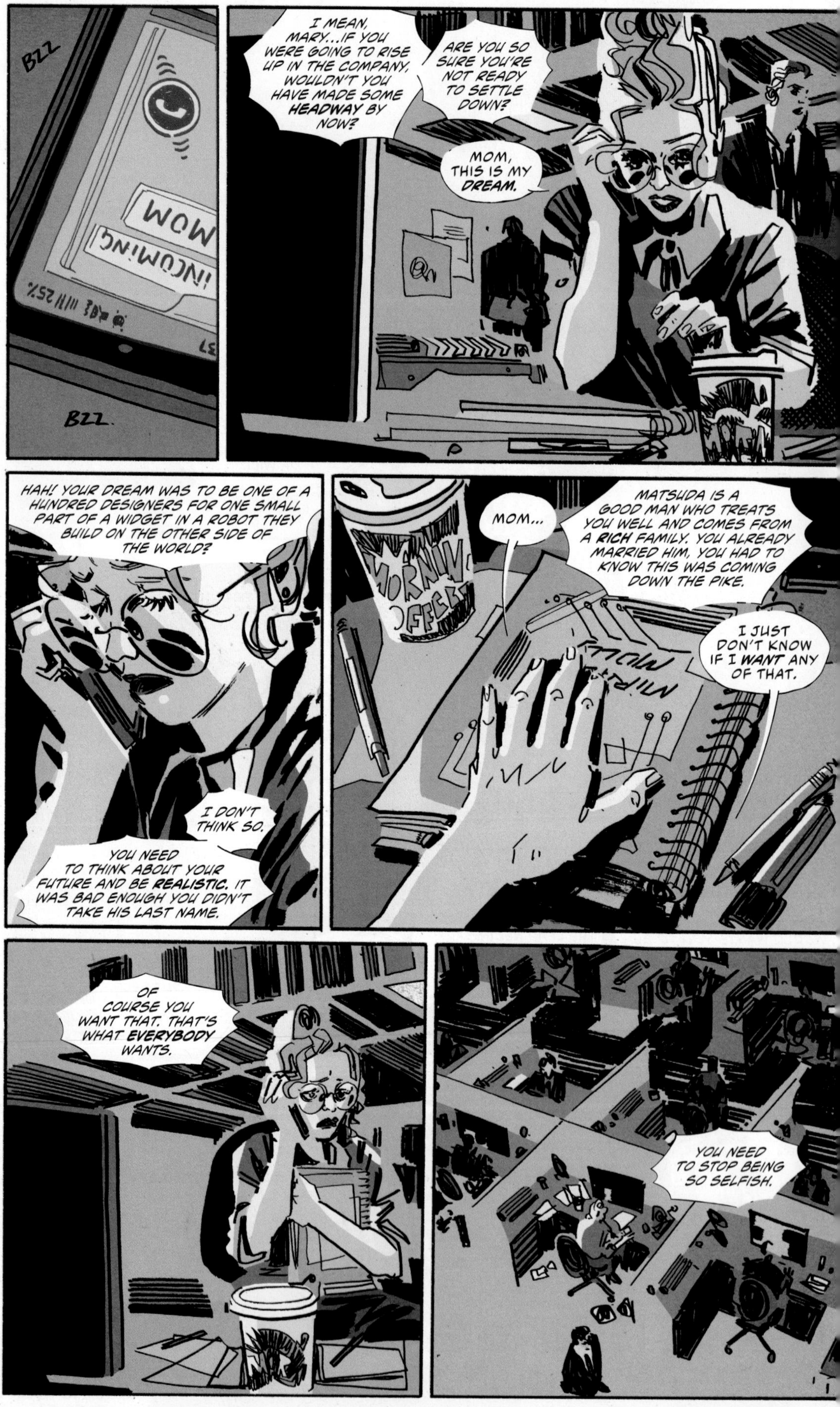
BZZ
INCOMING
MOM
BZZ
I MEAN, MARY...IF YOU WERE GOING TO RISE UP IN THE COMPANY, WOULDN'T YOU HAVE MADE SOME HEADWAY BY NOW?
ARE YOU SO SURE YOU'RE NOT READY TO SETTLE DOWN?
MOM, THIS IS MY DREAM.
HAH! YOUR DREAM WAS TO BE ONE OF A HUNDRED DESIGNERS FOR ONE SMALL PART OF A WIDGET IN A ROBOT THEY BUILD ON THE OTHER SIDE OF THE WORLD?
I DON'T THINK SO.
YOU NEED TO THINK ABOUT YOUR FUTURE AND BE REALISTIC. IT WAS BAD ENOUGH YOU DIDN'T TAKE HIS LAST NAME.
MOM...
MATSUDA IS A GOOD MAN WHO TREATS YOU WELL AND COMES FROM A RICH FAMILY. YOU ALREADY MARRIED HIM, YOU HAD TO KNOW THIS WAS COMING DOWN THE PIKE.
I JUST DON'T KNOW IF I WANT ANY OF THAT.
OF COURSE YOU WANT THAT. THAT'S WHAT EVERYBODY WANTS.
YOU NEED TO STOP BEING SO SELFISH.

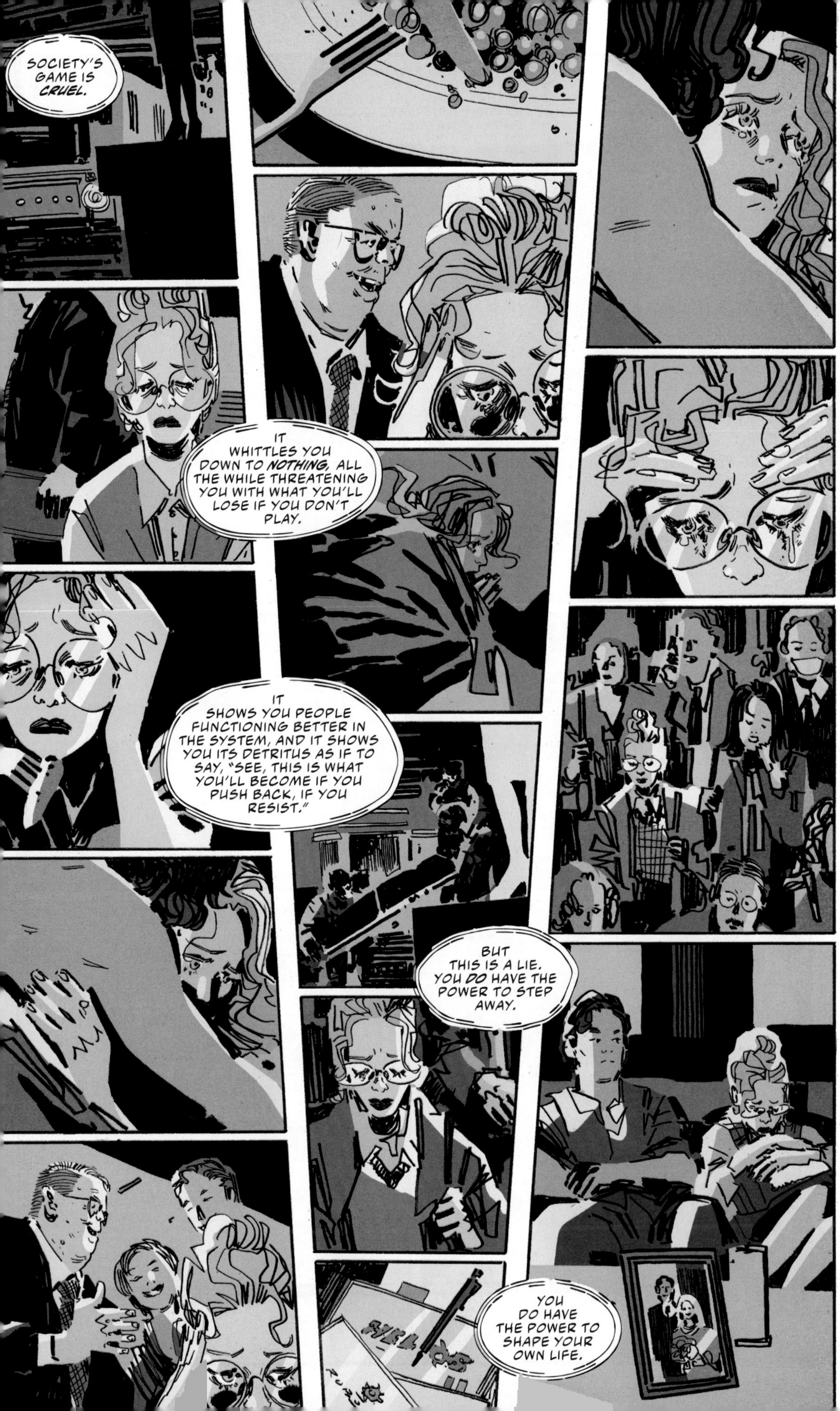
SOCIETY'S GAME IS CRUEL.
IT WHITTLES YOU DOWN TO NOTHING, ALL THE WHILE THREATENING YOU WITH WHAT YOU'LL LOSE IF YOU DON'T PLAY.
IT SHOWS YOU PEOPLE FUNCTIONING BETTER IN THE SYSTEM, AND IT SHOWS YOU ITS DETRITUS AS IF TO SAY, "SEE, THIS IS WHAT YOU'LL BECOME IF YOU PUSH BACK, IF YOU RESIST."
BUT THIS IS A LIE. YOU DO HAVE THE POWER TO STEP AWAY.
YOU DO HAVE THE POWER TO SHAPE YOUR OWN LIFE.

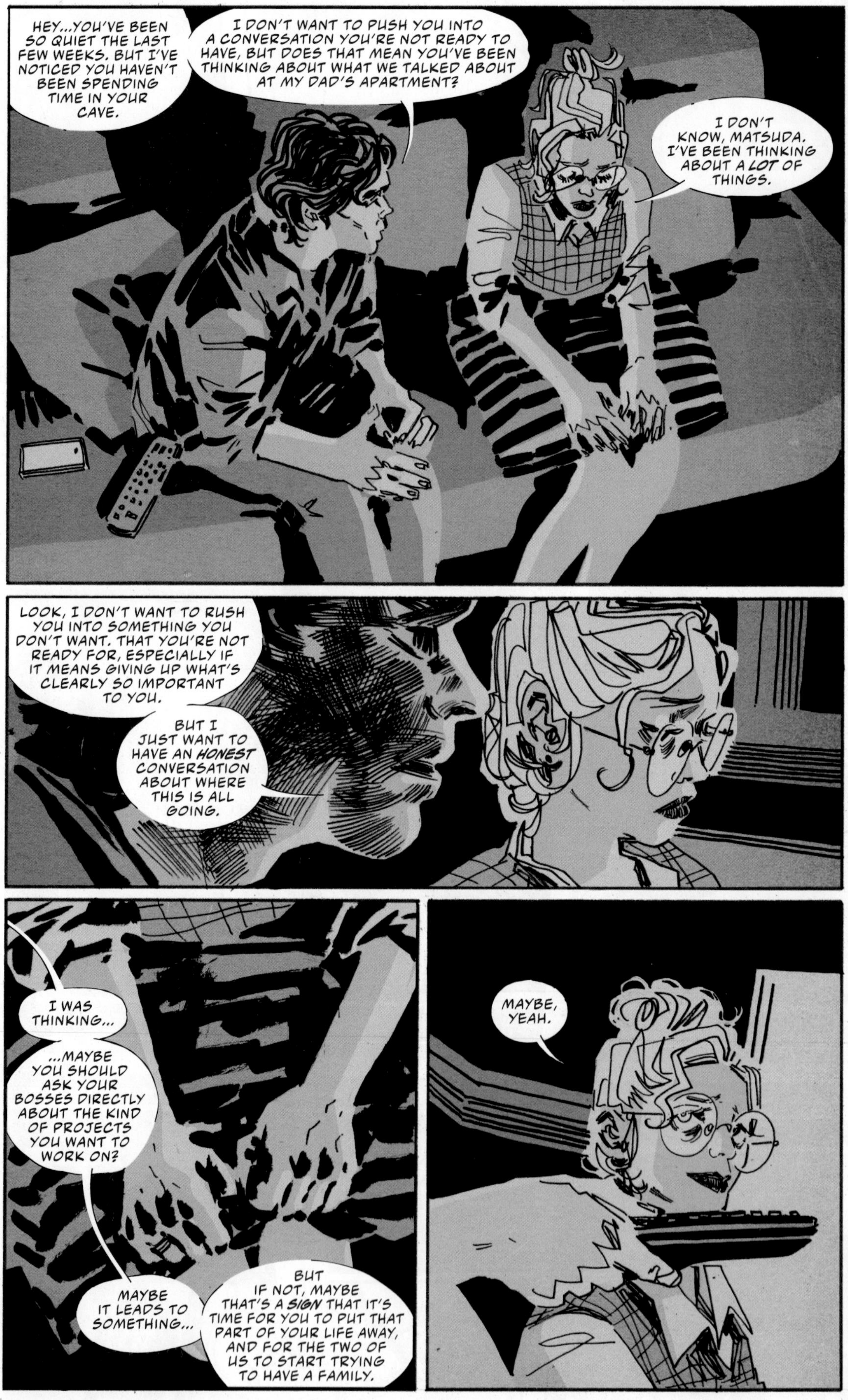
HEY...YOU'VE BEEN SO QUIET THE LAST FEW WEEKS. BUT I'VE NOTICED YOU HAVEN'T BEEN SPENDING TIME IN YOUR CAVE.
I DON'T WANT TO PUSH YOU INTO A CONVERSATION YOU'RE NOT READY TO HAVE, BUT DOES THAT MEAN YOU'VE BEEN THINKING ABOUT WHAT WE TALKED ABOUT AT MY DAD'S APARTMENT?
I DON'T KNOW, MATSUDA. I'VE BEEN THINKING ABOUT A *LOT* OF THINGS.
LOOK, I DON'T WANT TO RUSH YOU INTO SOMETHING YOU DON'T WANT. THAT YOU'RE NOT READY FOR, ESPECIALLY IF IT MEANS GIVING UP WHAT'S CLEARLY SO IMPORTANT TO YOU.
BUT I JUST WANT TO HAVE AN *HONEST* CONVERSATION ABOUT WHERE THIS IS ALL GOING.
I WAS THINKING...
...MAYBE YOU SHOULD ASK YOUR BOSSES DIRECTLY ABOUT THE KIND OF PROJECTS YOU WANT TO WORK ON?
MAYBE IT LEADS TO SOMETHING...
BUT IF NOT, MAYBE THAT'S A *SIGN* THAT IT'S TIME FOR YOU TO PUT THAT PART OF YOUR LIFE AWAY, AND FOR THE TWO OF US TO START TRYING TO HAVE A FAMILY.
MAYBE, YEAH.

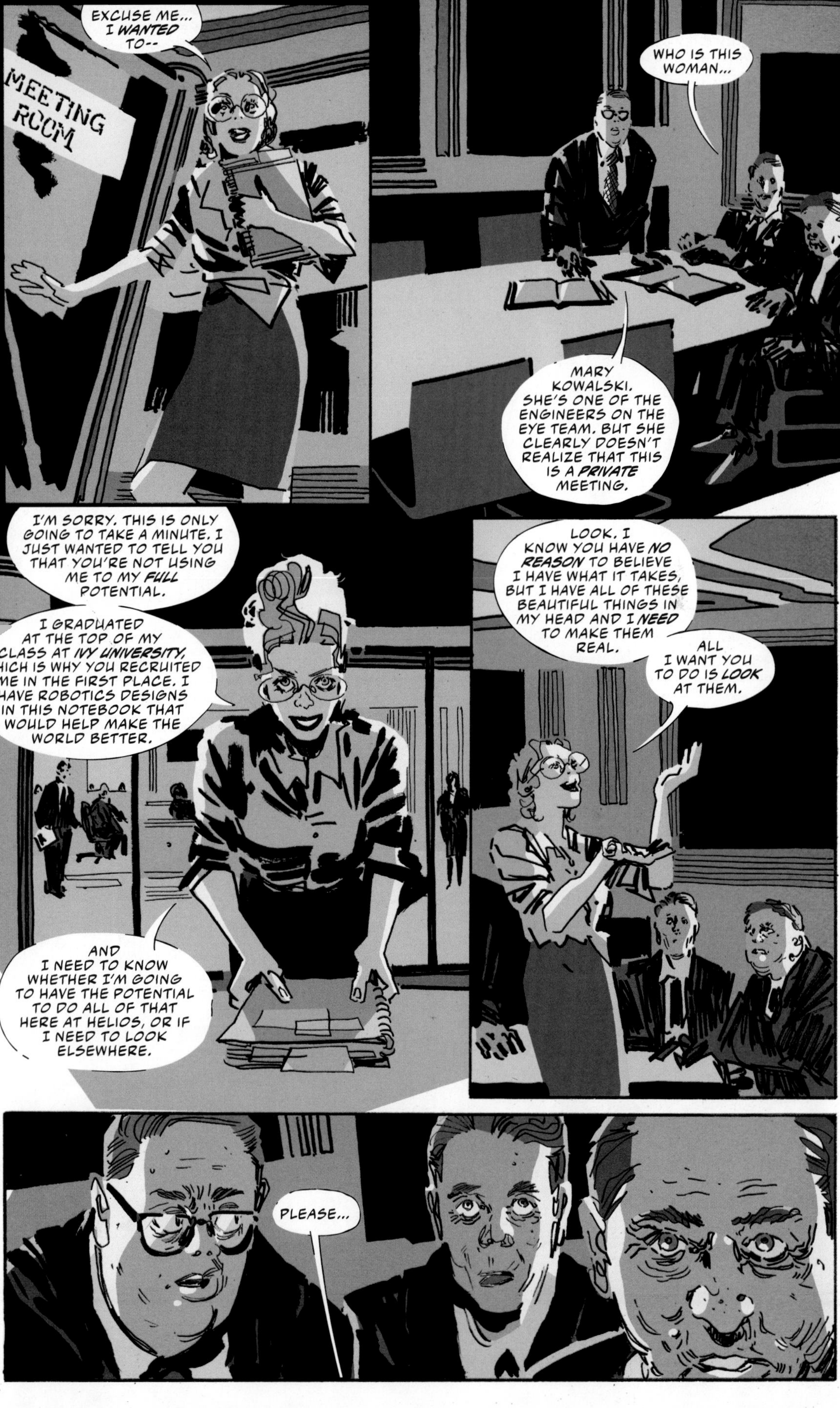
MEETING ROOM
EXCUSE ME... I WANTED TO--
WHO IS THIS WOMAN...
MARY KOWALSKI. SHE'S ONE OF THE ENGINEERS ON THE EYE TEAM. BUT SHE CLEARLY DOESN'T REALIZE THAT THIS IS A PRIVATE MEETING.
I'M SORRY. THIS IS ONLY GOING TO TAKE A MINUTE. I JUST WANTED TO TELL YOU THAT YOU'RE NOT USING ME TO MY FULL POTENTIAL.
I GRADUATED AT THE TOP OF MY CLASS AT IVY UNIVERSITY, WHICH IS WHY YOU RECRUITED ME IN THE FIRST PLACE. I HAVE ROBOTICS DESIGNS IN THIS NOTEBOOK THAT WOULD HELP MAKE THE WORLD BETTER.
AND I NEED TO KNOW WHETHER I'M GOING TO HAVE THE POTENTIAL TO DO ALL OF THAT HERE AT HELIOS, OR IF I NEED TO LOOK ELSEWHERE.
LOOK. I KNOW YOU HAVE NO REASON TO BELIEVE I HAVE WHAT IT TAKES, BUT I HAVE ALL OF THESE BEAUTIFUL THINGS IN MY HEAD AND I NEED TO MAKE THEM REAL.
ALL I WANT YOU TO DO IS LOOK AT THEM.
PLEASE...

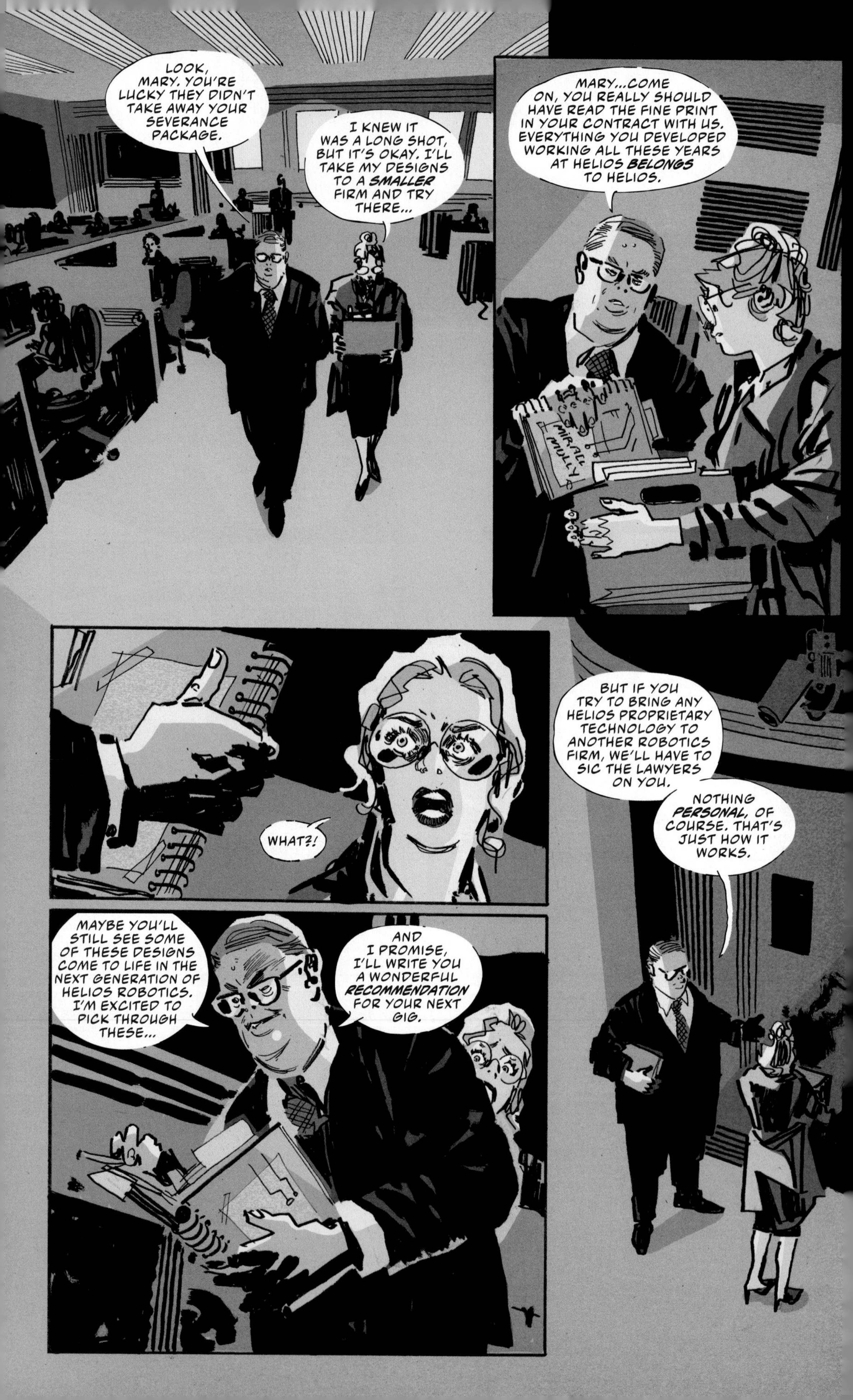
LOOK, MARY. YOU'RE LUCKY THEY DIDN'T TAKE AWAY YOUR SEVERANCE PACKAGE.
I KNEW IT WAS A LONG SHOT, BUT IT'S OKAY. I'LL TAKE MY DESIGNS TO A SMALLER FIRM AND TRY THERE...
MARY...COME ON, YOU REALLY SHOULD HAVE READ THE FINE PRINT IN YOUR CONTRACT WITH US. EVERYTHING YOU DEVELOPED WORKING ALL THESE YEARS AT HELIOS BELONGS TO HELIOS.
WHAT?!
BUT IF YOU TRY TO BRING ANY HELIOS PROPRIETARY TECHNOLOGY TO ANOTHER ROBOTICS FIRM, WE'LL HAVE TO SIC THE LAWYERS ON YOU.
NOTHING PERSONAL, OF COURSE. THAT'S JUST HOW IT WORKS.
MAYBE YOU'LL STILL SEE SOME OF THESE DESIGNS COME TO LIFE IN THE NEXT GENERATION OF HELIOS ROBOTICS. I'M EXCITED TO PICK THROUGH THESE...
AND I PROMISE, I'LL WRITE YOU A WONDERFUL RECOMMENDATION FOR YOUR NEXT GIG.

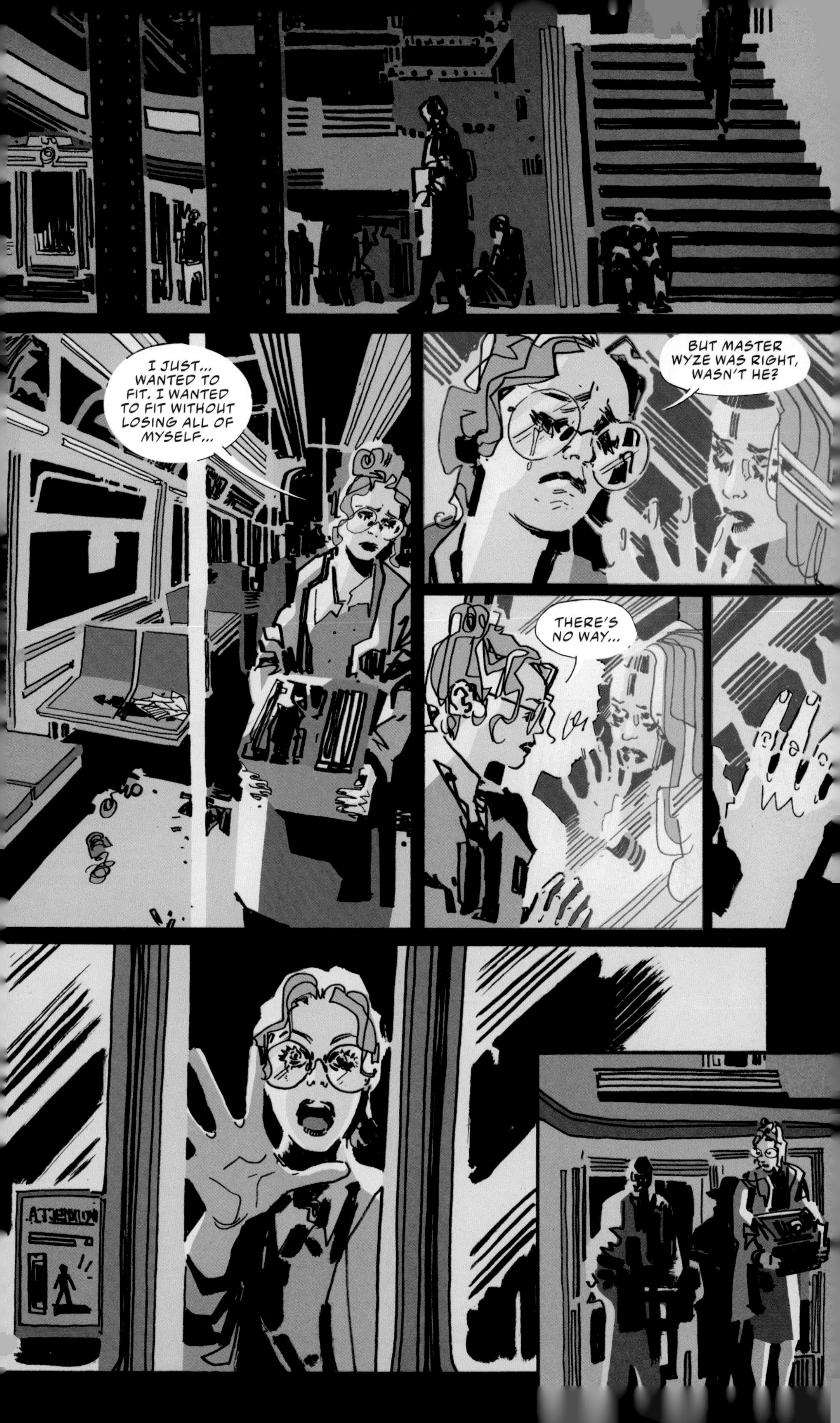
I JUST... WANTED TO FIT. I WANTED TO FIT WITHOUT LOSING ALL OF MYSELF...
BUT MASTER WYZE WAS RIGHT, WASN'T HE?
THERE'S NO WAY...

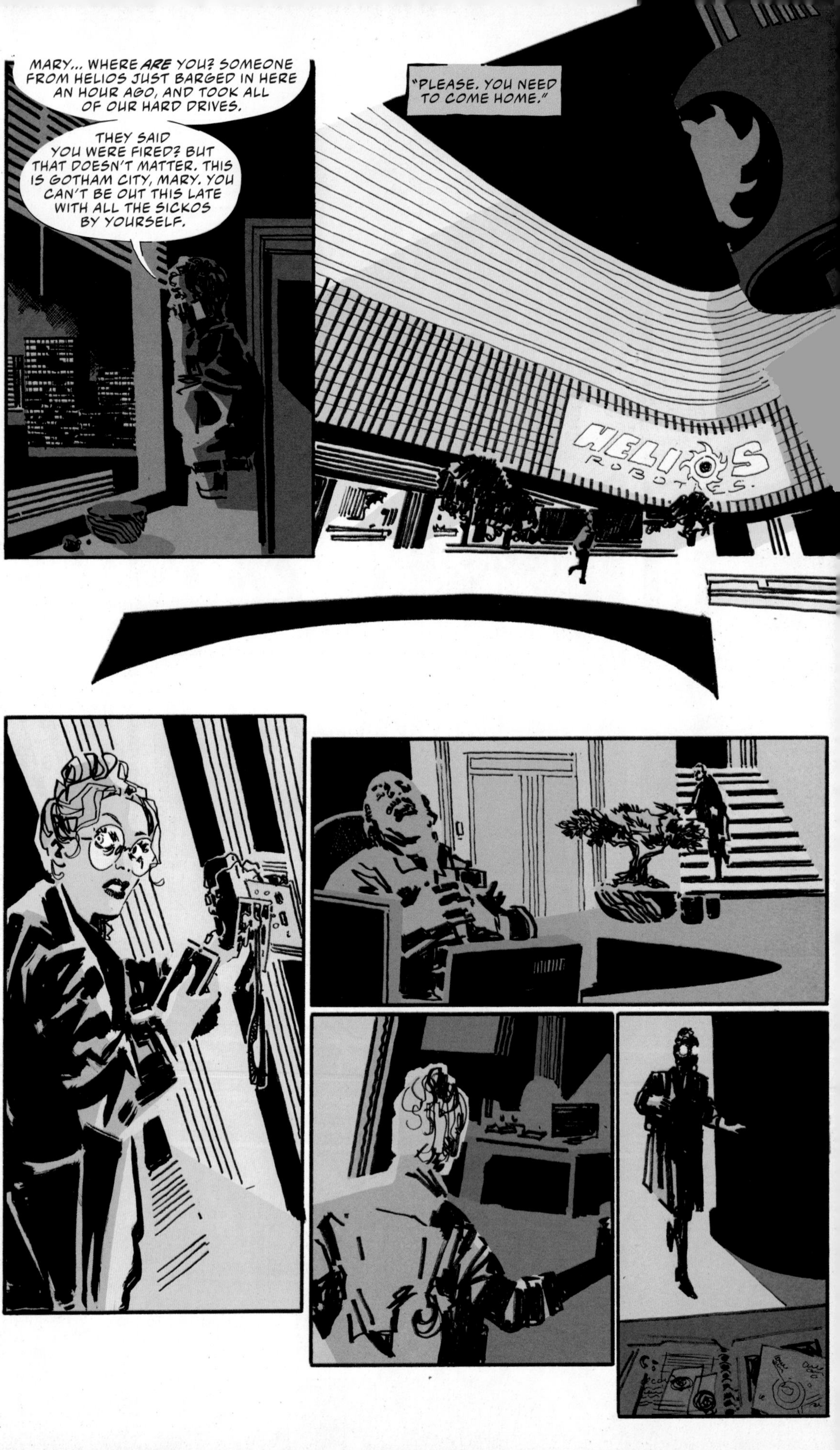
MARY... WHERE ARE YOU? SOMEONE FROM HELIOS JUST BARGED IN HERE AN HOUR AGO, AND TOOK ALL OF OUR HARD DRIVES.
THEY SAID YOU WERE FIRED? BUT THAT DOESN'T MATTER. THIS IS GOTHAM CITY, MARY. YOU CAN'T BE OUT THIS LATE WITH ALL THE SICKOS BY YOURSELF.
"PLEASE. YOU NEED TO COME HOME."
HELIOS ROBOTICS

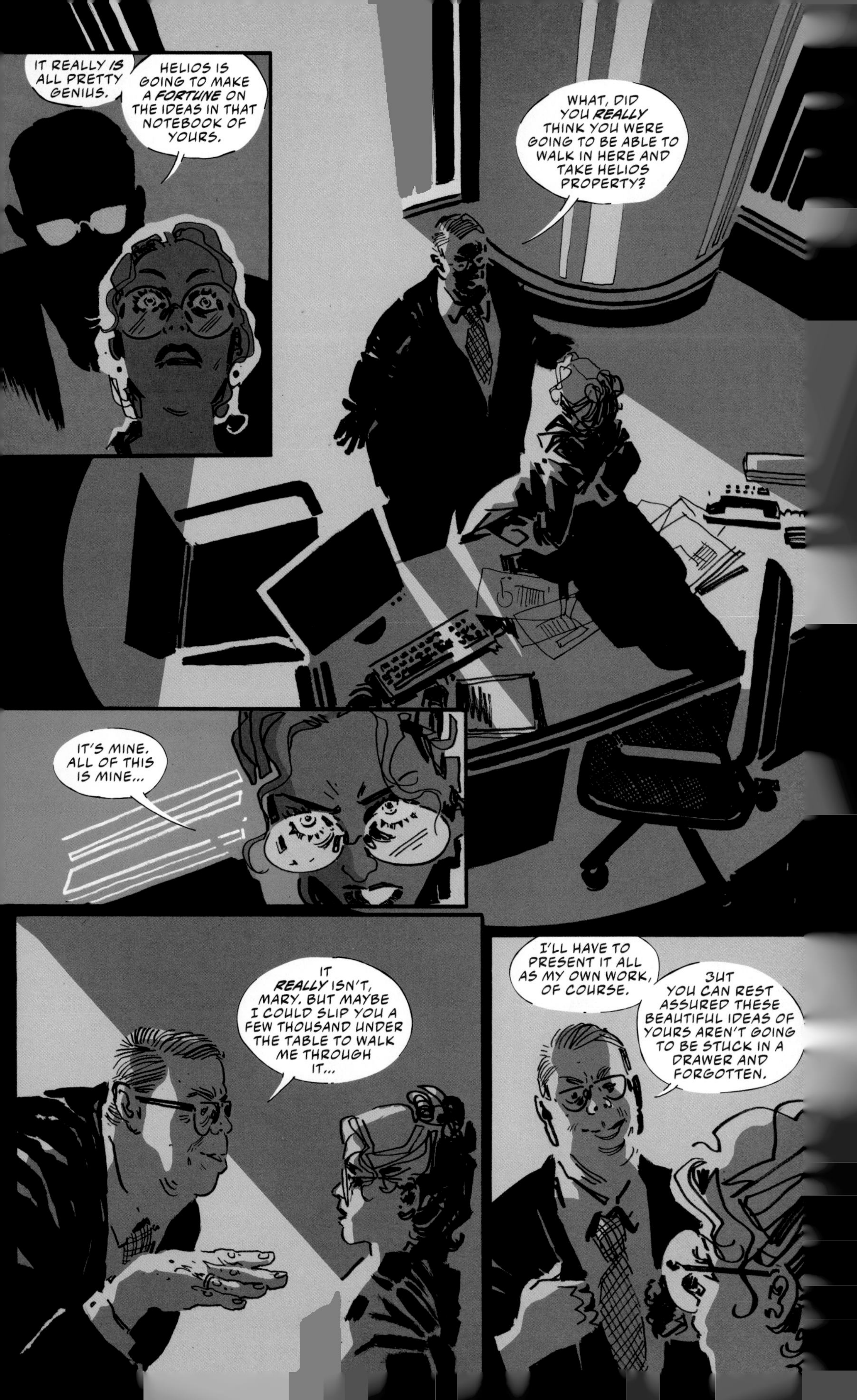
IT REALLY *IS* ALL PRETTY GENIUS.
HELIOS IS GOING TO MAKE A *FORTUNE* ON THE IDEAS IN THAT NOTEBOOK OF YOURS.
WHAT, DID YOU *REALLY* THINK YOU WERE GOING TO BE ABLE TO WALK IN HERE AND TAKE HELIOS PROPERTY?
IT'S MINE. ALL OF THIS IS MINE...
IT *REALLY* ISN'T, MARY. BUT MAYBE I COULD SLIP YOU A FEW THOUSAND UNDER THE TABLE TO WALK ME THROUGH IT...
I'LL HAVE TO PRESENT IT ALL AS MY OWN WORK, OF COURSE.
BUT YOU CAN REST ASSURED THESE BEAUTIFUL IDEAS OF YOURS AREN'T GOING TO BE STUCK IN A DRAWER AND FORGOTTEN.

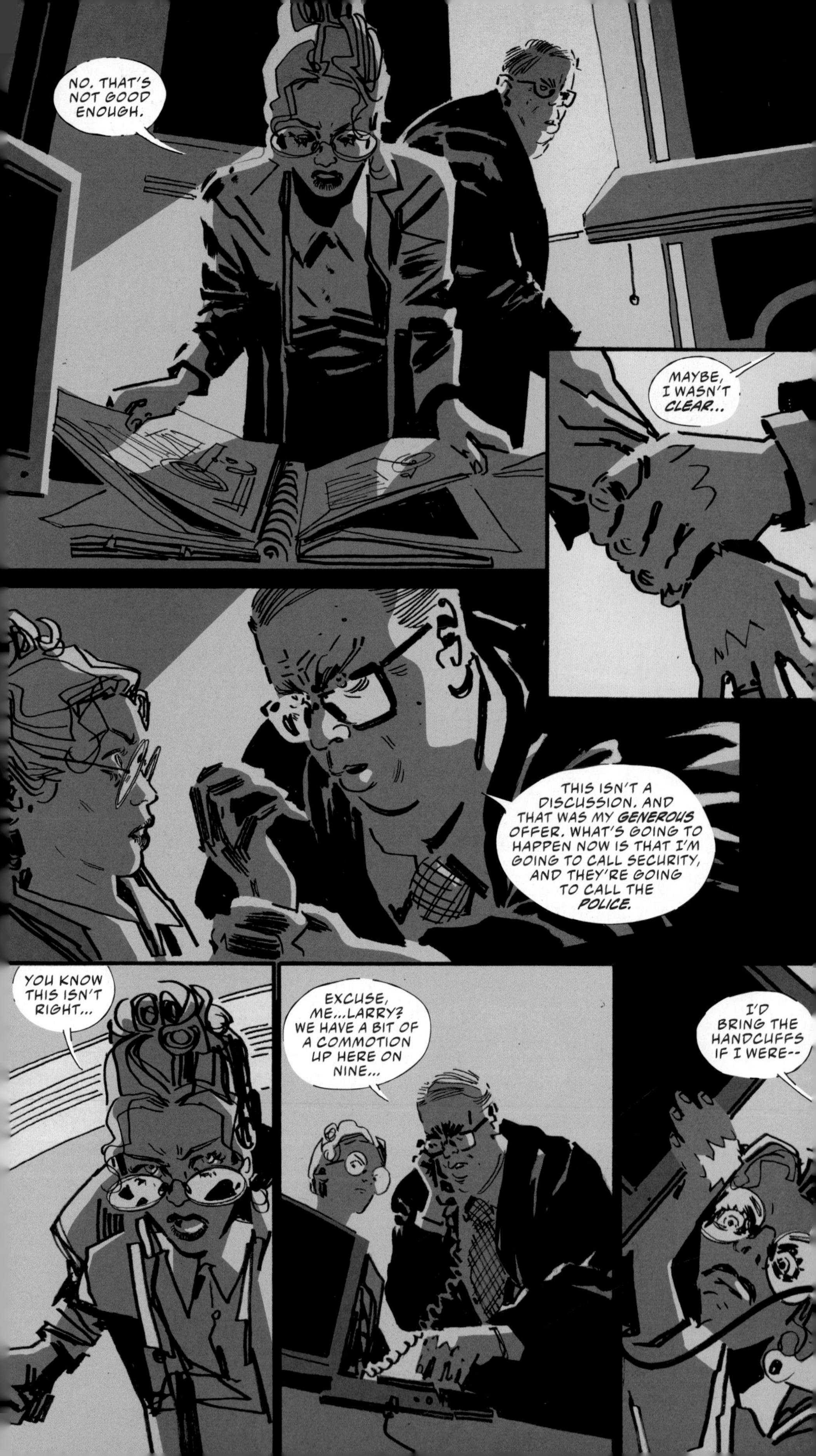
NO. THAT'S NOT GOOD ENOUGH.
MAYBE, I WASN'T CLEAR...
THIS ISN'T A DISCUSSION. AND THAT WAS MY GENEROUS OFFER. WHAT'S GOING TO HAPPEN NOW IS THAT I'M GOING TO CALL SECURITY, AND THEY'RE GOING TO CALL THE POLICE.
YOU KNOW THIS ISN'T RIGHT...
EXCUSE, ME...LARRY? WE HAVE A BIT OF A COMMOTION UP HERE ON NINE...
I'D BRING THE HANDCUFFS IF I WERE--

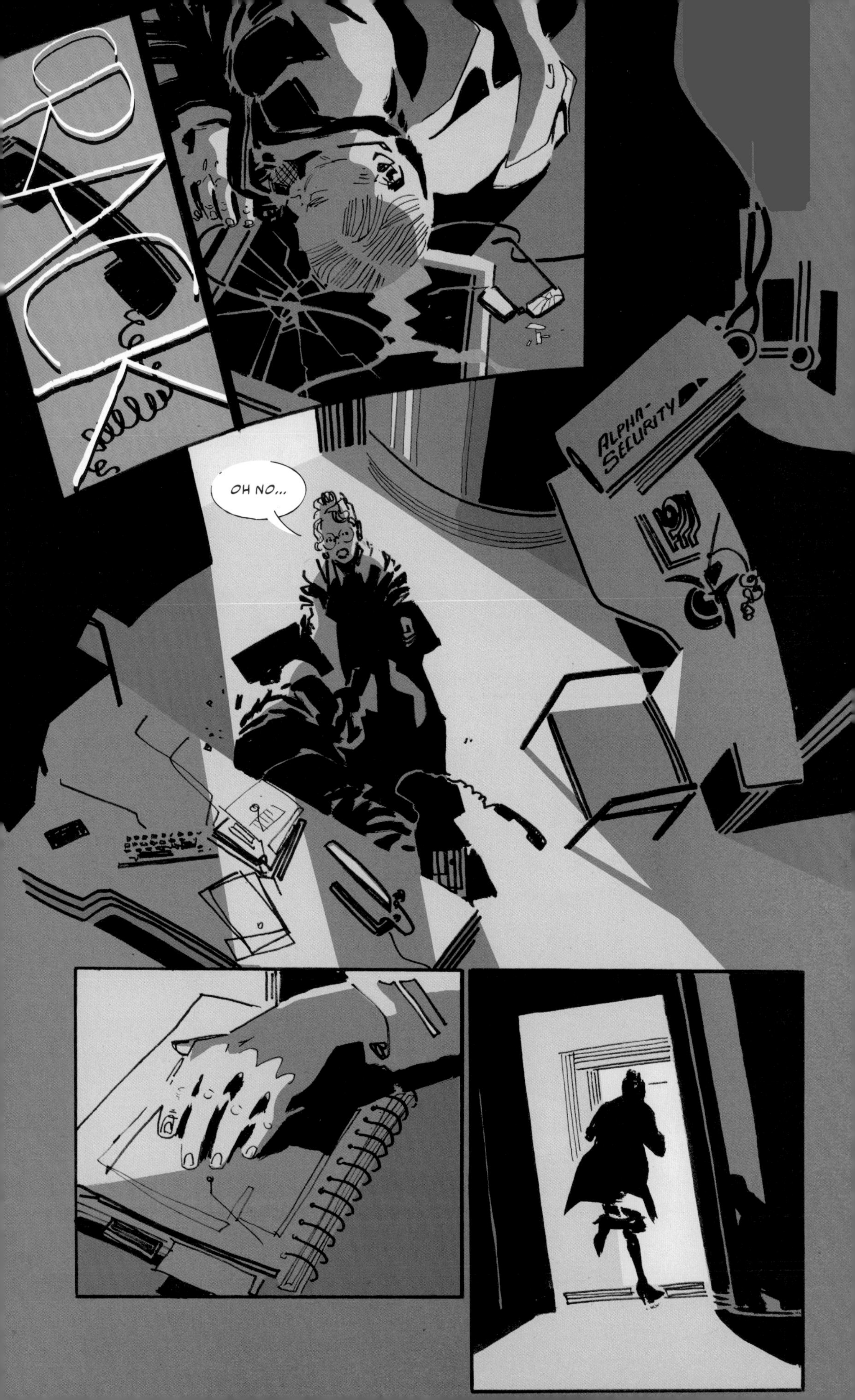
CRACK
OH NO...
ALPHA-SECURITY

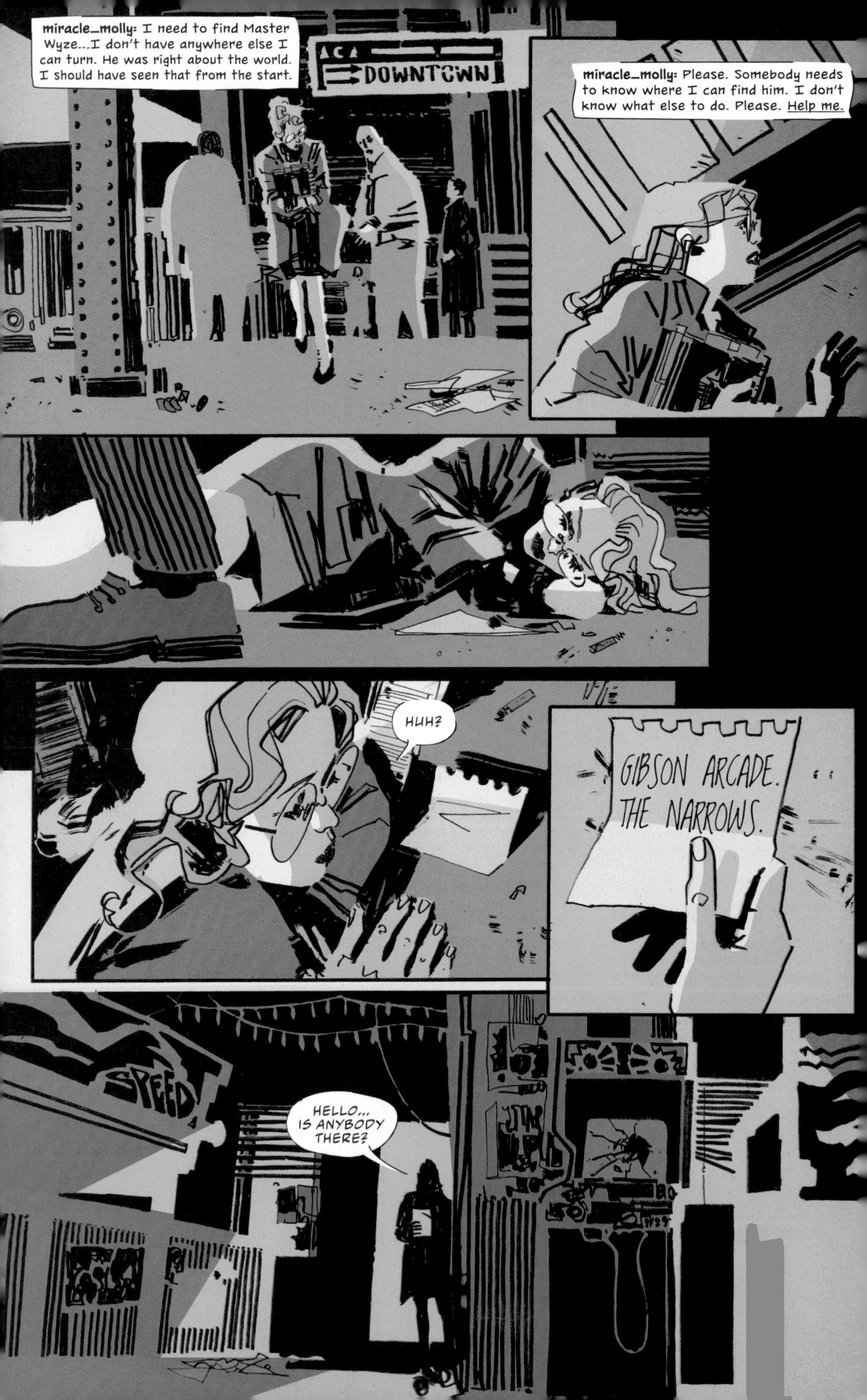
miracle_molly: I need to find Master Wyze...I don't have anywhere else I can turn. He was right about the world. I should have seen that from the start.
DOWNTOWN
miracle_molly: Please. Somebody needs to know where I can find him. I don't know what else to do. Please. Help me.
HUH?
GIBSON ARCADE. THE NARROWS.
SPEED!
HELLO... IS ANYBODY THERE?

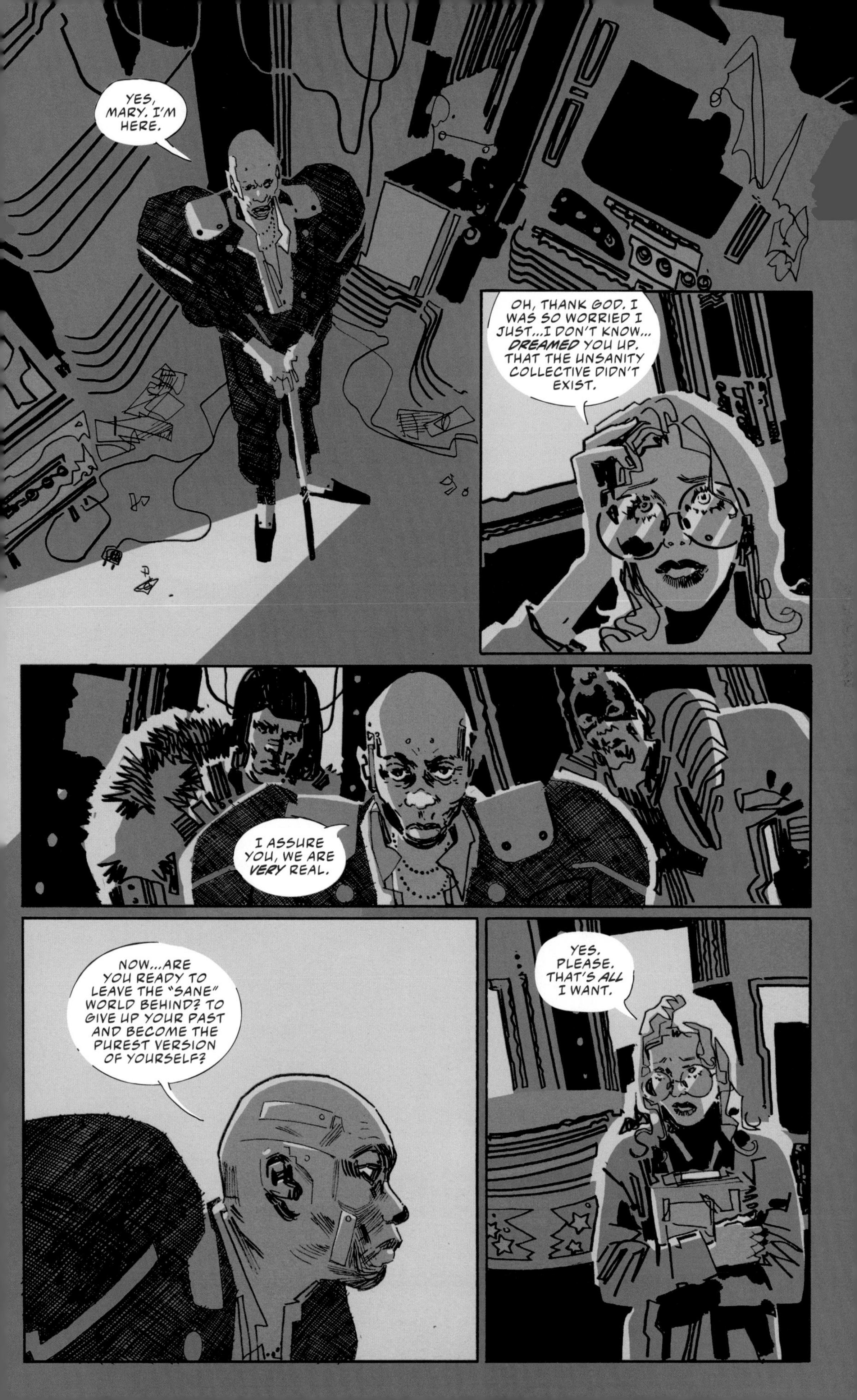
YES, MARY. I'M HERE.
OH, THANK GOD. I WAS SO WORRIED I JUST...I DON'T KNOW... *DREAMED* YOU UP. THAT THE UNSANITY COLLECTIVE DIDN'T EXIST.
I ASSURE YOU, WE ARE *VERY* REAL.
NOW...ARE YOU READY TO LEAVE THE "SANE" WORLD BEHIND? TO GIVE UP YOUR PAST AND BECOME THE PUREST VERSION OF YOURSELF?
YES. PLEASE. THAT'S *ALL* I WANT.

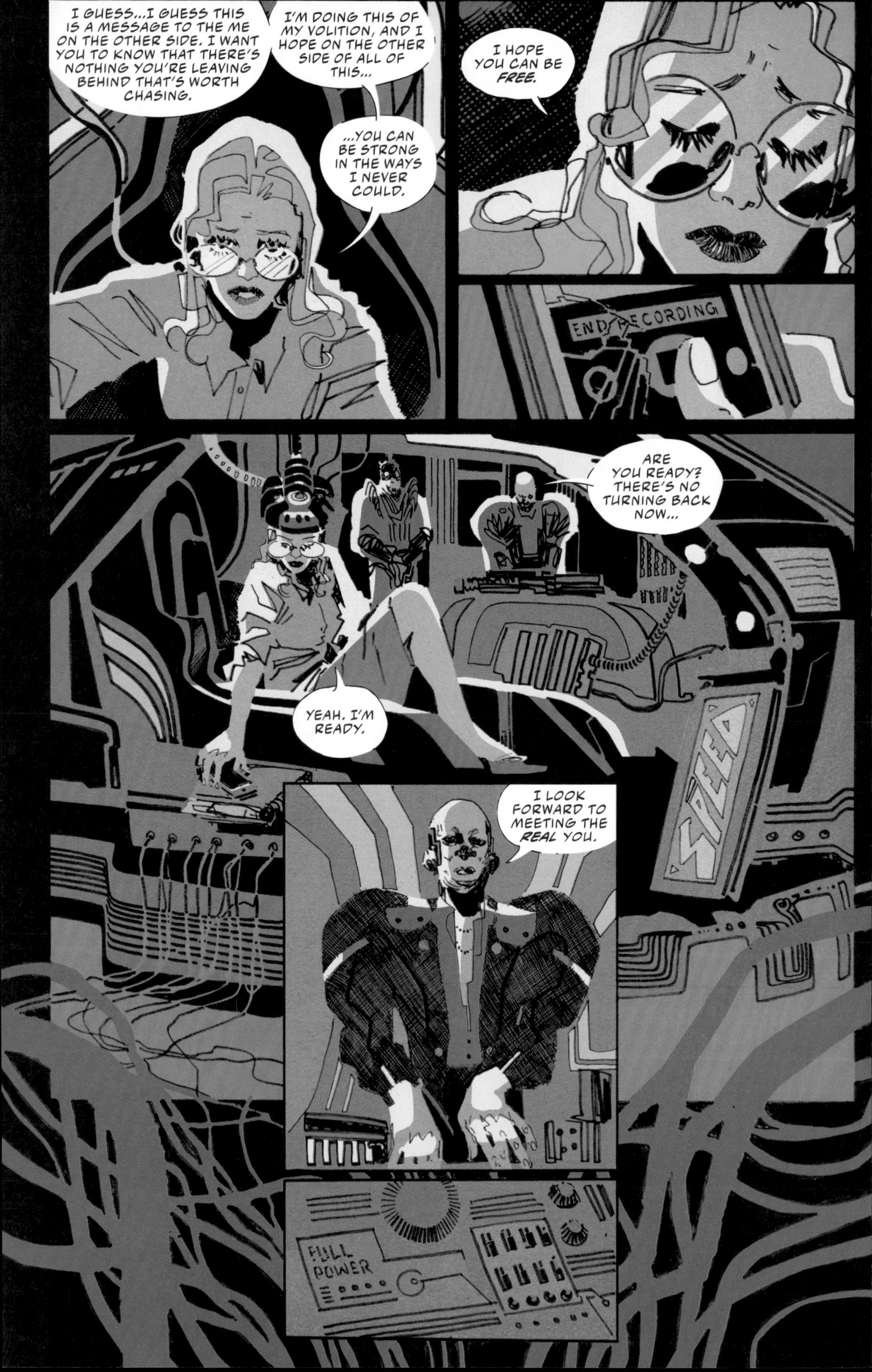
I GUESS...I GUESS THIS IS A MESSAGE TO THE ME ON THE OTHER SIDE. I WANT YOU TO KNOW THAT THERE'S NOTHING YOU'RE LEAVING BEHIND THAT'S WORTH CHASING.
I'M DOING THIS OF MY VOLITION, AND I HOPE ON THE OTHER SIDE OF ALL OF THIS...
...YOU CAN BE STRONG IN THE WAYS I NEVER COULD.
I HOPE YOU CAN BE FREE.
END RECORDING
ARE YOU READY? THERE'S NO TURNING BACK NOW...
YEAH. I'M READY.
SPEED
I LOOK FORWARD TO MEETING THE REAL YOU.
FULL POWER

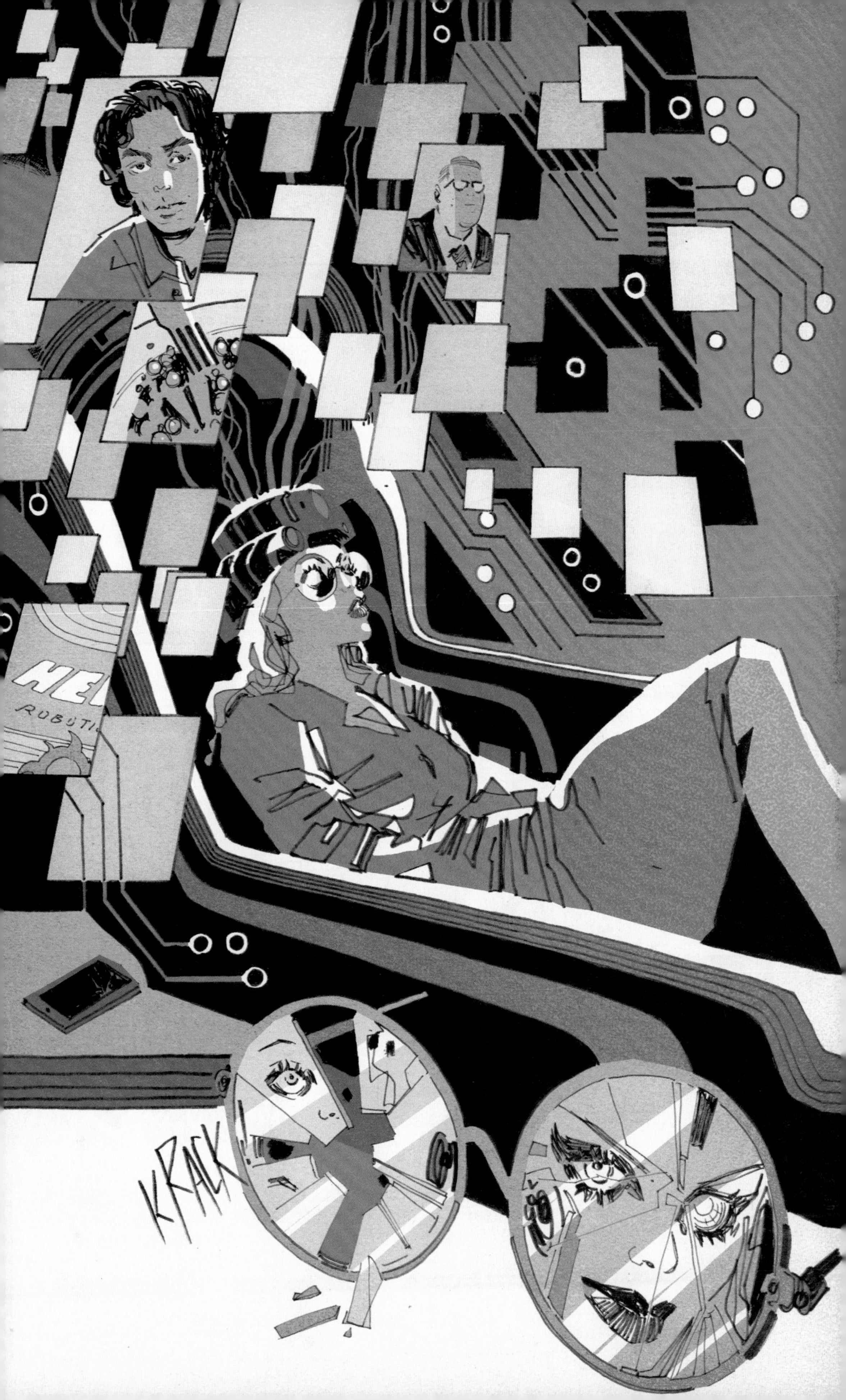
KRACK!

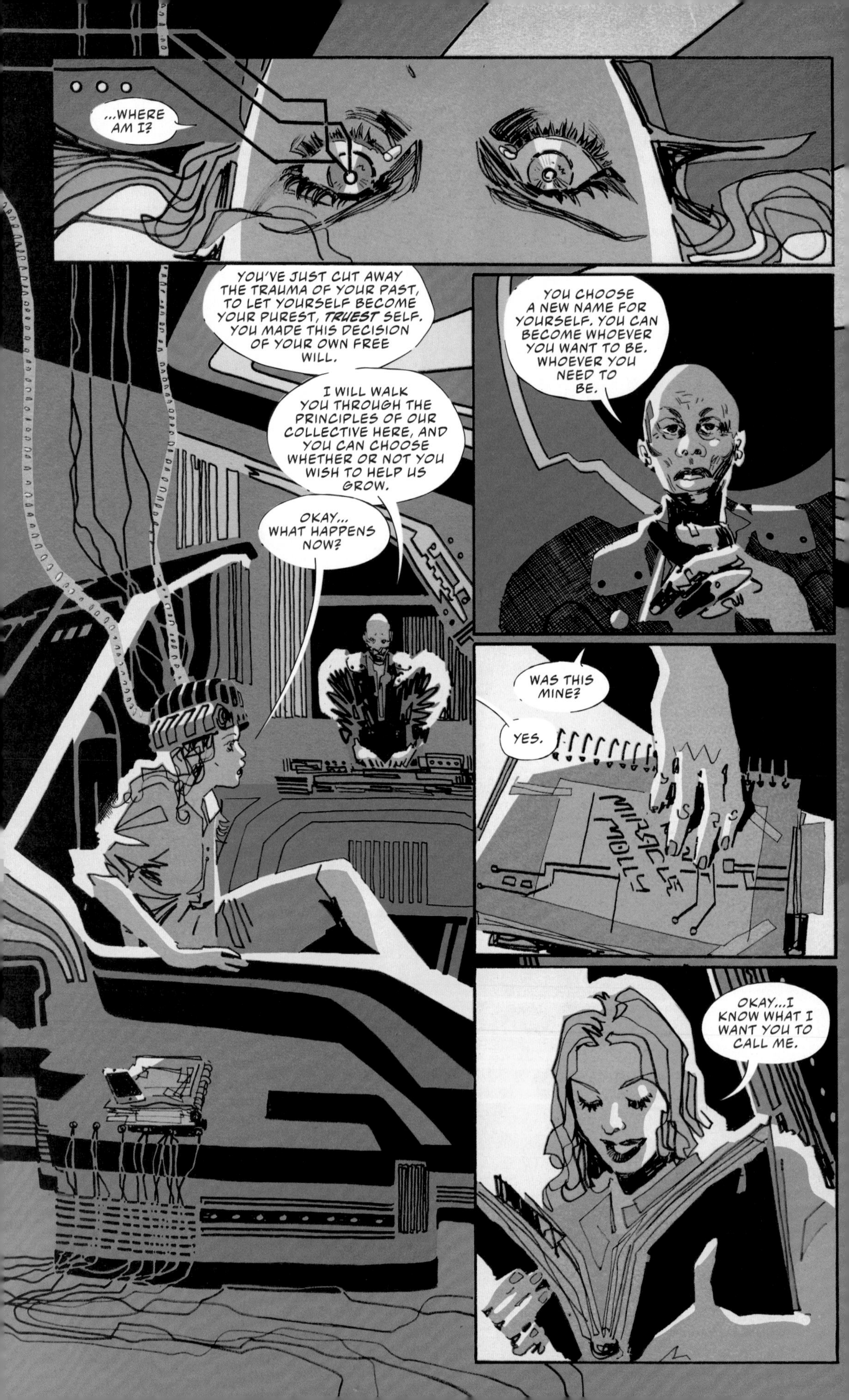
...WHERE AM I?
YOU'VE JUST CUT AWAY THE TRAUMA OF YOUR PAST, TO LET YOURSELF BECOME YOUR PUREST, TRUEST SELF. YOU MADE THIS DECISION OF YOUR OWN FREE WILL.
I WILL WALK YOU THROUGH THE PRINCIPLES OF OUR COLLECTIVE HERE, AND YOU CAN CHOOSE WHETHER OR NOT YOU WISH TO HELP US GROW.
OKAY... WHAT HAPPENS NOW?
YOU CHOOSE A NEW NAME FOR YOURSELF. YOU CAN BECOME WHOEVER YOU WANT TO BE. WHOEVER YOU NEED TO BE.
WAS THIS MINE?
YES.
OKAY...I KNOW WHAT I WANT YOU TO CALL ME.

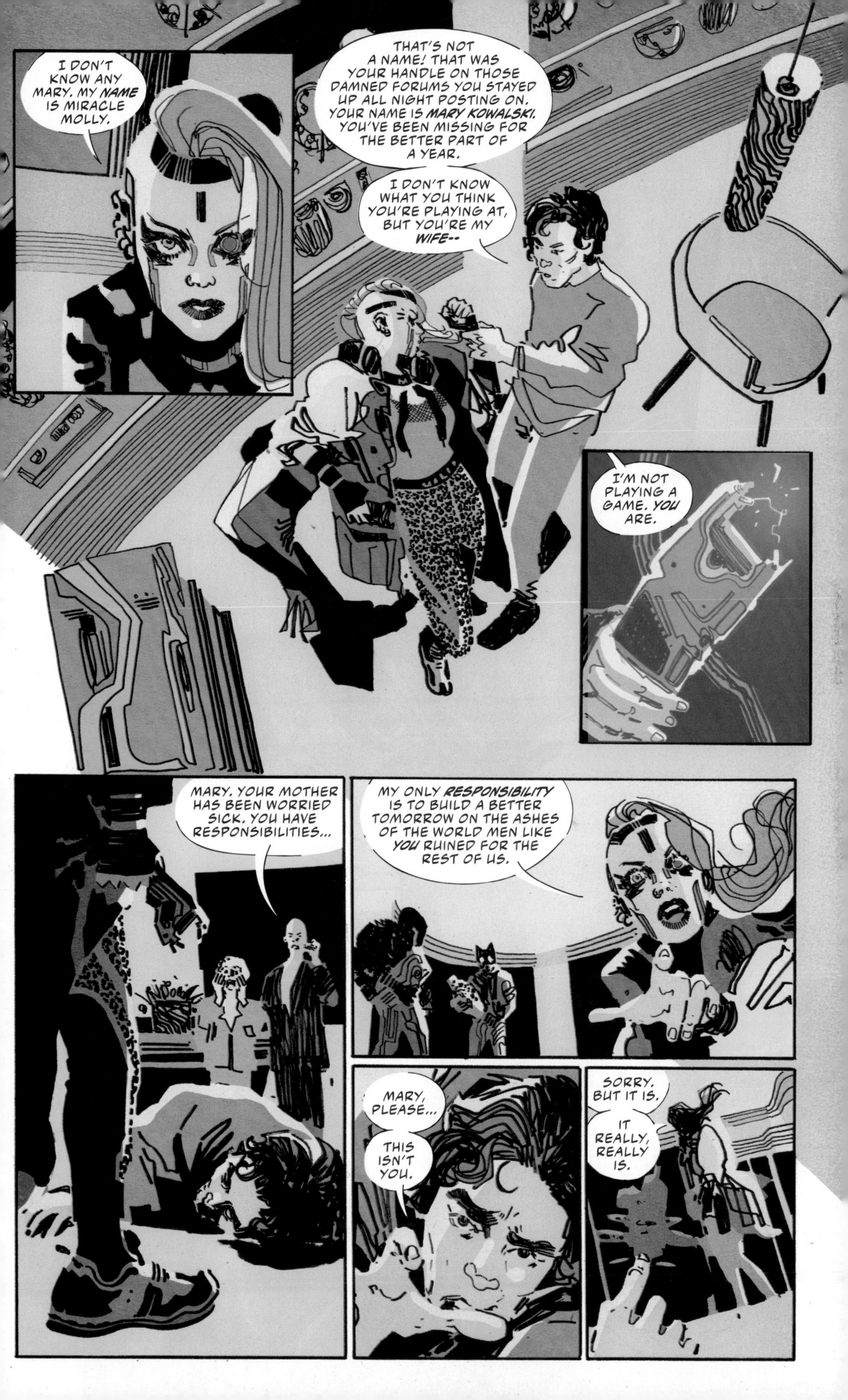
I DON'T KNOW ANY MARY. MY NAME IS MIRACLE MOLLY.
THAT'S NOT A NAME! THAT WAS YOUR HANDLE ON THOSE DAMNED FORUMS YOU STAYED UP ALL NIGHT POSTING ON. YOUR NAME IS MARY KOWALSKI. YOU'VE BEEN MISSING FOR THE BETTER PART OF A YEAR.
I DON'T KNOW WHAT YOU THINK YOU'RE PLAYING AT, BUT YOU'RE MY WIFE--
I'M NOT PLAYING A GAME. YOU ARE.
MARY. YOUR MOTHER HAS BEEN WORRIED SICK. YOU HAVE RESPONSIBILITIES...
MY ONLY RESPONSIBILITY IS TO BUILD A BETTER TOMORROW ON THE ASHES OF THE WORLD MEN LIKE YOU RUINED FOR THE REST OF US.
MARY, PLEASE...
THIS ISN'T YOU.
SORRY. BUT IT IS.
IT REALLY, REALLY IS.

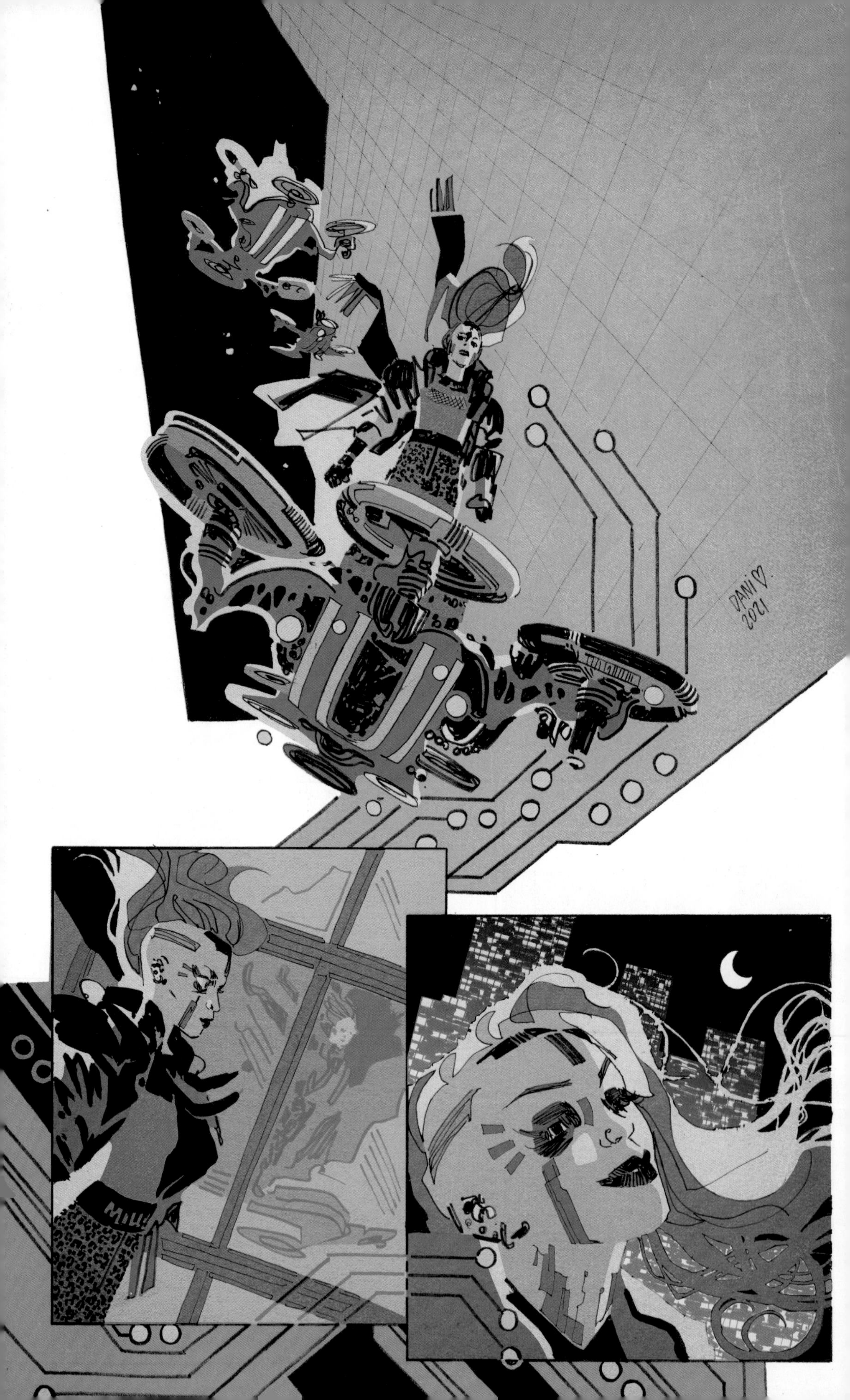
DANI
2021

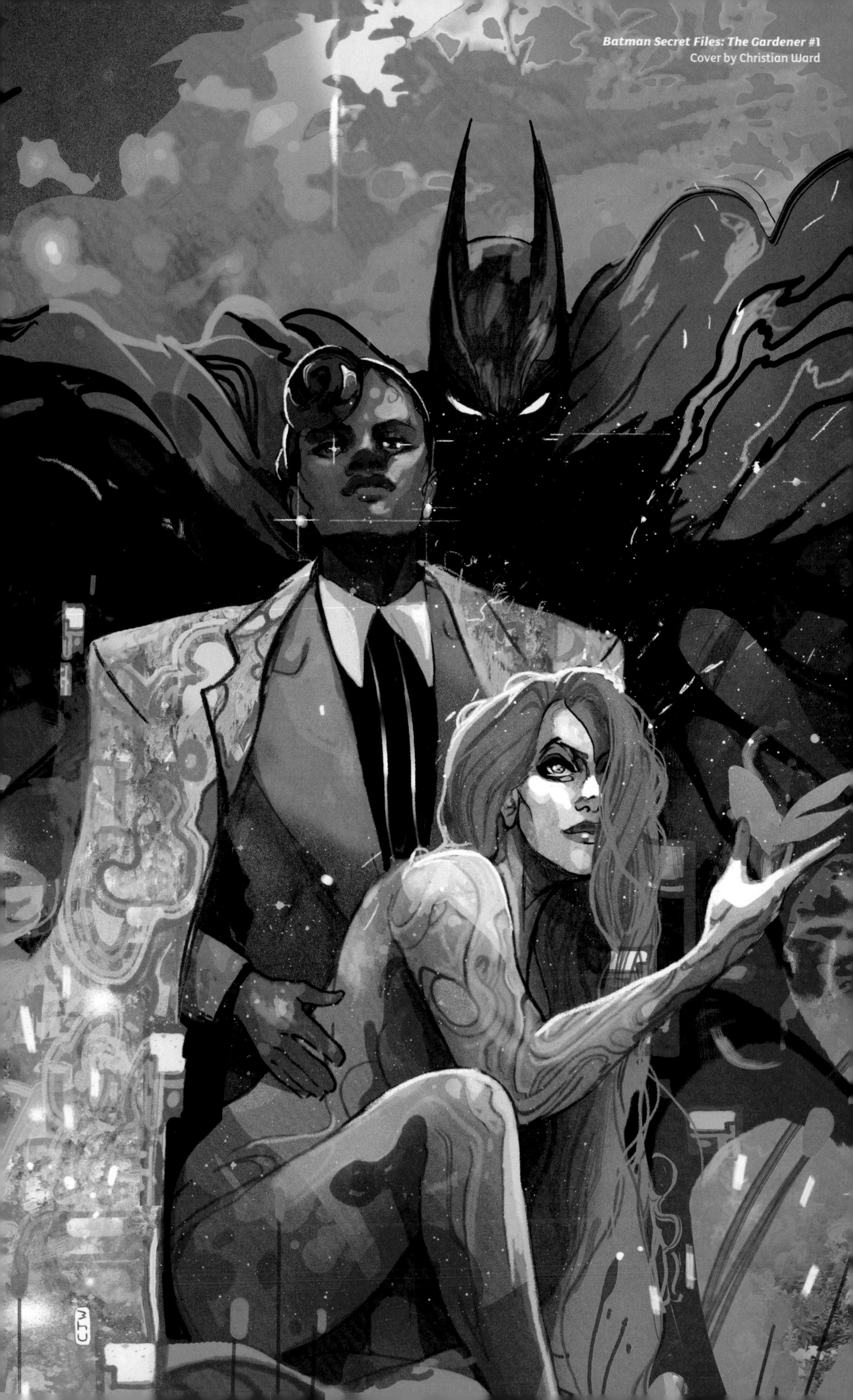
CTW

Batman Secret Files: The Gardener #1
Cover by Christian Ward

Batman Secret Files:
The Gardener

Written by
James Tynion IV

Drawn by
Christian Ward

Colored by
Christian Ward

Lettered by
Tom Napolitano

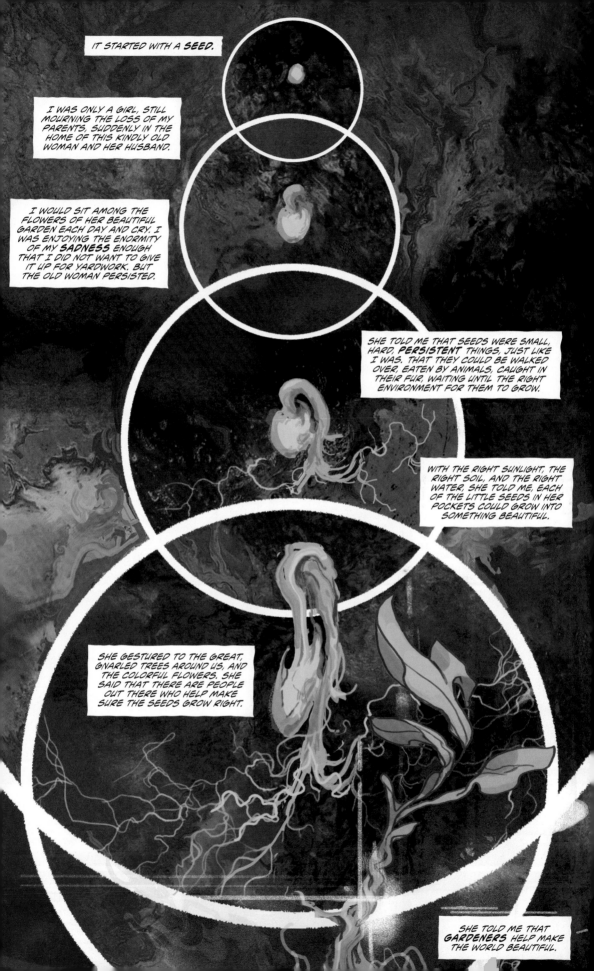

IT STARTED WITH A **SEED.**

I WAS ONLY A GIRL, STILL MOURNING THE LOSS OF MY PARENTS, SUDDENLY IN THE HOME OF THIS KINDLY OLD WOMAN AND HER HUSBAND.

I WOULD SIT AMONG THE FLOWERS OF HER BEAUTIFUL GARDEN EACH DAY AND CRY. I WAS ENJOYING THE ENORMITY OF MY **SADNESS** ENOUGH THAT I DID NOT WANT TO GIVE IT UP FOR YARDWORK. BUT THE OLD WOMAN PERSISTED.

SHE TOLD ME THAT SEEDS WERE SMALL, HARD, **PERSISTENT** THINGS, JUST LIKE I WAS. THAT THEY COULD BE WALKED OVER, EATEN BY ANIMALS, CAUGHT IN THEIR FUR, WAITING UNTIL THE RIGHT ENVIRONMENT FOR THEM TO GROW.

WITH THE RIGHT SUNLIGHT, THE RIGHT SOIL, AND THE RIGHT WATER, SHE TOLD ME, EACH OF THE LITTLE SEEDS IN HER POCKETS COULD GROW INTO SOMETHING BEAUTIFUL.

SHE GESTURED TO THE GREAT, GNARLED TREES AROUND US, AND THE COLORFUL FLOWERS. SHE SAID THAT THERE ARE PEOPLE OUT THERE WHO HELP MAKE SURE THE SEEDS GROW RIGHT.

SHE TOLD ME THAT **GARDENERS** HELP MAKE THE WORLD BEAUTIFUL.

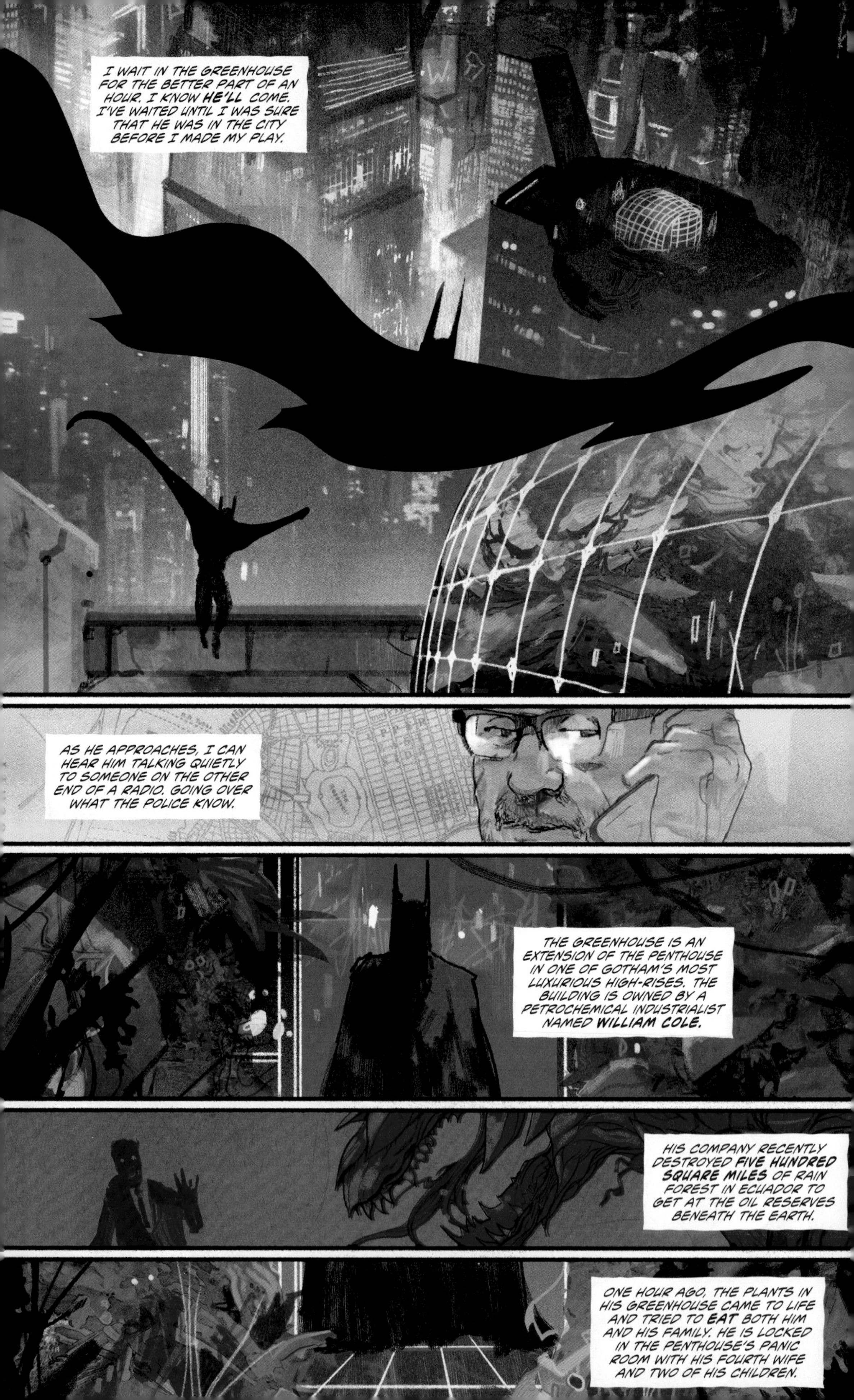
I WAIT IN THE GREENHOUSE FOR THE BETTER PART OF AN HOUR. I KNOW **HE'LL** COME. I'VE WAITED UNTIL I WAS SURE THAT HE WAS IN THE CITY BEFORE I MADE MY PLAY.
AS HE APPROACHES, I CAN HEAR HIM TALKING QUIETLY TO SOMEONE ON THE OTHER END OF A RADIO. GOING OVER WHAT THE POLICE KNOW.
THE GREENHOUSE IS AN EXTENSION OF THE PENTHOUSE IN ONE OF GOTHAM'S MOST LUXURIOUS HIGH-RISES. THE BUILDING IS OWNED BY A PETROCHEMICAL INDUSTRIALIST NAMED **WILLIAM COLE.**
HIS COMPANY RECENTLY DESTROYED **FIVE HUNDRED SQUARE MILES** OF RAIN FOREST IN ECUADOR TO GET AT THE OIL RESERVES BENEATH THE EARTH.
ONE HOUR AGO, THE PLANTS IN HIS GREENHOUSE CAME TO LIFE AND TRIED TO **EAT** BOTH HIM AND HIS FAMILY. HE IS LOCKED IN THE PENTHOUSE'S PANIC ROOM WITH HIS FOURTH WIFE AND TWO OF HIS CHILDREN.

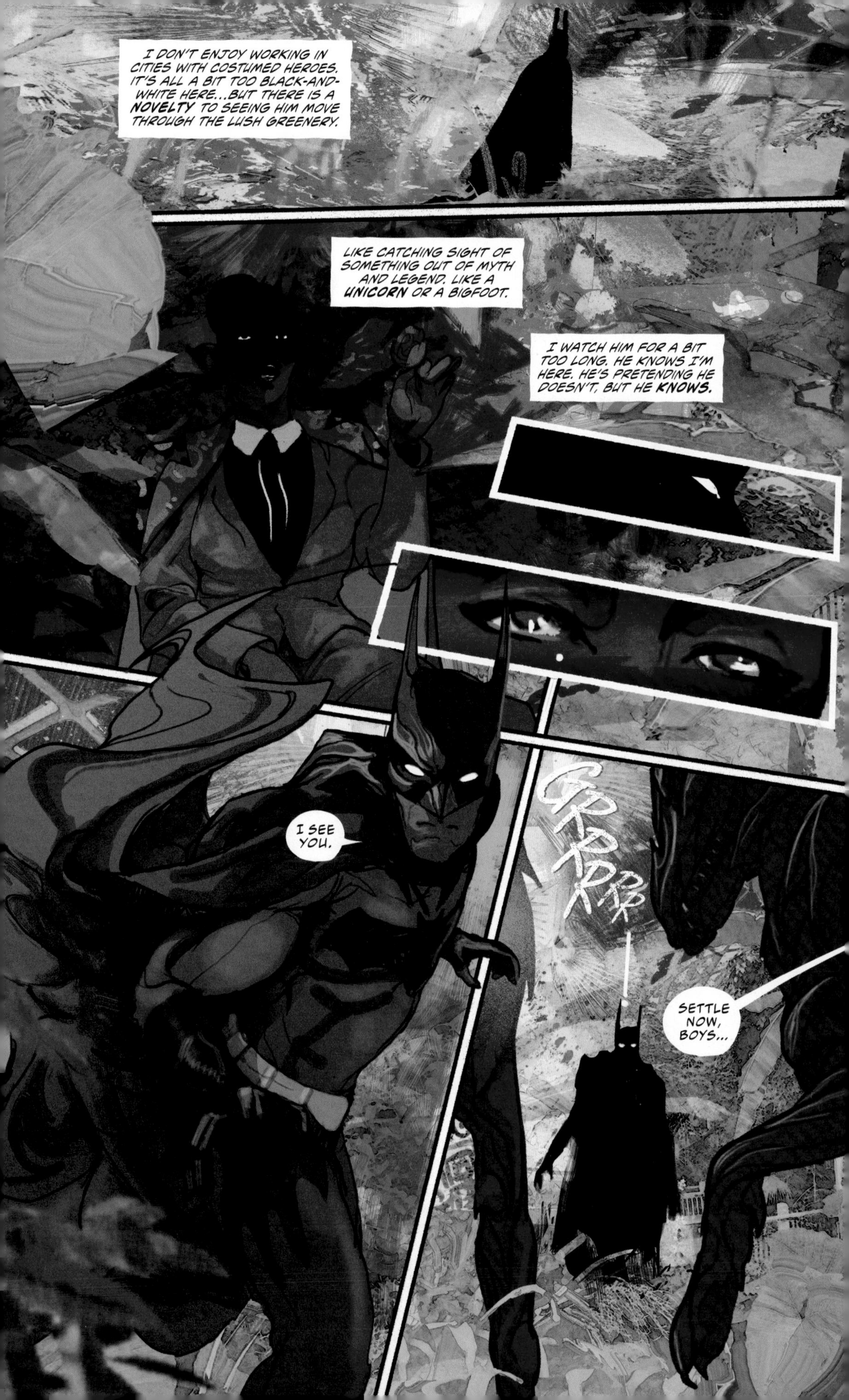

I DON'T ENJOY WORKING IN CITIES WITH COSTUMED HEROES. IT'S ALL A BIT TOO BLACK-AND-WHITE HERE...BUT THERE IS A **NOVELTY** TO SEEING HIM MOVE THROUGH THE LUSH GREENERY.
LIKE CATCHING SIGHT OF SOMETHING OUT OF MYTH AND LEGEND. LIKE A **UNICORN** OR A BIGFOOT.
I WATCH HIM FOR A BIT TOO LONG. HE KNOWS I'M HERE. HE'S PRETENDING HE DOESN'T, BUT HE **KNOWS.**
I SEE YOU.
GRRRRRR
SETTLE NOW, BOYS...

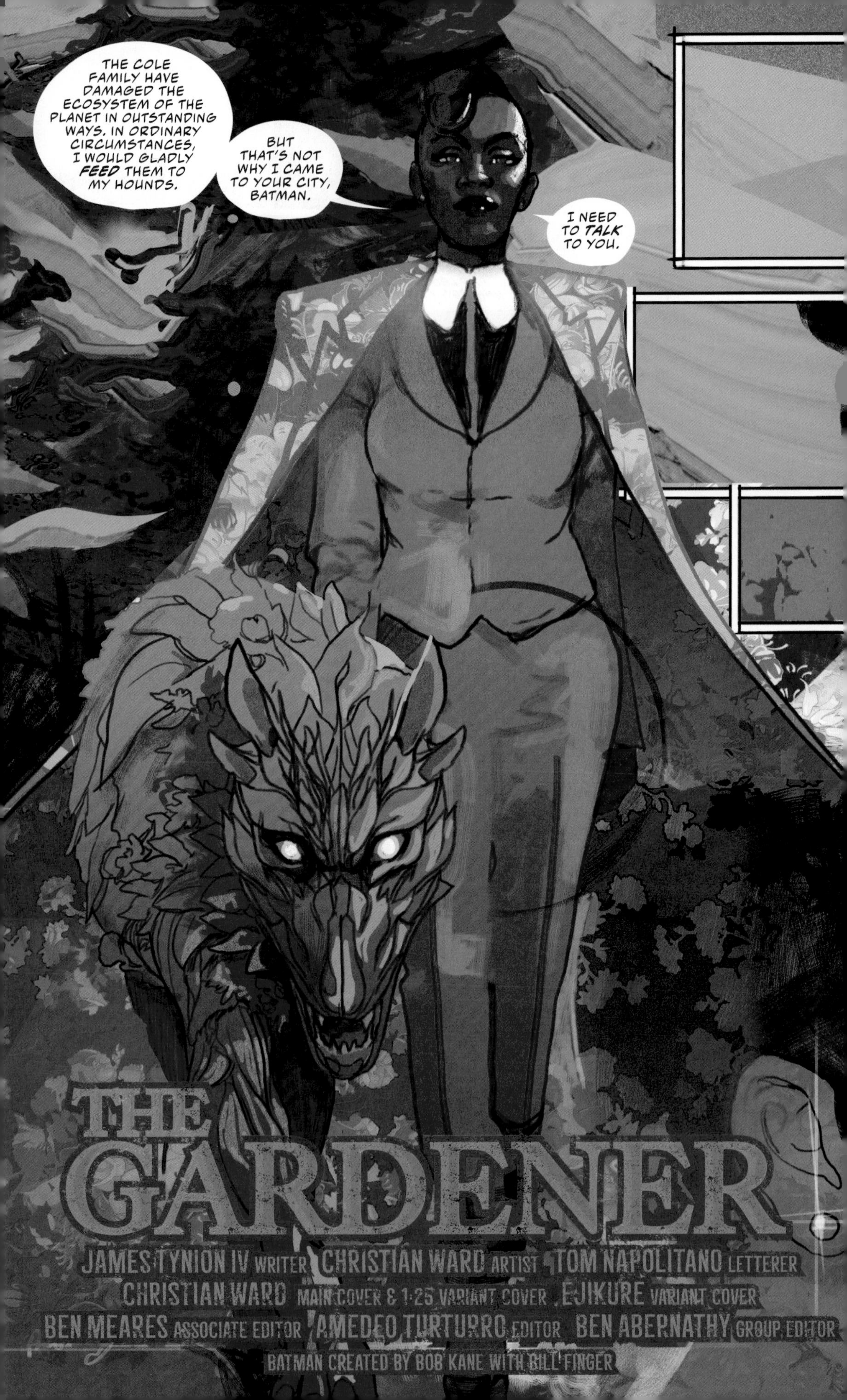
THE COLE FAMILY HAVE DAMAGED THE ECOSYSTEM OF THE PLANET IN OUTSTANDING WAYS. IN ORDINARY CIRCUMSTANCES, I WOULD GLADLY FEED THEM TO MY HOUNDS.
BUT THAT'S NOT WHY I CAME TO YOUR CITY, BATMAN.
I NEED TO TALK TO YOU.
THE GARDENER
JAMES TYNION IV WRITER CHRISTIAN WARD ARTIST TOM NAPOLITANO LETTERER
CHRISTIAN WARD MAIN COVER & 1:25 VARIANT COVER EJIKURE VARIANT COVER
BEN MEARES ASSOCIATE EDITOR AMEDEO TURTURRO EDITOR BEN ABERNATHY GROUP EDITOR
BATMAN CREATED BY BOB KANE WITH BILL FINGER

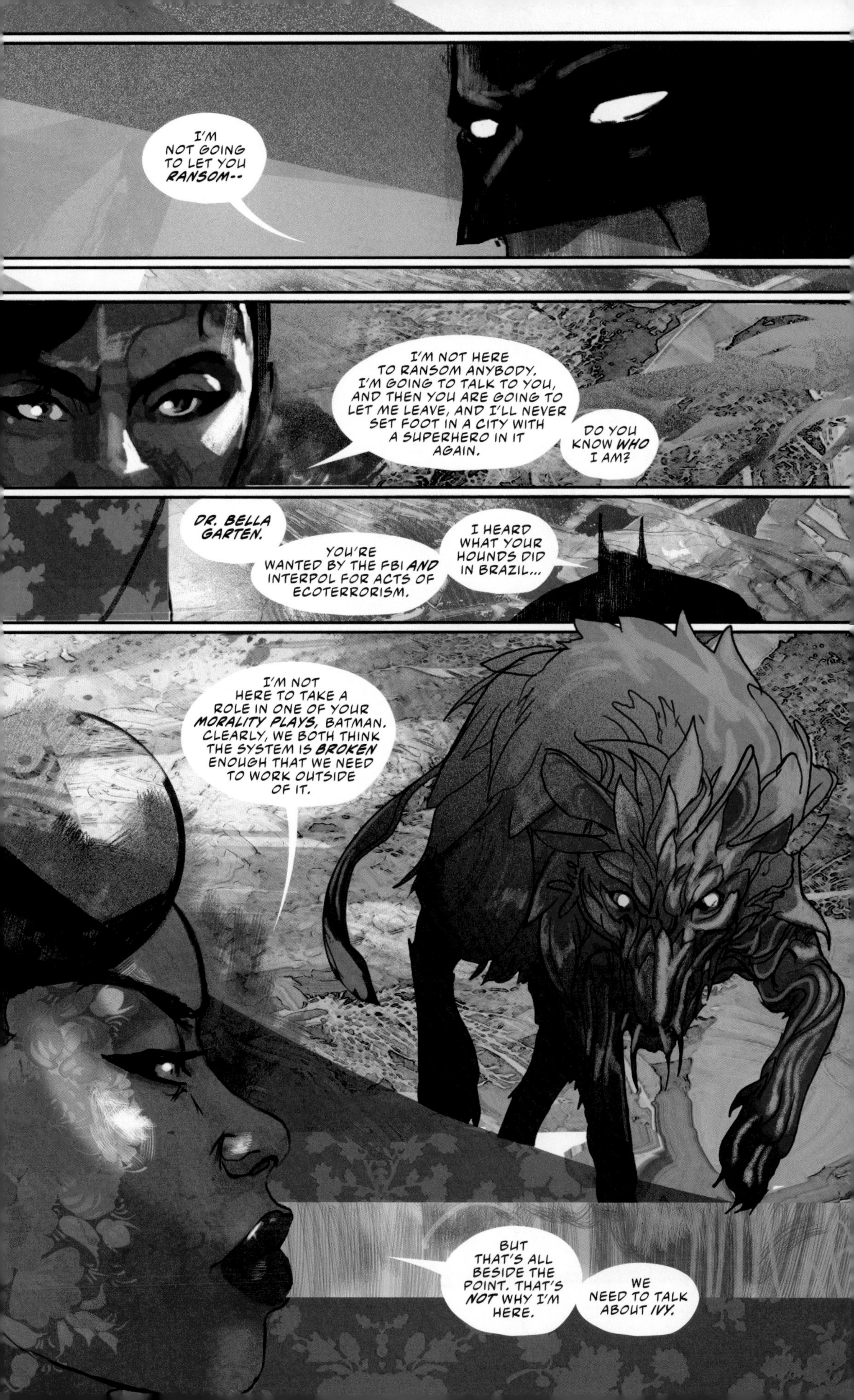

I'M NOT GOING TO LET YOU RANSOM--
I'M NOT HERE TO RANSOM ANYBODY. I'M GOING TO TALK TO YOU, AND THEN YOU ARE GOING TO LET ME LEAVE, AND I'LL NEVER SET FOOT IN A CITY WITH A SUPERHERO IN IT AGAIN.
DO YOU KNOW WHO I AM?
DR. BELLA GARTEN.
YOU'RE WANTED BY THE FBI AND INTERPOL FOR ACTS OF ECOTERRORISM.
I HEARD WHAT YOUR HOUNDS DID IN BRAZIL...
I'M NOT HERE TO TAKE A ROLE IN ONE OF YOUR MORALITY PLAYS, BATMAN. CLEARLY, WE BOTH THINK THE SYSTEM IS BROKEN ENOUGH THAT WE NEED TO WORK OUTSIDE OF IT.
BUT THAT'S ALL BESIDE THE POINT. THAT'S NOT WHY I'M HERE.
WE NEED TO TALK ABOUT IVY.

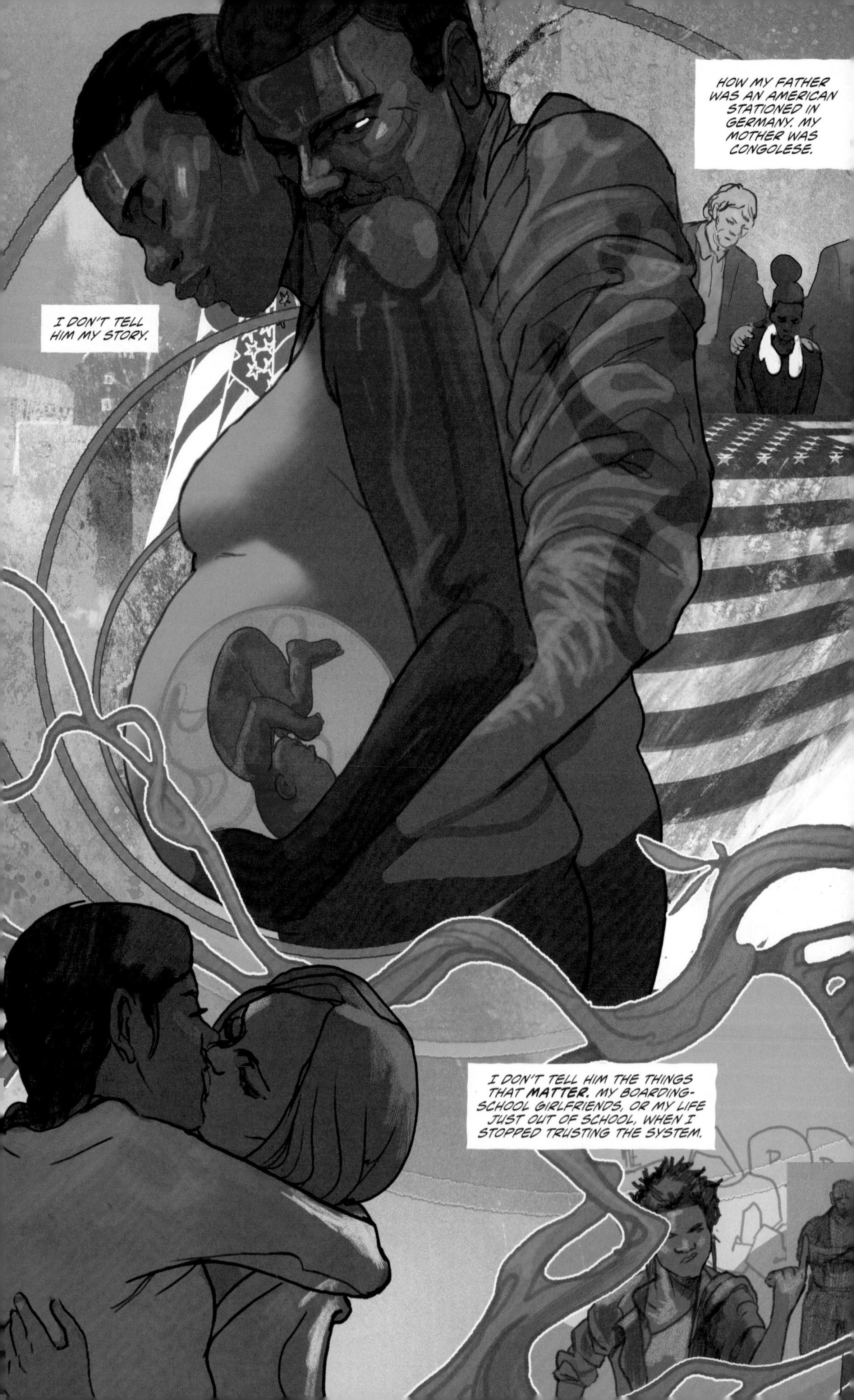
HOW MY FATHER WAS AN AMERICAN STATIONED IN GERMANY. MY MOTHER WAS CONGOLESE.
I DON'T TELL HIM MY STORY.
I DON'T TELL HIM THE THINGS THAT **MATTER.** MY BOARDING-SCHOOL GIRLFRIENDS, OR MY LIFE JUST OUT OF SCHOOL, WHEN I STOPPED TRUSTING THE SYSTEM.

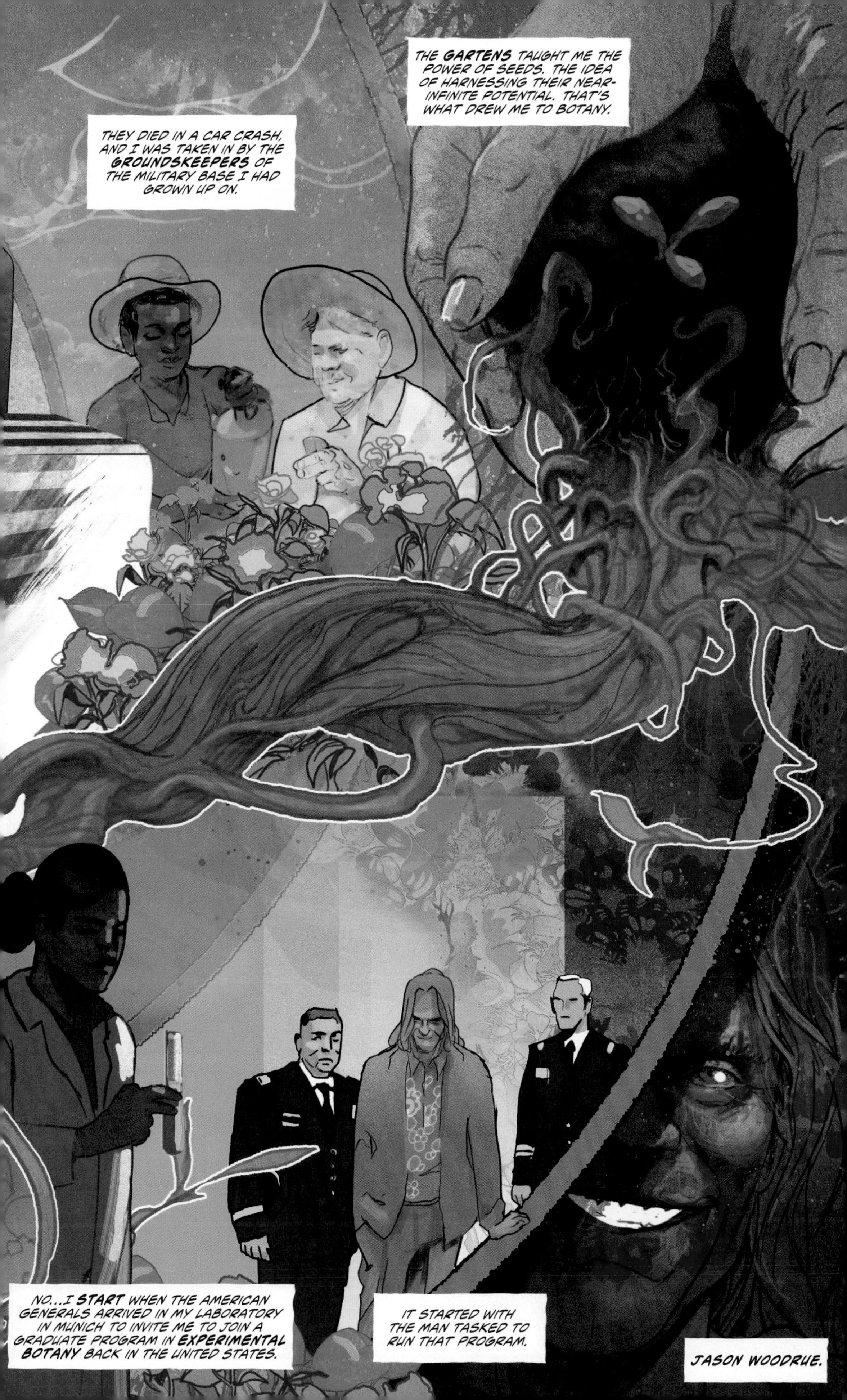
THE GARTENS TAUGHT ME THE POWER OF SEEDS. THE IDEA OF HARNESSING THEIR NEAR-INFINITE POTENTIAL. THAT'S WHAT DREW ME TO BOTANY.
THEY DIED IN A CAR CRASH, AND I WAS TAKEN IN BY THE GROUNDSKEEPERS OF THE MILITARY BASE I HAD GROWN UP ON.
NO...I START WHEN THE AMERICAN GENERALS ARRIVED IN MY LABORATORY IN MUNICH TO INVITE ME TO JOIN A GRADUATE PROGRAM IN EXPERIMENTAL BOTANY BACK IN THE UNITED STATES.
IT STARTED WITH THE MAN TASKED TO RUN THAT PROGRAM.
JASON WOODRUE.

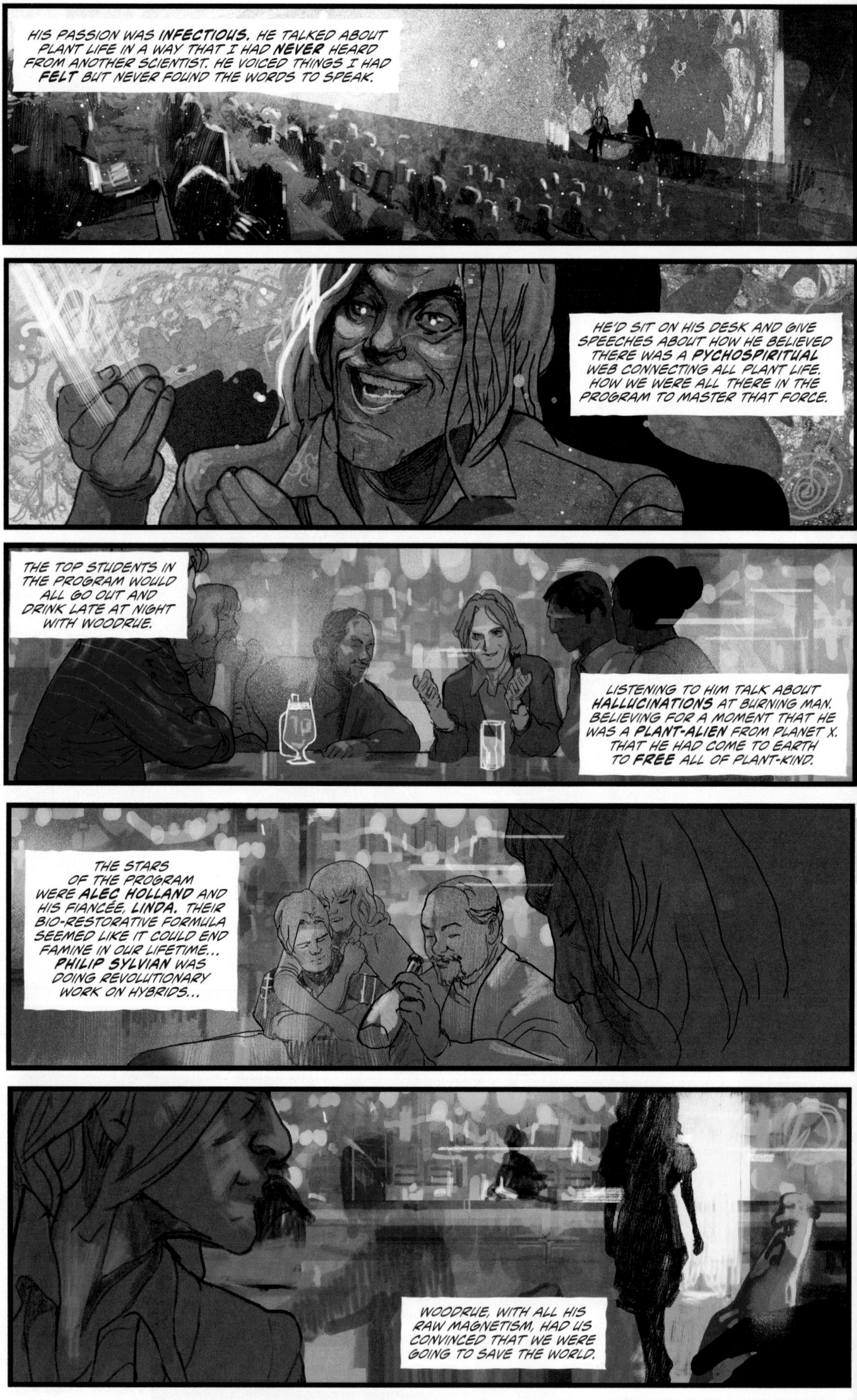
HIS PASSION WAS INFECTIOUS. HE TALKED ABOUT PLANT LIFE IN A WAY THAT I HAD NEVER HEARD FROM ANOTHER SCIENTIST. HE VOICED THINGS I HAD FELT BUT NEVER FOUND THE WORDS TO SPEAK.
HE'D SIT ON HIS DESK AND GIVE SPEECHES ABOUT HOW HE BELIEVED THERE WAS A PYCHOSPIRITUAL WEB CONNECTING ALL PLANT LIFE. HOW WE WERE ALL THERE IN THE PROGRAM TO MASTER THAT FORCE.
THE TOP STUDENTS IN THE PROGRAM WOULD ALL GO OUT AND DRINK LATE AT NIGHT WITH WOODRUE.
LISTENING TO HIM TALK ABOUT HALLUCINATIONS AT BURNING MAN. BELIEVING FOR A MOMENT THAT HE WAS A PLANT-ALIEN FROM PLANET X. THAT HE HAD COME TO EARTH TO FREE ALL OF PLANT-KIND.
THE STARS OF THE PROGRAM WERE ALEC HOLLAND AND HIS FIANCÉE, LINDA. THEIR BIO-RESTORATIVE FORMULA SEEMED LIKE IT COULD END FAMINE IN OUR LIFETIME... PHILIP SYLVIAN WAS DOING REVOLUTIONARY WORK ON HYBRIDS...
WOODRUE, WITH ALL HIS RAW MAGNETISM, HAD US CONVINCED THAT WE WERE GOING TO SAVE THE WORLD.

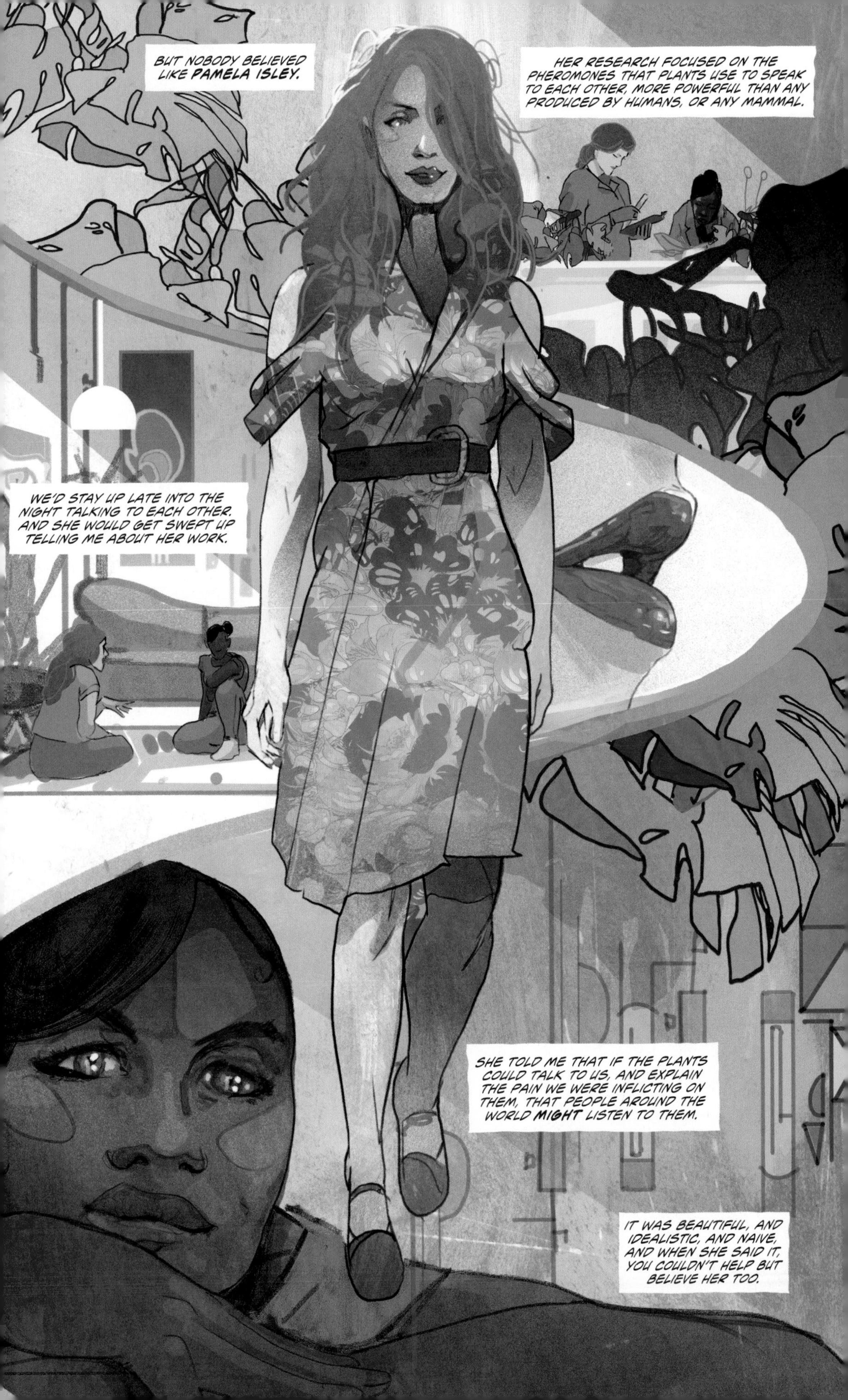
BUT NOBODY BELIEVED LIKE **PAMELA ISLEY.**
HER RESEARCH FOCUSED ON THE PHEROMONES THAT PLANTS USE TO SPEAK TO EACH OTHER, MORE POWERFUL THAN ANY PRODUCED BY HUMANS, OR ANY MAMMAL.
WE'D STAY UP LATE INTO THE NIGHT TALKING TO EACH OTHER. AND SHE WOULD GET SWEPT UP TELLING ME ABOUT HER WORK.
SHE TOLD ME THAT IF THE PLANTS COULD TALK TO US, AND EXPLAIN THE PAIN WE WERE INFLICTING ON THEM, THAT PEOPLE AROUND THE WORLD **MIGHT** LISTEN TO THEM.
IT WAS BEAUTIFUL, AND IDEALISTIC, AND NAIVE, AND WHEN SHE SAID IT, YOU COULDN'T HELP BUT BELIEVE HER TOO.

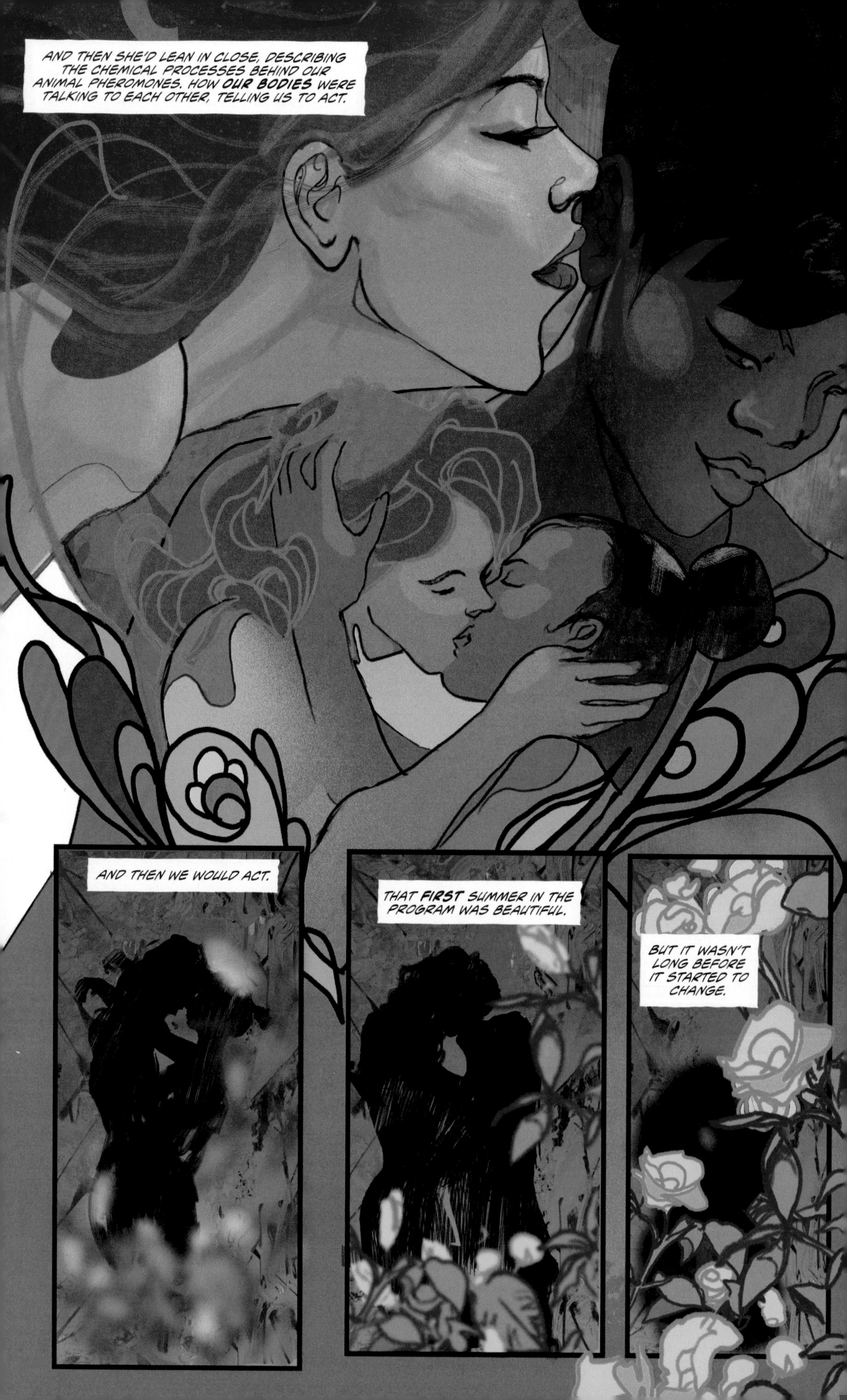
AND THEN SHE'D LEAN IN CLOSE, DESCRIBING THE CHEMICAL PROCESSES BEHIND OUR ANIMAL PHEROMONES. HOW **OUR BODIES** WERE TALKING TO EACH OTHER, TELLING US TO ACT.
AND THEN WE WOULD ACT.
THAT **FIRST** SUMMER IN THE PROGRAM WAS BEAUTIFUL.
BUT IT WASN'T LONG BEFORE IT STARTED TO CHANGE.

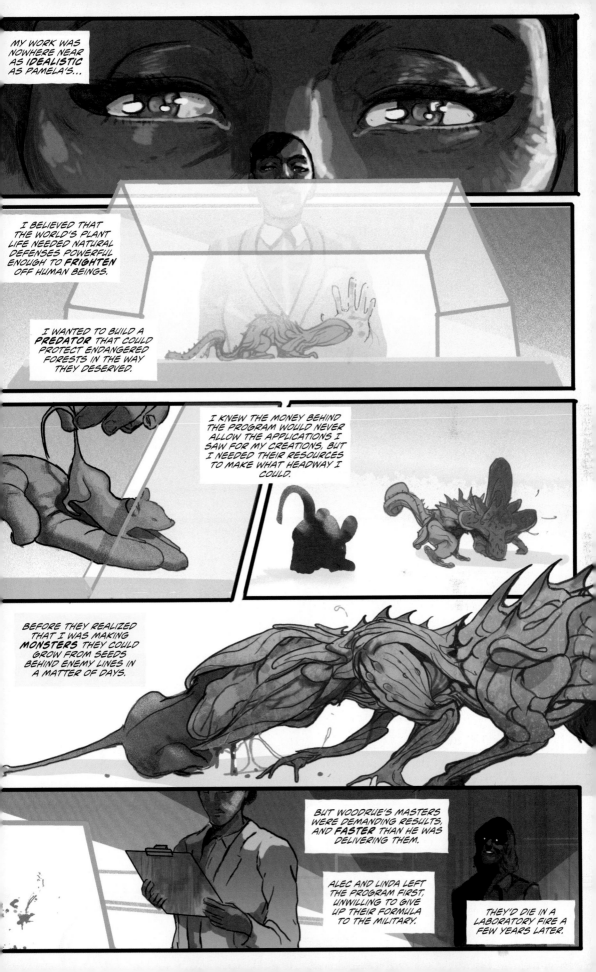

MY WORK WAS NOWHERE NEAR AS *IDEALISTIC* AS PAMELA'S...

I BELIEVED THAT THE WORLD'S PLANT LIFE NEEDED NATURAL DEFENSES POWERFUL ENOUGH TO **FRIGHTEN** OFF HUMAN BEINGS.

I WANTED TO BUILD A **PREDATOR** THAT COULD PROTECT ENDANGERED FORESTS IN THE WAY THEY DESERVED.

I KNEW THE MONEY BEHIND THE PROGRAM WOULD NEVER ALLOW THE APPLICATIONS I SAW FOR MY CREATIONS, BUT I NEEDED THEIR RESOURCES TO MAKE WHAT HEADWAY I COULD.

BEFORE THEY REALIZED THAT I WAS MAKING **MONSTERS** THEY COULD GROW FROM SEEDS BEHIND ENEMY LINES IN A MATTER OF DAYS.

BUT WOODRUE'S MASTERS WERE DEMANDING RESULTS, AND **FASTER** THAN HE WAS DELIVERING THEM.

ALEC AND LINDA LEFT THE PROGRAM FIRST, UNWILLING TO GIVE UP THEIR FORMULA TO THE MILITARY.

THEY'D DIE IN A LABORATORY FIRE A FEW YEARS LATER.

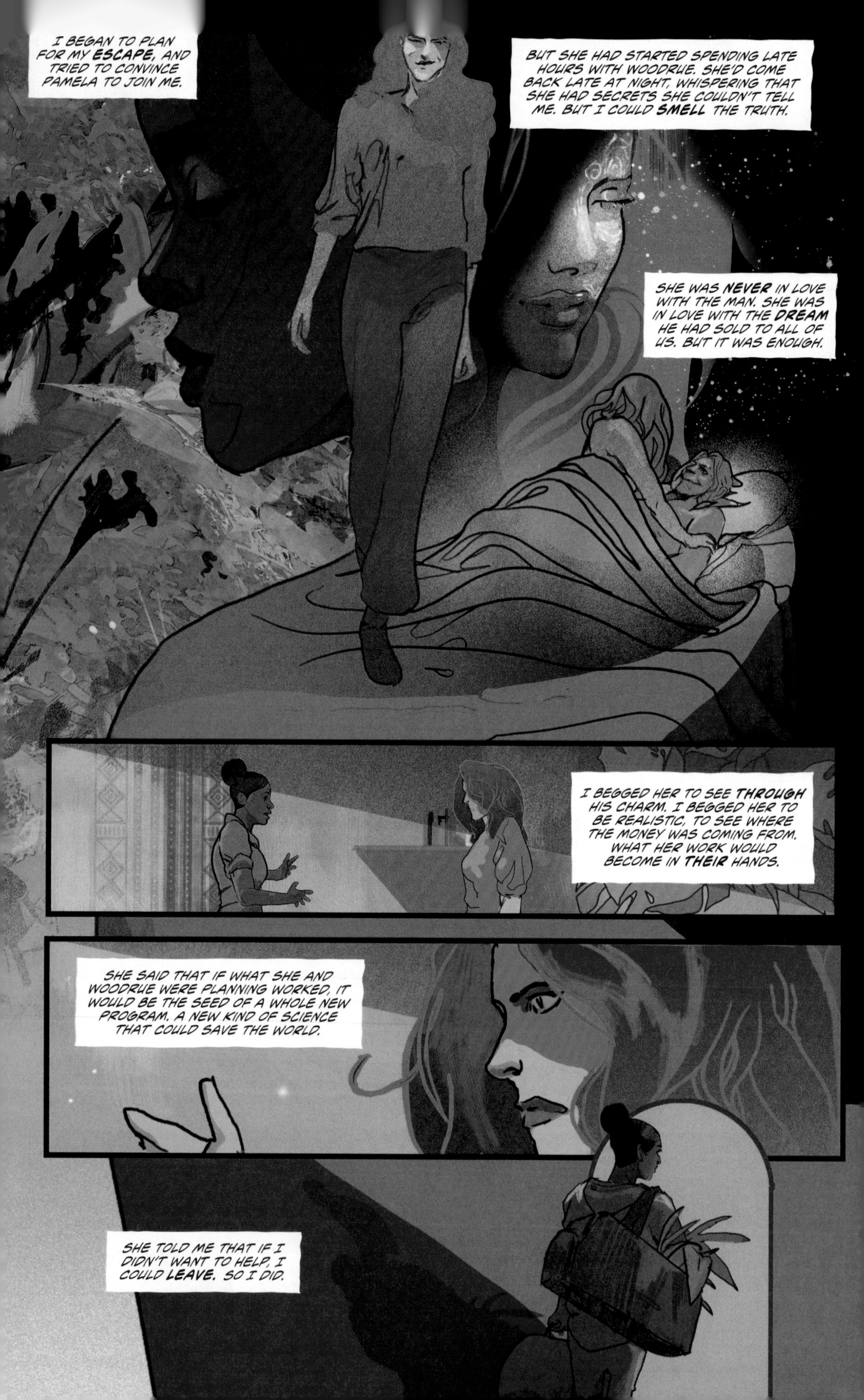
I BEGAN TO PLAN FOR MY ESCAPE, AND TRIED TO CONVINCE PAMELA TO JOIN ME.
BUT SHE HAD STARTED SPENDING LATE HOURS WITH WOODRUE. SHE'D COME BACK LATE AT NIGHT, WHISPERING THAT SHE HAD SECRETS SHE COULDN'T TELL ME. BUT I COULD SMELL THE TRUTH.
SHE WAS NEVER IN LOVE WITH THE MAN. SHE WAS IN LOVE WITH THE DREAM HE HAD SOLD TO ALL OF US. BUT IT WAS ENOUGH.
I BEGGED HER TO SEE THROUGH HIS CHARM. I BEGGED HER TO BE REALISTIC, TO SEE WHERE THE MONEY WAS COMING FROM. WHAT HER WORK WOULD BECOME IN THEIR HANDS.
SHE SAID THAT IF WHAT SHE AND WOODRUE WERE PLANNING WORKED, IT WOULD BE THE SEED OF A WHOLE NEW PROGRAM. A NEW KIND OF SCIENCE THAT COULD SAVE THE WORLD.
SHE TOLD ME THAT IF I DIDN'T WANT TO HELP, I COULD LEAVE. SO I DID.

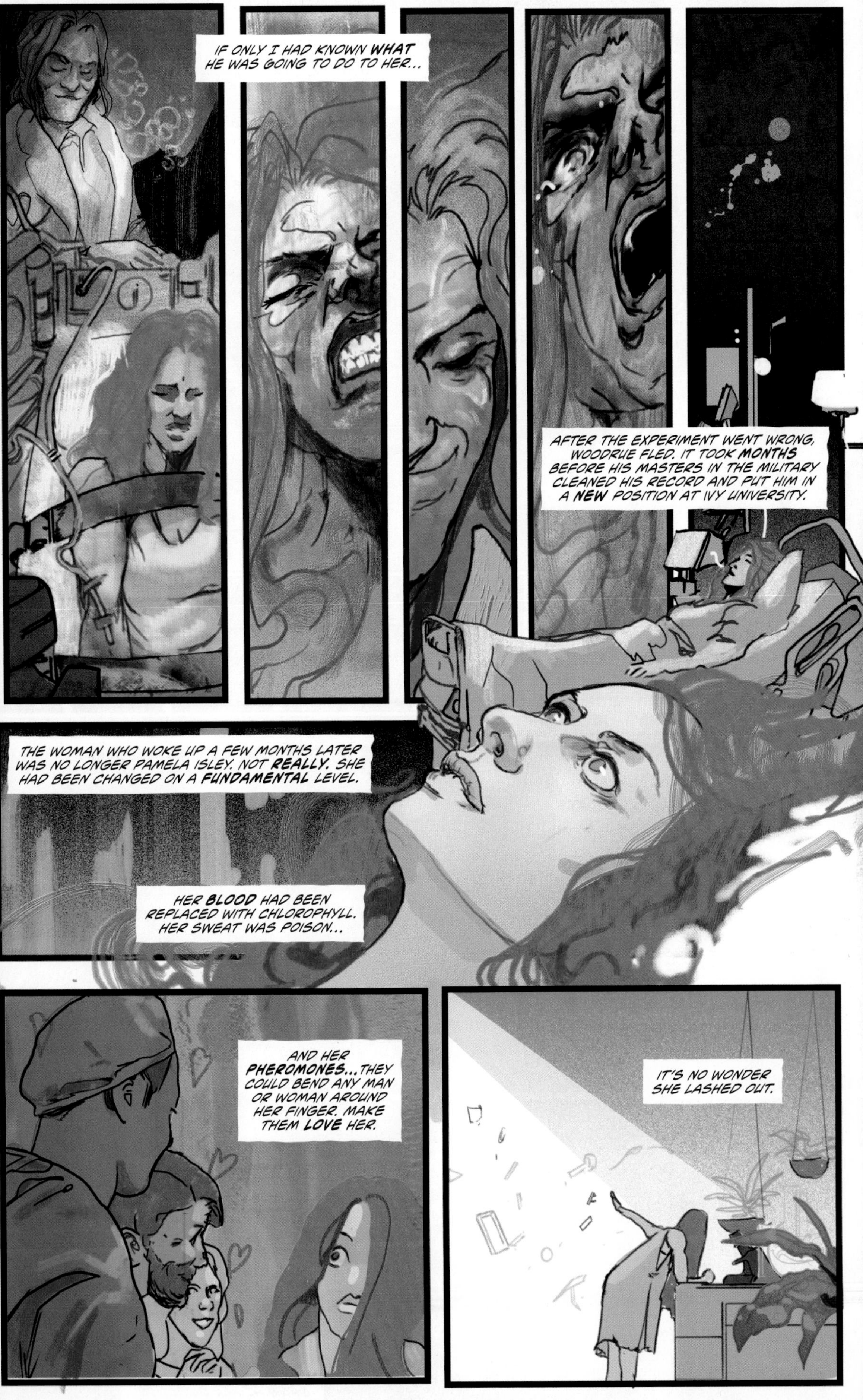
IF ONLY I HAD KNOWN WHAT HE WAS GOING TO DO TO HER...
AFTER THE EXPERIMENT WENT WRONG, WOODRUE FLED. IT TOOK MONTHS BEFORE HIS MASTERS IN THE MILITARY CLEANED HIS RECORD AND PUT HIM IN A NEW POSITION AT IVY UNIVERSITY.
THE WOMAN WHO WOKE UP A FEW MONTHS LATER WAS NO LONGER PAMELA ISLEY. NOT REALLY. SHE HAD BEEN CHANGED ON A FUNDAMENTAL LEVEL.
HER BLOOD HAD BEEN REPLACED WITH CHLOROPHYLL. HER SWEAT WAS POISON...
AND HER PHEROMONES...THEY COULD BEND ANY MAN OR WOMAN AROUND HER FINGER. MAKE THEM LOVE HER.
IT'S NO WONDER SHE LASHED OUT.

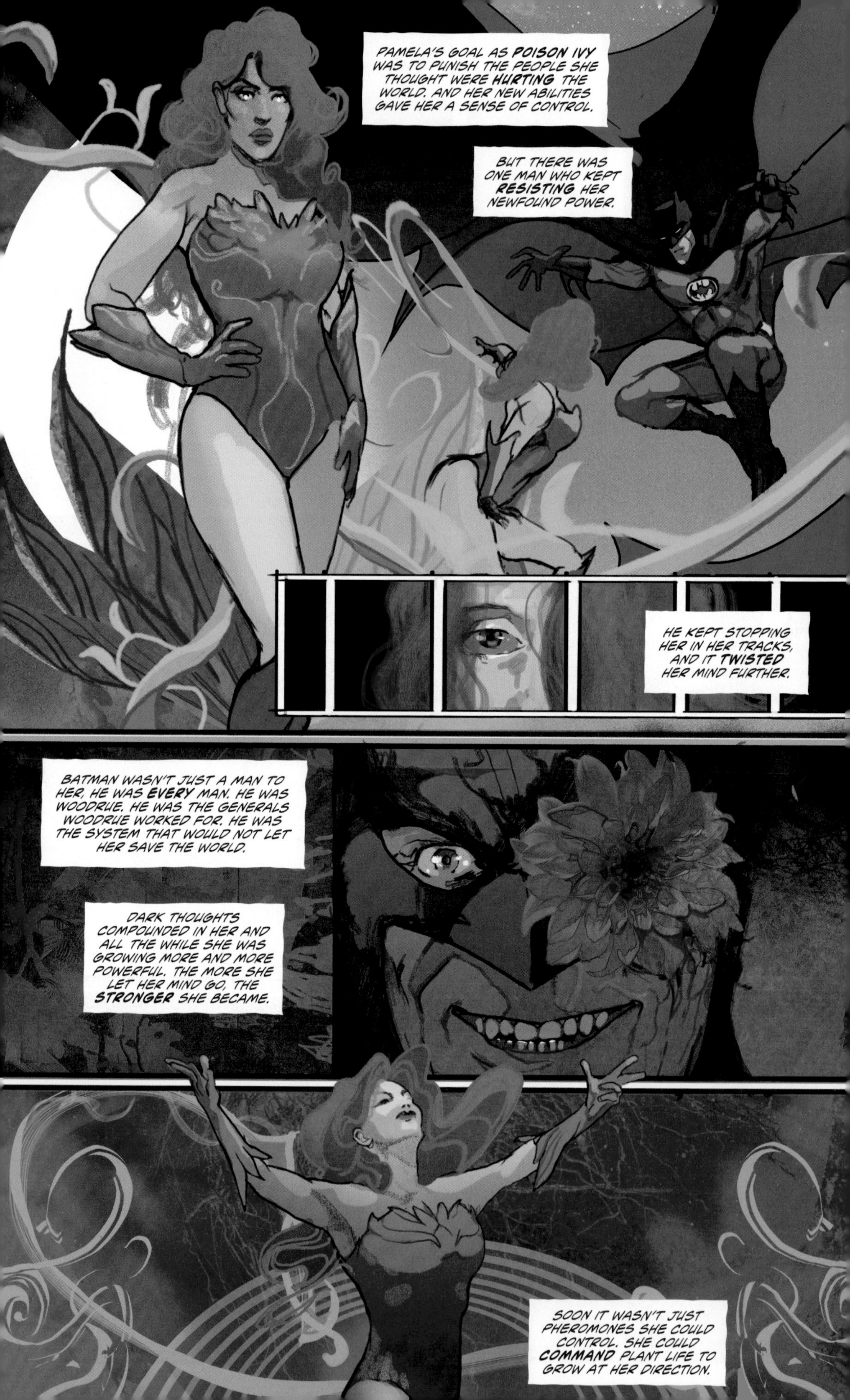
PAMELA'S GOAL AS POISON IVY WAS TO PUNISH THE PEOPLE SHE THOUGHT WERE HURTING THE WORLD, AND HER NEW ABILITIES GAVE HER A SENSE OF CONTROL.
BUT THERE WAS ONE MAN WHO KEPT RESISTING HER NEWFOUND POWER.
HE KEPT STOPPING HER IN HER TRACKS, AND IT TWISTED HER MIND FURTHER.
BATMAN WASN'T JUST A MAN TO HER, HE WAS EVERY MAN. HE WAS WOODRUE. HE WAS THE GENERALS WOODRUE WORKED FOR. HE WAS THE SYSTEM THAT WOULD NOT LET HER SAVE THE WORLD.
DARK THOUGHTS COMPOUNDED IN HER AND ALL THE WHILE SHE WAS GROWING MORE AND MORE POWERFUL. THE MORE SHE LET HER MIND GO, THE STRONGER SHE BECAME.
SOON IT WASN'T JUST PHEROMONES SHE COULD CONTROL. SHE COULD COMMAND PLANT LIFE TO GROW AT HER DIRECTION.

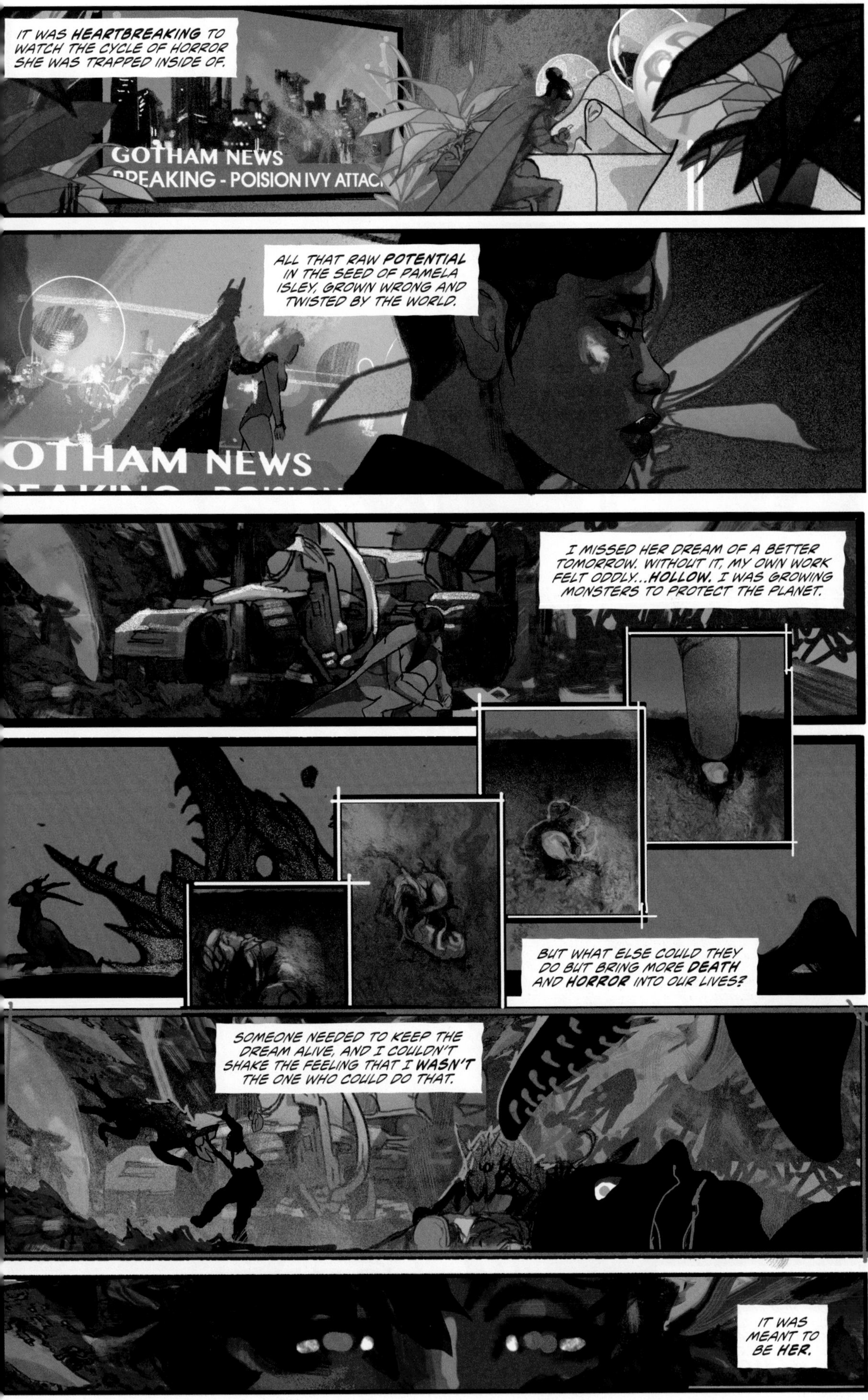
IT WAS **HEARTBREAKING** TO WATCH THE CYCLE OF HORROR SHE WAS TRAPPED INSIDE OF.
GOTHAM NEWS
BREAKING - POISION IVY ATTAC
ALL THAT RAW **POTENTIAL** IN THE SEED OF PAMELA ISLEY, GROWN WRONG AND TWISTED BY THE WORLD.
OTHAM NEWS
I MISSED HER DREAM OF A BETTER TOMORROW. WITHOUT IT, MY OWN WORK FELT ODDLY...**HOLLOW.** I WAS GROWING MONSTERS TO PROTECT THE PLANET.
BUT WHAT ELSE COULD THEY DO BUT BRING MORE **DEATH** AND **HORROR** INTO OUR LIVES?
SOMEONE NEEDED TO KEEP THE DREAM ALIVE, AND I COULDN'T SHAKE THE FEELING THAT I **WASN'T** THE ONE WHO COULD DO THAT.
IT WAS MEANT TO BE **HER.**

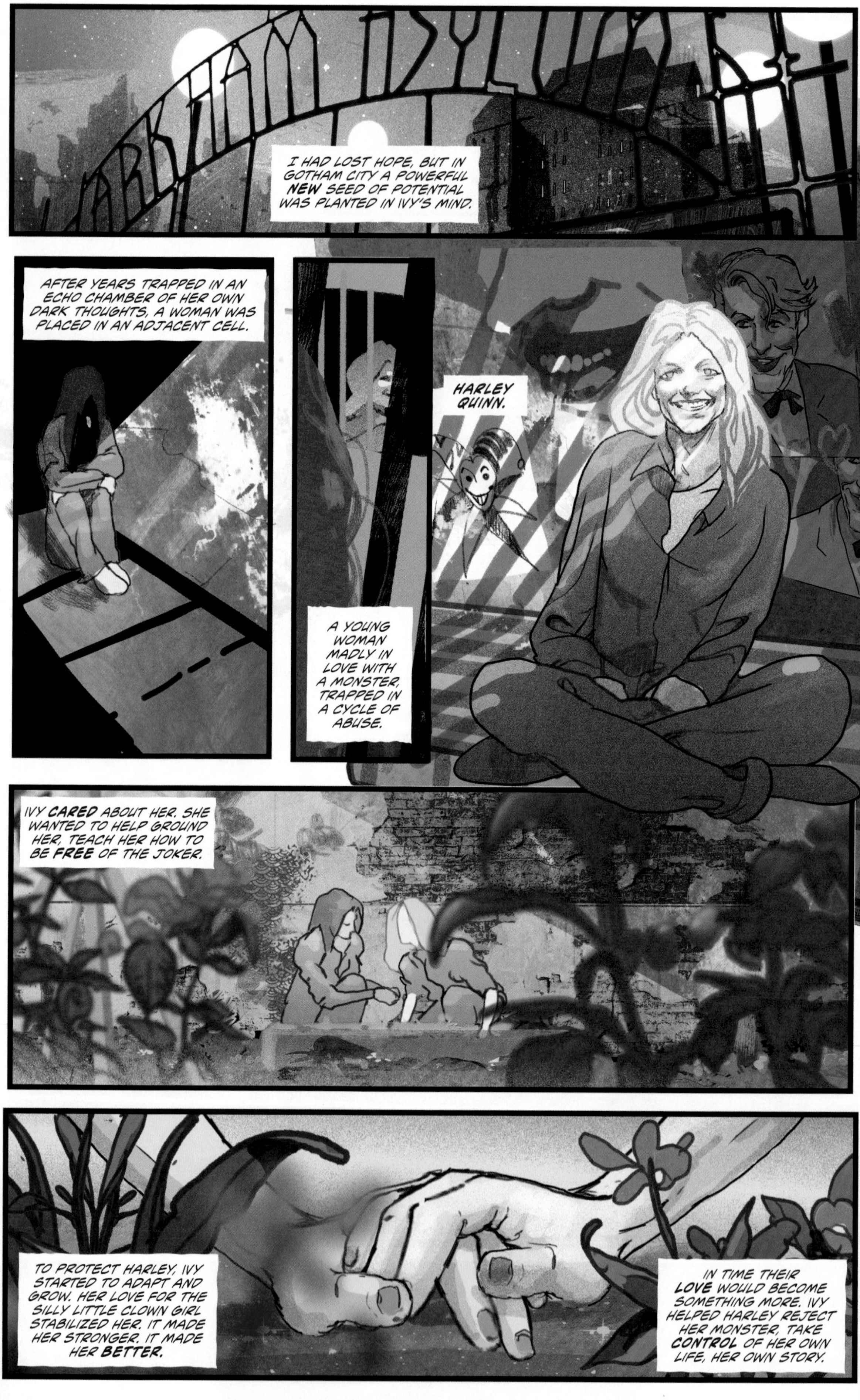

ARKHAM ASYLUM
I HAD LOST HOPE, BUT IN GOTHAM CITY A POWERFUL **NEW** SEED OF POTENTIAL WAS PLANTED IN IVY'S MIND.
AFTER YEARS TRAPPED IN AN ECHO CHAMBER OF HER OWN DARK THOUGHTS, A WOMAN WAS PLACED IN AN ADJACENT CELL.
HARLEY QUINN.
A YOUNG WOMAN MADLY IN LOVE WITH A MONSTER, TRAPPED IN A CYCLE OF ABUSE.
IVY **CARED** ABOUT HER. SHE WANTED TO HELP GROUND HER, TEACH HER HOW TO BE **FREE** OF THE JOKER.
TO PROTECT HARLEY, IVY STARTED TO ADAPT AND GROW. HER LOVE FOR THE SILLY LITTLE CLOWN GIRL STABILIZED HER. IT MADE HER STRONGER. IT MADE HER **BETTER.**
IN TIME THEIR **LOVE** WOULD BECOME SOMETHING MORE. IVY HELPED HARLEY REJECT HER MONSTER, TAKE **CONTROL** OF HER OWN LIFE, HER OWN STORY.

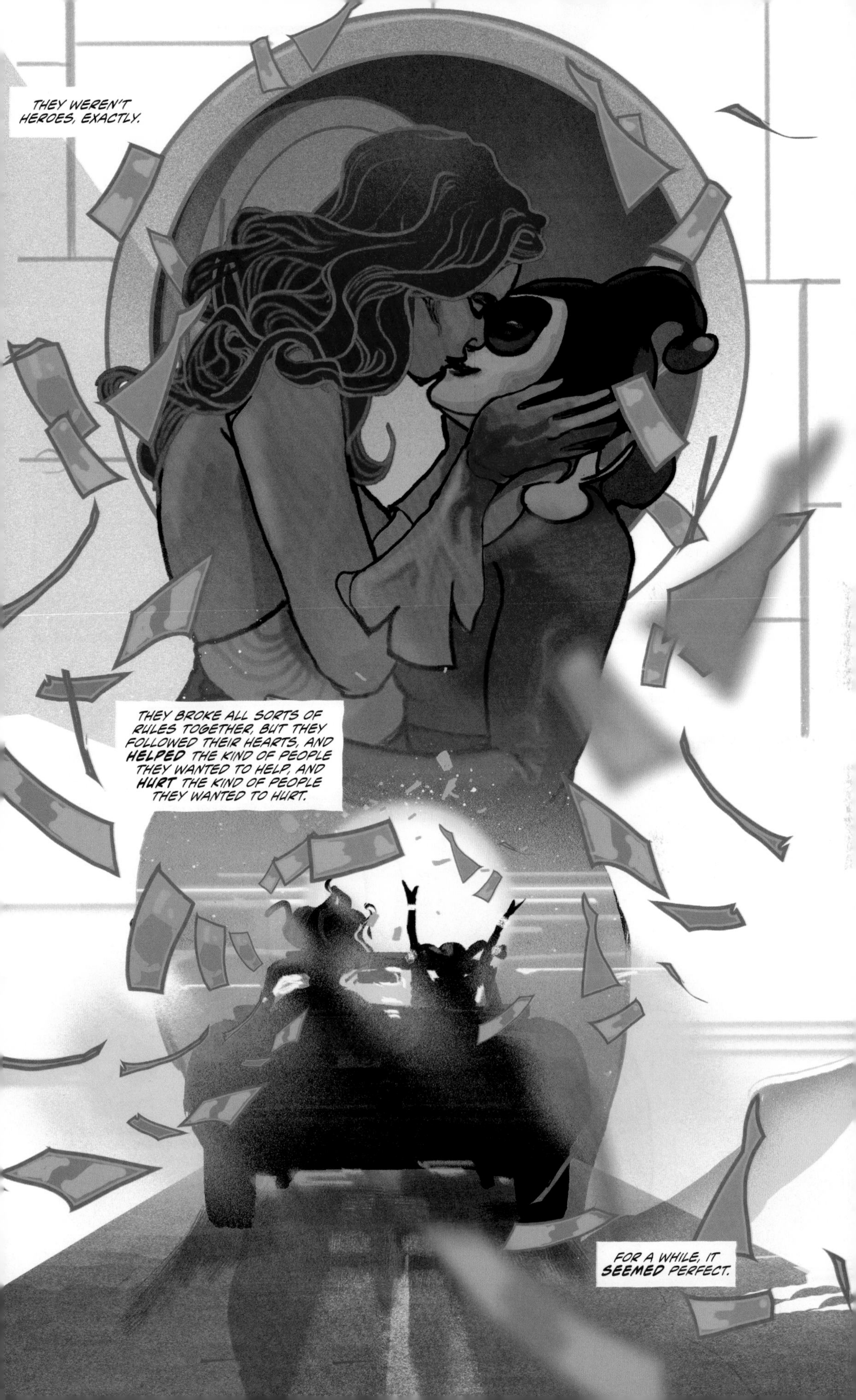
THEY WEREN'T HEROES, EXACTLY.
THEY BROKE ALL SORTS OF RULES TOGETHER, BUT THEY FOLLOWED THEIR HEARTS, AND HELPED THE KIND OF PEOPLE THEY WANTED TO HELP, AND HURT THE KIND OF PEOPLE THEY WANTED TO HURT.
FOR A WHILE, IT SEEMED PERFECT.

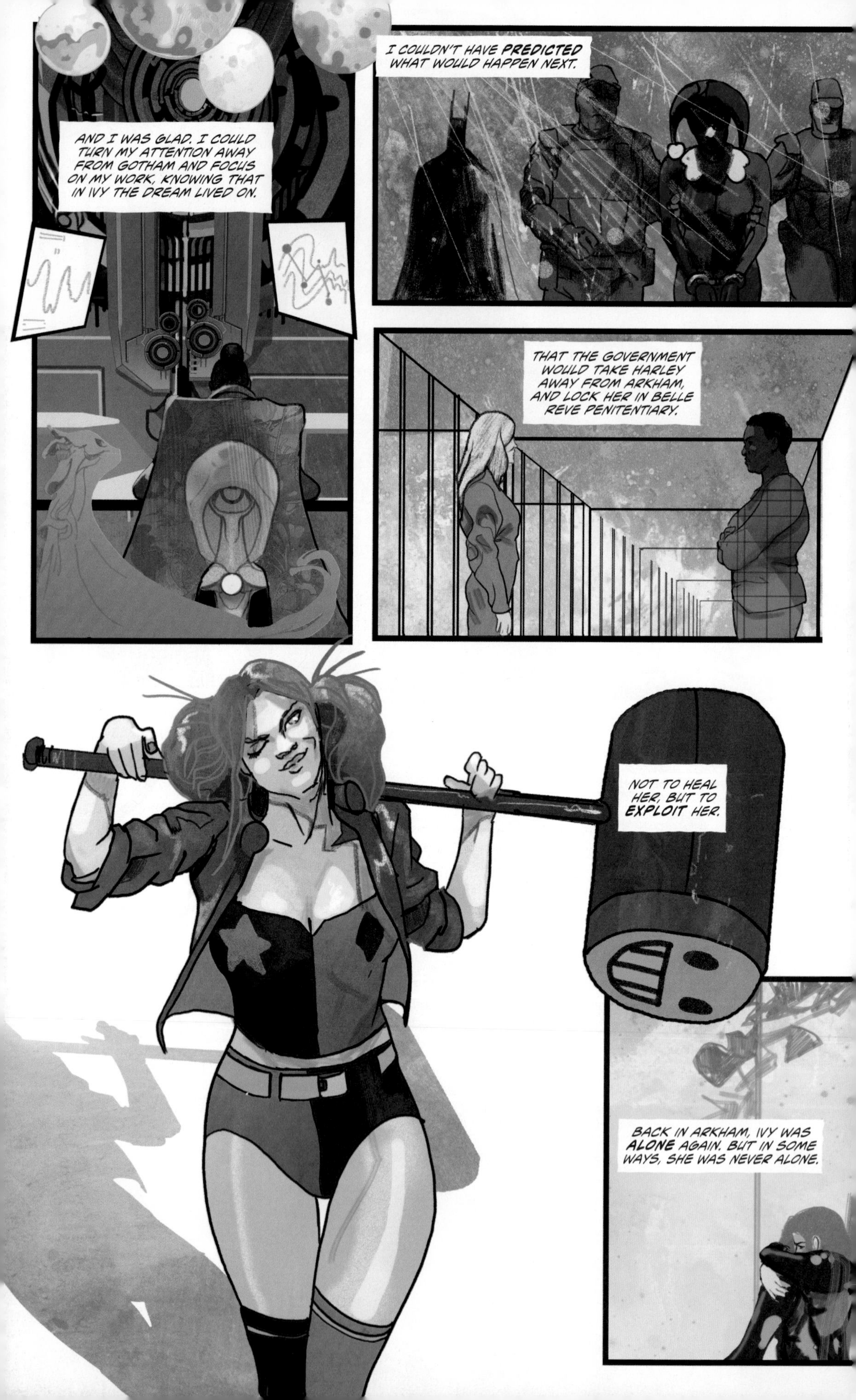
AND I WAS GLAD. I COULD TURN MY ATTENTION AWAY FROM GOTHAM AND FOCUS ON MY WORK, KNOWING THAT IN IVY THE DREAM LIVED ON.
I COULDN'T HAVE **PREDICTED** WHAT WOULD HAPPEN NEXT.
THAT THE GOVERNMENT WOULD TAKE HARLEY AWAY FROM ARKHAM, AND LOCK HER IN BELLE REVE PENITENTIARY.
NOT TO HEAL HER, BUT TO **EXPLOIT** HER.
BACK IN ARKHAM, IVY WAS **ALONE** AGAIN. BUT IN SOME WAYS, SHE WAS NEVER ALONE.

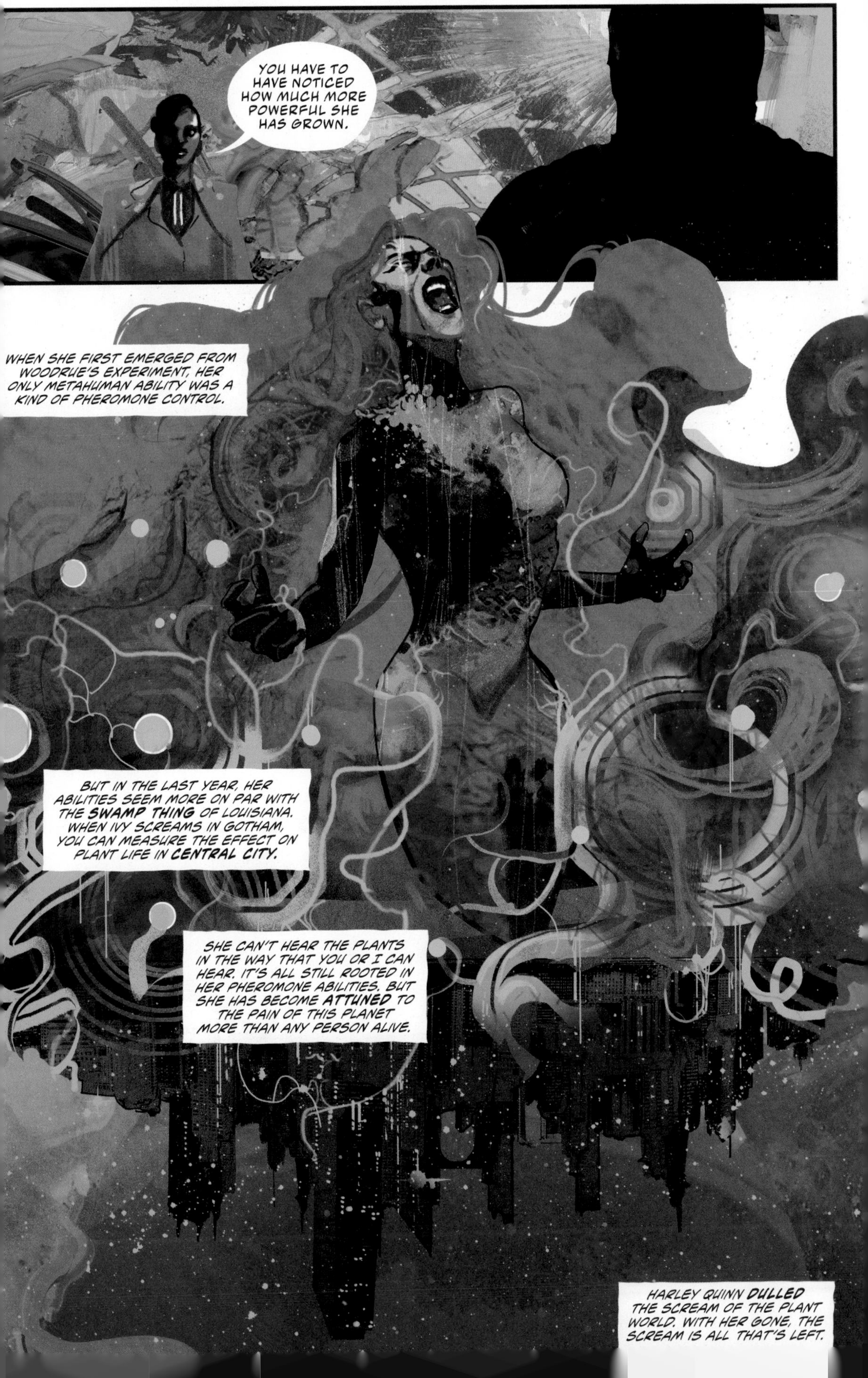

YOU HAVE TO HAVE NOTICED HOW MUCH MORE POWERFUL SHE HAS GROWN.
WHEN SHE FIRST EMERGED FROM WOODRUE'S EXPERIMENT, HER ONLY METAHUMAN ABILITY WAS A KIND OF PHEROMONE CONTROL.
BUT IN THE LAST YEAR, HER ABILITIES SEEM MORE ON PAR WITH THE SWAMP THING OF LOUISIANA. WHEN IVY SCREAMS IN GOTHAM, YOU CAN MEASURE THE EFFECT ON PLANT LIFE IN CENTRAL CITY.
SHE CAN'T HEAR THE PLANTS IN THE WAY THAT YOU OR I CAN HEAR. IT'S ALL STILL ROOTED IN HER PHEROMONE ABILITIES. BUT SHE HAS BECOME ATTUNED TO THE PAIN OF THIS PLANET MORE THAN ANY PERSON ALIVE.
HARLEY QUINN DULLED THE SCREAM OF THE PLANT WORLD. WITH HER GONE, THE SCREAM IS ALL THAT'S LEFT.

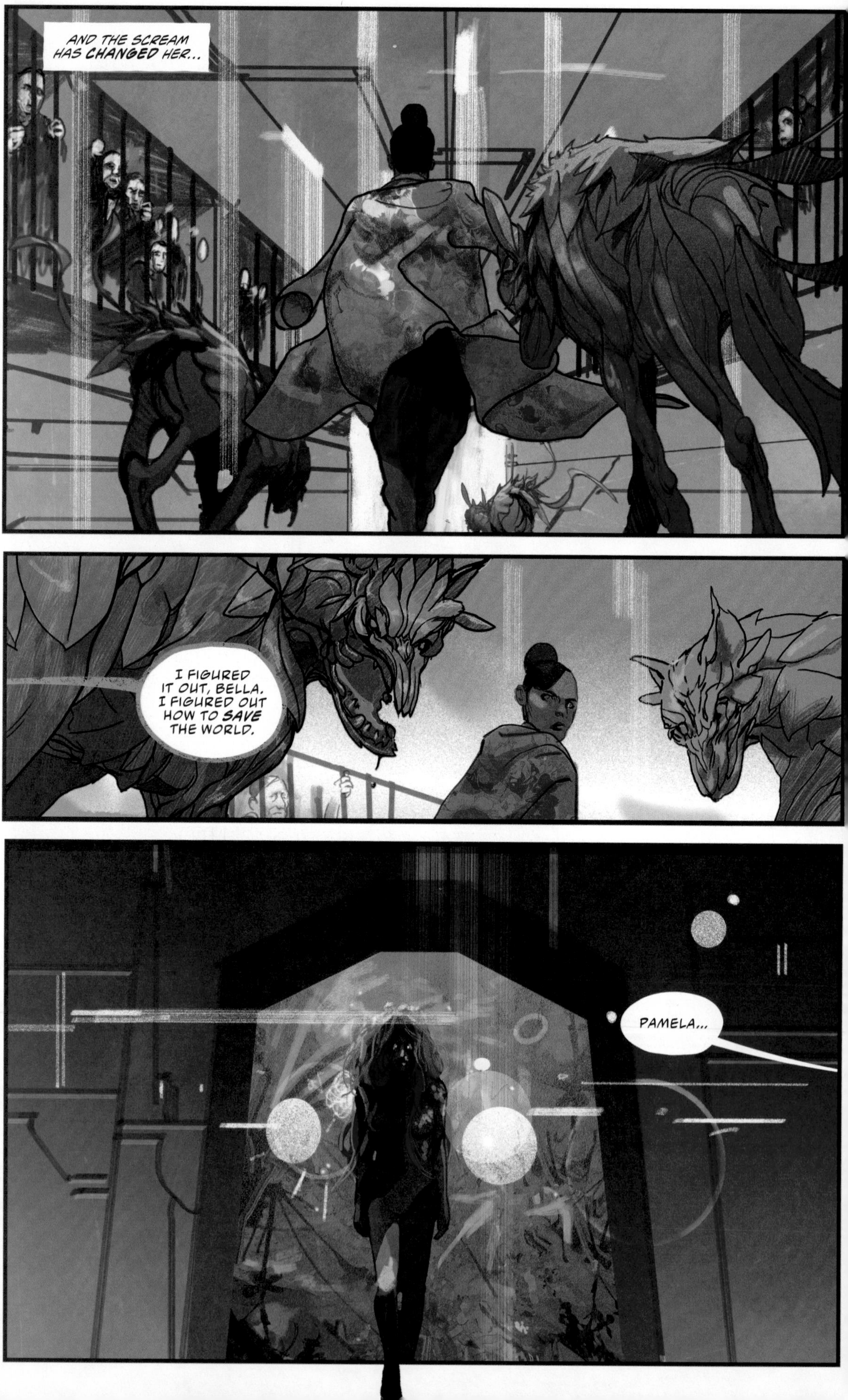
AND THE SCREAM HAS CHANGED HER...
I FIGURED IT OUT, BELLA. I FIGURED OUT HOW TO SAVE THE WORLD.
PAMELA...

I'VE BEEN TESTING MY ABILITIES FOR MONTHS NOW. I THINK I'M READY.

FOR WHAT?

I AM GOING TO USE MY PHEROMONES TO MAKE *EVERY* HUMAN ON THE PLANET FALL IN LOVE WITH ME, SO I CAN *MAKE* THEM ALL DO WHAT THEY NEED TO DO TO SAVE THE WORLD.

ARE... ARE YOU REALLY THAT POWERFUL?

WE LOVE YOU, IVY!

YES.

I *WANTED* TO TELL HER THAT SHE SOUNDED LIKE *WOODRUE* AT THE END. WHEN HIS DREAM HAD GONE RANCID IN HIM. I KNEW THAT AN ATTEMPT LIKE THIS COULD BREAK HER MIND, FOREVER.

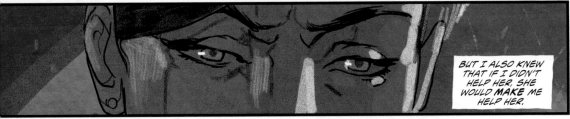

BUT I ALSO KNEW THAT IF I DIDN'T HELP HER, SHE WOULD *MAKE* ME HELP HER.

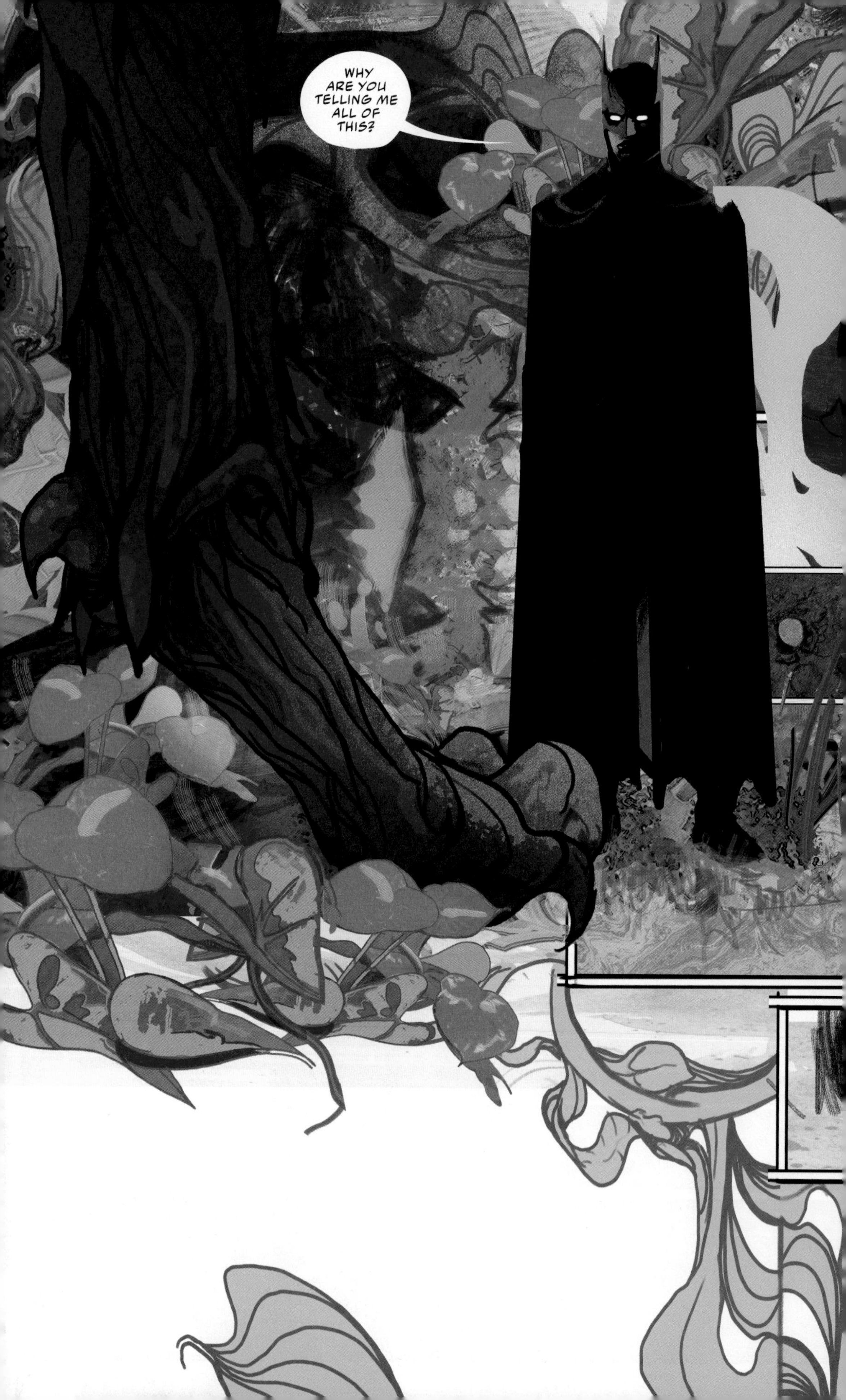
WHY ARE YOU TELLING ME ALL OF THIS?

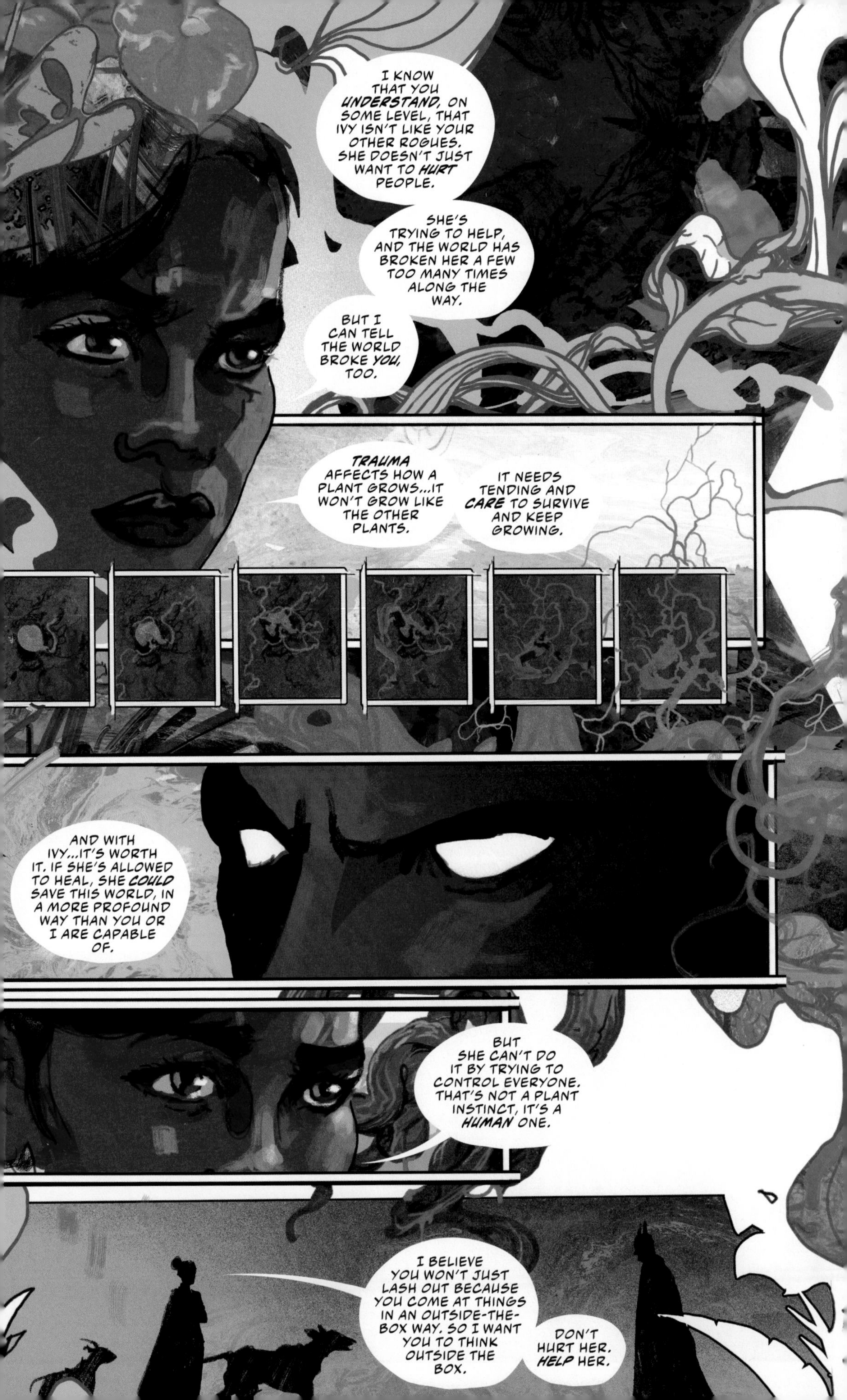
I KNOW THAT YOU UNDERSTAND, ON SOME LEVEL, THAT IVY ISN'T LIKE YOUR OTHER ROGUES. SHE DOESN'T JUST WANT TO HURT PEOPLE.
SHE'S TRYING TO HELP, AND THE WORLD HAS BROKEN HER A FEW TOO MANY TIMES ALONG THE WAY.
BUT I CAN TELL THE WORLD BROKE YOU, TOO.
TRAUMA AFFECTS HOW A PLANT GROWS...IT WON'T GROW LIKE THE OTHER PLANTS.
IT NEEDS TENDING AND CARE TO SURVIVE AND KEEP GROWING.
AND WITH IVY...IT'S WORTH IT. IF SHE'S ALLOWED TO HEAL, SHE COULD SAVE THIS WORLD, IN A MORE PROFOUND WAY THAN YOU OR I ARE CAPABLE OF.
BUT SHE CAN'T DO IT BY TRYING TO CONTROL EVERYONE. THAT'S NOT A PLANT INSTINCT, IT'S A HUMAN ONE.
I BELIEVE YOU WON'T JUST LASH OUT BECAUSE YOU COME AT THINGS IN AN OUTSIDE-THE-BOX WAY. SO I WANT YOU TO THINK OUTSIDE THE BOX.
DON'T HURT HER. HELP HER.

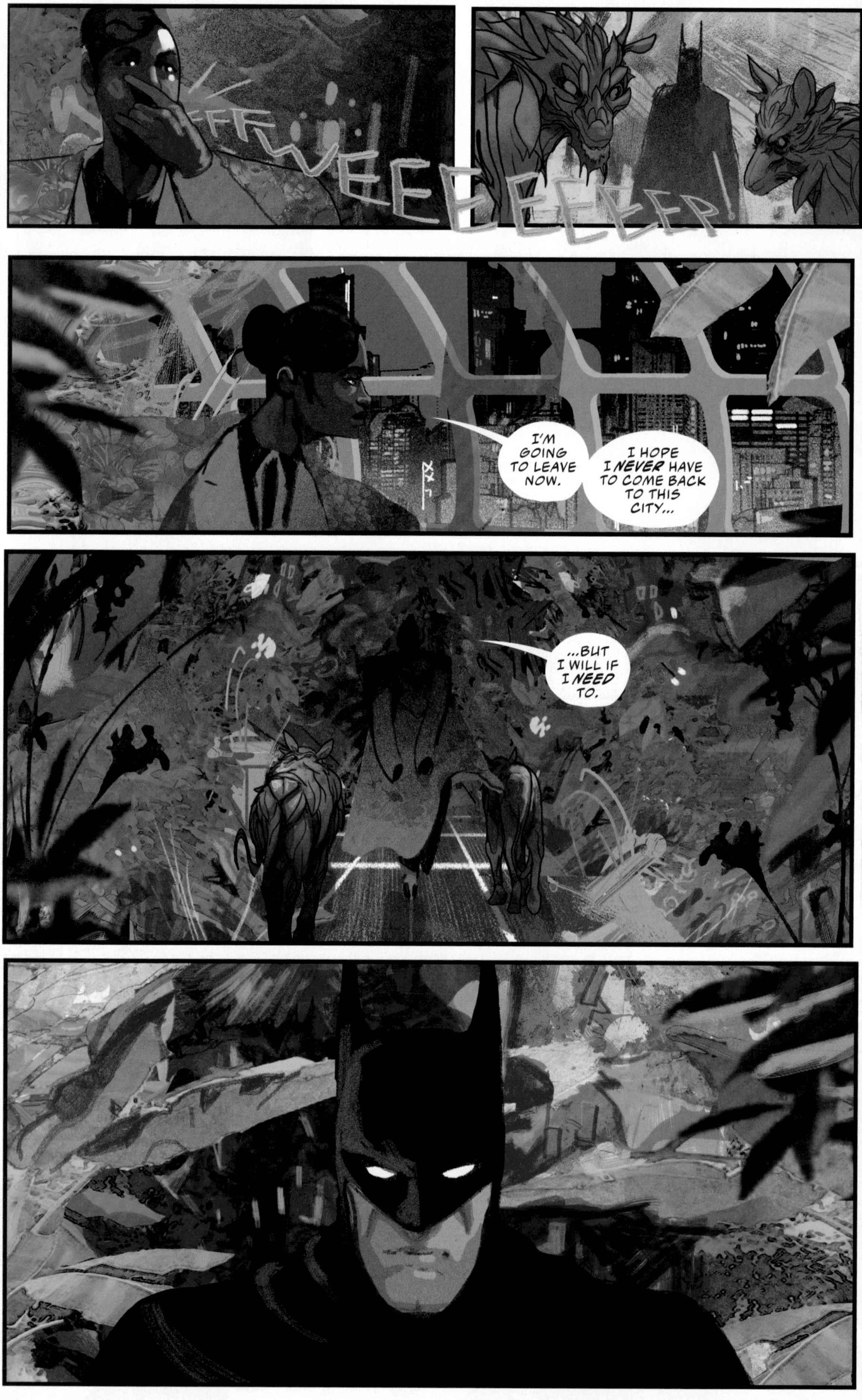
FFFWEEEEEEEEP!
I'M GOING TO LEAVE NOW.
I HOPE I NEVER HAVE TO COME BACK TO THIS CITY...
...BUT I WILL IF I NEED TO.

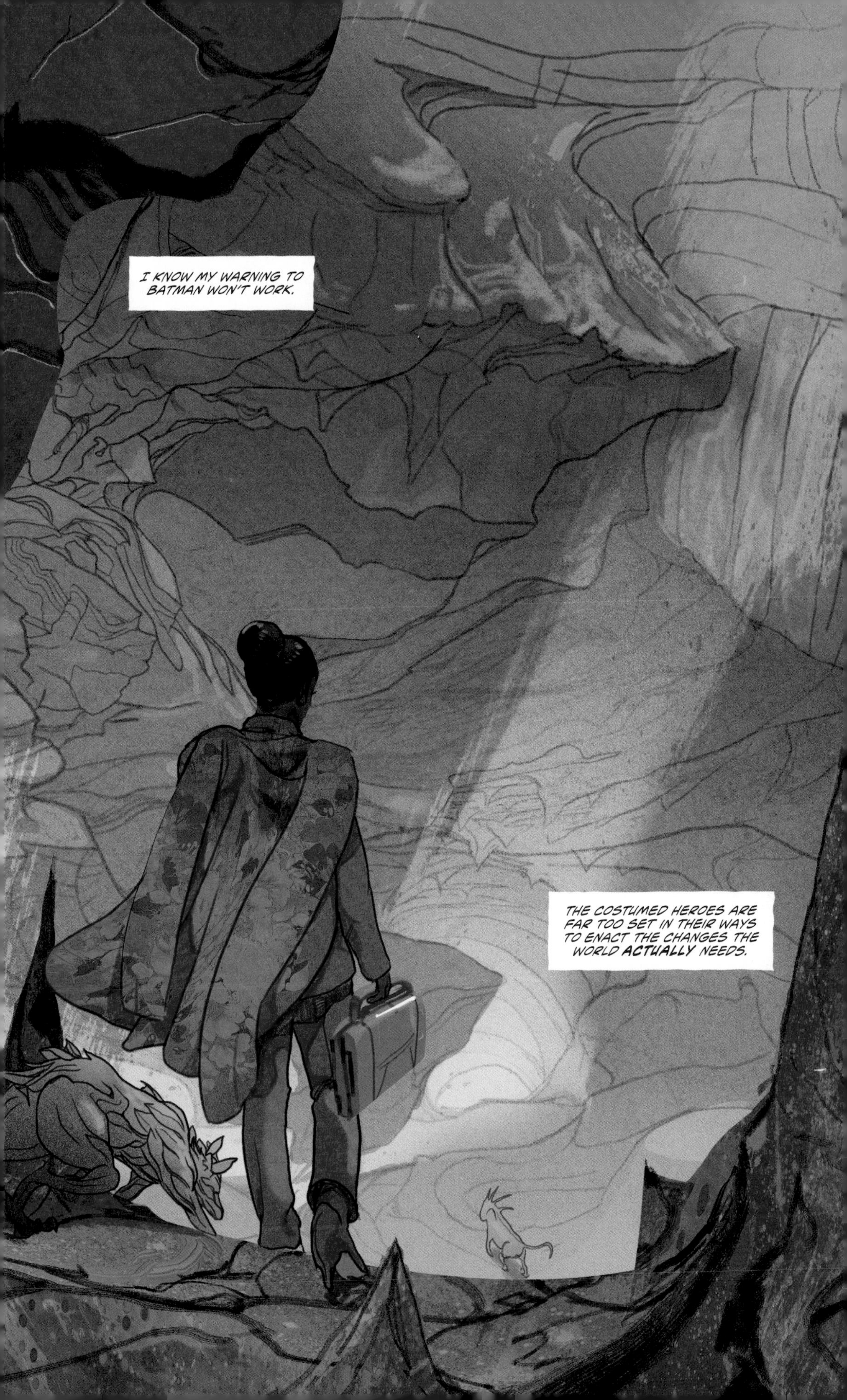
I KNOW MY WARNING TO BATMAN WON'T WORK.
THE COSTUMED HEROES ARE FAR TOO SET IN THEIR WAYS TO ENACT THE CHANGES THE WORLD **ACTUALLY** NEEDS.

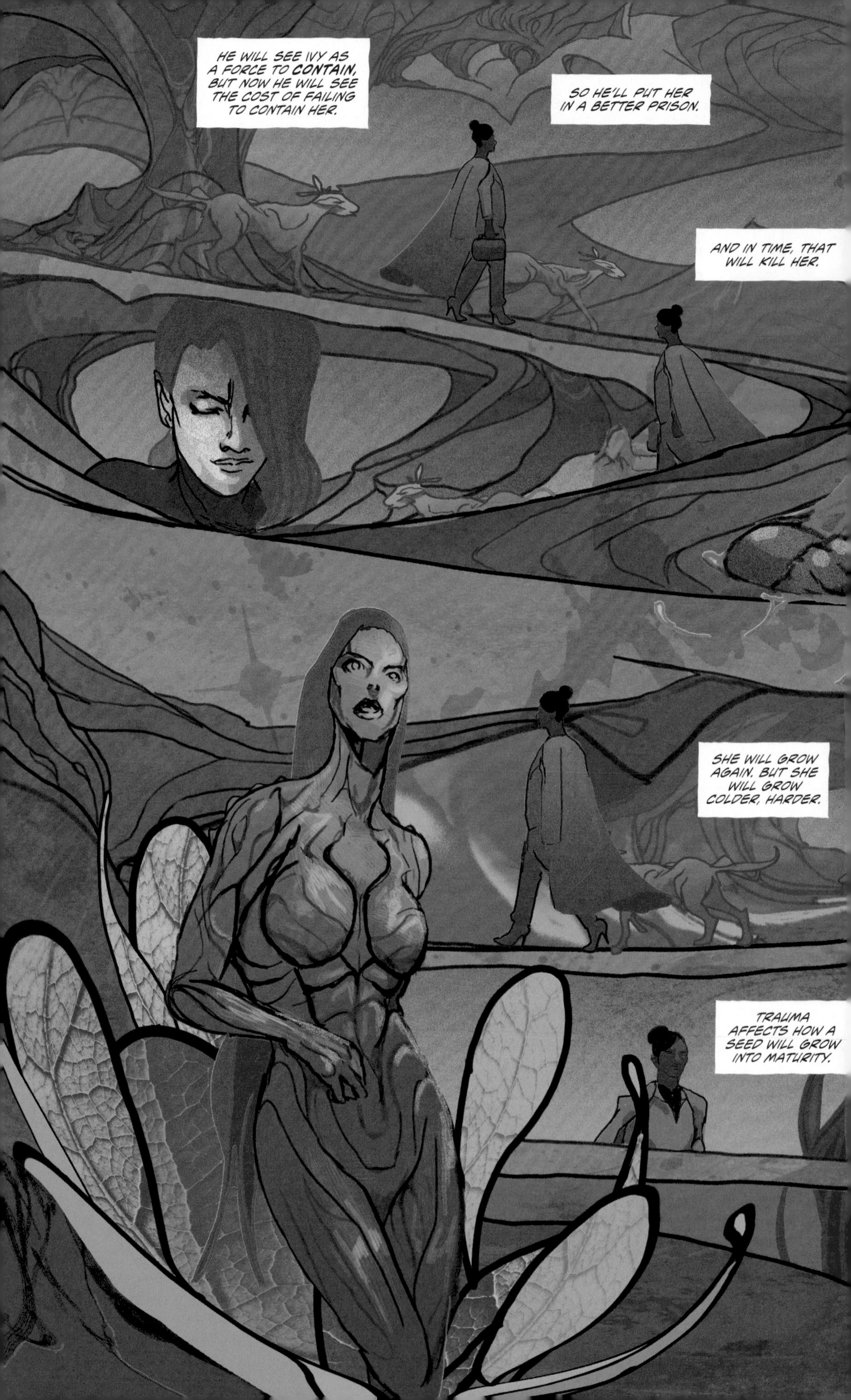
HE WILL SEE IVY AS A FORCE TO CONTAIN, BUT NOW HE WILL SEE THE COST OF FAILING TO CONTAIN HER.
SO HE'LL PUT HER IN A BETTER PRISON.
AND IN TIME, THAT WILL KILL HER.
SHE WILL GROW AGAIN. BUT SHE WILL GROW COLDER, HARDER.
TRAUMA AFFECTS HOW A SEED WILL GROW INTO MATURITY.

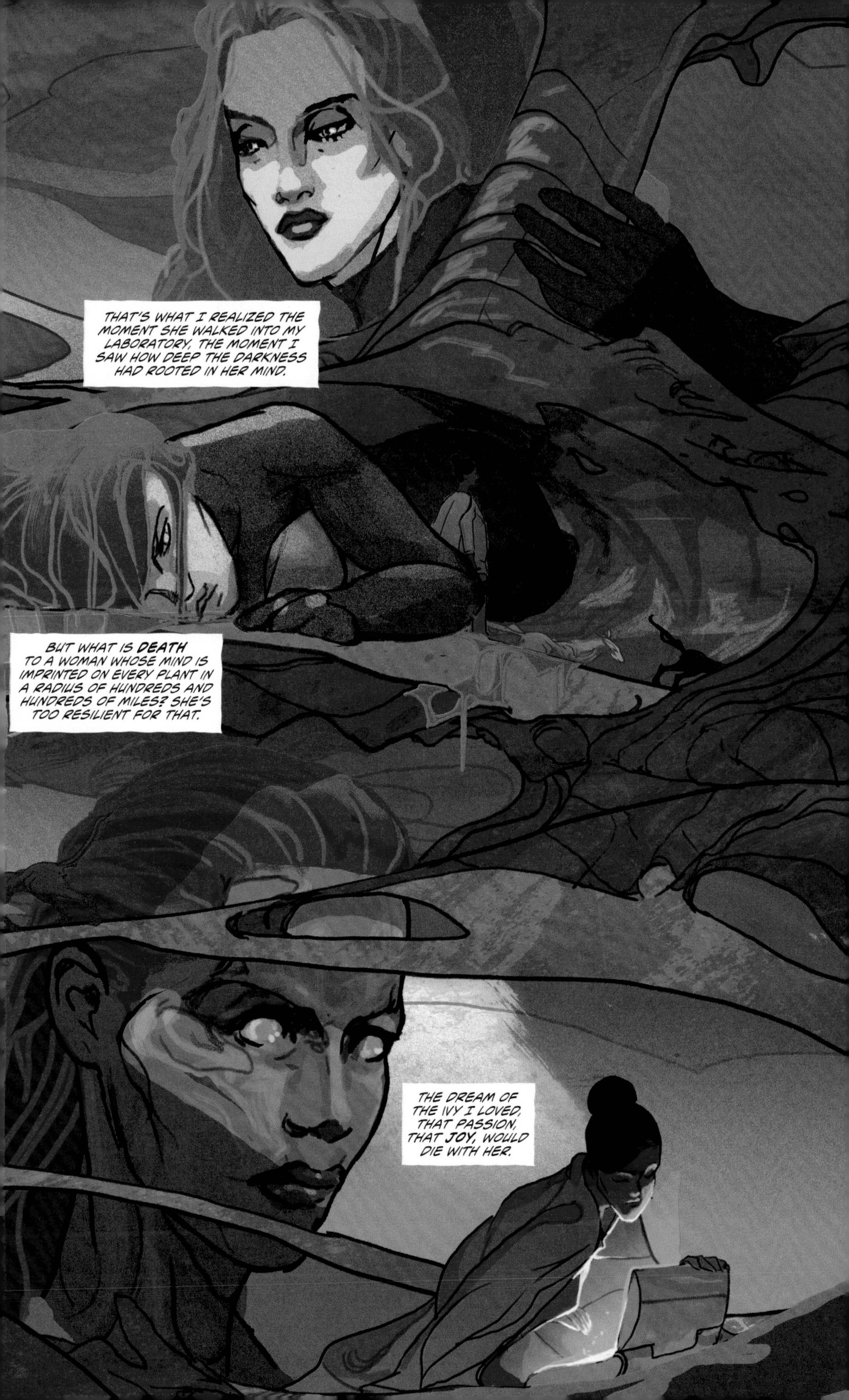
THAT'S WHAT I REALIZED THE MOMENT SHE WALKED INTO MY LABORATORY, THE MOMENT I SAW HOW DEEP THE DARKNESS HAD ROOTED IN HER MIND.
BUT WHAT IS **DEATH** TO A WOMAN WHOSE MIND IS IMPRINTED ON EVERY PLANT IN A RADIUS OF HUNDREDS AND HUNDREDS OF MILES? SHE'S TOO RESILIENT FOR THAT.
THE DREAM OF THE IVY I LOVED, THAT PASSION, THAT **JOY**, WOULD DIE WITH HER.

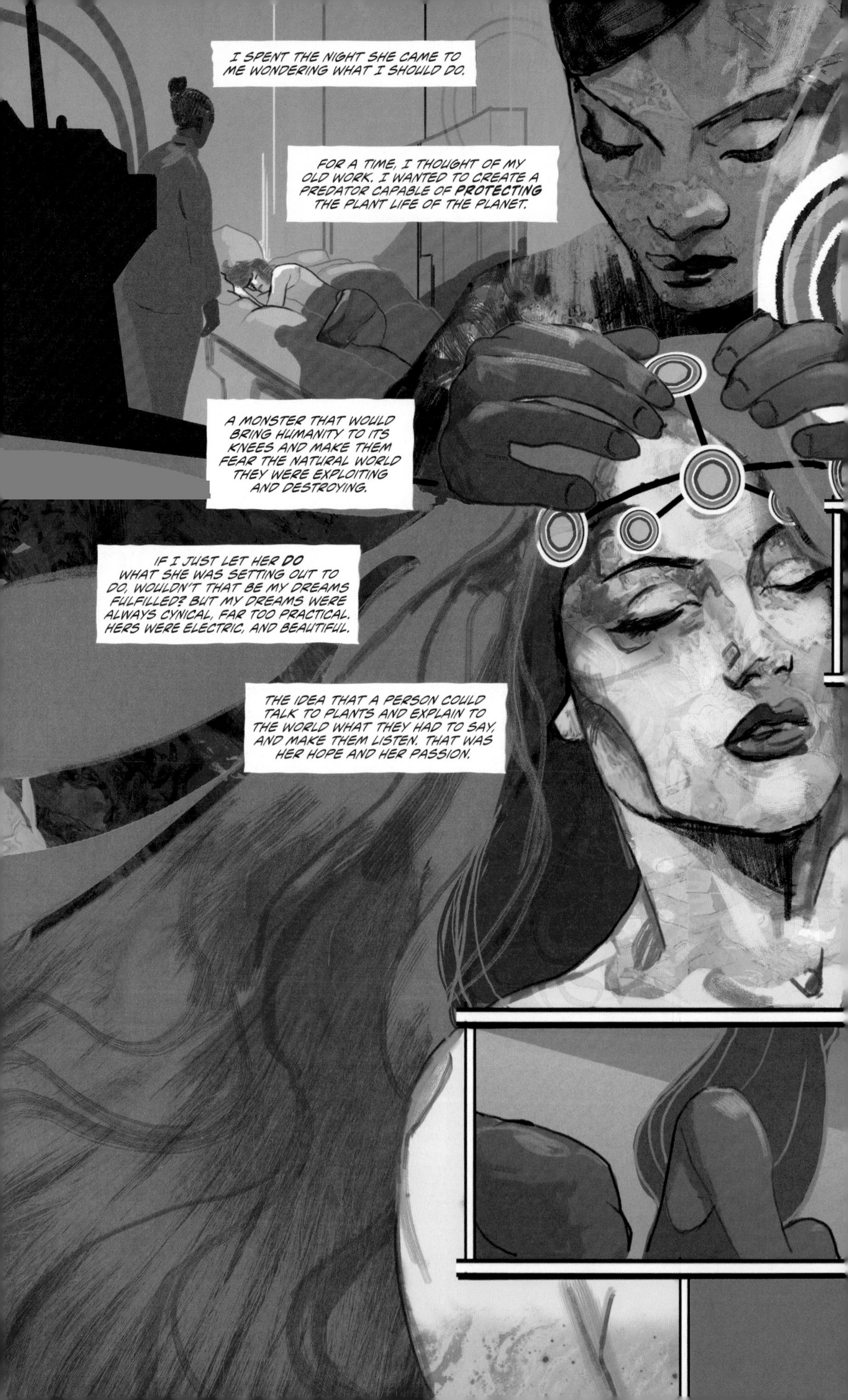

I SPENT THE NIGHT SHE CAME TO ME WONDERING WHAT I SHOULD DO.
FOR A TIME, I THOUGHT OF MY OLD WORK. I WANTED TO CREATE A PREDATOR CAPABLE OF PROTECTING THE PLANT LIFE OF THE PLANET.
A MONSTER THAT WOULD BRING HUMANITY TO ITS KNEES AND MAKE THEM FEAR THE NATURAL WORLD THEY WERE EXPLOITING AND DESTROYING.
IF I JUST LET HER DO WHAT SHE WAS SETTING OUT TO DO, WOULDN'T THAT BE MY DREAMS FULFILLED? BUT MY DREAMS WERE ALWAYS CYNICAL, FAR TOO PRACTICAL. HERS WERE ELECTRIC, AND BEAUTIFUL.
THE IDEA THAT A PERSON COULD TALK TO PLANTS AND EXPLAIN TO THE WORLD WHAT THEY HAD TO SAY, AND MAKE THEM LISTEN. THAT WAS HER HOPE AND HER PASSION.

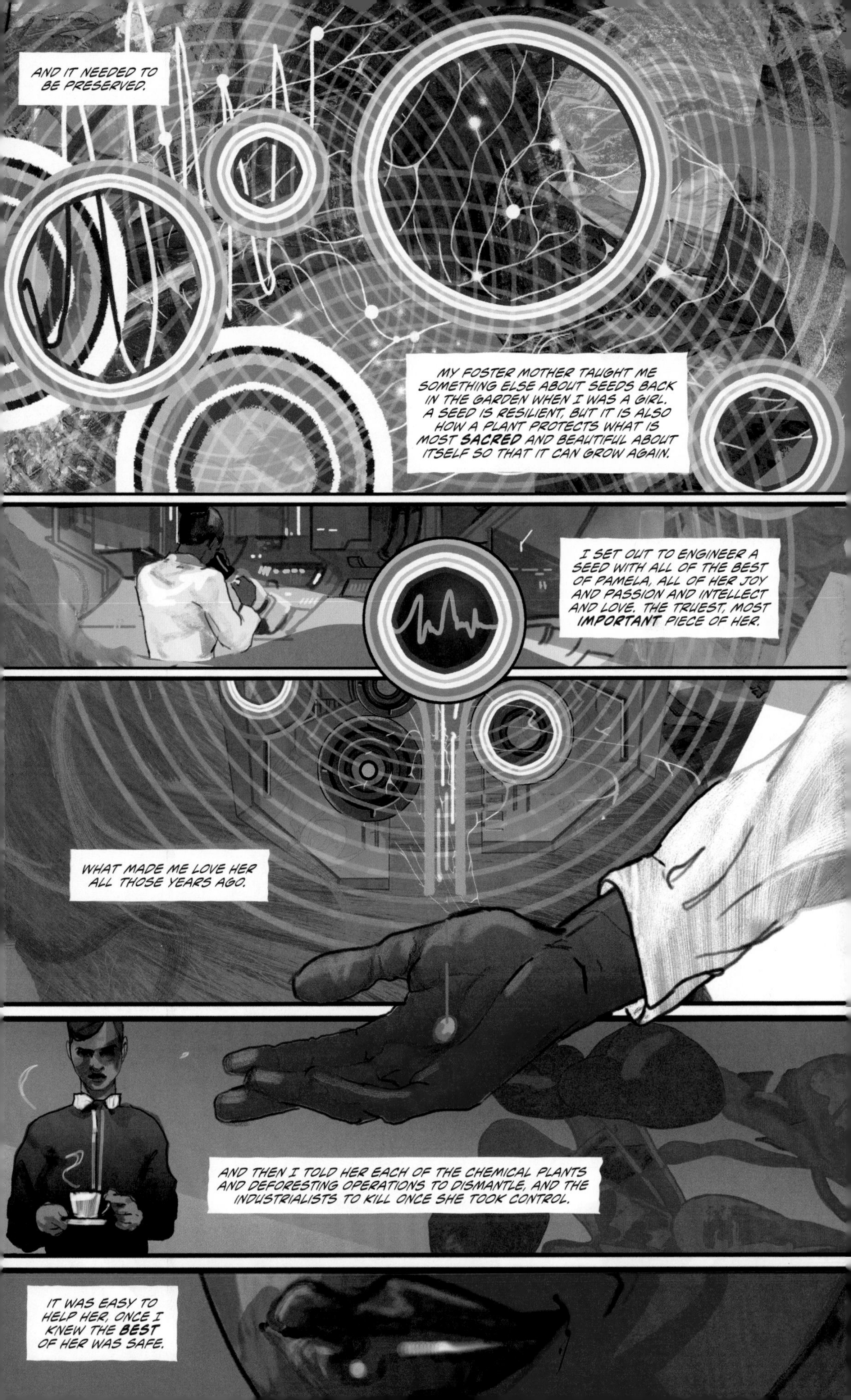
AND IT NEEDED TO BE PRESERVED.
MY FOSTER MOTHER TAUGHT ME SOMETHING ELSE ABOUT SEEDS BACK IN THE GARDEN WHEN I WAS A GIRL. A SEED IS RESILIENT, BUT IT IS ALSO HOW A PLANT PROTECTS WHAT IS MOST SACRED AND BEAUTIFUL ABOUT ITSELF SO THAT IT CAN GROW AGAIN.
I SET OUT TO ENGINEER A SEED WITH ALL OF THE BEST OF PAMELA, ALL OF HER JOY AND PASSION AND INTELLECT AND LOVE. THE TRUEST, MOST IMPORTANT PIECE OF HER.
WHAT MADE ME LOVE HER ALL THOSE YEARS AGO.
AND THEN I TOLD HER EACH OF THE CHEMICAL PLANTS AND DEFORESTING OPERATIONS TO DISMANTLE, AND THE INDUSTRIALISTS TO KILL ONCE SHE TOOK CONTROL.
IT WAS EASY TO HELP HER, ONCE I KNEW THE BEST OF HER WAS SAFE.

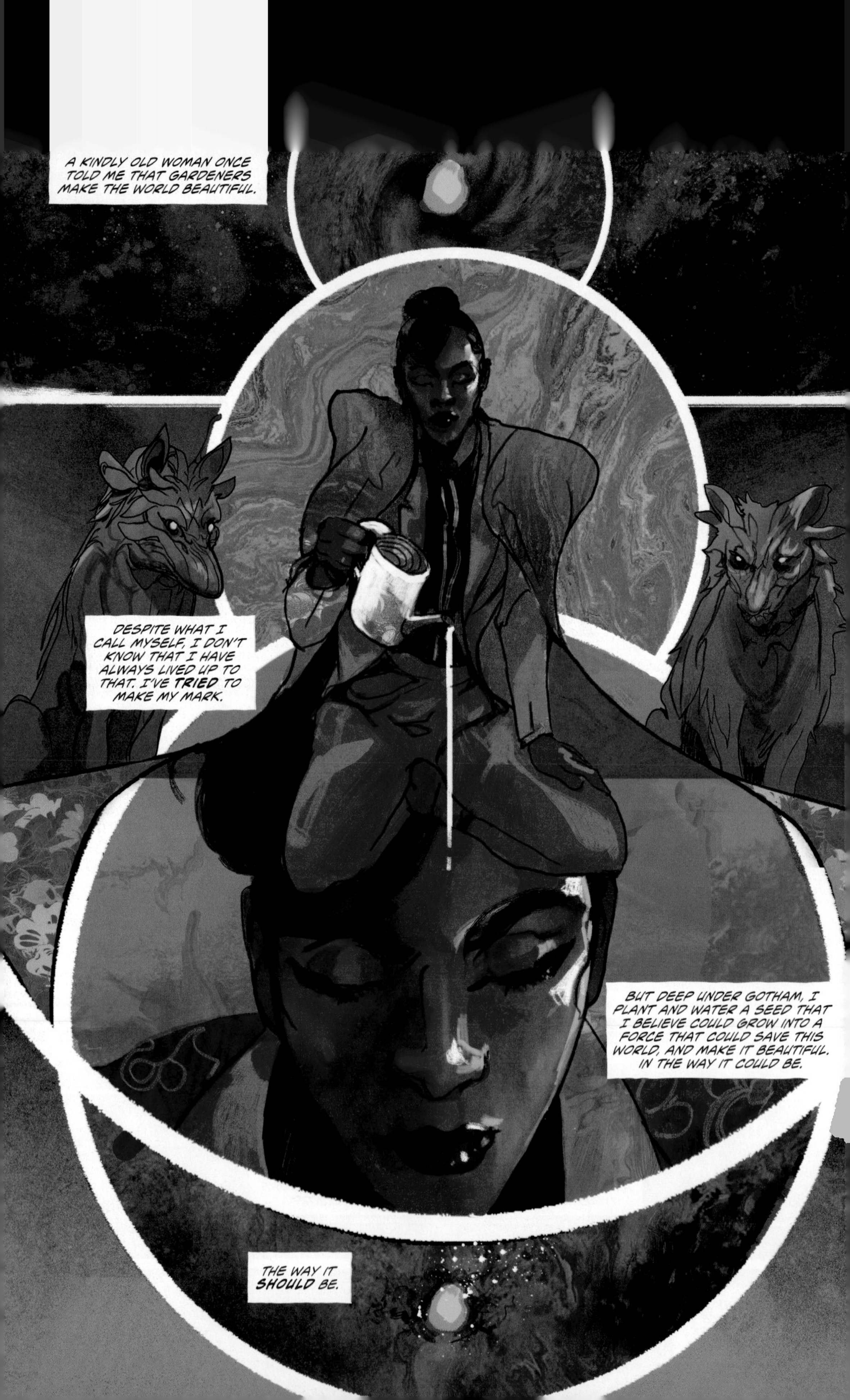
A KINDLY OLD WOMAN ONCE TOLD ME THAT GARDENERS MAKE THE WORLD BEAUTIFUL.
DESPITE WHAT I CALL MYSELF, I DON'T KNOW THAT I HAVE ALWAYS LIVED UP TO THAT. I'VE **TRIED** TO MAKE MY MARK.
BUT DEEP UNDER GOTHAM, I PLANT AND WATER A SEED THAT I BELIEVE COULD GROW INTO A FORCE THAT COULD SAVE THIS WORLD, AND MAKE IT BEAUTIFUL. IN THE WAY IT COULD BE.
THE WAY IT **SHOULD** BE.

VARIANT COVER
GALLERY

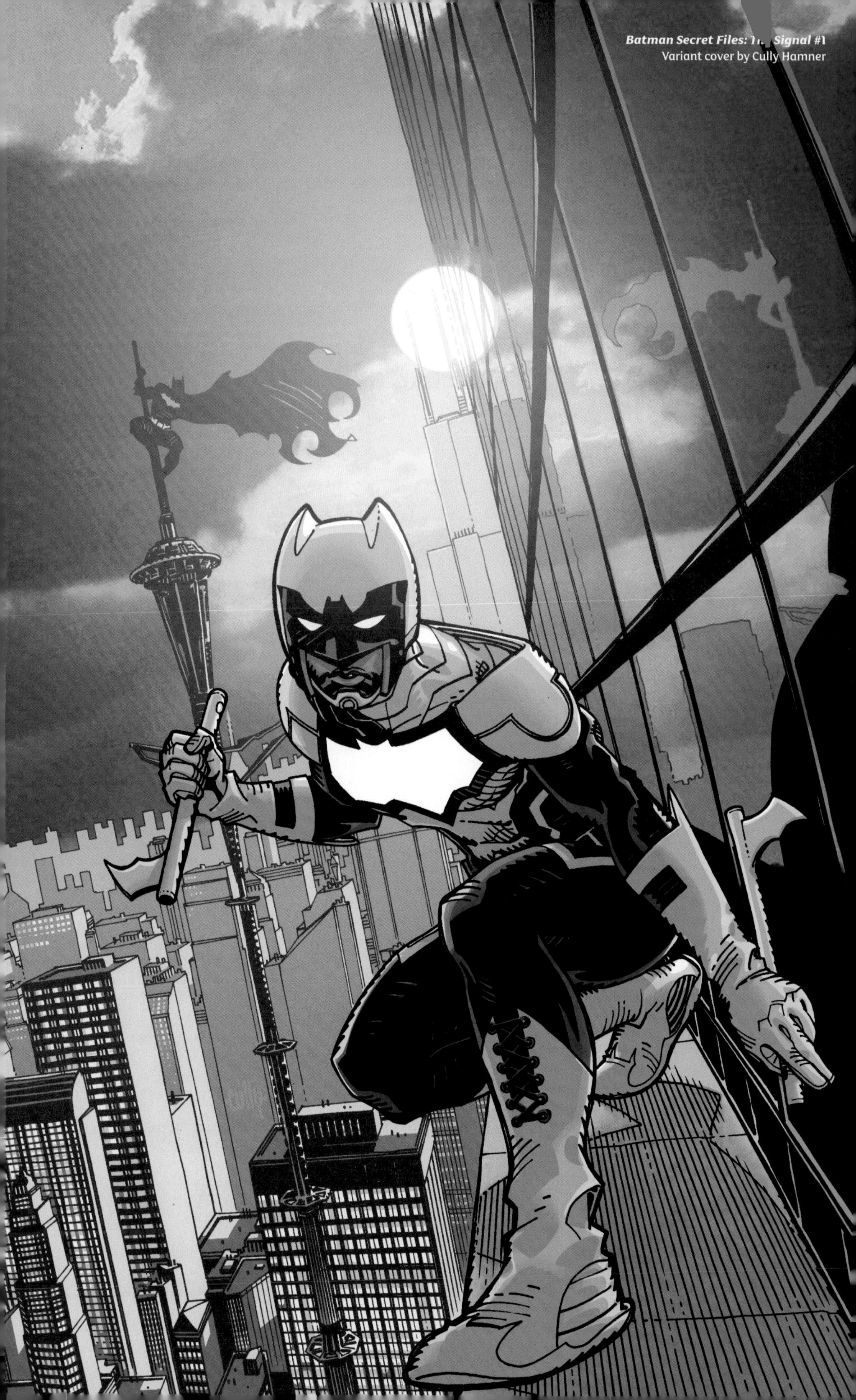

Batman Secret Files: The Signal #1
Variant cover by Cully Hamner

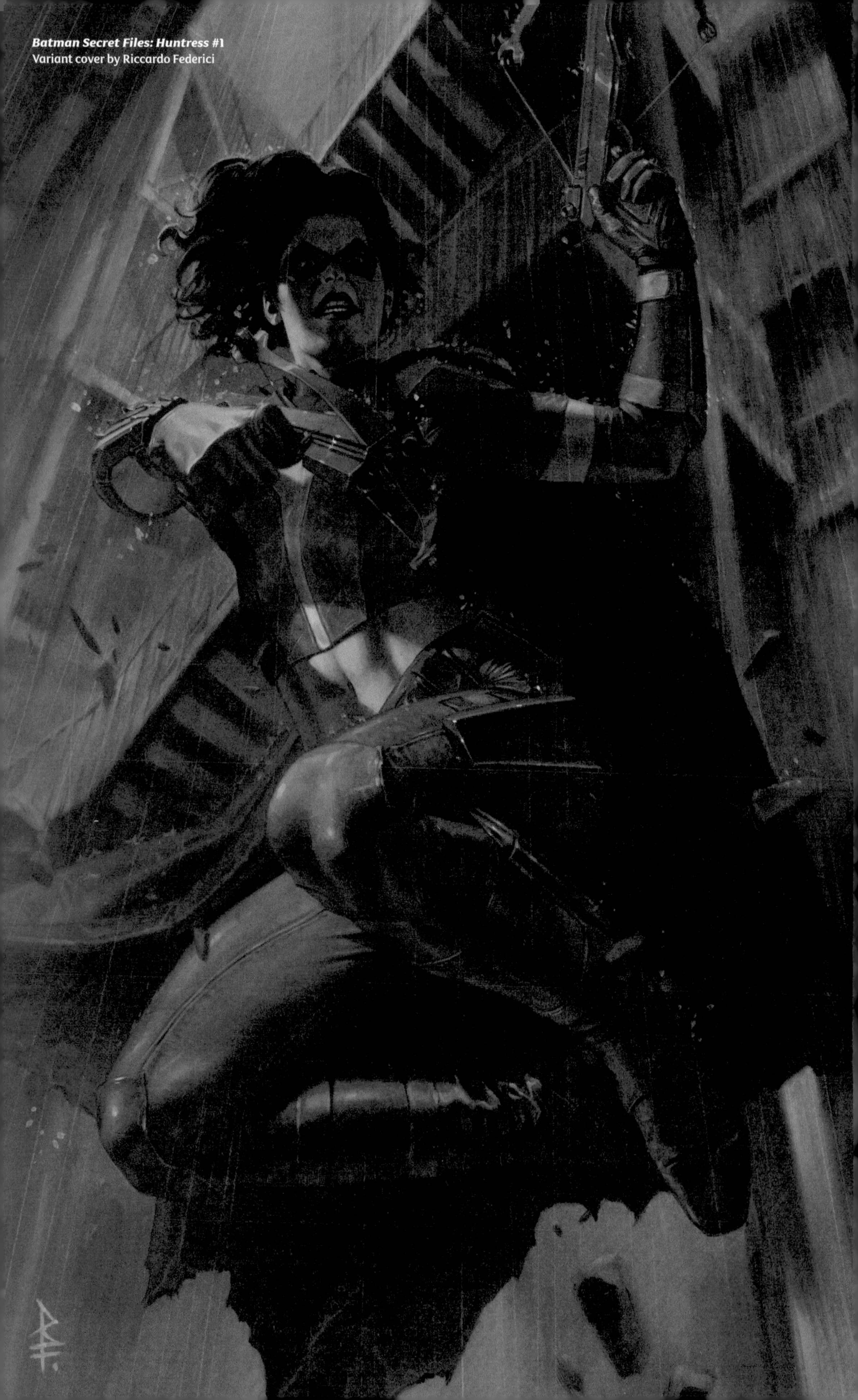

Batman Secret Files: Huntress #1
Variant cover by Riccardo Federici

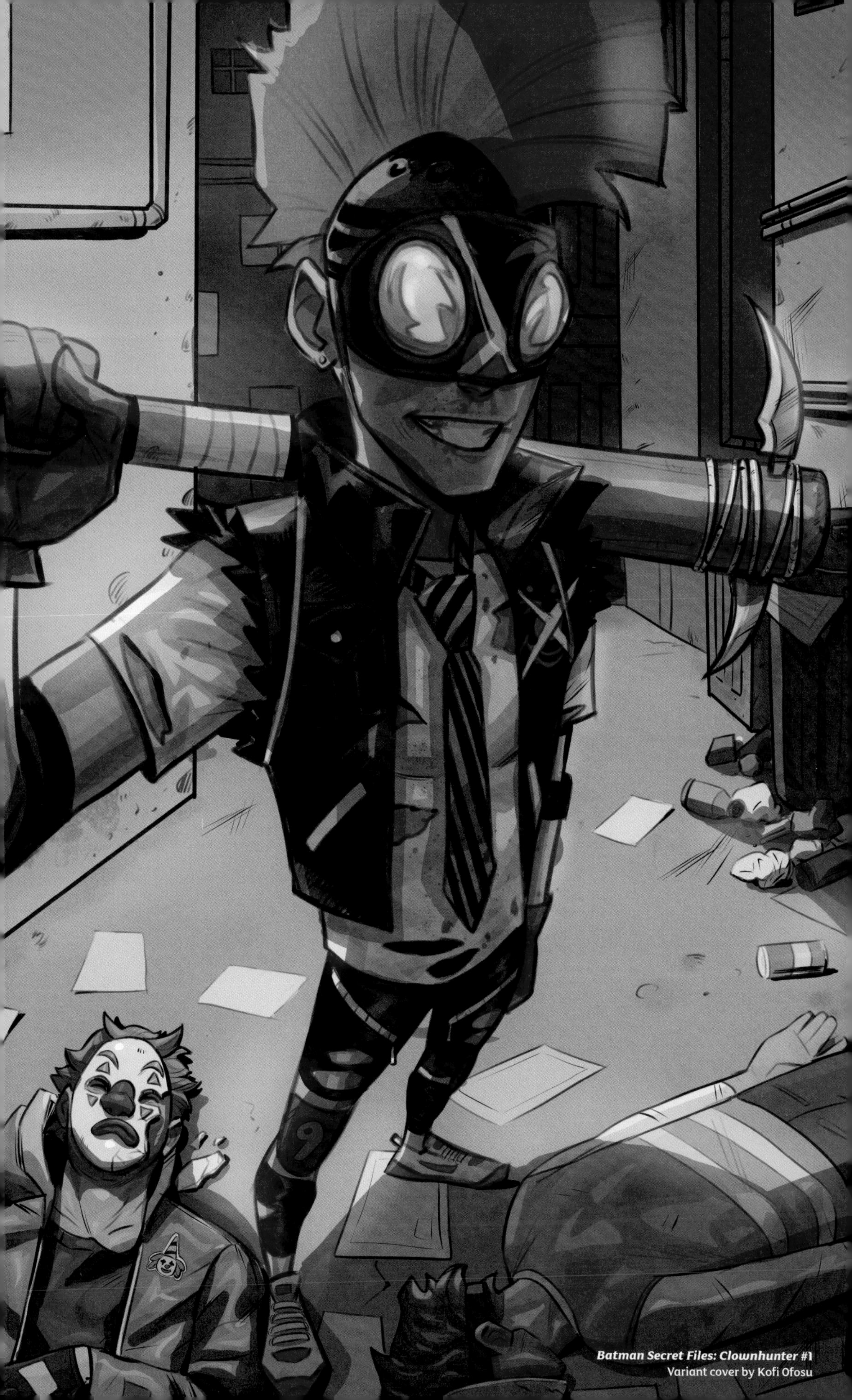

Batman Secret Files: Clownhunter #1
Variant cover by Kofi Ofosu

***Batman Secret Files: Peacekeeper-01* #1**
Variant cover by Tyler Kirkham & Alejandro Sánchez

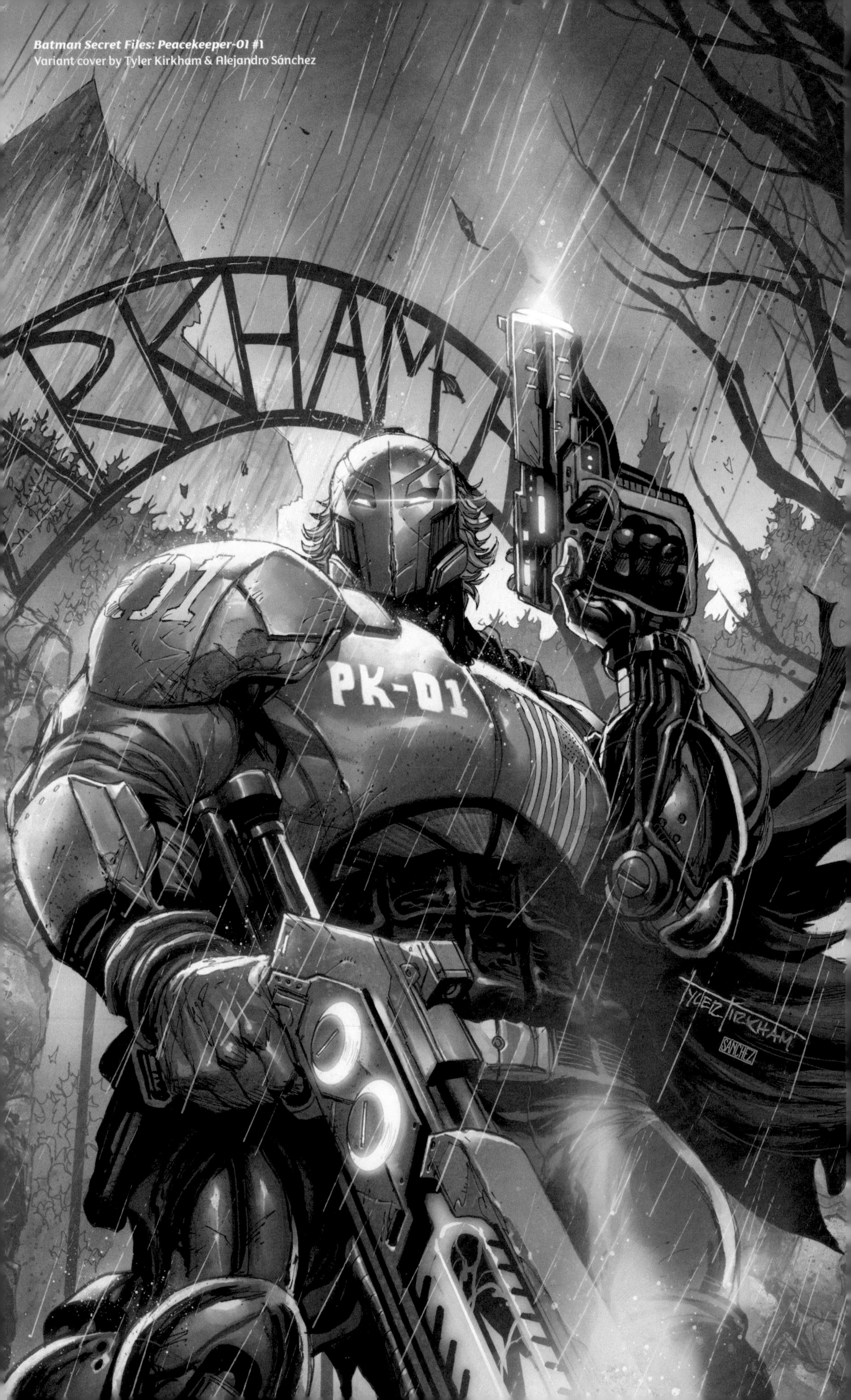
PK-01
TYLER KIRKHAM
SANCHEZ

***Batman Secret Files: Miracle Molly* #1**
Variant cover by Justine Frany

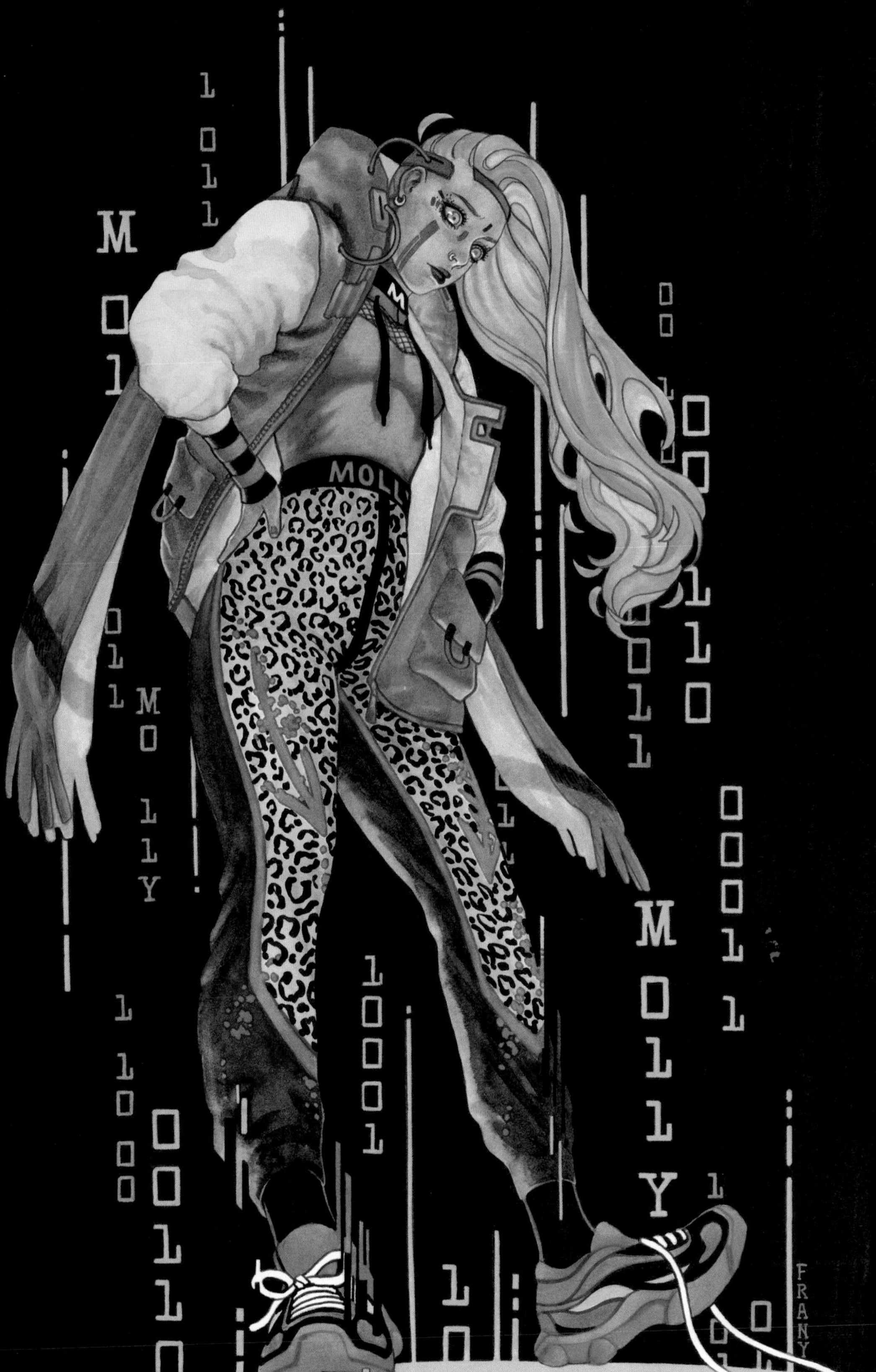
FRANY

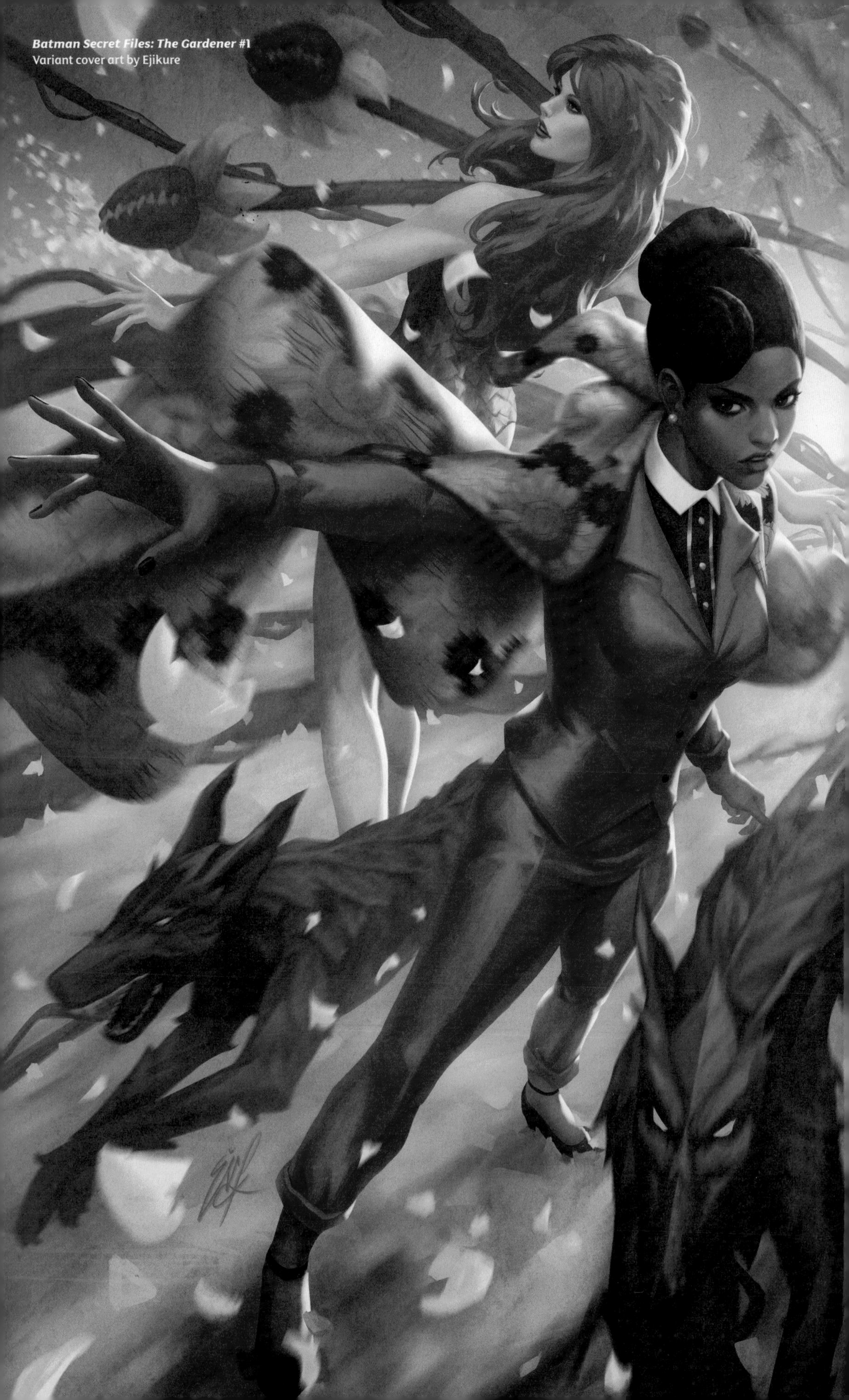

Batman Secret Files: The Gardener #1
Variant cover art by Ejikure